Centuries of Trial

A History of Ireland under English Rule until 1922

Volume 1
1171 - 1691

MICHEÁL MAC SEIRIDH

Published by *ÉIRE DUISIGH PRESS*

© *ÉIRE DUISIGH PRESS 2023*

www.centuriesoftrial.ie

Centuries of Trial Volume 1
A History of Ireland under English Rule Until 1922
Volume 1, covering the period 1171 until 1691.

All photos courtesy of Wikimedia Commons except p453 and p545 (author)

© MICHÉAL MAC SEIRIDH 2023

MICHÉAL MAC SEIRIDH asserts the moral right to be identified as the author of this work.

All rights reserved. No part of this publication may be reproduced, stored in a retrieval system, or transmitted in any form or by any means, mechanical, electronic, recording, photocopying or otherwise, without the prior permission of the publisher.

Jackket Image – Cromwell's Army at Drogheda, September 1649.

Jacket and book design by the author

"Centuries of brutal and often ruthless injustice…have driven hatred of British rule into the very marrow of the Irish race."

- David Lloyd George

"It has pleased the English people in general to forget all the facts in Irish history. They have been also graciously pleased to forgive themselves all those crimes."

- Daniel O'Connell

"If history is deprived of the truth, we are left with nothing but an idle unprofitable tale."

- Polybius

Do cum glóire Dé agus onóra na h-Éireann[i]

---

[i] For the glory of God and the honour of Ireland

Contents   Page

Map of Ireland	31
A Note on the Title	33
Author's Note	35
Foreword by Fr. Eóghan Monaghan	37
Prologue – Ireland, "Land of Warriors"	41
Part 1 – The Failed Conquest	61
Part 2 – For Faith and Fatherland	233
References	588

Prologue - Ireland, Land of Warriors

Kingdoms and Nation	41
- The Ruling Families	
- Division of the Land	
- The Class Structure	
- Brehon Law	
- Armies and Tribute	
- The Transfer of Power	
- The Importance of Poets	
The High King of Ireland	46
Brian Ború	48
Good Friday 1014 – The Battle of Clontarf	49
- Mailmora's Anger	
- The Battle	
- The Death of Brian Boru	
The Decline of The High Kingship	54
- The Return of Malachi Mór	
- A Diminished High Kingship	
England – The Norman Kingdom	56
- Who were the Normans?	
- The St. Brice's Day Massacre	

- 1066 – The Norman Invasion of England
- The Establishment of England as a Norman Kingdom

Part 1 – The Failed Conquest

Chapter 1 - Diarmuid McMurrough, King of Leinster

Becoming King	63
Challenges to Mac Murrough's Reign	64
- An Outrageous Act	
Becoming a Dominant Power	65
Ireland – "A Trembling Sod"	66
- A Contested High Kingship	
- A Failed Attempt at Peace	
The Queen of Breifne	67
- A Period of Church Regeneration	
- The Taking of Dervorgilla	
Mac Murrough at the Height of his Power	70
- MacMurrough's Rule of Leinster	
The Madness of the High King	72
- The Fall of Muircheartaigh MacLochlainn	
- "Revenge!"	
The Flight of Diarmuid MacMurrough	73

Chapter 2 - Ireland Betrayed

MacMurrough gives Allegiance to the English King	75
- On the trail of King Henry II	
- "Laudabilitur"	
- An Act of Treason	
Wales "The Warrior's Nest"	79

- Strongbow and the Geraldines
- An Agreement with Strongbow

MacMurrough Returns to Ireland   81

Chapter 3 - The Norman Landings

War and Peace   83
- The Capture of Wexford
- MacMurrough Submits to the High King

The Fall of Dublin   85
- Battle on the Beach
- The Arrival of Strongbow and the Battle for Waterford
- The Capture of Dublin
- The High King Kills his Hostages

The Death of MacMurrough   90

Chapter 4 - Expanding the Bridgehead

King Henry II Comes to Ireland   91
- The Return of the Ostmen
- The Contest for Dublin
- The Arrival of the English King
- The Submission of the Irish Kings
- The Synod of Cashel

"The Five Bloods"   96
- Norman Crimes Against the Irish People

Initial Attempt as Conquest   98
- The Plan for Complete Norman Conquest
- The Death of Tiernan O'Rourke
- The Capture of Limerick
- A "Peace Treaty"
- Native Help for the Normans
- The Death of Strongbow
- The Sidelining of Raymond LeGros

The Despoilation of the Irish Church	104
John deCourcy goes North	105
- The Battle of Downpatrick	
Prince John Comes to Ireland	107
- Hugh deLacy becomes Chief Justice	
- Prince John's First visit to Ireland	
- The Death of Hugh deLacy	
The Death of the Last High King of Ireland	109
Prince John Deputises for Richard "The Lionheart"	110

Chapter 5 - Fighting and Infighting

Divide and Conquer	112
The Normans and the O'Connors in Connacht	113
A Norman Rebellion	114
- Unrest among the Hiberno-Normans	
- "Black Monday"	
- William deBraose	
King John in Ireland	117
- Dealing with deBraose	
- King's John's rule of Ireland	
- King John and the native Irish Leaders	
- The Normans achieve control of West Munster	
The Reign of King Henry III	120
- Civil War in Connacht	
- The Murder of Richard Marshall	
- Infighting in Ulster	
- Arrival of The Gallowglass Warriors	
- Geraldine Setback in Munster	
- The Battle of Athankip	
The Reign of King Edward I	132
- "Mere Irish"	
- Murder on the Menu	

Chapter 6 - The Scottish High King

The Beacon of Bannockburn   135
The Bruce Military Campaign   136
- An Irish Scottish Alliance
- "We Shall Attack Them in Defence of Our Just Rights"
- The Arrival of Edward Bruce
- More Infighting in Connacht
- Beginning of The Great Siege of Carrickfergus
- Bruce Moves South
- "King of Erin"
- The Bloody Battle of Athenry
- Robert Bruce comes to Ireland
- The Attempted Capture of Dublin and Limerick
- The Battle of Dysert O'Dea

The Death of The Scottish High King   146
- The Battle of Faughart

Chapter 7 - Gaelic Irish and Degenerate English

Disquiet and Rebellion among the Anglo Irish   149
- English Mistrust of the 'Old English'
- Infighting Among the Anglo Irish
- The Murder of William deBurgo

The Reassertion of Gaelic Governance in East Ulster   152
The English Policy of Segregation against the Anglo Irish   153
The Black Death   155
- After Effects of the Black Death

"Hiberniores Hibernicis ipsis"   156
Lionel Duke of Clarence, Lord Lieutenant of

Ireland	158
The Statute of Kilkenny	159
- The Measures Introduced	
- The Effects of the Statute	

Chapter 8 - A Tale of Two Kings

Art MacMurrough, King of Leinster	163
- The English Pale "Beholden to a Captain of the Enemy"	
King Richard II Comes to Ireland	165
- The Submission of the Gaelic Chieftains	
The Killing of Roger Mortimer	168
- The Emergence of the Lancastrian Faction	
- The Death of the Heir to the Throne	
"MacMurrough - Dead or Alive"	168
- The Entrapment of the King	
The Death of Two Kings	172

Chapter 9 - Ireland During The Wars of The Roses

From HenryIV to Henry V	175
Regaining Lost Ground	176
The Reign of Henry VI	177
The Ulster Chieftains Attack South	178
The Cancer of Feuding	179
The Arrival of Richard Plantagenet	180
An Opportunity for Richard and the House of York	181
- Richard's Return to Ireland	
- Richard's Final Defeat	
An Anglo Irish War of the Roses	183
- The Geraldines Supreme	

The Execution of Thomas Fitzgerald,
Earl of Desmond 185
- Ireland after Thomas Fitzgeralds' Death

Chapter 10 – The Rise and Fall of the House of Kildare

The Tudors come to Power 189
The Pretenders 190
- Lambert Simnel
- Perkin Warbeck

Poynings Law – Anglo Irish Power Annulled 194
Garrett Mór Fitzgerald – "All but King of
Ireland" 195
- "The Fittest Man to govern all Ireland"

The Battle of Knocktow (Knockdoe) 197
A Report on the State of Ireland 199
The Accession of Henry VIII 200
The Death of Garrett Mór Fitzgerald 200
Lord Deputy Garrett Óg Fitzgerald 200
- The Undermining of Garrett Óg Fitzgerald
- Thomas Howard replaces Fitzgerald as Lord Deputy
- "Surrender and Regrant"
- The Return of Kildare as Lord Deputy

The Fall from Grace of Garrett Óg Fitzgerald 206
The Rebellion of "Silken" Thomas Fitzgerald 208
- The Plot
- The Revolt
- The Pardon of Maynooth
- The Capture and Death of Thomas Fitzgerald

Massacre at Carrigogunnell Castle	213
"The Geraldine League"	214

Chapter 11 – "Faithless Sons"

Introduction	217
The Reformation in England	218
- The Reformation in Europe	
- "Bewitched"	
- The Anglican Schism	
Henry VIII extends his Schism to Ireland	221
- The Parliament of 1536	
Dissolution and Destruction	224
- The Death of Lord Grey	
"Surrender and Regrant"	226
Henry VIII – King of Ireland	228
"For Shame"	232

Part 2 – For Faith and Fatherland

Chapter 12 – The First Plantation

The Religious Reforms of King Edward VI	235
- Opposition in Ireland to the Reforms	
English Law versus Brehon Law	238
- The Tyrone Succession	
Queen Mary Tudor	241
- The Restoration of The Catholic Faith	
- "King's County" and "Queen's County"	
- The Death of Queen Mary	

Chapter 13 – Shane O'Néill, King of Ulster

England Becomes Protestant	245

Scotland and Presbyterianism	246
1560 – The Irish Reformation Parliament	247
Initial Effects of the Reforms	249
Shane "The Proud"	250
- Gaelic Ulster	
- Shane "The O'Néill"	
The O'Néill at the Court of Elizabeth	252
The Battle of Glenshesk	253
Farsetmore – Shane O'Néill's Last Battle	254
The Death of Shane O'Néill	255

Chapter 14 – Rebellion, Massacre and Plantation

Enforcing the New Religion	258
- The Gaelic Order Under Threat	
War between the Earls of Ormond and Desmond	260
The First Geraldine Rebellion	262
- The Parliament of 1568	
- English Intentions Laid Bare	
- Rebellion in Munster	
- Slaughter of the Innocents	
- The End of the Rebellion	
Rebellion provoked in Connacht	266
An English Plantation Attempted in Ulster	267
- The Plantation of Sir Thomas Smyth	
- Mass Extermination of the Irish in North-east Ulster	
- The Murder of Brian O'Néill of Clandeboye	
The Mullaghmast Massacre	270
- "Righteous" Rory Óg O'More	
- Mass Murder at Mullaghmast	
The Second Rebellion of the Munster Geraldines	273
- Fitzmaurice Seeks help for Ireland	
- The Rebellion is launched	

- The Death of Fitzmaurice
- The Battle of Manister
- The Earl of Desmond Joins the Rebels
- The Battle of Carrickafoyle Castle
- Irish victory at Glenmalure

Massacre at the Fort of Gold   282
- Spanish and Italian help for the Rebels
- The English massacre their prisoners
- The End of the Rebellion

The Plantation of Munster   286

Chapter 15 – The Spanish Armada

Sir John Perrott as Lord Deputy   287
- Reign of Terror in Connacht
- The Kidnapping of Hugh Roe O'Donnell
- The Fall of Perrott

The Spanish Armada   294

Chapter 16 – Gaelic Ulster under Threat

Ulster – The Last Gaelic Stronghold   297
The Overthrow of Gaelic Rule in Monaghan   298
Hugh O'Néill – "The Queen's Man"?   300
- The English Upbringing of Hugh O'Néill
- Earl of Dungannon
- The O'Néill – Bagenal Marriage

Hugh Roe O'Donnell Returns Home   304
- Escape and Recapture
- The Second Escape
- Home to Donegal
- Evicting the English
- "The O'Donnell"

Chapter 17 – The Nine Years War 1 - Years of Victory

1593 – The Road to War	310
- Captain Humphrey Willis is sent into Fermanagh	
- Massacre at Enniskillen Castle	
1594 – Ulster Declares War on the Crown	313
- The Fording of the River Arney	
- The Northern Alliance goes West	
- Hugh O'Néill goes to Dublin	
O'Néill Declares War "For Faith and Fatherland"	315
- The Capture of The Blackwater Fort	
- Hugh Roe O'Donnell Under Siege in Sligo	
- Attack on Monaghan Town	
- The Battle of Clontibret	
- Hugh O'Néill is Inaugurated "The O'Néill"	
- The Battle of Mullabrack	
- A Truce	
The War in Leinster	323
- Massacre in Offaly	
- A Plea to the King of Spain	
- Russell Replaced by Borough as Lord Deputy	
- The Battle of Tyrrellspass	
- The English rebuild the Blackwater Fort	
- The Siege of Ballyshannon Castle	
The Battle of The Yellow Ford	329
- The Trap is Set	
- The Trap is Sprung	
Munster Rises Again	334
An Ominous Portent	335
"The Royallest Army"	336
- Ambush at The Cashel Pass	
- The Battle of The Yellow Pass	
The Duke of Essex Angers his Queen	339

Chapter 18 – The Nine Years War 2 – Years of Defeat

An English Victory at any Price　　　　　　　　341
- The Death of Hugh Maguire
- The Arrival of Blount and Carew
- Carew in Munster
- The Foyle Landings
- Man Made Famine
- Treachery Among the Irish
- Ulster Under Pressure

The Siege and Battle of Kinsale – September
1601 to January 1602　　　　　　　　　　　　347
- The Arrival of Spanish Aid
- O'Donnell's March
- Spanish Landing at Castlehaven
- Disaster at Kinsale

The Departure and Murder of Hugh Roe
O'Donnell　　　　　　　　　　　　　　　　　353
The Siege of Dunboy Castle　　　　　　　　　354
- Spanish Treachery
- The Dursey Island Massacre
- The Epic Defence of Dunboy Castle

The "Cleansing" of Munster　　　　　　　　　358
The Death March of The Clan O'Sullivan Beare　358
The Surrender of Hugh O'Néill　　　　　　　　360

Chapter 19 – The Flight of The Earls

James I of England　　　　　　　　　　　　　364
- James I – A Secret Catholic?
- The Act of Oblivion
- Puritanism
- The Gunpowder Plot
- The Effect of The Gunpowder Plot in Ireland

The Flight of The Earls   370
- Robert Cecil's Plot for the Removal of the Ulster Earls
- Hugh O'Néill is Summoned to London
- Departure from Rathmullan
- A Forlorn Hope

Chapter 20 – The Wholesale Robbery of Gaelic Land

Ulster Seized by the Crown   377
- The Attainder of Hugh O'Néill and Rory O'Donnell
- King James I Seizes Tyrone and Donegal
- King James Renounces the Act of Oblivion and Seizes a Further Four Counties of Ulster

The Rebellion of Sir Cahir O'Doherty   380
- The Seizure of The Culmore Fort
- The Sack of Derry
- Taking Advantage of O'Doherty's Rebellion

King James Bible – Exodus Chapter 20, Verse 15; "Thou shalt not Steal"   383
- The Plantation of Ulster

The Fate of the Native Irish   385

Plantation and Persecution   388
- Attempted Conversion of the Irish to Protestantism

Chapter 21 – Reasons for a Rebellion

Land Seizures in Leinster   392
- The Land Commission

The "Packed" Parliament of 1613   394
- A Catholic Parliament?
- A Rigged Election

- Pleading With the King

Renewed Catholic Persecution   397
- The Loyal City
- The Court of Wards

The "Graces" of King Charles I   399
- Tensions Between Crown and Parliament
- From His Majesty's Bounty
- "Boyle's Law"

Lord Deputy Sir Thomas Wentworth   404
- Wentworth's Parliament
- Dispossessing the People of Connacht

Wentworth's Enemies and the Slide Towards Civil War   408
- The London Companies lose "Londonderry"
- Scotland on the Brink of War
- Wentworth Introduces "The Black Oath" in Ulster
- The Scottish War
- The King Signs the Warrant for Wentworth's Execution

Chapter 22 – The Great National Rising of 1641-42

Ireland's Call   415
- A Deteriorating Situation
- Government Plans to drive the Irish into Rebellion
- Planning an Insurrection

The Gaelic Insurgency   419
- Disaster in Dublin
- Ulster
- Proclamations and Letters
- The Planters are Cast Out Without Mercy

Massacres   423
- Truth and Fiction
- Atrocity Propaganda

The Insurrection Widens   429
- The Catholic "Old English" are Goaded into Rebellion
- English Policy Towards the Insurrection
- "Slay and Destroy"
- The Beginning of the English Civil War
- A Scottish Army Sent to Ulster

Chapter 23 – The Catholic Government 1642 - 1649

The Establishment of The Catholic Confederation   439
- The Synods of Kells and Kilkenny
- Massacre Outside Naas
- Massacres in Meath
- "Murrough of The Burnings"
- The Return to Ireland of Eoghan Roe O'Néill
- For King or for Parliament?
- "Pro Deo, Pro Rege, Pro Patria Hibernia Unanimis"

A Divisive Truce   448
- Battles and Massacres
- An Opportunity for King Charles I
- A Truce is Signed

The Bridge at Finea   451
An Unrealistic Offer?   454
The Arrival in Ireland of Archbishop John Baptist Rinuccini   455
"Ormondists" and "Rinuccinists"   457
- Ormond Arrests the Earl of Glamorgan
- A Split in the Confederacy

- The Surrender of Bunratty

The Battle of Benburb   459
- Opposing Armies
- "A Fight for your Native Birthright"
- The Battle

Rinuccini Takes Charge   464
- Ormond's Treaty Rejected
- A Lost Opportunity

The Confederacy Defeated   466
- The Arrival of General Michael Jones
- Dungan's Hill
- The Sack of Cashel
- The Battle of Knockanos

The End of The Confederacy   471
- "Sooner Defeat than O'Néill"
- Inchiquin Switches to the Royalist Side
- Truce with Inchiquin – Death Knell of The Confederacy
- Rinuccini Leaves Ireland
- The Return of Ormond
- Struggle for Supremacy before the Coming of Cromwell

Chapter 24 – "With Bible and Sword"

Cromwell Comes to Ireland   479
- The Killing of the King
- The Levellers
- Ireland – A Land Divided Among British Factions
- The Arrival of Cromwell

"Cursed be he that Maketh not his sword starke drunk with Irish blood!"   482
- "This Marvellous Great Mercy" – Drogheda, September 1649

- Venables Goes North
- "This Other Mercy" – Wexford, October 1649

Cromwell Continues His Campaign   491
- The Killing of Eoghan Roe O'Néill
- Ormond's Disastrous Strategy
- Swift Progress for The New Model Army
- The Defence of Clonmel
- The Battle of Scarriffhollis
- Perfidious Albion
- The flight of Ormond
- The Siege of Limerick
- Ireton is Summoned into Eternity
- The Conquest of Connacht

General Surrender   504
The War Continues Against Tories and Priests   505

Chapter 25 – "To Hell or Connacht"

Ireland at the End of War   509
Cromwell's "Act of Grace" for Ireland   510
- The Down Survey
- The Division of the Irish Spoils

The Irish Slaves   514
"Cromwell's Slaughter Houses"   515
The Governance of Ireland under Cromwell   516

Chapter 26 – The Return of the King

The Restoration   519
- A "Fortunate Day"
- The Recall of the Monarch

Tinkering with Cromwell's Irish Settlement   520
- Great Expectations
- Another Act of Settlement

The Re-establishment of Anglicanism   524

- The Return of the Established Church and Parliament
- The Persecution of Presbyterians

The Execution of Archbishop Oliver Plunkett   525
- The Rise of Anti Catholic Sentiment
- The Titus Oates Plot
- The Effects of the Plot in Ireland
- The Trial of Archbishop Oliver Plunkett

The Catholic King   530
- The Change of Monarch
- Growing Disquiet over King James's Catholicism
- King James II – The Hope of Catholic Ireland
- Richard Talbot – Lord Lieutenant of Ireland

The "Glorious Revolution" and the end of English Monarchical Rule   533
- The Declaration of Indulgence
- The Arrival in England of William of Orange

Chapter 27 – The Catholic Rearguard

Ireland Prepares for War   536
- False Rumours
- The Apprentices Close Derry's Gates
- French Help for James II

The Siege of Derry   540
- Clearing the Passes
- "Lundy the Traitor"
- James II at the Walls of Derry
- The Course of the Siege of Derry
- The Breaking of the Siege

The "Patriot Parliament"   543

The Introduction of "Gun Money"   545

The Opening Phase of The Williamite War   546
- Slaughter at Newtownbutler

- Siege at Carrickfergus
- Skirmishing in Dundalk
- The Battle of Cavan Town
- The Siege of Charlemont Fort

The Battle of The Boyne — 550
- The Arrival of William of Orange in Ireland
- The Army of James II on the Eve of Battle
- Lead up to the Battle
- The Battle
- Retreat to Dublin
- James II Leaves Ireland

"Enjoy the War for the Peace will be Terrible" — 559

The First Siege of Athlone — 560
- "I will Defend Until I eat my Old Boots!"
- General Douglas Massacres Irish Civilians

The First Siege of Limerick — 561
- Limerick Taken Under Siege by King William
- "Sarsfield is the Man"
- The Epic Defence of Limerick
- The End of the Siege

The Duke of Marlborough Captures Cork — 567

The Second Siege of Athlone — 568
- The Arrival of The Marquis St. Ruth
- The English Army Advances on Athlone
- De Ginkell Enters Athlone
- "Are There Ten Men Who Will Die With Me For Ireland?"
- Athlone Captured
- The Jacobite Army Retreats Westwards

Aughrim – The Decisive Battle — 573
- Battle is Joined
- Defeat from the Jaws of Victory

Limerick – The Last Jacobite Bastion — 577
- The Capitulation of Galway and Sligo

- The Death of Tyrconnell
- The Second Siege of Limerick Begins
- Massacre at Thomond Gate
- Capitulation

The Treaty of Limerick   581
- The Civil Articles of the Treaty
- The Departure of "the bone and sinew of Ireland"

"Remember Limerick and Saxon Faith!"   587

References   589

"Already the curse is upon Her,

and strangers her valleys profane;

They come to divide – to dishonour,

And tyrants they long will remain.

But onward! – the green banner rearing,

Go flesh every sword to the hilt;

On our side is virtue and Erin,

On theirs is Saxon and Guilt."

Excerpt from;

"The Song of O'Rourke, Prince of Brefnie"

By

Thomas Moore, "The Bard of Erin"

1779 – 1852

Ireland

A Note on the Title

The title of this book is taken from a phrase in the Preamble to The Irish Constitution. The Preamble declares:

"In the Name of the Most Holy Trinity, from Whom is all authority and to Whom, as our final end all actions both of men and States must be referred.
We, the people of Éire,
Humbly acknowledging all our obligations to our Divine Lord, Jesus Christ, Who sustained our fathers through **centuries of trial**,[i]
Gratefully remembering their heroic and unremitting struggle to regain the rightful independence of our Nation,
And seeking to promote the common good, with due observance of Prudence, Justice and Charity, so that the dignity and freedom of the individual may be assured, true social order attained, the unity of our country restored, and concord established with other nations,
Do hereby adopt, enact, and give to ourselves this Constitution."

---

[i] This passage is based upon a phrase in the Irish Declaration of Independence as read to the assembled members of Dáil Eireann on January 21st 1919: "We humbly commit our destiny to Almighty God, who gave our fathers the courage and determination to persevere through long centuries of a ruthless tyranny..."

Author's Note

The story of these two volumes of Ireland's "Centuries of Trial" under English rule began in May of 2018 following Ireland's abandonment of the unborn child.

I have been passionate about history ever since I can remember and this has given me the habit of viewing modern events in an historical light.

In the Summer of 2018, following the referendum which overturned the protection given to the unborn child in Ireland, my mind was filled with thoughts of what our forefathers, who sought to free our country from a different tyranny would think of this crime against God and against our own people and nation.

Once more I immersed myself in the history of our land, seeking a way of escape from what I would regard as being the lowest point in our history. I finally felt compelled to record Ireland's historic struggle against English tyranny for the current generation. These two volumes are the result.

The sources which I have used in these two volumes are a mixture of primary and both ancient and modern secondary sources. To the authors of all sources, both living and dead, I owe a great debt of gratitude.

At every point I have attempted to sacrifice political correctness for accuracy. Events from English history which impacted on English rule in Ireland are also recorded.

Rather than being an academic work, this is instead a popular history.

Buiochas le An t-Athair Eóghan Monaghan, Maire, Peadar, Diarmuid, Liam agus mo Chlann.

Foreword

Patrick's Coming

In a pagan land far to the north, the druids and witch doctors were nervous. Their prophets had foretold the coming of a strange religion with a strange God.

"Pole-headed shall come from over the sea,
His staff crook-headed, his garment hole-headed,
His servants shall sit in the east of his house,
And they shall say Amen, Amen."

"Pole headed" was Patrick; the "crook-headed staff" was his crosier; the "hole-headed garment" was his chasuble.[i] Little did they know! The hand of God was moving and the days of the Scotti worshipping the sun and sacrificing their children to Crom on the "Fields of Slaughter"[ii] would soon be numbered. The worldly nephew of St. Martin had been taken prisoner and enslaved on Mount Slemish. He had been drawn to the desert. "And he watched over me before I knew him… and consoled

---

[i] Chasuble – outer vestment worn by the priest during the offering of the Holy Sacrifice of the Mass
[ii] Numerous Irish townlands derive their origin from the title "Fields of Slaughter" where pagan sacrifices took place before the coming of Patrick.

me as a father would his son"[i] he wrote. He found God in Ireland. Then he escaped from Ireland determined never to go back...

Then, one night, Patrick saw a man coming as if from Ireland with innumerable letters... "and he gave me one of them, and I read the beginning of the letter: "The Voice of the Irish', and as I was reading the beginning of the letter I seemed at that moment to hear the voice of those who were beside the forest which is near the western sea, and they were crying as if with one voice: 'We beg you, holy youth, come back and walk among us once more."

Just a dream? Then Pope Celestine sent him back.

The priests were ready, they saw the fire, they knew its meaning. "Unless that fire is extinguished tonight," they said, "it will never again be extinguished in Ireland."
Nor was it. For Patrick had brought the light of Christ to the end of the Earth where they never had any knowledge of God but, always, until now, cherished idols and unclean things. "They are lately become a people of the Lord, and are called children of God, the sons of the Irish and the daughters of the chieftains are to be seen as monks and virgins of Christ."

The Island of Saints and Scholars, the cradle of re-Christianised Europe...until the English invaded, and then apostatized. What of Ireland now, would it remain faithful? It did.
And the heretical English conquered the world for earthly glory – even as far as the ends of the earth. And wherever the English went, they were followed by the sons of Patrick. They brought the light of Christ they had received, and the Holy

---
[i] All quotations in the foreword are from "The Confession of St. Patrick"

Sacrifice was offered, and sins were forgiven, and souls were saved.

And now? When the Irish worship the sun once more and sacrifice their children to devils on the fields of slaughter? Now, it remains for us to be faithful.

"For this sun which we see, by God's command rises daily for our sakes, but never will it reign, nor will its splendour last; but all those who worship it shall go in misery to punishment. But we who believe in and worship Christ the true Sun, who will never perish, nor will anyone who doeth His will, but he will abide for ever, who reigneth with God the Father Almighty, and with the Ghost before the ages now and for ever and ever. Amen."

Fr. Eóghan Monaghan

Prologue

Ireland, Land of Warriors

"The great Gaels of Ireland
Are the men that God made mad
For all their wars are happy
And all their songs are sad."

G.K Chesterton

Kingdoms and Nation

<u>The Ruling Families</u>
For a country of its size, Ireland certainly had a lot of Kings. In the twelfth century, Ireland was divided into ten kingdoms that contained over one hundred small or "petty" kingdoms referred to in Gaelic as "Tuathanna". Each petty kingdom or "Tuath"[i] was governed by its own ruling dynasty, known as the "derb fine" or the "true family" from which the King or Chieftain was chosen.

---

[i] Tuath" is a Gaelic word meaning people. The actual number of Tuathanna varies depending on the source accessed, with some historians putting the number at well over 100.

In Gaelic, the word for children (or family) is "Clann", with each Chieftain being the "father" of his Clann. Generally, in books on Irish history, the anglicised term "Clan" is used to refer to the ruling family of one of the ten kingdoms with all the other families within the kingdom being referred to as "septs"[i] with the septs considered as constituent parts or members of the ruling Clan as of a tribe.

In reality, in Gaelic Ireland all families were Clans, with Gaelic or "Brehon" law setting down the structure and rules of interdependence and loyalty of the Clans of the kingdoms to the ruling Clans of the various Tuathanna, and of the Chieftains of the Tuathannna to the regional King. This regional King was also Chieftain of his own Tuath as was the High King of Ireland (Árd Rí na hÉireann) to whom these regional Kings owed their allegiance.

Division of the Land

The land of each tuath was divided into a number of "Ballybetaigh" and each Ballybetaigh was subdivided into twelve "Seasrach", with each seasrach consisting of about one hundred and twenty acres. Most of the land was designated as common freehold for the general population with every family being entitled to a share while the rest was reserved for the King, the nobility and members of honoured professions who could use the land allocated then as they saw fit or rent it out. On no account however, could it be sold or transferred to any person outside the tuath.

---

[i] The term "Sept" is not a period term but one that became popular about two hundred years ago at a time when there was a growing interest in Irish history. It is an English term used to refer to any family loyal to the leading family within the Tuath or more commonly to one of the ruling families of the Tuathanna who owed their loyalty to one of the regional kings. It is therefore common to read that such and such a sept were members of such and such a Clan

Economic affairs within each regional kingdom were carried on independently of its neighbouring kingdoms and each kingdom had access to the sea either directly or by river so that trade could be carried on without infringing the land border of its neighbours.

The Class Structure

The class structure of the time was unlike that in most other European countries in that there were no castes or serfs within the clan. Any lowly clan member who proved his worth could rise above his station and eventually rank among the nobility or the honoured professions.

Naturally there were class distinctions. Below the King, the nobility and the privileged were the general body of the people known as the "féine". The féine consisted of a number of social divisions which included free tenants (who rented land but owned their own livestock) and unfree tenants (who rented land and livestock and were bound by obligations to their superiors.) Finally there were the labouring classes, the "bothach" and the "sencleithe" who performed the menial tasks for which they received payment which they used to rent a small holding. There was also one final grouping in the tuath who did not belong to the clan but was rather its property. This grouping was known as the "Fuidir" or strangers and consisted of what might be considered as the flotsam and jetsam of the nation – prisoners of war, fugitives seeking refuge, slaves from abroad and criminals. Even the fudir in time could work their way up the social ladder as once they had proved their worth or completed their sentence no obstacle was placed in their way to the ascent of the social ladder.

Brehon Law

Drawn up with the well-being of the lower classes in mind, this system of law which was to remain in use in Gaelic controlled areas until the seventeenth century, regulated inheritance, property, contracts and much else besides.

For most crimes, the law did not demand excessive punishments and was much concerned with the payment of compensation for wrongs committed inflicting penalties such as the public shaming of wrong-doers who would not make restitution.

It says much for those who initially devised Brehon or Gaelic law, based as it was upon the natural law, that even after the coming of Christianity to Ireland, and its rapid acceptance by Ireland's kings, Brehon law remained almost unaltered in the centuries that followed.[i]

Armies and Tribute

The tuath king and the regional king to whom he owed loyalty both maintained an army. Aside from full time soldiers, all the healthy menfolk were required to perform a certain number of day's military service[ii] annually and to be ready for action in the event of war. The King would also choose his chief warrior or champion who was generally the strongest and most powerful of his men, known as the King's "Airechta"[iii] or "Defender". In the case of the provincial king, mercenaries were often used to bolster the ranks of his army.

Interstate warfare was common as kings often sought to take revenge for a real or perceived slight by a neighbouring kingdom by raiding over their borders in order to capture possessions or cattle herds. Alliances between kingdoms were often fickle, and if a king, after defeat in battle promised loyalty and tribute to another king this was generally assured by court hostages being given to his overlord. These hostages

---

[i] The Annals of the Four Masters record that the main body of Brehon law, the "Senchás Már" came into force in 438 AD
[ii] Referred to in Gaelic as "bonnacht"
[iii] Aireachta – from the Gaelic "aire" – to care for.

were usually family members of the vanquished king and could be put to death or blinded in the event of bad faith. The awful punishment of blinding was not peculiar to Ireland at this time but was common to many nations including England. In the reign of Henry IV some hundreds of years later a law was passed forbidding its use within his realm.

The system of tribute saw the petty kings contributing both taxes and warriors to the provincial king who in turn contributed to the High King of Ireland. There was also a system of tribute in force which operated in reverse. This acknowledgement tribute was known as "tuarastal". A regional King given a large "tuarastal" by the High King, could consider himself either well thought of or feared.

The Transfer of Power

Traditionally the succession of a Gaelic King was according to the law of the "derbfiné"[i] and by this law all male descendents of the King to the fourth generation were eligible for election as King by the Clan elders. In order to avoid disputes after the King's death, his successor or "Tánaiste"[ii] was generally chosen within his lifetime. During his reign as High King, Brian Ború sought to change this system to one of direct succession from father to son, but the old system did not die out. Whatever system was chosen it was required that the Tánaiste be without physical deformity. Law-breaking by the king left him open to being deposed by the clan and replaced by his Tánaiste, who following his election immediately began assembling a band of young eager men around him.

The king always needed to be vigilant that no members of the true family were getting ideas above their station and it was not uncommon practice at the time that if a king viewed a son

---

[i] "derbfine" – "true kindred"
[ii] Tánaiste" – ""Deputy Leader"

or any of his kinsfolk as a threat to his rule, the potential offender would be disabled and rendered unelectable, usually by blinding. If a king was not making a success of his rule or allowed his detractors to go unchallenged, he left himself open to being deposed in a revolt, not necessarily by his Tánaiste, but by a clan member with ambition, who could then present the clan electors with a "fait accompli"

Unchecked ambition within the clan could lead to rivalry culminating in a split of the clan and a power struggle for supremacy within the kingdom.

The Importance of Poets

Along with his warriors, also critical to the King's survival were his poets or bards whose importance and influence within the kingdom was enormous. In pre Christian times the position of bard or poet coincided with that of Druid but even after the coming of Christianity, poets continued to be regarded with awe and respect. If the King displeased his poet or did not give him sufficient payment for his work, the poet might use his art to compose a work ridiculing the king, perhaps destroying his reputation and making an object of ridicule in his kingdom.

Certain poets are recorded in the native annals as having the ability to perform "poetic miracles", or the ability to bring about discomfort or misfortune to those who crossed them by the composition of a poem condemning or making fun of them.

The High King of Ireland

The question is often asked why in the centuries following the Norman invasion, the Irish did not unite more effectively and drive out the invader, even when they possessed the military strength to do so? The answer must be approached by understanding that Ireland in the twelfth century has to be considered as a federation of independent kingdoms, loosely aligned under a High King, to whom many of the regional Kings gave but a grudging and enforced respect, while some felt militarily strong enough to ignore him completely. To all of the regional Kings, their kingdoms were more important than the Nation as a whole and they generally possessed a distrust of their neighbouring Kings as much as of any foreign invader.

For centuries, the High Kingship or overlordship of all Irish kings had alternated between branches of the Clan O'Néill, rulers of the kingdoms of Aileach and Meath. This was the race of the ancient warrior pirate King "Niall of the Nine Hostages" who brought the Apostle of Ireland, St. Patrick as a slave to these shores.

The two branches of the dynasty that were based in Aileach were the Cenél[i] Conaill (O'Donnell's) in Tirconnell or Donegal and the Cenél Eoghan (O'Néill's) in Tyrone with a third and weaker branch known as the Clan Méalaghlainn (Mc Loughlin) based in Co. Meath.

Following the Battle of Cloiteach in 789, the Cenél Connell had been excluded from both the rule of Aileach and the High Kingship. Since then the high kingship had alternated between the O'Néill and Méalaghlainn branches. Every time Meath held the position the strength of the High Kingship was regarded as inferior as Meath had neither the men or the wealth of resources which the Cenél Eoghan possessed, and also lacked its renowned heroism.

In ancient times, the traditional seat of the High King had been the Hill of Tara in Co Meath. However since the sixth century, Tara had been deserted on account of a curse pronounced against it by St. Rodan of Tipperary and since then the High King had lived in his native Kingdom. However the name of

---

[i] Cenél – Kindred

the ancient seat lingered and the High King of Ireland was still referred to as "The King of Tara"

Brian Ború

The man who succeeded in overthrowing the ancient line of succession of the High King was a certain Brian Ború[i] who hailed from the family of a Munster Chieftain, Cennétig MacLorcáin, rulers of a small petty kingdom near Limerick called "Dal gCais" and also rulers of the regional kingdom of Thomond. Brian Boru's elder brother Mahon became King of Munster in 964 and, after his assassination in 978, Brian succeeded him. The kingdom of Munster had long been a grudging acknowledger of the O Neill High Kings and by 1002 Brian had achieved such strength that he challenged the reigning High King, Malachy Mór, of the weaker O'Néill tribe of Méalaghlainn, who submitted to him without a fight after the northern O'Néill tribes ignored Malachy's plea for help. Brian's career of battle and struggle gave to both king and chieftain the example that greater power could be achieved by both drive and ambition.

The reign of Brian Ború as High King is rightfully regarded as a beacon in Irish history. Although his usurpation of the high kingship was to have long lasting consequences, his reign was brilliant. He strove in a few short years to undo the Viking curse of two centuries and bring about the resurrection of Ireland from the death of the Norse tyranny. For him, the soul of the nation could only be reclaimed if it returned from pagan chaos to Christian order. Numerous churches were built or rebuilt during his rule, monasteries revived, and books replaced with those that could be found abroad. His efforts in this regard were enormous and continued after his death.[ii]

---

[i] Called "Boru" after the name of the village where he was born.
[ii] Some surviving examples of the work of this restoration period include the Cross of Cong, the high cross at Monasterboice and Cormac's Chapel in Cashel.

All his life Brian had battled against the Viking invader whose dark shadow had first reached these shores just before the year 800, effectively bringing to a halt the burgeoning celtic Christian civilisation that was in its first flowering. Even when his brother Mahon agreed a truce with the Vikings in order to bring an end to the mutually destructive warfare, Brian would have no part of it. With less than twenty followers he continued fighting the Vikings using guerrilla tactics. Seeing his brother's resolve in the fight against the invader, Mahon relented and once again joined forces with him. By 970 they had succeeded in overthrowing the power of the Vikings in Munster. Their success guaranteed them enemies and in 976 Mahon was murdered at Bruree, Limerick, by an alliance of Norse and Irish leaders who had become jealous of Mahon's success and power. In the aftermath of Mahon's death Brian ensured that his brother's assassins paid for his murder with their lives.

Good Friday 1014 – The Battle of Clontarf

Mailmora's Anger

The pinnacle of Brian's life's work and the last great battle in Ireland between Christianity and paganism came in 1014. Maolmóra, King of Leinster, already unhappy with his lot in Brian's Kingdom,[i] was visiting Brian's palace at Kincora in Thomond. During a game of chess with Brian's son Murchad, the latter touched a raw wound when he brought up the subject of Maolmóra's defeat along with that of the army of Leinster by his father in 999 remarking that with Maolmóra's lack of strategy at chess, it was no wonder he was beaten in battle. At this remark, Maolmóra was completely consumed

---

[i] In 999 Brian Ború had defeated the army of Leinster, which was commanded by Maolmóra.

Ireland 1014 AD

by rage and anger. He stormed out of the High King's palace, determined to bring an end once and for all to the Ború rule of Ireland. Brian sent a messenger in his wake to summon him back to the King's court but when the messenger caught up with him Maolmóra killed him by beating in his skull with a yew branch. As soon as he returned to Leinster, Maolmóra, encouraged by his sister Gormflaith (the rejected wife of King Brian) contacted those Gaelic Kings that he believed would help him and also Sitric Silkenbeard, leader of the Vikings of Dublin. Seeing in this a chance for complete Viking domination of Ireland, Sitric sent for help from farther afield.

The Battle

A massive Norse force from the Isle of Man, the Hebrides, Scandinavia, France and Germany converged on the Norse city of Dublin and prepared for battle. Although unwilling to desecrate the day with a scene of carnage, the hand of King Brian was forced by the enemy, and battle was joined on Good Friday the 23rd of April 1014.

As the battle lines were drawn Brian rallied his army. With a sword in his right hand and a crucifix in his left, he gave his men a rousing speech in which he stirred up their anger by reminding them of the tyranny of the Vikings and of how they had desecrated many times both church and relic, murdering and plundering wherever they went.[i]

Although in his mid –seventies, Brian was nevertheless intent on leading his army into battle, but was persuaded by his chieftains to retire and hand over command in the field to his

---

[i] One of the worst Viking massacres occurred at a large monastic settlement in Bangor, Co.Down in the early 800s when 900 monks along with their Abbot were slaughtered in one day.

son Murchad and so King Brian remained in his tent at the rear praying for victory before the crucifix with which he had rallied his troops that morning.

All day the great battle raged with no quarter being given by either side. Murchad is recorded in the Danish account of the battle as having hewed his way with a battle axe towards the Viking standard bearer whom he slayed. Amongst those killed were the architect of the battle, Maolmóra of Leinster, and two Kings of the West who led Brian's Connacht contingent. Murchad (who commanded the army of Munster as well as being in overall command) and his son Turlough were both killed. After the battle, Turlough's body was found in the weir of the River Tolka through which part of the Viking army had tried to escape, his hands entangled in the hair of a dead Dane. By evening the Vikings and their Irish allies were on the defensive and after a final great effort by Brian's army (which fought with the Vikings of Waterford and Limerick), their lines were broken. Retreating towards the sea and their ships, they found their path blocked by the Meath army of the former High King Malachy Mór who had outflanked them, blocking their withdrawal. Trapped between the Irish armies, the Norsemen suffered very high casualties, with many who broke through to the sea drowning before they could reach their ships.

High King Brian Boru

The Death of Brian Boru

Seeing the Viking rout and thinking victory almost complete, Brian's bodyguards left him so as not to miss out on the last foray of battle. King Brian's manservant, Conaing[i] then saw some figures approaching and warned the High King, who reached for his weapon. The Viking King of the Isle of Man, Brodar, then entered the tent and lunged at Brian, cleaving open his head with an axe, even though Brian had managed to strike the first blows with his long double edged sword, cutting off both Brodar's legs below the knee.[ii] The Danish "Niala Saga" reports Brodar as having been captured alive, hung and eviscerated by King Brian's enraged bodyguards.

While the Vikings who had arrived from abroad sought to escape, the Vikings of Dublin and the remnants of Maolmóra's army retreated into the city proper. Such was the amount of blood spilt on that day, the army of the High King was unable to pursue them and complete the task. Afterwards, the body of the great King was carried in procession to the apostolic city of Armagh[iii] by the clergy and buried close to the high Altar of its Cathedral.

---

[i] Also referred to in some accounts as "Laiten"

[ii] According to the Book of Leinster;: "The High King gave him a sword blow that cut off the left leg at the knee and turning gave another, which took the right leg at the foot. Jarl Brodhir gave the King one stroke, which crushed his head utterly, and they fell mutually by each other."

[iii] After becoming High King, Brian visited Armagh. After attending Mass he placed a large amount of gold on the altar and commanded his scribe to write in the "Book of Armagh" the following "The holy Patrick when going to heaven, ordained that the whole fruit of his labour as well of baptism as of church matters and alms should be paid to the apostolic city which in Irish is called Ardmacha"

The Decline of the High Kingship

<u>The Return of Malachi Mór</u>

The death of King Brian along with that of his son and grandson at the Battle of Clontarf signalled the end of a promising dynasty which, if it had endured, could have changed Ireland's history, transforming the country into a strong and united nation. Rightly recalled as a brave and wise monarch, Brian's example in unseating the High King was in the long term set to plunge the country into decades of war and strife as now the High Kingship was to become an open book to those who coveted it and the country became disunited and weakened by the power struggles that ensued.

For eight short years after the death of Brian Ború, the High King that he himself had overthrown, Malachi Mór ruled Ireland once again in relative peace in what was to prove to be the swansong of the High Kingship as his rule was accepted by all save the men of Leinster whom Malachi finally succeeded in bringing to heel.

After the death of Malachi Mór almost all the Irish High Kings are referred to as "with opposition" meaning that there was one or more regional King who did not accept their rule. The Annals of Clonmacnoise are more explicit. They tell us that Malachy: "...was the last king of Ireland of Irish blood that had the crown but that there were seven kings after without crown before the coming of the English."[1]

In the aftermath of their defeat the Norsemen clung to their petty states along the coasts maintaining their position as sea merchants. They kept to themselves and were reluctant to get involved in any further power struggle unless it was clearly to their own advantage. Isolated from the greater Viking world they were referred to by the Irish as "Ostmen". Gradually they assimilated Irish habits and language and became Christian but still maintained their independence even as far as church matters were concerned, choosing their own bishops who were consecrated in England and building their own churches.

Only once more would the Vikings seriously attempt the conquest of Ireland when Magnus Barelegs landed with his army in 1098. He managed to gain control of Dublin but was killed in battle at Downpatrick in 1103.

A Diminished High Kingship

After King Malachy's death, there was an interregnum that lasted for some twenty years when Ireland was ruled by two learned men, Cuan O'Lochan, a poet, and Corcran Cléireach (the Cleric) a devout and holy man. For most of this time Corcran Cléireach ruled alone as in 1024 Cuan O'Lochan was murdered. It is recorded in the Annals of Kilronan that his murderers all died tragic deaths and that their offspring became known by the offensive odour they emitted. Following the death of Corcran Cléireach, another son of Brian Ború, Donnchad, King of Munster claimed the throne but was widely opposed, even by his own family. He eventually left Ireland for Rome, a broken man, apparently taking with him the crown worn by his father as undisputed king of Ireland which he presented to the Pope. The next High King with opposition came from the family of MacMurrough, Kings of Leinster since Clontarf. Diarmuid "na Mail na mBo"[i] Mac Murrough was a High King who extended his influence beyond these shores. He is famous for providing refuge to the surviving sons of King Harold Godwinson of England after the Battle of Hastings, providing them with ships and weapons for their attempted invasion of England. After his death in 1072 Turlough O'Brien of Munster claimed the throne also with opposition.

---

[i] " na Mail na mBo" - "Baldy of the Cattle"

According to the Annals of Lough Ce, the High King of Ireland and King of Munster Turlough O'Brien died in 1086 being succeeded by his son Muircheartaigh, who sought to continue the supremacy of Munster in the provision of the High King. The Kings of Connacht and Aileach had other ideas, especially the King of Aileach, Domhnalll MacLochlainn who came from the Clan O'Néill, which had provided the Irish with their High King for centuries. It was almost fifteen years before Muircheartaigh managed to suppress the northern challenge and make his "Circuit of the High King"[i]

Muircheartaigh O'Brien was an able High King, much interested in the welfare of the church and presided at the first synod of reform in 1110 at which the proposed division of the country into various dioceses became a reality. He also presented to the church the former seat of the King of Munster, Cashel. Upon his death in 1119 the High Kingship passed forever from the descendents of BrianBorú. The King of Connacht, Turlough O'Connor now claimed the crown.

England – The Norman Kingdom

Along with briefly recounting events in Ireland before the time at which this history begins, it is also worthwhile to recall how the Norman kingdom of England came to be.

Who Were the Normans?

As the Viking's had first plundered and then settled along Ireland's coast, they had accomplished the same along the northern shores of Gaul or Francia. (France). In this region

---

[i] A tour that the High King made in which the provincial kings pledged loyalty to him. Hostages were often taken to safeguard the profession of loyalty.

they gradually allied themselves with the upper echelons of society through intermarriage and trade.

In time, one of the Viking leaders, Rollo, was appointed by the French Emperor as ruler over the whole area after which what became known as the Duchy of Normandy was successfully established. These descendants of the Viking warrior bands became indistinguishable from other northern Frenchmen except for their singular character which retained many Viking traits. Their rule of the Duchy of Normandy was a success and saw the region develop as a well established power on the northern French coast.

The St. Brice's Day Massacre

Meanwhile, England continued to suffer greatly from Viking invasions and interventions whereby the Vikings eventually sought to take control of the governance of the country. The English King, Ethelred, had enough of their interference and decided to take decisive action, ordering a massacre of Viking leaders which took place on St. Brice's day, November 2nd 1002. However the massacre encompassed the sister of King Sweyn of Denmark, a woman named Brunhilda. On hearing of the murder of his sister, Sweyn ordered a punitive expedition to England, which finally led to the establishment of Viking control in England under Sweyn's son, Canute who became King of England. During Canute's rule an alliance with the Normans across the Channel was formed and strengthed through ties of trade and intermarriage beginning with that of Canute to Emma, the sister of the Duke of Normandy.

1066 – The Norman Invasion of England

After 1042, England was ruled by St. Edward the Confessor, who was a son of Emma and Canute. Edward had little interest in worldly power and wealth but yet impressed his people by and ruled them in a spirit of God fearing sanctity.

Edward had no direct heir and his two likely successors were William of Falaise, and Harold Godwin, both of whom were distant relations by marriage. The successor to Edward seemed to be settled when Edward promised William that he would be the next King of England. Edward's promise was further reinforced when some years later, Harold, while on a visit to Normandy personally swore to William that he would do all in power to ensure that William would be the next King of England.

However when Edward died on January 5th 1066, Harold was in London and William was not. Harold immediately had himself crowned as King of England, a move which not only divided loyalties in England but united many on the continent behind William.

William and Harold

After assembling a massive army of some 50,000 men, 14,000 of whom were mounted, William landed in England on September 29th 1066 at Pevensey Harbour.

When William landed, Harold was far to the north in York, having just defeated the army of his brother, Tostig, in battle at Stamford Bridge and it was three days before news of William's landing reached him.

Moving south as quickly as he could, Harold's exhausted army arrived outside Hastings on October 13th 1066 to find William's army occupying the town. Early the following day, William's army moved out of the town and took up positions on Telham Hill, and at nine o'clock battle was joined.

The battle (which lasted all day) was a close run affair and could have gone either way. At dusk, Harold's army, who were doubtless more exhausted than William's due to their previous battle and long march south gave way, and Harold was killed.

William "The Conqueror" was crowned King of England in Westminster Abbey on Christmas Day 1066.

The Establishment of England as a Norman Kingdom

In the years that followed William and his Normans extended Norman ways into England though not without conflict. By 1069, the introduction of new taxes was causing great unrest and a new Viking invasion threatened. After spending Christmas 1069 in York, William went north and with great violence suppressed all opposition. His reign was now secure.

Since Roman times, Britain had been regarded as one entity and William succeeded in becoming overlord of Scotland after the Scottish King Malcolm swore allegiance to him in 1072. In Wales his overlordship was established more gradually because of the resistance of the Welsh Lords.

Although the Norman government took central control, many of the local lords who had previously given their allegiance to Harold remained in place. In 1086, William summoned them all to Salibury plain where he exacted an oath of allegiance from them, above that which they owed to their feudal Lord.

In the middle of the twelfth century, England was subject to much turbulence and war following the death of King Henry I, (who was William's youngest son) due to arguments over the succession. In 1154 this turbulence came to an end when Henry Plantagenet, the son of Geoffrey of Anjou and the previously widowed Empress Mathilda was crowned King of England.

Henry Plantagenet was now one of the most powerful men in Europe. As well as being King of England and Overlord of

Normandy, Henry II had direct control over Anjou, Gascony, Aquitaine, Maine and Touraine. Henry II also claimed overlordship of Wales and Scotland.

Part 1

The Failed Conquest

Chapter 1

Diarmuid MacMurrough, King of Leinster

Becoming King

Born in the year 1110, in the Leinster petty kingdom of Hy Kinsella, Diarmuid was only five years old when his father, Donnacha who was King of Leinster was killed in battle while fighting the High King of Ireland, Muircheartaigh O'Brien, who was aided by the Ostmen of Dublin. According to the Gaelic "Book of Rights", the Ostmen of Dublin, Wexford and Waterford owed allegiance to the King of Leinster, but the High King had a higher claim on their loyalty.

In the same year that his father was killed, Diarmuid's eldest brother also died in battle while fighting in Munster, leaving his other brother Enna to shoulder the burden of state. But Enna's reign was also short-lived, and in 1126 at only sixteen years of age and against the articles of succession in Brehon law, Diarmuid was elected to the throne of Leinster after Enna died unexpectedly. Diarmuid had a hard act to follow for Enna had been a cunning ruler, not easily taken advantage of, being at times an ally of and a plotter against the High King, Turlough O'Connor of Connacht.

Challenges to McMurrough's Reign

With Enna dead and Diarmuid still coming to terms with his shortened youth, Turlough O'Connor was quick to see his chance to reduce the size of MacMurrough's kingdom. He launched a massive attack by land and sea, intending to split the kingdom and secure the north of it as a separate kingdom with his own son Conor at the helm. This fell through when his son was deposed by the Leinstermen and so instead the High King installed as his puppet Domhnall MacFaelain, a Leinster native of a former ruling family. Mac Murrough was incensed that a member of the Mac Faelain Clan whom the MacMurrough's had previously defeated in battle in order to gain the throne of Leinster should now be resurrected and granted half of the kingdom.

It was at this time that Diarmuid MacMurrough had his first experience of Tiernan O'Rourke; King of Breifne as the High King dispatched the one eyed O'Rourke to teach Diarmuid a lesson and put him in his place for once and for all. O'Rourke was in his very nature a man bred for warfare who loved battle. Pillaging of Diarmuid's kingdom followed, after which O'Rourke then retreated leaving the teenage King of Leinster to pick up the pieces and rebuild his kingdom.

An Outrageous Act

In the years that followed, Diarmuid caused the High King no trouble and was allowed to slowly recoup his strength until finally he decided to make his move. By 1131, Turlough O'Connor, the High King, was in trouble. Kingdoms from north and south were rebelling against his rule. With the High King thus distracted, Diarmuid seized his opportunity.

In those days, the appointment of the Abbess of the monastic settlement at Kildare (founded by St. Bridget) was not just a prestigious religious appointment but also a political one and MacMurrough decided that a candidate of his choosing should be Abbess. He ordered his soldiers to secure the town of Kildare and defile the Abbess, Mor Ui Faelain, thus rendering her ineligible to continue in her role, leaving him free to ensure that the position would be in his gift. This outrageous act was significant for the future as it showed that Diarmuid MacMurrough's method of operation was "the end justifies the means".

Becoming A Dominant Power

Having succeeded in Kildare, McMurrough began strengthening his power base making alliances with his neighbours by war wherever necessary. He renewed the allegiance owed him by the Norsemen of Dublin and then began a military campaign, striking south and west becoming overlord of the Kingdoms of Ossory and Thomond as well as of the Ostman city of Waterford. He made a pact of friendship and mutual assistance with Méalaghlainn, King of Meath, which was the buffer kingdom between Leinster and the Kingdom of Breifne. In 1138, Méalaghlainn called on McMurrough for help as his Kingdom was under threat from being overrun by the forces of the High King, Turlough O'Connor. McMurrough's military prowess was not inconsiderable at this time and when O'Connor saw the army that was arrayed against him; he withdrew from the borders of Meath without a fight.

By 1141 the petty kings of Leinster were intent on challenging McMurrough's dominance. These included his own brother in law MacFaelain, who had been installed by O'Connor years earlier, so it was perhaps under orders from the High King that the plan to unseat Diarmuid was hatched. In any event, on learning of the plot, Diarmuid acted before his enemies and dispatched an army commanded by his brother Murchad to round up the ringleaders, seventeen of whom were killed or blinded. This swift and ruthless action secured his rule of

Leinster for over two decades and enhanced his reputation for brutality.

Ireland; "A Trembling Sod"
<u>A Contested High Kingship</u>

The years that followed perfectly illustrate the chaos that resulted from a High Kingship that was not hereditary and so continuously open to challenge. The King of Munster, Conor O'Brien, now tried to gain the High Kingship for himself, even arriving at the gates of the Ostman city of Dublin, where he managed to secure the loyalty of McMurrough's Norse allies for himself. He then attacked Connacht which was the territory of the High King. Diarmuid MacMurrough saw trouble on the horizon. If O'Brien managed to overthrow the High King and become High King himself, his rule of Leinster could be under threat. In order to protect himself he now pledged allegiance and gave hostages to the High King, Turlough O'Connor. O'Connor was quick to take advantage of this and as soon as he had Diarmuid's hostages, he turned on McMurrough's friend and ally, Méalaghlainn, King of Meath knowing that McMurrough could not help him. Once Méalaghlainn was defeated, Turlough O'Connor once again tried to install his son Conor as King, this time of Meath. When King Turlough had previously installed him as King of Leinster in 1126, the men of Leinster revolted but this time his son was assassinated by the Meathmen as an unwanted foreign monarch. The revenge of the High King on Meath was swift and violent and after being overrun Meath was split between O'Connor's two allies but enemies of one another, O'Rourke of Breifne and MacMurrough of Leinster.

A Failed Attempt at Peace

Well aware of the injustice and damage to the country as a whole of this never ending warfare, the Archbishop of Armagh, Gelasisus, (Gilla Mac Liac) now intervened to try and bring peace and restore order. At a convention in Ormond to which all Kings and princes were summoned, O'Connor and O'Brian swore an oath of peace and Méalaghlainn was restored to his kingdom. However, in spite of this war soon broke out again between O'Brien and O'Connor for the title of High King of Ireland. However, behind their backs a new threat was rising far to the north in Ulster. Muircheartaigh MacLochlainn from the Clan of O'Néill, who had been watching from the sidelines, decided to try and reassert his family's ancient dominance. Having nurtured his forces and asserted his dominance in Ulster, he made his challenge. Seeing his rising power and great military strength, first Diarmuid MacMurrough and then Tiernan O'Rourke made their submission to him. MacMurrough's submission was such that he seems to have become firm friends with MacLochlainn and never again feared for the safety of his kingdom while MacLochlainn lived. A witness to his own decline, the King of Connacht and High King of Ireland Turlough O'Connor also submitted. In 1151, and without having to fight any major battle Muircheartaigh MacLochlainn became High King by forcing O'Connor to give hostages to him.

The Queen of Breifne

A Period of Church Regeneration

In spite of the turbulent times Church reform continued apace. In the year 1152, a national synod was held for the Irish church at Kells. Its published program was "in order to set forth the Catholic Faith, to purify and correct the morals of the people, to consecrate four archbishops and give them the pallia."[2] Pope Eugenius III sent his legate Cardinal Paparo to confer the pallia, declaring the Archbishop of Armagh as Primate and also elevating the Bishop of Lismore to the position of Papal Legate to Ireland. The Kings of Ireland assented to all the decrees passed including most importantly those against immoral unions and concubinage, as in Europe Ireland was widely regarded as being a permissive society where many still preferred to adhere to the old precepts contained in Brehon law which allowed for divorce. Before long, this assent was to come back to haunt MacMurrough.

During this period of regeneration for the Church and in that same year of 1152, the High King Muircheartaigh MacLochlainn and the former High King Turlough O'Connor met and made friends with each other under the staff of St. Patrick[i] and the relics of St Columcille.

The Taking of Dervorgilla

Around this time MacMurrough as King of Leinster met with these two Kings and together they decided upon the reconstitution of the Kingdom of Meath. Possibly this was at MacMurrough's instigation as he had been unable to come to the King of Meath's aid when his Kingdom had been previously abolished by O'Connor.

One person who was not happy at this state of affairs was the King of Breifne, Tiernan O'Rourke who very reluctantly would have to give back the part of Meath that he controlled.

---

[i] Known as the "Bachall Isa" or "the Staff of Jesus", due to the tradition that St. Patrick had received it from a hermit who lived on an island in the Etruscan Sea, who in turn had received it from the hands of Jesus with the instruction that it was to be given to St. Patrick. In 1173, it was seized by Strongbow from its shrine in Ballyboughal and was placed in a new reliquary in St. Patrick's Cathedral, Dublin, where it remained until 1538 when the Anglican Archbishop Browne ordered that its golden ornaments and precious stones be removed prior to it being publicly burned as a "superstitious relic" in the precincts of the Cathedral.

Emboldened by his friendship with the Ulster High King and deciding to teach O'Rourke a lesson (doubtless with revenge in mind for what he had previously suffered at O'Rourke's hands as a teenager), McMurrough embarked with his forces into Breifne and mauled O'Rourke's army also destroying his seat at Dangan. Not content that he had caused O'Rourke to lose Meath, he now reduced his kingdom further, splitting it and installing another O'Rourke more to his liking as ruler of the Southern part of Breifne.

Diarmuid Mac Murrough

Tiernan O'Rourke was married to Dervorgilla Méalaghlainn, the daughter of the King of Meath by an arranged marriage. At this time when her husband's back was to the wall, she allowed herself in spite of her pretended protestations to be carried off by MacMurrough taking with her everything that she had brought to Breifne as her dowry and bringing them to MacMurrough's castle at Ferns. Tiernan O'Rourke was on a pilgrimage to Croagh Patrick (or St. Patrick's Purgatory at Lough Derg according to some accounts) when this occurred.

It was not long before MacMurrough began to regret his elopement with Dervorgilla as it developed into something of a national incident with leaders of both Church and State condemning him. O'Rourke, who was shamed and humiliated by the incident, appealed to the King of Connacht for redress. The following year Dervorgilla was handed back after an expedition led by O'Connor entered Diarmuid's territory, but

O'Rourke longed for vengeance and determined to bide his time until fortune should turn against the King of Leinster.[i]

MacMurrough at the Height of his Power

In 1156 the elderly King of Connacht and former High King of Ireland Turlough O'Connor died. His son Rory succeeded him as King of Connacht and lost no time in ensuring that his reign would remain unchallenged – at least in Connacht. He imprisoned his three brothers and blinded the eldest and most promising of them.

In Leinster, MacMurrough was emboldened by his strong alliance with MacLochlainn. Safe in the knowledge that he would not be called to answer for his actions before the High King, MacMurrough now involved himself in arguments outside his kingdom. When his friend Méalaghlainn, King of Meath, died, his son Diarmuid succeeded him as King of Meath. This was not to MacMurrough's liking as Diarmuid Méalaghlainn then allied himself not with Leinster, but with Tiernan O'Rourke's Breifne. MacMurrough now waged war against both Meath and Breifne in order to ensure that a different son called Donnchad, who had promised MacMurrough his allegiance, became King of Meath. He also overthrew the King of Ossory and installed a ruler he deemed more suitable. Of this period in McMurrough's life, the twelfth century Norman historian and Deacon, Gerald of Wales, later wrote of him; "his hand was against every man, and every man's hand against him"[3]

---

[i]Much later, after her husband's murder at the hands of the Normans, Dervorgilla would retire to the Abbey of Melifont where she would spend the rest of her life doing penance.

McMurrough's Rule of Leinster

In these years of secure rule McMurrough also involved himself in other tasks such as building infrastructure in his kingdom and helping in the foundation of monasteries. At that time in Ireland many abbeys and monasteries were unaligned to the great religious orders possessing their own rule, with some of these displaying a marked laxity. MacMurrough assisted and gave grants of land for the foundation of those orders with a fixed rule such as the Augustinians and Cistercians. These actions, whilst both noble and commendable, were also self-serving as no Abbot of a major monastic settlement could now be appointed in Leinster without MacMurrough's approval. Such deeds also contributed to both his national and international prestige. In 1148, after contributing to the foundation of a Cistercian monastery at Baltinglass he received a personal letter from Bernard of Clairvaux addressed to "Diarmait, King of Ireland". St. Bernard went on to say "...your renown has reached this country and we rejoice exceedingly in the good reports of you"[4], balm indeed for Diarmuid's prestige! He had also remarried, his new wife being the sister of the Abbot of Glendalough, Mor O Tuathaill, and they had two children called Conor and Aoife.

The King of Connacht Rory O'Connor was meanwhile widening his sphere of influence, determined to make his own bid for the High Kingship. However, after O'Rourke threw in his lot with O'Connor, MacLochlainn decided to bring an end to his ambition and defeated their alliance in a major battle at Ardee in 1159. O'Connor now had no other choice but to submit and gave court hostages to MacLochlainn.

The saying "Absolute power corrupts absolutely" was now to become true of Muircheartaigh MacLochlainn. Overtaken by hubris, a minor argument with a petty king was to bring his edifice of power tumbling to the ground and with it that of his main ally Diarmuid MacMurrough.

The Madness of the High King
The fall of Muircheartaigh MacLochlainn
In 1165 the King of Dalaradia, Eochy MacDunleavy, caused offence in some way to the High King Muircheartaigh MacLochlainn. MacLochlainn would tolerate no dissent and, deciding to make an example of MacDunleavy, launched a punitive raid against his territory in which many innocent people were killed. MacDunleavy remained as King only when his daughter was handed over as a court hostage along with sons of the Chieftains of the other kingdoms of Ulster who had brokered the peace and vouched for MacDunleavy's future good behaviour.

For some unknown reason in the spring of 1166, MacLochlainn killed his hostages. On meeting Eochy MacDunleavy shortly thereafter, perhaps at a parley, MacLochlainn had him seized and blinded and the three men that accompanied him were killed. The fury of the Ulster Chieftains, some of whom had lost sons, knew no bounds at these outrages. From their armies the best troops were picked and assembled into a strike force with one purpose in mind – to run to ground and kill the High King. Seeking out MacLochlainn they encountered him on his native soil of Tyrone. Having only his personal bodyguard with him, MacLochlainn was heavily outnumbered but still decided to stand his ground and fight. In the battle that followed he was killed.

"Revenge!"
With MacLochlainn dead, Rory O'Connor lost no time in ensuring that the next High King would be from Connacht. He quickly made the rounds of provincial kingdoms, securing loyalties and taking hostages from some, including Diarmuid

MacMurrough. As MacMurrough was an inveterate supporter of Mac Lochlainn, the High King also decided to withdraw the kingship of Leinster from him. To the Ostmen of Dublin, O'Connor exhibited such grandiose generosity that they were compelled to support him. A tax of 4,000 cattle was levied on the rest of Ireland and given to them.

When MacLochlainn was alive, Diarmuid MacMurrough had not hesitated to involve himself in the affairs of other kingdoms. Those whom he had subjected to his tyranny were now more than anxious to square accounts with him. But there was one King who placed himself above these others for MacMurrough had not only taken his wife but had also made a fool of him. Tiernan O'Rourke, at long last saw his chance to get revenge for the humiliation he had undergone at the hand of Diarmuid MacMurrough.

With O'Rourke in the lead, accompanied by MacTurkill from Dublin and MacGilla Patraic of Ossory along with warriors from Breifne, Connacht, and all over Leinster, a strike force made ready to descend on McMurrough's home at Hy Kinsella.

The Flight of Diarmuid McMurrough

Well aware that he was a marked man and knowing that this time he would not be left to lick his wounds, MacMurrough made plans for his imminent departure from Hy Kinsella. Taking his wife and daughter with him along with a small number of followers, he fled Ireland, making for the port of Bristol on August 1st 1166, leaving his son Domhnall MacMurrough Kavanagh in charge.

O'Rourke duly arrived at the head of MacMurrough's enemies. Enraged that their prey had flown, they vented their spleen on MacMurrough's castle, after which hostages were taken. Apart from those hostages sent to the court of the High King, Enna, (Diarmuid's son and Tánaiste) was taken to the neighbouring kingdom of Ossory by the King, MacGilla Patraic. Part of the Kingdom of Leinster was also annexed by MacGilla Patraic with the remainder being left in the governance of Diarmuid's brother Murchad. As far as the Irish Kings were concerned, Diarmuid MacMurrough, like his protector Muircheartaigh MacLochlainn had been destroyed. But MacMurrough had not given up. He was still alive and determined at all costs to make a comeback.

Chapter 2

Ireland Betrayed

MacMurrough gives Allegiance to the English King
On the Trail of King Henry II

After departing Ireland, MacMurrough's ship made for the port of Bristol, where he went to the monastery of St. Augustine, which was home to an old family friend, Robert Fitzharding. Here he sought Fitzharding's advice about his predicament. Fitzharding had once been an important man and also a friend and advisor to King Henry II of England, but now he was in the autumn of his life and had retired to the monastery to "make his soul".

After relating to Fitzharding the fate that had overtaken him, MacMurrough told him of his determination to regain his kingdom at all costs. Fitzharding, doubtless with an eye to English advantage, advised him to seek out the King of England personally and ask for his assistance.

King Henry was not to be found in England. On learning that the King had travelled to Aquitaine in France to put down an insurrection, MacMurrough, in his eagerness, decided to follow him there.

When he arrived at the Court of the King, Diarmuid was well received by Henry who possibly had foreknowledge of this Irish King who was seeking his help. Diarmuid stated his case and agreed to swear loyalty to him in return for his help. The contemporary historian Giraldus Cambrensis (Gerald of Wales, 1146-1223) records his words as follows: "God, who dwells on high, guard and save you King Henry! May He in the same manner give you heart, courage and the inclination to avenge the shame and misfortune which my own people have brought upon me! Noble King Henry, hear of where I was born, of what country. Of Ireland I was born a lord, in Ireland I was acknowledged a King. But wrongfully my own people have cast me out of my kingdom. To you good Sire, I come to make complaint in the presence of the barons of your empire. From henceforth onwards, for all the day of my life I will become your liegeman on condition that you be my ally, so that I will not lose everything. I will acknowledge you as sire and lord in the presence of your barons and earls."[5]

"Laudabiliter"

Henry was pleased to accept Diarmuid's allegiance and saw an opportunity in his plight. He had had designs on Ireland for many years and had hoped one day to be able to invade the country. When Pope Anastasius IV had died in 1154 and an Englishman, Nicholas Breakspear, had succeeded to the throne of Peter, taking the name Adrian IV, Henry had lost no time in making representations to him in order to obtain his blessing for such an undertaking. He sent a monk by the name of John of Salisbury to Rome as his ambassador to the Holy See and John, acting on the King's instructions, filled the Pope's ear with tales of the declining state of the Church in Ireland and the need for the restoration of discipline and morals. He promised that if the Pope would bless the proposed undertaking, the payment of "Peter's Pence"[i] would be

---

[i] Peter's Pence" or "Alms of St. Peter" were originally monies voluntarily paid by the faithful for the support of The Holy See. The practice first began in Saxon

enforced from every house in the land. John of Salisbury later wrote: "In response to my petition the Pope granted and donated Ireland to the illustrious King of England, Henry, to be held by him and his successors...He did this in virtue of the long-established right, reputed to derive from the donation of Constantine, whereby all islands are considered to belong to the Roman Church."[6]

Shortly afterwards, Pope Adrian IV issued the Papal Bull "Laudabiliter"[i] which stated in part: "Thy greatness, as is becoming a Catholic prince, is laudably and successfully employed in thought and intention, to propagate a glorious name upon earth and lay up in heaven the rewards of a happy eternity...thou, dearest son in Christ hast likewise signified to us, that for the purpose of subjecting the people of Ireland to laws and eradicating vice from among them, thou art desirous of entering that land and also of paying from each house an annual tribute of one penny to St. Peter...We, therefore, with approving and favourable views commend thy pious and laudable desire...that thou enter that island and pursue those things which shall tend to the honour of God and the salvation of his people...that thou mayest merit an everlasting reward of happiness hereafter..."[7]

England and continued under the Normans, but now more as a form of taxation than a pious contribution.

[i] The existence of the Papal Bull "Laudabiliter" cannot be ascertained beyond all doubt. The only copy of the document exists in the papers of Giraldus Cambrensis (Gerald of Wales). There is no record of it in the Vatican archives. Furthermore, when Pope Alexander III wrote to the Irish bishops on September 20th 1172 concerning the then accomplished invasion, he makes neither mention of or reference to "Laudabiliter" but rather attributes the invasion to King Henry. Historians have generally relied on the works of Gerald of Wales as being "the only available historical document of the time. His works do indeed offer a rare and valuable firsthand account of the period of the Norman Invasion of Ireland but their complete reliability cannot be made sure of.

At the time when Pope Adrian IV issued "Laudabiliter", a mere two years had passed since the great synod of Kells in 1152 where, in the presence of the Legate of Pope Eugenius III, Cardinal Lecaro, the implementation of Church reform initiated decades earlier, had been greatly accelerated. It is a source of wonder that after such a short time, permission was given by an English Pope to an English King to enter Ireland to "regulate the Church" by force. It cannot be overlooked that the payment of "Peter's Pence" figures prominently both in King Henry's offer and in the Pope's document. At this time, the apostolic city of Armagh received or regulated and distributed within Ireland all Irish church alms, as St. Patrick had ordained. That a form of church taxation begun in Saxon England and continued under the Normans would be extended to Ireland if King Henry were ruler cannot but have appealed to Pope Adrian IV.

Having obtained the Pope's approval, the plan was shelved. Other more important matters had occupied Henry's time and his mother the Empress Mathilda was opposed to it. Here now was an opportunity for Henry to revisit the matter.

An Act of Treason

If Diarmuid was not already aware of the King's shelved plan to invade Ireland or the Pope's approval of it, it is difficult to imagine that Robert Fitzharding, the King's friend, had not put him in the picture. Or had Fitzharding withheld this information from him, advising him to seek the King's help, knowing that in MacMurrough's request the King would see his chance to finally execute his plan?

In any event, instead of directly seeking to hire paid mercenaries from abroad to help him (as had been the practice of Irish Kings in the past), Diarmuid instead approached the monarch of a foreign power to invite him to intervene directly in the affairs of Ireland in order to help him regain the throne of Leinster. Did MacMurrough really imagine that the King of England would help him take back his throne and ask for nothing more than his proffered hand of friendship and loyalty in return? He knew full well that there would be a price to be paid, a price much higher than the help given. In this lay Diarmuid's act of treachery and betrayal to the land of his forefathers. By promising allegiance to a foreign monarch in return for his help, he no doubt felt that one day the throne of Leinster would again be his and maybe, if everything went according to plan, even the throne of the High King of Ireland. If MacMurrough could have seen the centuries of trial that were to follow, would he have acted differently?

Wales – "The Warrior's Nest"
Strongbow and the Geraldines

King Henry II was too busy with his own affairs at this time, but he gave Diarmuid a letter encouraging any of his English or French subjects who so desired, to help him regain his kingdom. He wrote: "...We have admitted to our grace and favour Diarmuid, Prince of Leinster...If any person from within our wide dominions wishes to help in restoring him, as having done us fealty and homage, let him know that he has our goodwill and permission to do this."[8] Much encouraged by his audience with the King, Diarmuid returned to England and, after trying his luck in various quarters without success, he went to Wales and approached the former Earl of Pembroke and Strigul. His name was Richard Fitzgilbert de Clare, better known by his 'nom de guerre' – "Strongbow".

An Agreement with Strongbow

Strongbow was persona non grata with King Henry and his land had been confiscated by him due to his failure to support Henry at the time of his succession to the English throne. Moving to pastures new appealed to him. He agreed to assist Diarmuid in the restoration of his kingdom but in return wanted to marry Diarmuid's daughter Aoife and succeed Diarmuid as King of Leinster after his death. Diarmuid agreed to this and in so doing broke Brehon Law, as he did not have the right to name his successor to the throne of Leinster.

Strongbow

Having reached this agreement with Strongbow, Diarmuid then succeeded in getting help from other Cambro-Norman Knights and from Knights in the Welsh-Flemish colony where the descendants of those who had once helped the Normans conquer England lived. They were mostly all related, being descended from the progeny of the various liaisons of the Welsh Princess Nesta Ferch Rhys, wife of Gerald of Windsor and daughter of Rhys app Tewdwr Mawr, the last Welsh prince who had up to that time remained independent of the Normans. She was the mother-hen of the Norman-Welsh brood, being either mother or grandmother to many of those who Diarmuid now enrolled in his expeditionary force. The surnames of these Knights are Irish surnames now: Fitzgerald[i], deBarri (Barry), and deRoche to name but a few, commonly known as "The Geraldines" after Nesta's husband Gerald. Mac Murrough promised them land around Wexford, at that time an Ostman settlement.

These Norman knights did not regard themselves as a reconnaissance party for an invasion of Ireland by Henry II, but rather as adventurers moving on to pastures new. Doubtless they would have much preferred if Diarmuid MacMurrough had not gone cap in hand to King Henry. It would have been much more to their liking if he had come directly to them first. Then they could have given him the help he desired, the payment for which would have been a new home in Ireland. Leaving Wales and moving to Ireland could have meant escaping the over-lordship of King Henry, but now, thanks to MacMurrough, King Henry would keep a very close eye on their adventure.

MacMurrough Returns to Ireland

Diarmuid MacMurrough returned to Ireland in 1167 with a small force of Norman Knights and foot soldiers commanded by Richard FitzGodebert in order to establish a foothold for further operations. After spending the winter hiding out in a monastery, he returned to Ferns and his home at Hy Kinsella.

---

[i] Fitzgerald" from the French "fils du Gerald" or "son of Gerald". Many Irish surnames of Norman extraction begin in this way, for example Fitzsimons and Fitzmaurice. All trace their roots back to the Normans. However, the Irish surname "Fitzpatrick" is not of Norman descent. The ancient rulers of the kingdom of Ossory "Mac GillaPatraic" changed their surname to the Norman style during the reign of King Henry VIII after accepting English title at the time of the Tudor policy of "Surrender and Regrant". Other Irish surnames of Norman extraction have been altered since the Reformation, with the "Fitz" being dropped. Examples of this are: Fitzthomas and Fitzhenry which became Thomas and Henry respectively.

Word now got out of his return and before long his old enemy Tiernan O'Rourke came to Hy Kinsella to visit him. MacMurrough was full of friendship and contrition for his past misdemeanours, portraying himself as a man who wanted to spend his final years in peace at home with his family. He finally gave to O'Rourke the gold that was the price of honour for carrying off Dervorgilla, as required by Brehon law. Ever the fox, he was playing for time until a larger force of Normans should arrive. His family was told of the help he had been promised abroad but the fact that he had also given away the right of succession to his kingdom was not divulged. By the second half of 1168, the promised Welsh help still had not appeared. Growing a little anxious, Diarmuid was spurred into action by the return home of his son and Tánaiste Enna, who had been held hostage in Ossory. On hearing of MacMurrough's return, MacGillaPatraic had blinded him before setting him free.

Enraged by this, MacMurrough longed to retaliate but was powerless to do so. Where were those Norman Knights? He immediately sent his trusted secretary Maurice O'Regan to Wales to remind Strongbow and the others of their promise to him.

Chapter 3

The Norman Landings

War and Peace

The Capture of Wexford

On May 1st, 1169, Maurice de Prendergast, Robert de Barry and Robert FitzStephen arrived on the Irish shoreline with thirty knights, six hundred archers and a force of men at arms under their command. Accompanied by attendants and their baggage train, the total landing force is reckoned at about 2,000 men. Strongbow's uncle Hervey Mountmaurice also accompanied them. Landing at Bannow Bay (Baginbun) on the south Wexford coast, they immediately established earthwork fortifications in case of attack. As soon as news of their arrival reached the MacMurrough's home at Hy-Kinsella, Diarmuid and his son Domhnall departed with 500 men to join forces with them, after which their joint army marched against the Ostman City of Wexford. Ireland had never seen anything like it before: foot soldiers and archers flanked by squadrons of horsemen, heavily armed and armoured, with huge shields and long lances. The Norman war machine had arrived in Ireland. Having no answer to this medieval blitzkrieg, the Ostmen were soon besieged behind Wexford's walls and before long they sued for peace.

After granting Wexford to Robert Fitzstephen and Maurice Fitzgerald, Diarmuid MacMurrough and his new allies went to

Ferns where they rested and plotted for three weeks without being molested. Greatly heartened by this lack of response from the High King Rory O'Connor, who, with sheer weight of numbers alone, could have easily snuffed out the Norman adventure, MacMurrough planned his next move.[i]

With his strength renewed, MacMurrough now turned his attention to Ossory to get revenge for the blinding of his son Enna. The men of Ossory fought bravely but after being decoyed out from a position of defence into one of attack, they were overwhelmed by the battle prowess of the Norman cavalry.

MacMurrough was now to lose some of his foreign contingent. Maurice dePrendergast decided he had had enough of this adventure and wanted to return to Wales with his personal contingent of 300 men. Diarmuid was not prepared to let him go and prevented his departure. The dispute turned to rancour with dePrendergast finally deciding that if Diarmuid would not let him go then he would fight on the side of Diarmuid's enemies. He now determined to join forces with MacGiolla Patraic who had survived the ravaging of Ossory.

MacMurrough Submits to the High King

On hearing that the men of Ossory had been overwhelmed by Diarmuid and his army of foreigners, the High King Rory O'Connor finally began to sit up and take notice of what was

---

[i] Of this initial period the eminent historian Martin Haverty writes "Never did a national calamity, so mighty and so deplorable, proceed from a commencement more contemptible than did the English occupation of Ireland."

As mentioned in Chapter 1, it was not unusual for the regional Kings to strengthen their armies with mercenaries and it is likely that MacMurrough's foreigners were viewed as such and not a force that would ever be a threat to the nation.

going on. He headed south-east towards Wexford with his army. After a few half-hearted skirmishes, peace talks began and, to the High King's surprise, MacMurrough was more than eager to come to terms with him. It was agreed that Diarmuid would be King of all Leinster outside of Dublin on condition that the foreigners would leave Ireland. Diarmuid then pledged allegiance to Rory O'Connor as High King of Ireland and gave him hostages, including his youngest son Conor, who was also his favourite. In return, the High King promised his daughter in marriage to Conor.

Rory was satisfied with Diarmuid's pledge of loyalty and left to return to Connacht. But as soon as his back was turned, Diarmuid, greatly heartened by O'Connor's lack of enthusiasm for battle, sent word to Strongbow in Wales to come to Ireland with all possible haste.

The Fall of Dublin

Battle on the Beach

By this time Strongbow was almost ready to make his move. Preparatory to his own arrival, he sent some more knights and archers under Raymond Fitzgerald (known as "le Gros") to reinforce the garrison at Bannow Bay. No sooner had they arrived there than a large army of Ostmen from Waterford accompanied by Irish from the surrounding areas came and attacked their water's edge fortress. Once more the military prowess of the Normans won the day and the Ostmen were forced to retreat, leaving behind many of their number, both dead and prisoners of the Normans. Seventy of these prisoners were high ranking Ostmen and a large ransom was offered for their release, but the Normans rejected it as they had thought of a better use for them. After having had their limbs broken by the soldiers, the seventy were hurled from a nearby cliff into the sea, in the knowledge that news of the atrocity would spread far and wide and strike fear into the hearts of both Ostmen and Irish alike.

The Arrival of Strongbow and the Battle for Waterford

As Strongbow made the final preparations for his Irish adventure, a messenger arrived from King Henry II commanding that the planned expedition to Ireland should not proceed as King Henry had intended that MacMurrough's help should be provided by loyal subjects of the crown and not those who were disaffected. News had reached Henry of the success that the small number of Normans who had already landed in Ireland had achieved and he now feared that if Strongbow and his men succeeded in gaining control of Ireland, an independent Norman kingdom might be the result. The King was not prepared to tolerate such a scenario. Nevertheless, in spite of this direct order, Strongbow decided to disobey. The throne of Leinster (not to mention Diarmuid's daughter Aoife) would not be his if he obeyed the King.

On August 23rd, 1170, Strongbow landed at Baginbun with two hundred knights and one thousand foot soldiers and after joining forces with Raymond le Gros wasted no time in attacking Waterford where the Ostmen of Waterford were joined in their defence of the city by the native Irish from the surrounding hinterland. The Norman atrocity at Baginbun had failed in its purpose. Aware of what had happened to the prisoners there, all were prepared to fight to the death in case a similar fate befell them. Twice the Norman attack failed before the city wall was breached by the toppling of a house on which its supports depended. Having made themselves an entrance, the besiegers swarmed through it. No quarter was shown to the defenders. When the battle was over, Diarmuid arrived with his daughter Aoife just as the Normans were about to put to the sword Reginald, a Lord of Danish extraction and the

O'Phelan, Prince of the Déisi[i], who had taken refuge in a tower. MacMurrough intervened on their behalf and they were spared, along with the now unresisting population.

In the midst of the carnage, the marriage between Strongbow and Aoife then took place as promised. There was no time to celebrate, however, since Dublin beckoned. MacMurrough and his allies departed Waterford at once.

The Capture of Dublin

By now fully aware of Diarmuid's double-dealing, the High King of Ireland, Rory O'Connor, finally acted along with Tiernan O'Rourke and moved to save Dublin from Norman occupation. Having set up their encampment at Clondalkin, all the approaches to Dublin were guarded, or so they thought. Diarmuid, however, succeeded in leading the Norman army on unknown paths through the Wicklow and Dublin mountains past Glendalough. To the horror of the Ostmen the joint armies of Diarmuid and Strongbow appeared in full battle array at the city walls, as if out of nowhere.

The Ostmen of Dublin, along with their King Hasculf MacTurkill were by now well aware of the battle prowess of the Normans and the swift defeats inflicted on the other Ostmen settlements of Wexford and Waterford. Deciding that discretion was the better part of valour, MacTurkill decided to sue for peace and sent the Archbishop of Dublin, Laurence O'Toole to open negotiations with the Normans. Rory O'Connor was so outraged that the Ostmen were parleying that he decided to leave them to their fate.

---

[i] The Déisi were an ancient Gaelic tribe originally from the area of modern day south Meath / north Kildare. Prior to the eighth century, they were expelled from this area, thereafter moving to and conquering Waterford. Waterford is still often referred to as "The Déise"

As the peace talks dragged on, a band of Normans led by two of Strongbow's Lieutenants, Raymond le Gros and Milo deCogan, launched a surprise attack and broke through the Norse defences at their weakest point after which an all out attack followed. Within a short time, they had captured the city, slaughtering many of its inhabitants and, in their desire for plunder, did not spare the city's churches. Those Norsemen who could escape, (including Hasculff) retreated to their longboats and left, vowing to return and retake the Norse city. Dublin was now in Norman hands and Milo de Cogan was appointed City Commander.

The High King Kills his Hostages

Now that much of Leinster was his and Rory O'Connor had not seen fit to attack him, MacMurrough felt that it was time to look further afield. First on the list was his old enemy O'Rourke. If he succeeded in defeating O'Rourke, he had decided on a battle against the army of O'Connor in order to secure the High Kingship for himself. What Strongbow's ultimate objectives were remain unclear.

The Alliance marched through Meath and on into Breifne, leaving terrible destruction in its wake. Many churches were plundered and destroyed including Slane, Dowth and Kilskeery. The important monastic town of Kells was burnt to the ground. One Gaelic Chieftain, Domhnall of Bregia (East Meath), who had been previously deposed by Rory O'Connor, joined the side of the Normans. However, MacMurrough's old enemy Tiernan O'Rourke evaded him. Twice O'Rourke had attacked a part of the Norman army and then quickly retreated, after which he moved westward to unite his army with that of the High King.

Despite all that had happened since the return of Diarmuid MacMurrough to Irish shores, the High King had avoided meeting him and his Norman army in battle. At this stage, could he have had any doubt that the Normans were in Ireland for the long haul? Still vacillating, he decided to give Diarmuid one last chance to retreat back to Leinster for he still had an ace in the hole – Diarmuid's favourite son Conor remained in his court. Messengers were dispatched to MacMurrough with an ultimatum: "Contrary to the conditions of our treaty of peace, you have invited a host of foreigners into this island, and yet as long as you kept within the bounds of Leinster we bore it patiently. But, now, forasmuch as, regardless of your solemn oath, and having no concern for the fate of the hostage you gave, you have broken the bounds agreed on, and insolently crossed the frontiers of your own territory...either restrain in future the irruption of your foreign warbands, or we will certainly have your son's head cut off and we will send it to you."[9]

On receipt of the message, Diarmuid either regarded it as a bluff or "would have preferred the gratification of his revenge to the lives of all his children".[10] He returned the messengers to the High King with the following message: "We will not desist from the enterprise we have undertaken...until we have obtained with it the monarchy of the whole of Ireland"[11].

On receiving MacMurrough's reply, the High King was reluctant to carry through on his threat. Rory O'Connor knew that if he killed the MacMurrough hostages, Connacht might pay a terrible price in blood.

As the High King continued to vacillate, Tiernan O'Rourke was at hand and he advised that Conor MacMurrough and the other hostages should be killed. At his urging, Rory carried out his threat and executed the prisoners – a son, a grandson (son of Domhnall MacMurrough Kavanagh) and a foster nephew of Diarmuid MacMurrough – at Athlone. Tiernan O'Rourke also killed the hostages he had previously taken from East Meath which had now gone over to the MacMurrough side.

The Death of MacMurrough

Shortly after the executions, MacMurrough was taken ill and retreated to his Castle at Ferns where he died of some unknown disease on May 1st 1171, aged 81.

Diarmuid MacMurrough has gone down in Irish history, reviled by the native Irish as the man who brought the English to Ireland, becoming known as "Diarmuid na nGall" or "Dermot of the Foreigners".

His obituary in the ancient chronicles of Ireland (compiled from older monastic manuscripts and records of Ireland's history by the O'Clerys, who were the hereditary historians to the princes of TirConaill (Donegal) in the sixteenth and seventeenth centuries), commonly known as "The Annals of the Four Masters", is unequivocal in its judgement of him. For the year 1171 the following is recorded:

"Diarmait Mac Murchada, King of Leinster, who had spread terror throughout Ireland after putting the English in possession of the country, committing excessive evils against the Irish people, and plundering and burning many churches among which were Kells, Clonard and others, died this year of an intolerable and uncommon disease. He became putrid while living, by the miracles of God, through the intervention of Columcille, Finian and other saints of Ireland for having violated and plundered their churches. He died at Ferns, without making a will, without penance, without the Eucharist and without Extreme Unction, as his evil deeds deserved." [12]

Chapter 4

Expanding the Bridgehead

King Henry II Comes to Ireland
The Return of the Ostmen
As Strongbow visited his dying father-in-law, the Norsemen returned to Dublin on a mission of reconquest and vengeance. Their deposed King Hasculf MacTurkill had kept his promise, bringing back to Dublin with him a huge Norse army commanded by John "the Wode" or "the Mad", so called because he was a Berserker warrior.[i]* A large armada of ships from the Isle of Man, Norway, and the Hebrides had ferried the Norse army on its mission of reconquering Dublin.

Once ashore, their iron phalanx took a heavy toll on the Normans who were forced to retreat from their forward positions back into the city. The Viking ranks were only broken after Milo de Cogan's brother Richard emerged unseen from Dublin's South Gate and attacked the Norsemen in the rear

---

[i] A Berserker was a Norse warrior who fought wearing a skin of a bear, a wolf or a boar. He entered battle in a trance-like fury, the cause of which is disputed (possibly magic mushrooms, hypnosis or both). Foaming at the mouth and biting his shield, he invariably provoked terror among the enemy before battle commenced and accounted for large numbers of them after battle was joined. The Norse god Odin was his patron. When the fury wore off, the Berserker experienced a dullness of mind that could last for days.

with heavily armoured knights on horseback and archers using armour-piercing arrows.

John the Wode was killed and Hasculf was captured and later beheaded due to his insistence that, if he were freed, he would lead an even larger force to recapture Dublin.

The Contest for Dublin

After this bruising encounter, the Normans had scarcely time to draw breath before the High King Rory O'Connor led a massive Irish army against Dublin, determined to bring the burgeoning invasion to a conclusion. For a time, a national army existed with the common purpose of defeating the Normans. This was after the Archbishop of Dublin, Laurence O'Toole, had successfully persuaded the Irish Kings to put aside their differences for the good of Ireland and drive these adventurers out of the country.

Outnumbered and cut off from the sea by Norse ships that had sailed from the Isle of Man, the Normans were under siege in Dublin for two months, during which time Strongbow was offered the Kingship of Leinster by the High King. He refused the offer. Desperately short of food and with surrender not something that the Normans would contemplate, it was decided to try the unexpected. Three companies slipped out of the city unnoticed, one led by Strongbow and the other two led by Carew and de Cogan. While O'Connor and some of his men were bathing in the Liffey, the Norman bands descended on the Irish camp at Castleknock, taking the High King's army completely by surprise. Panic and mayhem ensued, as the Irish struggled to reach their weapons and resist this unexpected attack. Many of them were slain and their supplies were captured. The siege was broken and the Irish routed. O'Connor narrowly escaped, while many of his men succumbed to the waters of the River Liffey after being fired on as they desperately tried to reach safety.

The Arrival of the English King

King Henry II[i] had been following events in Ireland with interest. With the Normans – led by his disaffected and disobedient knight Strongbow – now masters of the battlefield and ready to expand their bridgehead, he had no intention of giving Strongbow the time and space to establish a rival Norman Kingdom in Ireland which in time could pose a threat to the security of England. Deciding to make plain, not so much that Ireland was his, but rather that he would be King of all Norman possessions be they in England, France or Ireland, the King assembled a large army, ready to overthrow whatever Norman or Gaelic force might pose an obstacle to his rule. As he prepared to set sail, a visitor arrived begging to enter his presence. It was Strongbow. He knew of the King's imminent arrival in Ireland and feared that if he waited until the latter's coming in order to ask forgiveness for his disobedience, then it might be too late. He was eventually allowed to enter the King's presence to express his remorse and promise his allegiance anew. He sailed with the King who departed England in a fleet of 240 ships which landed in Waterford on October 17th, 1171, with a huge army of 500 knights and 4,000 archers. The total strength of his expedition was estimated to be around 10,000. On landing, he was met by the King of Desmond, Dermot MacCarthy, who renounced his allegiance to Rory O'Connor and offered King Henry his submission.

The Submission of the Irish Kings

King Henry II came to Ireland with all the trappings of state that he could muster in order to create a good impression on the Irish leaders. His plan was not to get them to submit by

---

[i] The son of the Empress Mathilda, King Henry II was known to the Irish chieftains as "Henry Fitzempress".

force of arms but rather by a display of military might and the use of all the charm and wile at his disposal thereby avoiding a sea of blood.

After his arrival, King Henry and his army marched towards Dublin along the East coast, their journey being more like a victory parade than an army marching towards battle.

After the King reached Dublin a huge encampment was set up, which was so large that the city of Dublin could not hold it and the tented town was erected outside the city walls. A great hall made of willow branches was constructed as the King's hall of state. As word spread over the coming weeks of the arrival of this powerful and statesmanlike Angevin[i] King, it was to this Dublin hall that the Irish Kings made their way in order to submit to him. These Kings were treated as they had never been treated before. There was nothing left wanting in the hospitality shown to them. Opulence and wealth, not to mention the trappings of Norman military might were everywhere on display.

King Henry II

King Henry made a good impression on the Gaelic kings. He made much of his apparent displeasure that the Norman adventurers had acted against his will and when Fitzstephen, who had been captured by the Irish during an attack on Carrick Castle in Wexford, was handed over to him, the latter's chains were not removed for some

---

[i] Angevin – literally from the French region of Anjou. The Angevin Kings of England were Henry II, Richard I and John.

days as an apparent punishment for the disobedience he had shown to his Monarch.

After all the decades of war, it seemed to many of the Irish Kings and bishops that there was a chance for respite with the arrival of Henry. However reluctant they were to offer their submission to someone who was not of their own race, they knew that their submission was equivocal. For them to support Henry, he and his Normans in their turn could not mistreat them. Here perhaps was an overlord powerful enough to bring peace and stability to the country and an end to the incessant feuding. The land that the Normans had already taken was the price to be paid for this, but the kingdoms of most of the Irish Kings were intact and Henry demanded very little of them. Submission to a High King was in the past something that they had done without compromising their own kingdoms. If a High King were not to their liking, they had gone their own way and suffered the consequences or given their support to a different contender. In the minds of the Irish Kings, the consideration of their own small kingdoms was paramount, the interest of the country as a whole being very much in second place. Each King made up his own mind regarding what was the best thing to do. They were completely devoid of an overall unity of purpose or action and lacking in the leadership that should have been shown them by the High King.

The High King himself, Rory O'Connor, did not attend the Dublin festivities but instead prepared for battle to protect his own Kingdom of Connacht. Henry dispatched emissaries to meet with him on the banks of the Shannon, after which he is reputed to have sent his submission by messenger, while the Northern O'Néill did not submit. The bishops, including the Archbishop of Dublin, Laurence O'Toole, also paid Henry their respects as they welcomed the peace that his overlordship could bring.

The Synod of Cashel

Henry's visit to Ireland occurred at a time when he was out of favour with the Pope because of the murder of the Archbishop of Canterbury, Thomas a Becket, which he himself had instigated. The King had even thought it necessary to take the precaution of closing the Channel ports before he left England so that any arriving Papal ambassadors who might stir up trouble would be kept out of the country while he was away. In order to regain favour with Rome, he called a synod of Bishops that took place in Cashel at the beginning of 1172. Since the decayed state of the Irish church was the pretext for a planned invasion, it is important to note that at the synod nothing was found wanting in the Irish Church regarding doctrine and the only reforms enacted were with regard to practice. Mundane articles such as the provision of catechism for children were passed, along with regulations on baptism and marriage. "Peter's Pence" was also introduced, and native liturgical rites were formally ended.

"The Five Bloods"

In histories of the coming of the Normans to Ireland, it has often been recorded how King Henry II extended Anglo Norman laws and customs, not only for the use of the Normans in Ireland but also for "The Five Bloods" or the chief families of the five provinces of Ireland (being Leinster, Meath, Connacht Munster and Ulster).

In his account of the arrival of Henry II, the twelfth century historian Matthew Paris writes that: "King Henry assembled a council where the laws of England were by all freely received and confirmed with due legal solemnity"[13] However the historian "on the spot" who was Giraldus Cambrensis (Gerald of Wales) makes no mention of this. What is certain is that the Gaelic ruling families of the five provinces (referred to by the Noramans as "The five bloods") and their families were allowed either by Henry II or by his son King John, the right to plead in a Norman court, as among the plea rolls in Birmingham's Tower in Dublin Castle during the reign of Edward II were the names of: "... O'Néill de Ultonia, O'Molaghlin de Midia, O'Connoghor de Connacia, O'Brien de Thotmonia et MacMurrough de Lagenia."[14] This right was to be retained by them until "The Statute of Kilkenny" was promulgated in 1366, after which the entire Gaelic nation was legally cast aside, thereafter being regarded as and legally referred to as "The King's Irish Enemies".

Norman Crimes Against the Irish People
As the "Five Bloods" were but a fraction of the Gaelic Irish, the remainder of the people of Ireland were ipso facto placed outside the law even in the parts of Ireland ruled by the Normans. As Daniel O'Connell (1775 – 1847) recounts: "They were treated as perpetual enemies, whom it was lawful to rob or kill, at the pleasure or caprice of an English subject"[15]
There are many recorded cases of how the native Irish suffered as a result of the willingness of English judges to regard them as being outside the law. In the common plea rolls of 4 Edward II, the following is recorded: "William Fitz Roger being arraigned for the death of Roger (O'Hederiscal) by him feloniously slain, comes and says that he could not commit felony by means of such killing; because the aforesaid Roger was an Irishman, and not of free blood...and therefore the said William, as far as regards the aforesaid felony, is acquitted. But inasmuch as the aforesaid Roger O'Hederiscal was an Irishman of our Lord the King, the aforesaid William was re-committed to jail, until he shall find pledges to pay five marks to our Lord the King, for the value of the aforesaid Irishman."[16] The nineteenth century Irish historian Fr. Jeremiah Vaughan (speaking at an Irish rally in New York in 1866) related to his audience how in the aftermath of the coming of the Normans:

"A trial had taken place in which two Englishmen convicted of having committed a rape, were released because the victim was only an Irishwoman. Any Englishman could legally drive away an Irishman from his land and settle on it himself. It was a crime to have any commercial relations with Irishmen. It was high treason to marry an Irishwoman or to employ an Irish nurse. So terrible were the sufferings of the Irish people under this state of things, that they offered a thousand marks – a very large sum in those days – to be admitted to the rights of English citizenship but were refused equal justice even on those terms. And when at last in the reign of Henry IV, the poor Irish people began to leave the country, a law was enacted prohibiting: "the further departure of the Irish enemy". In the course of centuries these unnatural laws have been, to a certain extent, modified, as civilization and enlightenment have advanced; but though not enforced, many of them may yet be found un-repealed on the English statute books."[17]

Although the legal protection of English law was sparsely granted to the Gaelic Irish, it would appear that Henry II had a special place in his heart for the Ostmen of Ireland's coastal cities who had descended from the same bloodline as the Normans. To the Ostmen of Waterford he granted: "that they should have and enjoy in Ireland the laws of England, and according to that law be judged and inherit"[18]

Initial Attempt at Conquest
The Plan for Complete Norman Conquest
After the conclusion of the synod, it was time for the more important business of confirming the Norman Knights as rulers of the lands they had already seized, while other parts of the country which the Normans planned on seizing were allotted by the King. Henry evidently had no intention of keeping faith with the Irish Kings. His division and allocation

of the land of Ireland to his Barons was an act which was to set the tone for the centuries that followed. The entire country was split into sections and divided among ten men.[i] Although they had as yet only conquered a fraction of the country, the English King unlawfully gave them title to it all, with not one square mile being allocated to the Irish.

To Strongbow was given Leinster, apart from the city of Dublin, which was granted to the citizens of Bristol. To Hugh deLacy was given Meath and he was also appointed as Governor of Dublin and, as such, Justiciar or Chief Justice. This was the most important role within the Hiberno Norman government as the Chief Justice would be directly answerable to the King for the conduct of Norman affairs within the country and would also command the King's army in Ireland. To John de Courcy was granted Ulidia (north east Ulster). In this division of spoils, Henry ensured that no one man was too powerful and that, by limiting Strongbow's grant to Leinster and placing de Lacy in command in Meath, Strongbow and his ambition would be hemmed in.

Henry's visit to Ireland lasted until April of 1172, although he would have left earlier in order to deal with the threat of a Papal interdict hanging over his head, but the storms raging in the Irish Sea prevented his departure.

The Death of Tiernan O'Rourke

No sooner had Henry departed than the Normans turned their attention to fulfilling the land allocations which had been given them by the King to the detriment of the native rulers, as had been their practice in Wales. Hugh de Lacy set about extending his domain beyond the boundaries of the old Kingdom of

---

[i] The ten men were Richard Fitzgilbert deClare (Strongbow), Robert Fitzstephens, Myles deCogan, Philip Bruce, Sir Hugh deLacy, Sir John deCourcy, William Fitzadelm deBurgo, Sir Thomas deClare, Otho deGrandison and Robert LePoer.

Meath and into the territory of Diarmuid McMurrough's old rival Tiernan O'Rourke. It was here that O'Rourke met his end as, during a supposed parley with deLacy, he was killed by a lance thrown by one of de Lacy's knights named Griffith. Once dead, O'Rourke's head was cut from his body and both parts of him were sent.to Dublin to be prominently displayed in the city, his body being hung by the feet.

The Irish quickly became familiar with the strengths and weaknesses of the Norman war machine and successfully adapted their battle tactics to suit. When Strongbow tried to extend his Leinster kingdom by raiding along the Offaly border, he lost a large number of men including his son in law, deQuenci. And when, in 1174, he advanced in a south-westerly direction, he was defeated in Thurles, Co. Tipperary, by the army of the King of Thomond Domhnall O'Brien and lost over 700 men, including four knights. Pursued by O'Brien, Strongbow took refuge in Waterford where he remained under siege until LeGros returned from Wales to come to his rescue.

The Capture of Limerick

On a mission of vengeance for the trials of his master, LeGros and his army attacked deep into the interior and as far as Limerick, the capital of Thomond on the West coast. Terrible slaughter and plunder followed, after which a Norman garrison was installed in the city under the command of Myles deCogan.

The McMurrough's of Leinster now launched a bid to regain their old Kingdom. A brother in law of Diarmuid Mac Murrough, Domhnall Kavanagh McMurrough, tried to overthrow Strongbow's grip on Leinster but was defeated and killed in battle, apparently by two Norman agents in his own army who attacked him from behind.

Even territory as far south as Cork and Kerry was not safe from the Norman grasp and these areas were attacked by Norman troops led by Robert Fitzstephen.

A Peace Treaty?

Tired of the unending Norman raids, the High King Rory O'Connor decided to send emissaries, including the Archbishop of Dublin Laurence O'Toole, to Henry II to inform him (in case he was in any doubt) of what his Norman Knights were up to in Ireland. The negotiations that followed ended in the signing of a peace treaty in 1175. Known as "The Treaty of Windsor", it was supposed to restrict the Norman expansion. It formally recognised Rory O'Connor as King of Connacht and also as High King of Ireland under the overlordship of Henry, who took the title "Lord of Ireland".[i] O'Connor also pledged to collect taxes from the Irish Kings that were to be paid to the English King. Any of the Irish who had fled from their territories that were now occupied by the English were to be free to return to their homes and live in peace. In this treaty, Henry formally took for himself the kingdoms of Leinster and Meath which were to be the core of English rule in Ireland, becoming known as "The Pale". The Pale was essentially an extension of England and English law, with the French language and Norman customs being the norm. In the centuries that followed, the amount of land in this area expanded and contracted many times with the fortunes of war. The Treaty of Windsor was really of no consequence, as the Normans paid very little if any heed to it. In reality it was really nothing more than an English deception. Any hopes

---

[i] "The King of England has granted to Rory, his liegeman, King of Connacht, as long as he shall faithfully serve him, that he shall be king under him, ready to his service, as his man. And he shall hold his land, as fully and as peacefully as he held it before the lord king entered Ireland..." – Treaty of Windsor, from Acts of Henry II, (W. Stubbs, London 1871)

that the Irish had placed on Henry bringing some sort of peace and stability to the country had long since proven to be without foundation. In effect, both before and after the treaty, Henry made little attempt to control his land-hungry barons, either personally or through his Chief Justice. Areas which they had invaded were granted retrospectively to the control of lesser barons, while Henry himself or his sons granted land that then had to be fought for, these being referred to by the Crown as "speculative grants".

Native Help for the Normans

All illusions regarding English designs on Ireland had long since evaporated. The Irish Kings now fought tooth and nail to resist all further intrusions into the areas the Normans had no right to enter and also to regain territory lost before the treaty was signed. Some temporarily sided with the Normans for their own benefit, such as Domhnall O'Brien who, after losing Limerick, hoped to gain favour with the Normans by helping them infiltrate the kingdom of Desmond in 1177. In Connacht too, the Normans were helped in their mission of conquest, this time by the son of the High King, Murchad O'Connor. The undertaking was a failure however and Murchad was afterwards blinded by his father Turlough for his treachery.

Division, which had hitherto been a weakness in the Kingdom of Ireland, now became something of a strength. Being divided into so many kingdoms, the country could not be easily conquered; not by one battle or the capture of one city could the Normans conquer Ireland. The Brehon law of succession also proved its worth. If a Clan Chieftain fell in battle or was murdered, there was always someone to replace him – to the fourth generation.

The Death of Strongbow
At the beginning of April 1176, Raymond LeGros who was in the south of the country received an urgent message from his wife Basilea who was also Strongbow's sister. It read: "Be it known to you that the great jaw tooth which used to trouble me so much has fallen out. Wherefore, return with all speed"[19]. Deciphering the cryptic message, LeGros realised that Strongbow was dead and that Basilea, knowing what a tenuous hold the Normans had in Dublin, was endeavouring to keep his death a secret until Raymond LeGros arrived. Strongbow, the warrior to whom the King of Leinster Dermot MacMurrough had given not only his daughter but also his Kingdom, met his end due to an infected foot wound. He was entombed in the newly rebuilt Christchurch Cathedral.

The Sidelining of Raymond LeGros
Much as King Henry II had feared Strongbow's ambition, he feared Raymond Le Gros' more. For some time, Strongbow's uncle Hervey Mountmaurice had been whispering in the King's ear that LeGros wanted Ireland for himself. Henry had recalled Raymond to England to answer to this charge, but it had been rescinded, due to an uprising in Limerick by Domhnall O'Brien that had triggered attacks against the Normans across the midlands. LeGros' leadership was badly needed, and he could not be spared. In any event, Henry was not going to allow LeGros to bring any big ideas that he may have had to fruition. He appointed William FitzAdelm deBurgo as Chief Justice with Miles deCogan, Robert Fitzstephen and John deCourcy as his assistants, thus sidelining LeGros completely. LeGros acquiesced and retired to his estates in Wexford until his death in 1182.

As Henry's new Chief Justice, deBurgo gained no friends among his countrymen since he tried to curb the excesses of the invaders and wanted to bring peace to the country and end the cycle of war and violence. However, his desire was at naught compared to the desire for land and booty that the Normans possessed.

Shortly after DeBurgos' appointment, the Normans suffered a serious setback when their large settlement and castle of Slane was attacked by MacLochlainn, Prince of the Northern Clan O'Néill. The settlement was used as a base from which raiding parties were sent into the surrounding counties. The O'Néill's were also supported by the army of the Kingdom of Oriel and overwhelmed the defenders, slaying the entire garrison of around 500 men, after which the outpost was abandoned along with three others in the surrounding area.

The Despoilation of the Irish Church

Descended from the Vikings, the Normans (even though they had long since converted to Christianity) did not spare the Irish holy places from destruction and the Irish were more than once reminded of their Norse ancestors.

In 1177, as Hugh deLacy tried to extend his territory westward beyond the Shannon in flagrant breach of the Treaty of Windsor, he entered and plundered the ancient monastic settlement of Clonmacnoise in such a way as would have done the Vikings proud. As he advanced westwards, he was defeated by the army of Rory O'Connor and retreated back across the Shannon. His action was but one of a series of crimes committed by the Normans against the Irish Church which was regarded by them as unworthy of any consideration, except for the obtaining of wealth. They often used the spoils of their plunder in the foundation of new monasteries and churches, with the clergy for these being imported from England.

In any area where the Normans were in control, no Irish monk was allowed into a Norman monastery or Irish nun into a Norman convent. Irish Bishops and priests were driven from their flocks and replaced with Norman clerics when the occasion arose, and Irish bishops were passed over for more senior positions within the Church.[20] From the beginning, the Norman policy was one of apartheid within the Church.

Gerard of Wales was himself a witness to much that befell the Church in Ireland. In his book "Expugnatio Hibernica" or "The Conquest of Ireland", written in 1189, he wrote: "The miserable clergy are reduced to beggary in the island. The cathedral churches mourn, having been robbed by the aforesaid persons and others along with them, or who came over after them, of the lands and ample estates which had been formerly granted to them faithfully and devoutly. And thus the exalting of the Church has been changed into the despoiling or plundering of the Church. While we conferred nothing on the Church of Christ in our new principality, we not only did not think it worthy of any important bounty, or of due honour; but even having immediately taken away the lands and possessions have exerted ourselves either to mutilate or abrogate its former dignities or ancient privileges"[21]

John DeCourcy Goes North

The Battle of Downpatrick

King Henry II had granted Ulidia to John de Courcy, a grant which he was determined to realise. In January 1177, he organised an expeditionary force consisting of over 300 knights and archers and their attendants and headed northwards. At the beginning of February, his force descended on the town of Downpatrick, the capital of the northern kingdom and home to a large monastic settlement. Town and monastery were not spared as his men laid waste to the area, killing and looting as they went.

DeCourcy's rampage coincided with a visit to the town of the Papal Legate, Cardinal Vivianus. Horrified by what he saw, Vivianus wanted to bring an end to the outrages but deCourcy would allow no intercession by him. Within a short time, a large Irish force led by a local Chieftain, Rory MacDunleavy, had assembled to oppose deCourcy. DeCourcy was now forced to fortify his position in order to prepare for the expected onslaught. As MacDunleavy advanced towards Downpatrick, Norman reinforcements arrived from Dublin and the battle that followed was a lengthy affair with many attacks and counter attacks, with neither side being strong enough to gain the upper hand. Finally, the Irish were driven back from the Norman lines by intensive arrow-fire followed up by a charge of knights on horseback led by John DeCourcy's brother Amory.

DeCourcy had established a foothold in Ulster but in the years that followed he suffered many reverses. In 1178 he lost over 400 men in battle outside Newry and on another occasion, while raiding further North, he was defeated by the army of the Dalaradian King, Cumee O'Flynn. He escaped from this battlefield with only a handful of companions and for two days and nights the Norman band was pursued until they finally reached Norman lines. In the years that followed, DeCourcy continued to show his penchant for resilience. Ulster had been granted to him and he was determined that his it would be. A prolific builder, he founded towns, abbeys and castles, and made smaller grants to his friends in order to surround himself with those of like mind. In 1194 he succeeded in killing his old adversary Cumee O'Flynn and also put to death after blinding, O'Carroll, King of Oriel whom he had captured the year before. Try as he might, he never succeeded in enlarging his territory past Antrim and Down. Despite repeated attempts, the English were never to establish a solid foothold west of Lough Neagh until the seventeenth century.

Prince John Comes to Ireland

Hugh deLacy becomes Chief Justice

In 1178, King Henry decided to replace the unpopular Chief Justice de Burgo with the man who was his greatest critic - Hugh deLacy.

By this time deLacy was in possession of around half a million acres of some of the best land in the country. He was also responsible for the construction of the largest Norman castle ever built in Ireland, in Trim Co. Meath. Despite his numerous battlefield encounters with Rory O'Connor, he still succeeded in gaining the hand of O'Connor's daughter Rose in marriage, an act that greatly angered King Henry as he suspected some sort of grubby arrangement between deLacy and O'Connor, namely that deLacy should succeed O'Connor as High King. Not unlike Raymond LeGros before him, deLacy's ambition caused the King some disquiet. With the country still in a state of unrest and afraid that deLacy was becoming too powerful, the King decided to send his youngest son, Prince John, to Ireland. After being knighted and receiving the title "Lord of Ireland", John set sail with a large retinue of followers, including Gerard of Wales, who was his tutor and secretary, and his butler, Theobald Walter, from whom descended the Butler dynasty. Military reinforcements, including 300 knights, were also in the Waterford-bound convoy.

If it was the intention of the King that the visit of John to Ireland should usher in a period of peace and order to the country, the Prince's appearance on the Irish scene in April 1185 had quite the opposite effect. Instead of pacifying the country, John and his court wasted no time in causing trouble.

Prince John's First Visit to Ireland

As soon as Prince John disembarked, his first official act was to make land grants to members of his retinue of parts of the country which were still in the possession of the Irish and that were now to be taken from them by force.

Unaware of this, numbers of the Irish Kings and Chieftains came to Waterford to pay their respects to the Prince. Instead of being treated with respect, they were instead loudly ridiculed by John's immature and foppish friends. In Ireland, head and facial hair were considered to be manly and symbols of maturity. As the Irish chieftains wore their hair long and their beards thick, Prince John's retinue insulted and poked fun at them by plucking their beards and making fun of their dress. Greatly insulted by this, the Irish Chieftains withdrew and decided to pay back with interest the welcome that the Prince and his friends had shown them. Within a short time, the Normans were attacked at many of their more remote settlements and in many places were driven from the countryside. Many of the reinforcements that John had brought with him from England were killed in the engagements that followed. Dismayed by the aftermath of John's arrival, King Henry recalled him and appointed deCourcy to replace deLacy as Chief Justice. On his return to England, the Prince would not accept any blame for the failure of his mission and laid the responsibility for the increase in attacks against the Normans squarely at deLacy's door.

The Death of Hugh deLacy

If King Henry now planned on recalling deLacy to England to answer the charges that Prince John laid against him, he never got the chance. On July 26th 1186, Hugh deLacy was inspecting his new castle at Durrow which was built on the site of St. Columkille's Monastery which he had personally ordered demolished. Suddenly a young Irishman appeared from the shadows and, drawing an axe from under his cloak, cut off the Baron's head in revenge for the destruction of the monastery.

The Death of the Last High King of Ireland

Despite trying to keep the Normans at bay, the Irish often continued with their mutually destructive battles of old, so much so that they have been described as fighting each other with one hand and fighting the English with the other.

In 1185, King Rory O'Connor decided to abdicate and handed the reins of power in Connacht to his son Conor Moinmoy, only to change his mind two years later. He then employed Norman mercenaries to help him in his bid to regain the throne and the kingdom of Connacht was split for a time before Conor Moinmoy got the upper hand. Conor was assassinated shortly afterwards during a rebellion of chieftains who felt that he should bow to the wishes of his father. After his death, Rory attempted to rule once more but there were now two other claimants to the throne, Rory O'Connor's half-brother Cathal "Crovderg"[i] O'Connor and Conor Moinmoy's son, Cathal Carrach. After Cathal Crovderg saw off the challenge of Cathal Carrach, the last Gaelic High King of Ireland, Rory O'Connor, finally accepted the demise of his rule and retired to the Abbey of Cong in Mayo to do penance. After his death in 1198, his remains were taken to Clonmacnoise, where they were interred near the high altar.[ii]

This infighting was to be the first in a long series of internal battles and power struggles within the Clan O'Connor that would ensure (with the help and encouragement of the invader) their self destruction and splintering into scattered factions.

---

[i] From the Gaelic "craobh dearg" meaning "red branch"
[ii] If the King of Leinster Dermot McMurrough has provoked the ire of succeeding Irish generations for bringing the English to our shores, Rory O'Connor has not escaped a portion of the same for his failure to take decisive action when the Norman adventure in Ireland was in its infancy, reacting too late and doing too little.

Prince John Deputises for Richard "The Lionheart"

When King Henry II died in early July 1189, his son Richard I "The Lionheart" succeeded him. At this time, the Christian government of the Holy Land had been overthrown and all Christians there had been put to the sword by an Islamic army under Saladin. The Monarchs of Europe, including Richard, had abandoned their domestic affairs and were at war in the East in an effort to defeat the Moslems and regain the Christian holy places. Richard's mother, Queen Eleanor of Aquitaine, was Regent during Richard's absence, assisted by Prince John who was placed in charge of the King's affairs in Ireland. Ireland, however, was not to the fore of John's thoughts as he was actively intriguing to succeed to the throne of England if Richard should die while fighting on the Crusades. The next in line to the English throne after Richard was his infant nephew, Arthur, and John hoped to usurp the succession if the opportunity arose.

Prince John appointed the son of the slain Hugh deLacy, also named Hugh, as Justiciar (Chief Justice), to the annoyance of John deCourcy who was very much his senior in the Irish Norman hierarchy. Under Prince John's tenure, one Justiciar succeeded another in quick succession as his appointees struggled to achieve what the Prince demanded. However under John's rule a policy of "incastellation" was more firmly established as the Normans sought to extend their control by the establishment of castles and forts in parts of the country where they could gain no firm foothold. These castles served as strongpoints against native aggression and also as bases from which punitive expeditions were launched. This was especially true in Munster where the King of Thomond, Domhnall Mór O'Brien and his men were as a brick wall to the ambition of the Normans. When the avaricious intentions of the Normans became clear in the wake of Henry II's departure, he was among the first to renounce the submission he had given to the King. Until his death in 1194, his sword was scarcely ever sheathed in defence of his kingdom. In 1193, William deBurgo married O'Brien's daughter, the marriage producing two sons, Richard and Walter of whom more will be told. After the death of Domhnall Mór O'Brien, his sons fell under deBurgo's sway and together they encroached into the territory of Desmond, where the O'Briens settled old scores of their own. This also allowed deBurgo to gain a foothold for further expansion.[i]

During his reign, King Richard never set foot in Ireland and spent only a short time in England. The rest of his time was spent either on the Crusades or in his French territories. He was imprisoned for almost two years by the Holy Roman Emperor, Henry VI, until a ransom demanded by Henry for his release could be arranged by his mother.[ii] He was killed in France in March 1199, being mortally wounded while putting down a revolt in Limousin. He had named his younger brother Prince John as his successor as he felt that his nephew Arthur had fallen under the power of the French king, Philip II.

---

[i] According to the Annals of Inisfallen it was on the occasion of this encroachment into Desmond that Auliffe O'Donovan, the last King of the Clan Cairbre Eva – enemies of the O'Briens for over two centuries – was killed.
[ii] His brother John along with Philip II of France offered the Emperor money to keep Richard imprisoned.

Chapter 5

Fighting and Infighting

"Divide and Conquer"

Even in the face of Norman expansion, Irish national disunity and infighting among the native kingdoms had not abated, indeed it might be said that since the arrival of King Henry II, any effort at national unity had dissolved. Each Gaelic King was effectively on his own and for the most part was determined to defend his own territory no matter what quarter the danger came from, whether it was from "Clan Norman" or any other Clan. From time to time, regional alliances emerged when the Normans threatened neighbouring kingdoms but more often than not these dissolved once the danger had passed.

For their part, the Normans were only too happy to help one Irish army fight against another and were adept at exploiting any situation to their own advantage. Aside from payment received, they helped themselves to whatever booty was available and had the pleasure of seeing and helping the Irish destroy themselves, since they were the ultimate beneficiaries of internal Gaelic discord, always ready to seize power when the opportunity arose.

From the very beginning until the final conquest of Ireland was complete over five centuries later, the motto of the invader was to be "Divide et Impera" (Divide and Conquer). By making promises of power and wealth to certain factions among the Irish in return for help and information the invader would receive inestimable help in the task they had set themselves. Those who assisted them were for a while courted, sometimes rewarded and then invariably cast aside (or worse) once they were of no more use.

The Normans and the O'Connors in Connacht

When King John succeeded his brother Richard I as King of England in 1199, Connacht was in the midst of an O'Connor power struggle between the King of Connacht, Cathal Crovderg O'Connor and Cathal Carrach O'Connor who was the grandson of the last High King, Rory O'Connor. As the nephew of the last High King, Carrach felt that he had a greater right to rule Connacht than Crovderg who had only been Rory O'Connor's half-brother. After engaging the services of William deBurgo and his men to fight for him as mercenaries, Cathal Carrach succeeded in overthrowing Cathal Crovderg.

In 1200, Crovderg, who was determined to regain Connacht, also engaged the Normans as mercenaries and employed the army of John deCourcy to help him in his venture. As deCourcy made his way to engage Carrach in battle, the latter was lying in wait for him and ambushed his army at Kilmacduagh in Co.Galway, with terrible loss of life on the Norman side.

In spite of this defeat, Crovderg did not give up. If deCourcy had failed him, he would try elsewhere. Knowing that the Normans sold their services to the highest bidder, Crovderg approached deBurgo, and persuaded him to change sides. In 1201, as the Crovderg / deBurgo army lay quartered in the Abbey of Boyle they were tracked down and attacked by Carrach's army. In the battle that followed Carrach was killed, and so the way was now clear for Crovderg to resume the rule of Connacht.

Following the battle, Crovderg and deBurgo went to Cong Abbey for the Holy Week ceremonies and deBurgo's men were billeted among the local populace for the duration. Shortly after they arrived, a rumour quickly spread among the population that deBurgo had been killed in the Abbey. The apparent killing now became the catalyst for an all-out attack on deBurgo's army by the people of Connacht. His men were unprepared and were at the added disadvantage of being distributed piecemeal among the population in their various billets. According to the Annals of Kilronan, around 700 of deBurgo's men were slaughtered.[22] DeBurgo and the surviving Normans escaped back to Munster with DeBurgo vowing that he would return for revenge on Connacht and its people, a feat he accomplished three years later when he returned and, according to the Annals of Kilronan, plundered the whole territory "both lay and ecclesiastical."[23]

A Norman Rebellion
Unrest among the Hiberno-Normans
Events in the wider Norman world often had their effect in Ireland. In August of 1202, King John took his young nephew Arthur prisoner at Mirebeau Castle in Normandy, after which Arthur was never seen again. Word spread abroad that King John had personally murdered him. Since his father Geoffrey's death in a jousting tournament, Arthur had been Duke of Brittany and as such, Normandy and the other French Norman possessions were in his domain, but King John had never relinquished control of them to him.

King John of England

After Arthur's death became public knowledge, John deCourcy openly spoke out against King John, describing him as a usurper and a murderer, which was eagerly reported to King John by Hugh deLacy. King John lost no time in proclaiming deCourcy a traitor to the Crown and ordered that he be captured. He sought refuge with the native Irish of Tyrone but was ultimately taken prisoner at Downpatrick just before Easter of 1204 and spent the rest of his life in the Tower of London. With deCourcy gone from the scene, deLacy was rewarded for his tale-telling, being appointed Earl of Ulster in deCourcy's place. Within a few years however, deLacy himself would fall foul of the King.

Infighting among the Normans in Ireland was now common. Not content with having relieved the Irish of much of their land, they turned on each other and there were numerous battles over territory. Their remoteness from England seemed to encourage a certain cavalier or "devil may care" attitude to authority. King John also had a habit of confiscating land already granted and regranting it to someone more to his liking, which was the cause of endless rancour and infighting among the barons.

Some of the Hiberno Norman barons, most notably Hugh and Walter deLacy, now sought to distance themselves from their allegiance to King John. To do this, they used the death of young Arthur as a pretext, as well as the fact that Pope

Innocent III had excommunicated King John due to his efforts to relieve the Church of her wealth. In 1207, Strongbow's son-in-law William Marshal came to Leinster. He was also out of favour with King John, and it was not long before he was also at war with the army of the Lord Justice.

"Black Monday"
In the middle of all the Norman infighting of the early 1200's, there was a great massacre of the citizens of Bristol, who had inhabited Dublin after it had been granted to them by King Henry II. "Cullen's Wood", located at the city's southern edge, was a popular beauty spot at the time and the Bristolians had a habit of going there on their days off. On Easter Monday of 1209, there was a large crowd there relaxing in the holiday atmosphere, when they were attacked by members of the Gaelic Clans of O'Byrne and O'Toole whose lands they now occupied. Around three hundred people were killed in the massacre that followed, and for many years afterwards the day was referred to by the Normans of the Pale as "Black Monday".

William deBraose
By 1210, Ireland had become such a hotbed of Norman dissent against King John that he felt that he had no option but to return, not to make war against the Irish but rather against his own Norman kin. One of the chief dissenters was a certain William deBraose, who had once been a great friend of King John. He had come to Munster years earlier after having received a large grant of land and since then, he had fallen on hard times and was now in debt to the tune of thousands of marks to the King's treasury because of unpaid rents. In the year 1200, he had been awarded the city of Limerick for which a debt of five thousand marks was still outstanding. As deBraose was unable to pay his debts, the King had ordered his youngest son to be seized as a hostage, but the boy's

mother had refused to give him up, citing what had happened to King John's own nephew Arthur. When His Majesty's debt collectors arrived to seize his home in Wales, he and his sons revolted, destroying their own property along with the local town of Leominster. A number of King John's soldiers were killed in the process. After this he had fled with his family to Ireland where they were given shelter by William Marshall.

King John in Ireland

Dealing with deBraose

Taking no chances regarding any measures his disloyal barons might have prepared in order to resist him, King John prepared a massive armada of some 700 ships packed with a vast army, including 800 knights and their warhorses. He landed at Crook, near Waterford, on June 20th, 1210. Before the King set sail, William Marshal arrived from Ireland, begging forgiveness for any disloyalty he had shown and swearing fealty, just as Strongbow had done with King Henry II.

News of the vast armada preceded John and by the time he arrived the troublemakers had flown. The deLacys and deBraose had escaped to France but deBraose's wife Maude and his youngest son fell into the King's clutches while trying to escape by boat to Scotland. Since he was unable to settle accounts with deBraose himself, Maude and her son now bore the brunt of John's revenge. They were imprisoned without food in Corfe Castle on the island of Purbeck in Dorset, England. Within a fortnight they were both dead.

King John's rule of Ireland

With little or no fighting to be done, the King concerned himself with the government of the Norman controlled parts of Ireland, dividing them into shires or counties after the Norman fashion[i]. In these areas, Norman law was to be obeyed by the Norman inhabitants, but the vast majority of the Irish had no recourse to it. The problem arising from this was that when the Normans abused the Irish, there was no way to bring them to justice. Knowing that the Irish had no recourse to Norman Justice, the Norman barons did not hesitate to apply death or mutilation to the native Irish in their assizes, punishments seldom used under Gaelic law.[24]

This state of affairs was nothing new however as since the invasion, the Irish people in the occupied areas had suffered much, especially by loss of rank. Free tenants were reduced to serfdom or bondage. Many Clans which had once given their loyalty to the Gaelic nobility were now subject to a Norman Lord, paying him dues and services in return for a patch of land.[ii] When laws were introduced to protect freeholders in the early 1200's, they had no retrospective effect, but even after this they were a dead letter to the Irish as it was well nigh impossible for an Irish freeholder to apply to the Normans for justice.

While in Ireland King John ordered that a mint be set up so that Norman money would be coined in Ireland to the same standard as it was in England.

King John and the native Irish leaders

During his stay, around twenty Gaelic chieftains including Cathal Crovderg renewed their submission. Crovderg had already come to terms with the Normans in Connacht and had given up two thirds of his Kingdom to Norman taxation on condition that he would be left in peace on the remaining one

---

[i] These were Uriel, (Louth) Waterford, Tipperary, Kerry, Connacht, Cork and Limerick.

[ii] The Norman term for this class of person was "Villein"

third. King John had high regard for Cathal, who was a fine scholar and an excellent chess player and wanted to bring Cathal's son back to England with him, promising to educate him and take special care of him. Cathal initially agreed but quite wisely did not produce him.

Hugh O'Néill of Tyrone was also summoned to appear before John. He had never previously submitted and did not intend to do so now. He came to meet the King, bringing an army with him so as not to be caught off guard. His army set up their encampment beside the Normans and when they left, they carried off a considerable amount of purloined booty away with them from the Norman encampment. Hugh O'Néill retained the strength of character required in order to resist the temptation to give his allegiance to King John, despite the actions of many of his peers. After the King departed, O'Néill teamed up with O'Donnell of Tirconnell. Temporarily putting their differences to one side, they attacked and defeated the Norman garrisons on Lough Erne and in Carlingford. In maintaining their opposition to the invaders, the Cenél Connell (O'Donnells) and the Cenél Eoghan (O'Néills) would maintain unbroken Gaelic rule in their kingdoms for a long time to come.

Before his arrival, the King had replaced Meyler Fitzhenry with Bishop John deGray as Lord Justice. Under his administration, the process of incastellation continued, especially in the South. He in turn was replaced by Henry of London, (nicknamed "Burn Bill" by the Irish[i]) who was also appointed Archbishop of Dublin. He claimed for himself the title "Primate of Ireland"

---

[i] The story of his nickname "Burn Bill" is as follows. After becoming Archbishop, he apparently called his Irish tenants together, telling them to bring the deeds of their properties along with them. Once he had the deeds in his hands (on the pretence of inspecting them), he cast them into a nearby fire in an attempt to dispossess them.

in opposition to the Gaelic Archbishop of Armagh. Under his tenure, the building of Dublin Castle was begun, and he is recorded as having knocked down several Irish Churches so as to provide an adequate supply of masonry for its construction.

The Normans Achieve Control of West Munster

In 1215, King John pardoned Walter deLacy and regranted Meath to him. At this time, the Normans also became involved in the internal strife within the Kingdom of Desmond where Diarmuid and Cormac Finn MacCarthy had gone to war with each other over the succession. The Geraldines were the ultimate victors and succeeded in strengthening their foothold in Cork and Kerry as a direct result of the conflict.

When Thomas Fitzgerald (son of Maurice Fitzgerald) had settled in Shanid near Limerick, he had two sons John and Maurice. John's family were to become the Earls of Desmond, while from Maurice came the family of Fitzmaurice, Barons of Kerry. After Meiler Fitzhenry died without any heir in 1220, the brothers took over his former holding and the whole area became a Geraldine stronghold.

King John died the following year on October 19th, 1216, while engaged in a military campaign against an invasion of Britain by King Louis of France who was supported by many of the Norman barons. During the campaign, William Marshal led 500 Irish-based Norman knights across the Irish Sea to Britain and on to Canterbury to join the King in battle.

The Reign of King Henry III

The unexpected death of King John in October 1216 meant that he was succeeded by his nine year old son Henry III. Henry's first appointee as Lord Justice was William Marshall, who now arranged a pardon for Hugh deLacy so that he could return to Ireland, but Marshall only returned to him some of the land of which he had previously been in possession. When William

Marshall died, his son, also called William Marshall inherited and Hugh deLacy decided to take advantage of his inexperience, going to war with him in order to regain the rest of the land which he had once possessed.

Meath and Louth were both torn apart in the fighting that followed and the Irish peasantry suffered greatly.

Civil War in Connacht

When the King of Connacht, Cathal Crovderg O'Connor died in 1224, his death ushered in yet another O'Connor power struggle between Cathal's son Hugh who planned to succeed his father and Hugh's cousin Turlough, son of the former High King Rory O'Connor. Turlough was supported in his bid for power by his brother, also called Hugh.

O'Néill of Tyrone now took a hand in affairs, urged on by Donn Og MacGeraghty, a disgruntled chieftain who had been deprived of his lands by Cathal Crovderg. The arrival of O'Néill signalled a general insurrection of Connacht chieftains against Hugh O'Connor who now fled Connacht and sought the help of the English who acted as a mercenary force, first helping one side and then the other, but all the while content to see the Irish dissipate their military power in the madness that followed. For three years, Connacht was completely ravaged by war, famine and plague and many towns were left completely without inhabitants as the cousins vied with each other for supremacy.

Unknown to the warring parties, their fate had ultimately been decided. Connacht had been marked down by Henry III in 1225 as a target for ultimate English supremacy since the terms of Cathal Crovderg's land grant had been so ambiguously phrased as to exclude his heir. Richard deBurgo was waiting in the wings for his chance to enforce this when the time was ripe.

When Hugh O'Connor was killed in 1228, his cousins, the two brothers Turlough and Hugh, then went to war with each other for the throne of Connacht, only to be joined in the fray by Cathal Crovderg's youngest son Feilim who felt that with his brother's death the throne of his father was by right his.

Hugh was favoured by the English and was crowned King with their help. Once King, his Chieftains told him they could not remain loyal to a man who was a Norman puppet. Rather than lose the loyalty of his men and the throne of Connacht, Hugh now cast aside his friendship for the English and attacked them with his much depleted army. In the battle that followed, he was roundly defeated. Richard deBurgo then entered Connacht with as large an army as he could muster in order to unseat Hugh and kill the powerful Donn Og MacGeraghty. Feilim O'Connor, the young son of the deceased Cathal Crovderg, now became King. After having his cousin Hugh killed, he embarked on the same journey as Hugh by trying to rid Connacht of the English. Nevertheless, he suffered the same fate. In 1235, seeing Connacht at their mercy, the English invaded by both land and sea and Feilim was forced to flee to O'Donnell of Tirconnell, leaving the enemy to plunder what spoils they could. Many of the local population fled the advancing English army, making for the islands of Clew Bay, but even here they were not safe. When the English arrived, many were killed, and the islands were totally despoiled of livestock by them.

Feilim eventually submitted to deBurgo who allowed him to remain as nominal King, but the English were now free to extend their policy of incastellation into Connacht. Feilim's power was confined to the feudal territory of the O'Connor's, five cantreds[i] in size, referenced on maps of the period as "the

---

[i] Cantred was a Welsh / Irish term for the division of land. One *cantred* consisted of almost 4,000 acres.

King's five cantreds" since by English law Feilim held them in trust for the King of England and paid him rent for them.

While Feilim O'Connor professed himself content with this state of affairs, his son Hugh was not and decided to do what he could to bring about an English reversal. In 1248, he gathered to himself an army of young men of noble Gaelic blood, many from the Clan O'Flaherty[i]. Using guerrilla methods, they raided and burned the English settlements to such an extent that the English could find no security outside their castles. In order to avenge the damage done to the settlers, the Lord Justice Maurice Fitzgerald arrived in 1249, bringing with him two armies. Being responsible for the actions of his son, Feilim had no option but to flee, heading north as usual to the safety of the Tirconnell border, bringing with him all the movable assets that he could lay his hands on. Finding the nest empty, Fitzgerald decided to install a willing puppet in his stead, Feilim's nephew Turlough. But Feilim was not gone for good. The following year, after recouping his strength, he raided his native soil, and drove out Turlough. He did not have enough power to remain and face Fitzgerald, and so made good his escape, once again taking with him everything he could lay his hands on. In light of this and knowing that they would have little peace, the English now sought to make peace with Feilim. In 1255, his son Hugh met with Lord Justice Alan de la Zouch and a deal was reached whereby Feilim was given a King's charter for the five cantreds.

---

[i] The O'Flaherty's were renowned for the ferocity in battle. Norman controlled Galway is reputed to have had the inscription "From the Ferocious O'Flahertys O Lord Deliver Us" on its walls. The Clan descended from Flaithbheartach Maceimhim who lived in the 10th century A.D.

The Murder of Richard Marshall

When William Marshall the younger died in 1233, his brother Richard succeeded to his estates. Being out of favour with the King due to his support for the Welsh rebels under Prince Llewellyn, he fled to Ireland after hearing that the Norman Barons Maurice Fitzgerald, Hugh and Walter deLacy, Richard deBurgo and Geoffrey deMarisco had seized the family's Irish holding. Without him knowing it, he was the subject of a plot by the Crown, a minister of which had told the aforementioned barons that they could divide up the land between them if they would kill Richard Marshall.

Having got back to Limerick, Richard Marshall was summoned by his brother barons to attend a peace conference on the Curragh of Kildare. It was an old trick of the Normans to call an adversary to a peace conference at which their enemy would either be taken prisoner or killed, as the former King of Breifne Tiernan O'Rourke (among others) had found out to his cost. Richard must have been well aware of this, but what he was not aware of was that his followers were in the pay of Geoffrey deMarisco. After arriving at the appointed meeting place on the Curragh, his treacherous followers abandoned him to his fate, leaving him with only his young brother Walter and his personal bodyguard of fifteen knights who had come with him from England. When he saw what was happening, Richard had Walter escorted away in order to save his life before his small body of men were engulfed by his adversaries. For a while they held off their attackers but, in the end, there could only be one outcome. Finally, Richard was unhorsed and knifed in the back, dying later in his own castle that had been taken over by Maurice Fitzgerald.

Infighting in Ulster

Tyrone had long been a thorn in the side of the Normans as the Cenél Eoghan were some of the most resolute in maintaining their defence against the invader. In Connacht and Munster, the English had used the method of "Divide and Conquer", and it had worked admirably for them. Now they would try the same in Ulster.

After the death of the Gaelic Lord of Tyrone Hugh O'Néill in 1239, he was succeeded by Domhnall MacLochlainn. There was however a different claimant to the Lordship of Tyrone, Brian O'Néill whom the Normans decided to assist in his opposition to Mac Lochlainn

Accompanied by Hugh deLacy, the Lord Justice Maurice Fitzgerald led an army northward and drove out MacLochlainn, leaving O'Néill in his place. MacLochlainn had escaped, however, and had no intention of leaving things as they stood. Before the year was out, he had regained his old position after defeating Brian O'Néill at the Battle of Carnteel, only to be overthrown again in 1241 when Brian regained control, this time assisted by the army of the Gaelic Lord of Tirconnell, Mélaghlainn O'Donnell.

Fitzgerald and his army returned again in 1247, this time to Tirconnell, killing O'Donnell and defeating his army at Ballyshannon. Now came the situation that English intentions thrived on. With O'Donnell dead, a power struggle encouraged by the English ensued between two rival claimants for the title: Godfrey O'Donnell and Rory O'Canannan. While the attention of the men of Tirconnell was diverted to this power struggle, there could be no united front against the invader and now another English army under the command of Theobald Butler succeeded in breaking through to Tyrone and subduing it. In 1252, the Gaelic Lord of Tyrone Brian O'Néill made his submission to Maurice Fitzgerald, and Fitzgerald felt that the time was now right to take control of the land of the Cenél Eoghan, something that was outside the terms of O'Néill's submission. When Fitzgerald and his army arrived in Tyrone in 1253, the army of the Cenél Eoghan, who were prepared to die rather than surrender control of the land of their fathers, met them in battle and succeeded in putting them to flight after great slaughter on both sides.

In 1257, Maurice Fitzgerald, now back in the role of Lord Justice, determined to bring West Ulster under English rule for once and for all. On this occasion, Tirconnell was once again in his sights. Taking his army through Sligo, he was met head on by the army of the Gaelic Lord of Tirconnell, Godfrey O'Donnell, at a place called Creadran Cille (The Rosses), where a furious battle ensued. During the battle, Godfrey and Maurice met each other in hand to hand combat, with both of them being severely wounded. The battle raged on for most of the day but the men of Tirconnell finally succeeded in routing the invader. Previously, the English had erected a huge castle at Belleek, on the River Erne, as a base for attacking into Tirconnell, and O'Donnell now ordered it destroyed.

After the battle, the badly wounded Fitzgerald retired to a Franciscan Monastery in Youghal where he took the Franciscan habit. Within a short time, he was dead.

Meanwhile in Tirconnell, Godfrey O'Donnell was also near death on an island in Lough Neagh. His neighbour, Brian O'Néill of Tyrone, thought of using the fact that Godfrey was at death's door to his advantage and tried to attain overlordship of Tirconnell by demanding hostages from him. Even though he knew his end was near, Godfrey ordered that his men should be assembled for battle. He would not allow them enter battle without their chief and had himself carried at the head of his troops to the battlefield on a stretcher and held up high in view of his warriors. Battle was joined near the River Swilly and the Tirconnell men won the day, While Godfrey was being borne hom his stretcher bearers became his pall bearers as Godfrey died at Conwal, near Letterkenny, while being brought home.

Arrival of the Gallowglass Warriors

With Godfrey dead, Brian O'Néill struck again, this time demanding hostages as a sign of his overlordship of Tirconnell. While the leadership of the Cenél Connell were deliberating as to what they should do next, a youth of eighteen years stepped forward and asked to be heard. He was Domhnall Og O'Donnell (son of the former Chieftain Domhnall Mór O'Donnell), just returned from Scotland where he had been fostered. He was married to Caitríona Mac Sweeney, and she had brought her brother with her who commanded a band of Scottish mercenaries known as Gallowglasses[i] who wore chain mail armour and fought with long swords. They were of mixed Gaelic and Viking blood, descended from a Viking Lord of the Isles named Somerled. For the next three centuries, these tough warriors were to become the backbone of many a Gaelic Lord's army and wherever there was hard fighting to be done they would not disappoint. In Tirconnell, the Clan Mac Sweeney and its Gallowglasses were to become a cornerstone of its defence against the invader until the seventeenth century. Greatly impressed by Domhnall Og the Clan electors wasted no time in voting for him as Chieftain. Domhnall Og O'Donnell now proved their confidence in him. He was successful in throwing off the O'Néill claim and also in defending the territory of his forefathers. By the time of his death in 1283, Sligo and Fermanagh were the borders of his territory.

Finally putting aside their differences in 1260, an alliance of Gaelic Lords of both Ulster and Connacht, led by Brian O'Néill, King of Tyrone – whom they proclaimed as High King of Ireland – sought to overthrow English power in Ulster.

---

[i] Taken from the Gaelic "galloglaigh" which means "young foreign warrior". The Irish surname "Gallogly" remains as a reminder of these brave warriors.

However, the alliance was defeated at The Battle of Downpatrick with the loss of around 350 warriors on the Irish side. The fighting is reported as having taken place not in the countryside, but rather in the streets of Downpatrick, which may have been the reason for the heavy Irish defeat, as the Irish were unused to urban warfare.

Geraldine Setback in Munster

The success at arms of the English at Downpatrick was followed the year after by a heavy defeat for them at the Battle of Callan near Kilgarvan, Co. Kerry. Having made strong gains in the area during and after the war of the MacCarthy succession, the descendents of Diarmuid MacCarthy, under the command of their chieftain Domhnall MacCarthy, now sought to regain lost territory from the Geraldines. They did this with great success and heavy loss to the Normans when their armies met at Callan. Those killed included members of the Fitzgerald family, fifteen knights, and many foot soldiers. The Geraldine line of Fitzthomas was almost wiped out in the battle. The Geraldines were forced to abandon most of the castles they had constructed in Desmond and these were subsequently knocked. The MacCarthys were back in business and were now undisputed rulers in an area stretching from the Lakes of Killarney to Bantry and as far east as Macroom.

The Battle of Athankip

When Feilim O'Connor died in 1265, his son Hugh who had previously caused havoc to the English of Connacht, succeeded him. Now that he held the reins of power he resolved once more to take the fight to the English and around 1267 he began launching a series of attacks against the forces of Walter deBurgo who was also Earl of Ulster due to his marriage with the daughter of Hugh deLacy. At length deBurgo found himself unable to cope with the situation and requested help.

The Lord Justice Sir Walter de Ufford led an army into Connacht to aid him in a bid to quell this O'Connor insurrection against English rule. After joining forces with deBurgo, the English army marched in pursuit of Hugh O'Connor and his men who were reinforced by Gallowglasses. The two armies met at a fording place on the River Shannon close to modern day Carrick-on-Shannon, known as Athankip. DeBurgo must have been surprised at the size of Hugh O'Connor's army as The Annals of Clonmacnoise record that "the Normansmen advised the Earle to make peace."[25] In any event, deBurgo proposed peace talks but Hugh O'Connor was well versed in English methods and was wary of falling into a trap. He agreed to the proposal but requested that deBurgo's brother William be handed over to his side as a hostage while he was at the peace talks. When William deBurgo and his party came into the O'Connor encampment, he was seized as a prisoner and in the melee some of the English were killed. DeBurgo was incensed at this and, throwing caution to the wind, attacked O'Connor's army the following morning but paid heavily for his rashness. In one of the largest battles on Irish soil since the coming of the Normans, DeBurgo and his men were routed by a force of Connacht men and gallowglass warriors.

The course of the battle is best told by quoting The Annals of Clonmacnoise:

"The Connoughtmen pursued the Normansmen, and made their hindermost part runn and break upon their outguard and foremost in such manner and foul discomfiture, that in that instant nine of their chiefest men were killed upon the bogge about Richard ne Koylle (Richard of the Wood) and John Butler who was killed over and above the said knights. It is unknown how many were slain in that conflict, save that only a hundred horses with their saddles and a hundred shirts of mail were left (of the enemy)".[26]

Thus, English fortunes in Connacht suffered a serious reversal. Following his success, Hugh O'Connor gave the English no respite, constantly attacking their settlements. In 1272, he recommenced his campaign, destroying Roscommon Castle, which had been completed by deUfford shortly before the Battle of Athankip. Crossing the River Shannon, he ventured as far as Granard in Co. Longford, which was home to a Norman settlement founded by Richard deTuite in 1199. After raiding and burning the area, he returned to his native turf via Athlone where he crossed the bridge over the Shannon, destroying it in the process so that he could not be pursued by this gateway into Connacht.

The death of this brave man, who had sought to drive out the invader from his youth, came about two years later and heralded years of incessant feuding among the Clan O'Connor. Between his death in 1272 and the year 1280, four different Kings were elected, each being murdered in his turn by rival factions within the Clan.

The year after Athankip, Walter deBurgo died. He was succeeded by his son Richard, better known as "The Red Earl of Ulster". Richard was only a child when his father died and did not come of age until 1280. In 1286, he returned to Connacht and exacted revenge for Athankip. Weakened as they were by their unending feuds, the Connacht men were unable to mount any significant resistance to him and were quickly overwhelmed. The Red Earl plundered at will and did not spare the native churches and monasteries. To crown the defeat, he conscripted the warriors of Connacht into his army and then turned north, heading for Tirconnell and Tyrone where he laid low both kingdoms, forcing their chieftains to say that he was Lord of their lands, that they ruled in his name, and also that they would provide him with men for military service.

Territory Conquered by Anglo Normans
TERRITORY UNCONQUERED (some under Anglo Norman influence)

The Height of the Norman Conquest – 1300 AD

The Reign of King Edward I

In 1272, King Henry III died and was succeeded by his son Edward I (known as "Longshanks"). Keen on further Irish expansion, he had no desire to admit any rights in law to the native Irish, even though his Lord Justice de Ufford recommended him to do so. It was not until 1292 that English law was granted, but only to an Irishman that demanded it. King Edward resumed the policy of "speculative grants" and it was during his reign that the first Bunratty Castle was built by Thomas deClare after he was granted Thomond (Clare). DeClare had to fight continuously against the O'Briens to retain control of Thomond, and in 1284 Bunratty Castle was destroyed by them while he was in England. In 1287, he rebuilt it, larger and better defended than before, but still the attacks on him continued unabated. The years of King Edward's reign were ones of incessant feuding among the land hungry Norman barons, and when Sir John deWogan was appointed as Lord Justice he attempted to bring order among the colonists and reinforce the dictates which prevented them from fraternising with the native Irish.

"Mere Irish"

DeWogan's first act was to try and bring peace among the settlers as in common with many of the Irish their infighting was causing them to lose sight of the task at hand. He successfully arranged a truce between the warring Geraldines and deBurgos, which was to last for a period of two years. He then summoned the first parliament of the Anglo Irish that was held in Kilkenny and revised the division of the country that King John had arranged. He also ordered all the borders of the English controlled areas to be guarded against the Irish and that all English absentee landowners should pay a tax as a contribution to the defence of the colony. Furthermore, any Englishman who was at war with the native Irish was forbidden to make peace with them without his permission. At a later parliament in 1310, a law was passed reinforcing the lapsed practice of forbidding Irish entrants to English monasteries: "No mere Irishman shall be received into a religious order among the Normans in the land of peace"[27] (the land of peace being the English occupied areas). However, the law was successfully appealed to the King by Archbishop Joyce of Armagh and revoked.

DeWogan was to serve three terms as Lord Justice, but often had to lead contingents of both Anglo and native Irish to fight for the King in his Scottish wars. It was also during his tenure that the notorious massacre of the Chieftains of the various dependent Clans belonging to the Clan of O'Connor Faly of Offaly took place, masterminded by Sir Peter deBermingham at his castle at Carrick-Carbury in Kildare.

Murder on the Menu
The Clan of O'Connor Faly had gained a fearful reputation among the English and succeeded in perpetrating many successful raids against them. On one occasion, they infiltrated the English Castle of Kildare and succeeded in destroying all accounts and records that they had accumulated there. They were also successful on the field of battle, accounting for many English knights, the most prominent of these being Meyler deExeter.

We have already seen how it was the practice of the English to invite their foe for a peace conference and then murder them. In a variation of this, all the Clan chieftains of the Clan O'Conor Faly, including Maurice and Calvagh O'Conor Faly, Princes of Offaly, were invited for dinner to deBermingham's castle on Trinity Sunday of 1305 during a period of truce. When the meal was over, the guests were in the process of rising from the table when every Irishman among them was attacked simultaneously from behind and murdered (some thirty in total) in an attempt by the "Treacherous Baron" (which became his nickname) to completely wipe out the "derbfine" of the Clan O'Conor Faly. He did not succeed in this. DeBermingham, the founder of the feast, did not soil his own hands with the Chieftains' blood, but left it to his loyal henchman, Jordan Cumin (founder of the Monastery of Trim) to organise the mass murder. For this foul act, deBermingham was rewarded by the English government in Dublin with the sum of one hundred pounds and also had a ballad composed in his honour praising this "hunter of the Irish"[28].

DeBirmingham met his own end a few years later in battle against the Irish in the year 1308.

Chapter 6

The Scottish High King

The Beacon of Bannockburn

In March of 1286, the King of Scotland Alexander III died after falling from his horse. Having no direct heir still living, the next in line to the Scottish throne was Alexander's infant granddaughter, Margaret, who was known as the "Maid of Norway"[29] as her father was King of that country. The child died while on her way from Norway by sea in order to take possession of her kingdom, and the succession was then thrown open to two other claimants: John Balliol and Robert Bruce, both distant relations of the dead King.

Balliol succeeded in his claim as he was more closely related, and on becoming King swore allegiance to King Edward I of England. His oath of allegiance to the English Crown did not go down well with the independent minded Scots and Balliol, eager to redeem himself, then renounced his allegiance to England. He now allied himself with the French against the English after which he engaged in sabre-rattling against the latter. King Edward would not allow this change in loyalties to go unchallenged and invaded Scotland in 1296, easily defeating Balliol. He then took the country completely under his charge, appointing a Lord Justice to deputise for him. Some Scots continued to resist, most notably under the leadership of William Wallace who was eventually captured and butchered.[i] Robert Bruce, grandson of the original Bruce claimant to the throne of Scotland, now succeeded Wallace as the prime mover for Scottish independence.

A wanted man, Robert Bruce more than once sought sanctuary on Rathlin Island off the north Irish returning to his homeland when the search for him had abated in order to continue the guerrilla war against the English with his scattered bands. His cause was one that was dear to the hearts of the Irish and on one occasion a small Irish army gathered by the Ulster chieftains went to help him. News of their arrival was possibly betrayed to the English authorities as the Ulstermen were immediately ambushed and cut to pieces by English troops when they landed on the Scottish coast.

The Scots gradually united behind Bruce and his guerrilla bands and his struggle developed into a mass movement that drove the English out, apart from one final stronghold held by them at Stirling. The English King Edward II led an army to relieve Stirling Castle, but this force was roundly defeated at Bannockburn on June 24th, 1314. News of the Scottish victory was received with joy in Ireland and seen by the Irish kings as a beacon of hope that they in their turn could drive out the invader.

The Bruce Military Campaign
<u>An Irish-Scottish Alliance</u>
Following this great Scottish victory over the English, the King of Ulster Domhnall O'Néill, speaking on behalf of all the Ulster chieftains, appealed to Robert Bruce to help them in their attempts to rid Ireland of the English invader. It was proposed to Robert that if he sent his brother Edward to Ireland at the

---
[i] * Wallace was hung, drawn and quartered.

head of a Scottish army to fight with the Irish then he could become the High King of Ireland.

Robert Bruce was delighted with this proposal because, since the victory at Bannockburn, his brother had wanted a share in the rule of Scotland, whereas now he could have Ireland for himself. Furthermore, if everything went according to plan, an anti-English alliance between the two countries would be the result.

"We Shall Attack Them in Defence of Our Just Rights"

As Bruce prepared his expedition, O'Néill and the Gaelic Lords of Ulster wrote and dispatched a document to Pope John XXII, outlining their arguments for the course of action they were following. The document stated the right of the Irish to be free from foreign interference and demonstrated the tyranny of the English with examples. It outlined how the Irish Church had been repeatedly desecrated and plundered and how the English refused to permit Irish entrants to the monasteries and convents. The document also spoke of the danger in which the Irish had been placed by being denied recognition under English law, to the extent that the murder of an Irishman was not punishable since the man killed was considered as "mere Irish". The remonstrance also summarised various atrocities committed by the English since their arrival in Ireland, including the massacre of the Chieftains of Offaly by deBermingham while they were seated at the latter's dinner table. The document concluded in part: "...Let no person, then, wonder if we endeavour to preserve our lives and defend our liberties, as best we can, against those cruel tyrants, usurpers of our just properties, and murderers of our persons...nor can we be accused of rebellion, since neither our fathers nor we did at any time bind ourselves by any oath of allegiance to their fathers or to them...We shall attack them in defence of our just rights, and never lay down our arms until we force them to desist..."[30]

The Arrival of Edward Bruce

On May 26th, 1315, Edward Bruce landed at Larne on the Antrim coast with an army of 6,000 soldiers and many Scottish noblemen. They were promptly joined by the armies of Ulster led by Domhnall O'Néill. The Bruce landing aroused great excitement and optimism among the Irish and filled the northern Anglo-Irish with dread. Leaving nothing to chance, Edward Bruce wanted to ensure that the professions of loyalty accorded to him by the Gaelic Lords of Ulster would not wane and demanded hostages from them.

The east coast of Ulster was soon liberated without much difficulty and the joint Scottish / Irish force moved south into the Kingdom of Oriel, where there was much destruction. The towns of Dundalk and Ardee were both burned, and in Ardee the church of the Carmelite Friary that had become a place of refuge for the Anglo-Irish was set on fire while the refugees were still inside.

The "Red Earl of Ulster", Richard deBurgo, and the Lord Justice Sir Edmund Butler quickly responded to this new threat. DeBurgo's army was mainly from Connacht and included the forces of the King of Connacht, Feilim O'Connor, while Butler's army marched northwards from Leinster.

After Oriel, Bruce turned northwest and by the time the Anglo-Irish army caught up with him, the rival forces were on opposite sides of the River Bann, unable to engage, except for the archers who fired across the river on their respective opponents.

More Infighting in Connacht

As deBurgo attempted to marshal his army Feilim O'Connor was forced to return home to Connacht with his force to deal with another episode of the seemingly never-ending internal strife that plagued his Clan. This time the trouble in the province stemmed from the actions of a young chieftain and head of the Clan Murtough named Rory O'Connor, who had declared for Bruce and had risen up against both the English and King Feilim, whom he considered to be an English lackey. However as Feilim prepared to set out for home, Bruce had secretly made contact with him and Feilim had given the Scotsman his allegiance. When this occurred, Bruce sent a messenger to Rory O'Connor telling him that going to war against the English was fine but that Feilim was to be left alone since he had now changed his loyalties. Rory O'Connor ignored this and refused to make any distinction between the English and King Feilim, no doubt hoping to take the latter's place as King of Connacht.

When Feilim arrived in Connacht, he found that most of his chieftains, including his own foster father, had renounced their allegiance to him and joined with Rory. For the remaining months of 1315 and into the early months of 1316, a pitiless civil war was fought in the province. In order to gain the upper hand, Feilim now used the Anglo-Irish to his own advantage. They were still unaware of his allegiance to Bruce, and so with the men who had remained loyal to him and a force of English under Richard deBermingham, he sought out Rory's army in north east Galway. Rory had been watching their approach from the top of a hill and had his men attack them, but in spite of this his army was defeated and he was killed. With Rory dead, Feilim managed to re-unite the factions in his kingdom by speaking openly of his support for Bruce whose presence in the country he used to re-invigorate in his tired warriors the desire for freedom from the English.

Beginning of The Great Siege of Carrickfergus

Meanwhile in Ulster, the Anglo Irish had caught up with Bruce's army. When the two forces finally met near Ballymena, the English, weakened by the loss of Feilim O'Connor's army, came off worst and were routed. William deBurgo, brother of the Red Earl, was taken prisoner along with a number of knights, and while some of the remnants of deBurgo's army retreated back to Connacht, the main body of his men took refuge in Carrickfergus Castle. These men were followed there by Edward Bruce's army and the castle was placed under siege. The fortress was well prepared for such eventualities and the stand-off looked set to last for some time. The besieged were confident that they would be able to hold out long enough for a relief force to eventually come to their aid.

Bruce Moves South

At the beginning of December 1315, Bruce, who had now received large reinforcements from Scotland decided to detach a part of his army and leave it to carry on the siege of Carrickfergus Castle while he moved south with the main body of his men, travelling by a circuitous route into the midlands through Kells, Finea, and Granard and on to Ballymore in Westmeath where the route march was adjourned for Christmas. In early 1316 he defeated an English army led by Sir Edmund Butler at Athy in Kildare.

The approach of Bruce precipitated uprisings by the native Irish and many of the old Norman outposts were destroyed. The English fled for safety to the large strongholds of Trim and Dublin. Even the heart of English rule, the Pale, was not safe and Arklow and Bray were set on fire by the Clans of O'Byrne and O'Toole. However, an uprising in Laois by the O'More Clan was unsuccessful, being suppressed by Edmund Butler with large loss of life.

"King of Erin"

Bruce now decided to return to Ulster and while his army retraced their steps through Kells they were met by another English army led by Sir Roger Mortimer. The battle was a disaster for the English who were soundly beaten, the blame for their defeat being laid at the feet of the Anglo-Irish families of deLacy and Verdan who had defected to the side of

The Coronation of Edward Bruce

Bruce. On reaching Dundalk, a coronation took place at the hill of Knocknemelan where the Scotsman Edward Bruce was crowned "King of Erin".

By now King Edward II was aware of the perilous situation of the Anglo-Irish and sent a special envoy in the person of Lord John Hotham to try and provoke a united response from them, but the success of this initiative was limited. There was great distrust among the Anglo-Irish since they did not know which of their number might be a closet supporter of Bruce. This Clandestine backing for the Scotsman stemmed from the fact that as far as many of the Anglo-Irish were concerned, if they fought against Bruce, their Irish holdings would be lost in the event of his campaign turning out to be a success.

The Bloody Battle of Athenry

By the summer of 1316, Feilim O'Connor was in open warfare with the English. Encouraged by the successes of Edward

Bruce, all Connacht had united behind him and he had also been joined by the O'Briens from the kingdom of Thomond, as well as by Mélaghlainn of Meath and O'Rourke of Breifne. The largest English force remaining in Connacht was in the town of Athenry in Galway where an army commanded by William de Burgo (known as "The Grey Earl") was well prepared to defend itself. The English stronghold was well fortified, and the troops were well armed but in spite of this King Feilim threw caution to the wind and decided to attack this stronghold.

The most heavily armed soldiers Feilim possessed were the Scottish Gallowglasses. By contrast, the Irish infantry or "kerns" were for the most part lightly armed, using spears and short swords. Additionally, most of them would not have worn body armour, except perhaps a helmet. The Irish, who performed well in guerrilla type engagements where they could get up close to their adversary, were not prepared for the confrontation which followed, which bordered on suicidal. On the tenth of August 1316, battle was joined, with the Irish attacking the enemy head-on. The archers of deBurgo's army were armed with powerful crossbows and killed many of the Irish infantry. No first-hand account of the battle survives but Irish losses were in the thousands and included very large numbers of the native Irish nobility, so much so that some bloodlines were almost rendered extinct. The Irish dead also included the twenty-three-year-old King Feilim, who fell beneath his leopard battle standard.

Robert Bruce Comes to Ireland

Meanwhile, after his coronation, Edward Bruce returned to the north. There, he involved himself in issues of governance before returning to Carrickfergus where the siege was not yet over. Things had not gone according to plan during his absence, as the Scottish garrison had been attacked in the rear by an English force led by Sir Thomas Mandeville. Mandeville's cohort had not been strong enough to lift the siege. Instead, it fought its way through and entered the encircled castle as reinforcements. Word of the siege reached Robert Bruce and in September 1316 he arrived at his brother's side, bringing advice and help, hoping to inject new life into his campaign. By this stage, the castle's resolute defenders had resorted to cannibalism rather than surrender. When a parley had been organised by the Scots, a delegation had been sent into the fortress for talks, but instead of talking, the English had promptly seized the Scots and having killed them, butchered them, and used them for food.

Eager to bring the siege to an end, Robert Bruce succeeded in re-opening negotiations with the besieged garrison, offering them surrender with honourable terms which they accepted.

After the winter had passed, Edward Bruce, still accompanied by his brother Robert, determined to renew his attack on the English, this time striking at the centre of English rule in Ireland, Dublin.

Attempted capture of Dublin and Limerick

The Bruce army that approached Dublin numbered around 20,000, plus a considerable force of Irish. Their advance left a trail of destruction in its wake. Panic now seized the Palesmen, fuelled by the distrust the Anglo-Irish had for each other.

The Mayor of Dublin Robert de Nottingham now ordered the arrest of "The Red Earl" who had previously been defeated by Edward Bruce outside Ballymena. The reason for this order was the fact that the Earl's daughter was married to Robert Bruce. DeBurgo was now in retirement at St. Mary Abbey in Dublin and had relinquished his sword of office. During his arrest, seven of his servants were killed and the abbey was partially destroyed.

Towards the end of February 1317, the Bruce army arrived at Castleknock and took the castle of Henry Tyrell for its headquarters. Tyrell was captured.

Robert deNottingham and his men now had the suburbs of Dublin evacuated and burned to the ground while the population retreated into the city proper. Even churches in the suburbs were knocked and their stones used to construct walls and barricades in order to hinder the path of the advancing Bruce army into the city.

Both Robert and Edward Bruce were very much dismayed at how prepared the capital was for defence and realised that a siege of the city was not really a viable option. The two brothers considered their alternatives for a few days and finally decided to go west and attack Limerick instead. Everywhere the Bruce army marched was marked with fire and sword. In their search for booty, even the tombs of the dead were opened, and shrines robbed. On reaching Limerick, they found the city as well if not better prepared for defence as Dublin. Caught in the open as winter approached, the Bruce army was now hampered by lack of suitable quarters and a shortage of provisions. In their reckless advance, they had lived from hand to mouth, destroying what they did not need and now that they could not enter Limerick, they had almost no food. Unable to take Limerick under siege, even if they had wanted to, they retreated in search of food and shelter but found only the devastation that they had created a short time before and many of Bruce's men fell victim to sickness and famine.

Since the beginning of the Bruce campaign, there had been no thought for the welfare of the native population and in his battles in the north and his advance southward there had been great destruction of property and crops, with a policy of scorched earth being widely carried out. As a result, many parts of the country had a very bad harvest, with many places suffering famine during the Winter of 1318. Initially, news of Edward Bruce's arrival had been greeted with joy among the Irish but now it seemed to them that things had gone from bad to worse. News of Bruce's advancing army was greeted with dismay since any area it passed through was sure to lose livestock and crops, with its inhabitants perhaps even losing the roofs over their heads. During the winter of 1317–18, the native Irish suffered terribly, and large numbers died of hunger.[i] Children were stolen and used as a source of food, as were the dead[31].

Once again the Bruce army retraced its path northwards to its Ulster stronghold where it sought to regain its strength. Robert Bruce now returned to Scotland, much to the relief of the English, as this signalled that the Irish campaign was taking a lower place in his priorities. However, even though Edward Bruce had a greatly reduced army, he was not for giving up on his Irish Kingdom.

The Battle of Dysert O'Dea

At this time, a great Irish victory took place in Thomond. The decades old war between the O'Briens and the deClares came to a head on the 10th of May 1318 at the Battle of Dysert O'Dea when Richard deClare attacked the home of Conor O'Dea, a chieftain of the Clan O'Brien. To deClare, O'Dea's men appeared to be few in number and initially seemed to retreat but when the Englishman advanced with his army the majority of O'Dea's men quickly appeared on his flanks. The heavily armed English fell foul of the flexible attack methods used by

---

[i] In many accounts Bruce's army is given all the blame for the hunger and disease that fell upon Ireland at this time, but this is not fully accurate. The period in question saw bad weather and failed harvests, with disease spreading among both animals and men. Both Ireland and England suffered but Ireland's suffering was made far worse by the widespread conflict and destruction.

the lightly-armed and fast-moving Irish warriors. During the battle, reinforcements arrived for O'Dea from other septs of the Clan and the English were surrounded. Finally forming themselves into a "battle hedge", they were slain to a man, including Richard deClare and his son. Following the battle, the victors made for the deClare stronghold of Bunratty Castle and found it ablaze. The fortress had been set on fire by deClare's wife before she made good her escape to Limerick, never to return.

The Death of the Scottish High King
<u>The Battle of Faughart</u>
During the summer of 1318, the fortunes of Bruce and his chances of significant reinforcement from Scotland suffered a setback. The Scottish supply lane across the North Channel to Ireland was cut and Thomas Dun, Bruce's transport chief, was captured. Meanwhile, the English poured reinforcements into the country under the command of Roger Mortimer, and full attention was given by them to the uprisings that had taken place all over the country as well as to those Anglo-Irish who had aided Bruce. The deLacys were summoned to appear before the Chief Justice and when they did not show up an envoy, Hugh de Custes, was sent to summon them and was killed. Mortimer now lost all patience with the deLacys and embarked on a mission of vengeance, plundering their property, and driving them underground. He succeeded in capturing John deLacy, who was sentenced to be pressed to death.[i] Notably, Mortimer also brought a proverbial carrot

---

[i] Pressed to Death" could either be a form of torture to procure information or a sentence of death for a defendant who would not enter a plea. The defendant was held in the lying position, while a door or panel of wood was placed on their chest after which heavy weights or large rocks were placed on top either until the defendant agreed to talk or was killed. The most famous example of

with him from England - permission from the King to admit the Irish to full use of English law.

In the Autumn of 1318, a strong English army under John deBermingham was moving northwards hoping to face the diminished force of Edward Bruce in battle. Bruce's army now only numbered less than three thousand men, plus the Irish contingent that still accompanied him, as well as the Anglo-Irish who had opted to fight under his banner. Bruce took up positions on the hill of Faughart outside Dundalk and prepared to face the numerically superior foe in open battle.

On October 14th, 1318, battle was joined and the outcome decided by the actions of one man, an English knight called Sir John Maupas. Maupas correctly sensed that without Edward Bruce the Scottish and Irish force would lose heart. Rushing into the thick of the enemy, he engaged Bruce in combat and killed him. Maupas was then slain by Bruce's men and after the battle his pierced body was found lying on top of Bruce's. The Scots, having lost their leader and the heart to fight, were overcome by the Anglo-Irish force and suffered appalling casualties.

DeBirmingham showed no respect whatsoever for the body of the dead King and subsequently had it cut up, displaying various pieces of it in different parts of the country as trophies of victory, the head being sent to King Edward II. For this and for his victory over Bruce, he was made Earl of Louth.

The death of Edward Bruce signalled the end of the Bruce involvement in Irish affairs. Although this Scottish intervention failed in its objective, the results were nonetheless noteworthy. It had torn asunder the unity of the Anglo-Irish in their aim of domination over the native Irish. In those parts of Ulster which had been cleared of colonists, the native Irish

---

pressing to death was of the Englishwoman Margaret Clitherow who was executed by this method on Good Friday in 1586 for hiding Catholic Priests.

were able to resume control of their ancestral lands, and this was repeated to a limited extent throughout the country. England at this time was in a state of turmoil, as Edward's French Queen Isabella had taken Roger Mortimer as her paramour and launched a rebellion against the King. In the years following the death of Bruce, the power of the English in Ireland was very weak. Nevertheless, the famine that was in part due to Bruce's arrival continued, and for much of the fourteenth century the people of Ireland lived a precarious existence in the shadow of hunger and pestilence

Chapter 7

Gaelic Irish and Degenerate English

Disquiet and Rebellion among the Anglo-Irish
English Mistrust of the "Old English"
The Bruce adventure in Ireland had come with a high cost to both native and Anglo-Irish, but it had also confirmed English suspicions that many of their Irish settlers were not wholly to be relied on. The "Bruce Effect" would resonate in Ireland for a long time to come. The Anglo-Irish as a body seemed to have lost the trust of their English masters, and for many of these, the trust of England no longer seemed to matter.

This situation was partly as a result of the actions of the King's Irish government that had long made a distinction between those of English birth and those of English descent, always preferring to appoint those of English birth to higher office. This passing over of the "Old English" settlers so angered them, that it drove many of them out of the arms of the English administration and into the arms of the native Irish.

This trend was to continue in the decades that followed as the English government in Ireland failed to remedy the rot that had set in among the families of their first settlers, many of whom now abandoned for good the old Norman policy of conquest.

The Irish were not slow to take advantage of any situation that presented itself for the remedying of old grievances, and the return into native hands of Irish land and property was always a priority. In the face of this and in order to protect themselves, not just from the Irish but also from the infighting of their Anglo-Irish brethren, many Anglo-Irish families became completely independent of the English government in the Pale and allied themselves with the native Irish, taking for their own the dress, customs, law and language of the Irish while also changing their Norman surname for one of an Irish style[i].

Infighting among the Anglo Irish

The years following the Bruce invasion were ones of stagnation and infighting for the English settlers. This infighting frequently ended in large-scale massacres. In 1329, two such massacres took place, the first in Ardee where the man who had claimed the credit for the defeat of Edward Bruce, John deBermingham was himself murdered along with the menfolk of his family and extended family after being lured into a trap by members of the Savage and Gernon families of Anglo Irish descent, while in Munster Lord Philip Bodnett and almost 150 of his kin were killed by members of the deBarry and deRoche families.

Like King John before him, King Edward III saw his settlers as a greater menace than the native Irish and hoped to bring the Anglo-Irish to heel by the appointment of a strong Lord Justice in the person of Sir Anthony Lucy. Arrests and some executions followed. Among those arrested were Sir William

---

[i] Examples of this were the Norman family of "de Angulo" which adopted the surname "Costello". In Cork the English family of "Jeffries" adopted the Gaelic surname MacSeffraigh which later became anglicised as "Sherry", (not to be confused with Sherry of Ulster who are descended from the Clan Mac Seiridh of Armagh, ancient rulers of the petty Kingdom of Dál Buinne which was located between Armagh and Lough Neagh.)

deBermingham and one of the most powerful of the Anglo-Irish, the Earl of Desmond, Maurice Fitzgerald, both of whom had been implicated in a plot against the Irish government. For his part in the plot Maurice Fitzgerald spent close on two years in prison.

The Murder of William de Burgo

It was the murder in 1333 of the 21 year old William deBurgo, (known as "The Brown Earl" of Ulster and grandson of the "Red Earl") that saw many of the deBurgos throw off the authority of the crown.
William had been responsible for the death by starvation of Walter deBurgo, a prominent member of the deBurgo family.
Walter's sister Gyle was married to Richard deMandeville who was William's uncle by marriage. It is believed that deMandeville, encouraged by Gyle, killed William while he was on his way to Mass in Carrickfergus along with some companions one Sunday morning. The young Earl was well liked and revenge for the murder was swift and encompassed all those who might have had any part to play. 300 people suffered the consequences and were killed. The young Earl's widow Maud fled to England with their one-year-old daughter and heir, Elizabeth. Realising that the future husband of young Elizabeth would inherit the family land, the deBurgos of Connacht seized all of the dead Earl's property in that province and promptly renounced English law, language and dress. They also threw off the name of deBurgo and took the name "MacWilliam", with three different branches of this family being established[i]. It was almost 100 years since the Norman

---

[i] The murdered Earl had two first cousins, Ulick and Edmund, both sons of his uncle William "the Grey". Ulick took for himself all the deBurgo lands of Co. Galway and this branch of the family became known as the "Clanrickard Burkes" or "Upper Mac William". Edmund seized all the land the family had acquired in Co. Mayo and his branch of the family became known as the "Mayo Burkes" or

deBurgos had succeeded in gaining power in Connacht for the English; now the English had lost it and would not regain it again for more than two hundred years.

The native Irish Clans, including the descendents of the former ruling family of O'Connor, now saw their chance to regain control of their native soil. As a result, the Clan of MacWilliam did not have things all their own way, and were hard put to keep what deBurgo had previously taken.

The Reassertion of Gaelic Governance in East Ulster

In Ulster, the Irish who just a short time before had been subject to deBurgo were not slow to act. With the Brown Earl dead, and his wife and daughter now in England, the Gaelic families of mid Ulster were able to reassert their dominance, and new territories came into being. In Fermanagh, the Maguires, in Cavan the O'Reillys, in Leitrim the O'Rourkes, and in Monaghan the MacMahons, all assumed governance of their native soil. In the former heartland of the deBurgo stronghold of Ulidia, a new force came into being – The O'Néills of Clandeboye[i], an offshoot of the Clan O'Néill which now ruled a large part of the dead Earl's former territory that included north Down and stretched from Belfast to the Antrim Glens. Another area of Ulster that reverted to Gaelic control was a large swathe of land along the north coast, which became known as "The Route", territory of the Clan MacQuillan which had previously been in the hands of the

---

"Lower Mac William". A third branch of the family also existed, founded by a younger son of the "Red Earl", named Edmund. This branch lived on the borders of Limerick and Tipperary and became known as "ClanWilliam".

[i] Clandeboye –from the Gaelic "Clann de Buidhe" or "The Yellow Family"

deMandeville family.[i] Only along parts of the Eastern coast did the Anglo-Irish retain anything approaching their former power but in time even this area of control came under threat and the English were forced to pay "black rent" or protection money to keep their borders safe from attack. The name of deBurgo had all but vanished from Ulster.

The disappearance of the deBurgo dynasty and the speed with which much territory had been regained also proved an encouragement to the Irish still living under English rule. One example of this occurred in 1340 when O'More of Leix, after gathering all the forces he could muster, launched a campaign against the occupiers in which many castles and outposts were destroyed, including the huge castle on the Rock of Dunamase, home of Roger Mortimer. A notable reappearance also occurred in Leinster. After the Carlow-based Norman family of LeBygod became extinct, Domhnall MacMurrough Kavanagh, who was descended from Diarmuid MacMurrough, reclaimed much territory, including the family's ancient seat of Hy Kinsella, and the Gaelic kingdom of Leinster was successfully reinstated.

English Policy of Segregation against the Anglo-Irish

A new Lord Justice Sir John Morris took office in 1341. Instead of attempting to breathe new life into the Anglo-Irish families that remained loyal to the crown, his approach was to cast them off completely as he sought to reclaim all debts that had been cancelled during previous administrations.

Worse was to come for the established Anglo-Irish. An edict of King Edward III was published in 1342 by which he sought to

---

[i] Accorrding to some historians, the Clan MacQuillan were previously the de Mandevilles. In the aftermath of the murder of William deBurgo a son of Hugelin de Mandeville adopted the surname "Mac Uighlín" (or son of Hugelin) which later became anglicised as MacQuillan.

completely break the power of the old Anglo-Irish families. Anyone, either of Irish or English descent, who had estates and land only in Ireland or was married to an Irishwoman was to be relieved from public office. All public office was now to be held by English-born subjects who had property in England.

The Anglo-Irish were incensed. Many of them refused to attend a session of Morris' parliament called to allay their fears and talk of armed resistance abounded. In the end, the King needed troops to fight in the war against the French and also could not risk an Anglo Irish revolt while his army was abroad. So, the edict was revoked on condition that the Anglo-Irish would send men for the King's army. Matters further deteriorated in 1344 when Sir Ralph deUfford was appointed as Lord Lieutenant. He attacked the territory of Maurice Fitzmaurice, Earl of Desmond after the latter refused to attend an Irish Parliament which deUfford had summoned. DeUfford was married to Maud, widow of the murdered Brown Earl, William deBurgo, and she reputedly kindled his tyrannical streak, perhaps feeling that revenge was due to the Anglo-Irish who had stood by, while her first husband's territories were dismembered. DeUfford's army seized estates and castles in Desmond's territory and murdered a number of his knights after the Earl refused to supply "coyn[i] and livery" to his army, which was the provision of food, money and entertainment for the soldiers and fodder for the horses. In time deUfford hoped to capture Fitzmaurice himself and to destroy the power of the Geraldines in Munster. Eventually the Earl of Desmond was captured and thrown into prison but before de Ufford could complete the task he had set himself, he fell ill and died in April 1346. After this, Fitzmaurice was released. Now he had the chance to present his case in person to King Edward III and

---

[i] from the Gaelic word "cothabhail", meaning maintenance.

hastened to England where he was pardoned as the King needed his troops to fight against France.

After this, any concerted effort to reduce the power of the old Anglo Irish families petered out, but there was to be a further weakening of ties between the Anglo Irish and the Crown, the result of a terrible plague of biblical proportions known as "The Black Death".

The Black Death

In 1348, the first and by far the worst of the three great plagues that occurred during the reign of King Edward III arrived in Ireland. The Black Death had made its appearance on the continent of Europe in 1347 and it arrived in Ireland at the busy port of Howth in Dublin during midsummer 1348. The primary carriers of the disease in the first instance were fleas hosted by black rats. When the rat died of the disease, the flea moved to a new host which all too often was a man or woman. Common symptoms were painful tumours under the armpits, around the groin or on the neck. Hallucination and delirium were also common. The native annals of this period have little space for anything other than listing the deaths of Gaelic noblemen from the plague. An eyewitness of these deadly times was Friar Clyn and in his annals he recorded: "It first broke out near Dublin at Howth and Dalkey; it almost destroyed and laid waste the cities of Dublin and Drogheda in so much that in Dublin alone from the beginning of August to Christmas 14,000 souls perished...The pestilence deprived of human inhabitants villages and cities, castles and towns so that there was scarcely found a man to dwell therein; the pestilence was so contagious that whosoever touched the sick or the dead was immediately affected and died, and the penitent and the confessor were carried together to the grave...scarcely one ever died alone in a house; commonly husband, wife, children and servants went the one way and death was assured."[32] The

Black Death affected the more highly populated areas and many of the native Irish who lived in the countryside escaped its grasp but those that lived in the Pale and other urban centres suffered terribly. It also took a high toll on the Anglo-Irish. Once it entered their estates, everyone from the lowest servant to the Baron were in danger and many of them abandoned their castles and left the country in an attempt to escape its grasp, which further weakened their presence in the country. In their flight, they had nowhere to escape to as all Europe was reeling in the plague's deathly vise.

The Effect of the Black Death
The Black Death proved to be something of a watershed moment in European history as in its wake came transition and decline, resulting in abuses, nepotism and corruption in both civil and church governance that culminated in the Protestant Reformation of the sixteenth century.
In the aftermath of the plague, a new language took hold in England. So many of the monks and nuns had died that the bringing up and education of children was left to servants or poorly trained teachers who used a semi-French Anglo-Saxon dialect that eventually permeated to the highest levels of society. This language became known as "English".

"Hiberniores Hibernicis ipsis"
In Ireland, the effect of the Black Death on spoken language was the same, but the result was different. English did not take hold outside the Pale and the Anglo-Irish in the country at large changed from speaking French to Irish. "If the speech is Irish the heart is also Irish"[33] was the verdict of the English government. As the decades of the fourteenth century passed, this difference in language only served to deepen the divide between the Anglo-Irish and their English masters who now disparagingly referred to them as "the Degenerate English"[34]

(a term first used by Chief Justice deWogan in 1297 to describe those settlers who wore their hair long in the Irish fashion. One English writer of the period expressed the view of English officialdom in latin. Many of the Anglo-Irish were "Hiberniores Hibernicis ipsis" or "more Irish than the Irish themselves."[35]

The old Norman families were not the only ones to change. Norman ways too had their effect on the native Irish who often adopted their method of warfare and mimicked their heraldry and castles. As the generations passed, the lines between many Norman and the Gael often became blurred.

It also cannot be overlooked that in this time before the Reformation, in spite of the measures often adopted by the English to segregate the two races, they nevertheless shared the same Catholic faith, and therefore the same Catholic culture and beliefs. Following the Reformation, the difference in religion would be an insurmountable stumbling block to any form of integration of the plantation families that would pour into Ulster in the seventeenth century.

Over time, some practices adopted by the Anglo Irish served to convert many of them to something approaching a love and appreciation of things Gaelic. The first of these was intermarriage between Norman Lords and the daughters of Gaelic Chieftains. These young Irishwomen were widely regarded for their chastity, beauty, intelligence and wit[36] and were much sought after as brides by eligible Anglo Irish gentlemen.[i] Another such practice was the adoption by many Anglo-Irish families of the Gaelic custom of fosterage whereby a son of the family was raised by a Gaelic family and treated as a son of the house, with the parents of the family becoming, in effect, his foster parents. Two boys nursed on the same milk

---

[i] The eminent historian Seumas MacManus writes concerning the marriage of Aoife to Strongbow: "On the blood-soaked battlefield of Waterford (1170), the Irish conquest of the Norman conquerors was begun".

were called foster brothers, and while one boy was Anglo Irish, the other was the blood son of his Irish nurse. This practice was despised by the English government because: "...fostering hath always been a stronger alliance than blood"[37] and with regard to the family it was considered that the foster children "...do adhere unto them in all fortunes with more affection and constancy."[38]

Lionel, Duke of Clarence, Lord Lieutenant of Ireland

When it came to reform of his Irish colony, King Edward III was like a dog with a bone. Foiled several times, he continued to gnaw. In 1360, he appointed his third son Lionel as his Irish Lord Lieutenant and gave him special powers. Lionel arrived in Ireland in the middle of September, bringing with him his wife Elizabeth (daughter of the murdered Brown Earl William deBurgo) and 1,500 men at arms. The Prince also ordered that all those Lords residing in England who had large Irish possessions should accompany him or have their lands confiscated. Sixty-four absentee landlords boarded ship with him.

On arriving in Ireland, he immediately resurrected the policy of distinction, whereby those of English birth were preferred to those of English descent. But he went further than before. Those of English descent were now considered Irish and a proclamation was issued forbidding anyone of Irish birth from coming anywhere near his army. Furthermore, those of Irish birth could not be advanced to any high position, either governmental or ecclesiastical. Once again, the old Anglo-Irish families were affronted, and once again the King's policy was foiled. One night, a hundred of Lionel's best soldiers were mysteriously killed, after which he relented and called all those who considered themselves to be subjects of the King to rally behind his flag.

Having failed with the Anglo-Irish, he hoped for better luck in his other projects. As husband of the heiress of Connacht and Ulster, the Earldom was his and now he hoped to regain the real estate that went along with it. In Connacht, his attempts met with failure, while his efforts in Ulster had limited success. He had better luck when he attacked the Irish Clans who were encroaching on the Pale and succeeded in capturing Art MacMurrough, Gaelic King of Leinster. In Cork, too, he managed to recover some territory for the Anglo-Irish, but for him Ireland was a backwater and he longed to be with his father, the King, on the battlefields of France where he felt glory awaited him.[39]

The Statute of Kilkenny

Lionel's parting shot came before he left Ireland for good. Embittered by his failure to achieve his aim of regaining the former territory of the de Burgos and realising that the native Irish could not be overcome by any power at his disposal, Lionel determined to try and halt the already advanced state of "Hibernisation" of the Anglo-Irish before he left Ireland for good. He resolved to cordon them off from their Gaelic neighbours in all respects and by so doing to save the English colony from demise. The act was really an admission of failure, as in England after 1066 the Saxons and Normans had gradually melded together, the whole country becoming Norman, whereas in Ireland nothing of the sort had been achieved.

In 1367, during his last weeks in office, he called an Anglo-Irish parliament to be held in Kilkenny where he introduced an act known as the "Statute of Kilkenny". To describe this legislation as draconian would be an understatement.

The Measures Introduced

The act was lengthy, consisting of thirty-five chapters, and prescribed the severest measures for the smallest breach of its code. On its passing, it became high treason to engage in any type of intimate relationship with the native Irish. Anyone found guilty of offences such as intermarriage or fosterage was subject to execution. Any settler who changed his name into the Irish style, adopted the Irish language or dress, or rode a horse bareback in the Irish fashion was to have all his property confiscated and be imprisoned until he provided adequate sureties for his conduct.

The Anglo-Irish were also forbidden to make war on the native Irish without the special permission of the government, not so as to place any restrictions on any unilateral action that the settlers might take against the native Irish, but rather "so that the Irish enemies shall not be admitted to peace until they be finally destroyed or shall make restitution fully of the costs and charges of that war"[40].

There was also a restatement of the racial segregation insisted on by the government within the Church. In the areas of the country under English control, it was forbidden to appoint a native Irish cleric to any ecclesiastical office or to allow the native Irish join a monastic order; "…no house of religion which is situated among the English shall in the future receive any Irishman to their profession…"[41]

What the Anglo-Irish might do in their hours of relaxation was also not overlooked in the act. They were forbidden to allow themselves to be entertained by any Gaelic Irish minstrel or bard and even Gaelic news-tellers were to be banned from their homes.

Apart from the provision regarding the Anglo-Irish, there were also measures in the act aimed at the native Irish living in the areas under English rule. Along with stipulations concerning pasturing, they were forbidden from speaking their native tongue under pain of loss of property and imprisonment.

The Effects of the Statute

The most important aspect of the Statute of Kilkenny was its enshrinement in law of the English land grab. It was the first time that the "titles" and "rights" of the crown were enshrined in a legal document. It would be referred to in the centuries to come by a different generation of invaders and planters who would use its provisions to eject Irish intruders from the "King's land", thus perpetuating and enlarging the robbery and injustice for centuries to come.

In its attempt to sever all connections between the Anglo-Irish and the native Irish, the Statute was totally impractical and unworkable. In large centres of the Anglo-Irish population, the act was not necessary, while in the countryside the Anglo-Irish often existed as islands in a sea of Gaelic Irish. Small in number and lacking a substantial cultural tradition of their own, the Anglo-Irish in these areas would find it almost impossible to undo what already had been done and once Lionel had departed, they for the most part regarded the act as a dead letter.

The native Irish, on the other hand, viewed the Statute as yet another measure designed for their repression as it labelled the whole race as "the King's Irish enemies" and also denied them of their right to inherit and hold land. Fearing that the passing of the act signalled an upsurge in attacks on their sovereign lands, the Gaelic Chieftains put aside their differences and attacked their common enemy.[i] The Anglo-Irish were put

---

[i] "The native Irish apprehending that the real object of a law enacted and proclaimed with so much pomp and appearance of authority was to root them altogether out of the land, naturally combined together for safety, and some of the more powerful chieftains resolved upon immediate hostilities. O'Conor of Connacht and O'Brien of Thomond for the moment laid aside their private

under such pressure during this time that had the native Irish Clans united to free the country of their rule, they could well have succeeded. But the native Irish Chieftains were only concerned with their own local situation and gave no thought to the restoration of the High Kingship. Such was the haemorrhage of land back into native hands that in 1368 an act was passed whereby all landlords had to either return to their Irish holding or provide troops to maintain the security of their holding. Any landlord who failed to adhere to this act had his lands confiscated by the Crown.

---

feuds, and united against the common foe. The earl of Desmond, Lord Justice, marched against them with a considerable army, but was defeated and captured in a sanguinary engagement fought in A.D 1369, in the county of Limerick. O'Farrell, the chieftain of Annaly committed great slaughter in Meath. The O'Mores, Cavanaghs, O'Byrnes, and O'Tooles, pressed upon Leinster, and the O'Néills raised the red arm in the north. The English of the Pale were seized with consternation and dismay, and terror and confusion reigned in their councils, while the natives continued to gain ground upon them in every direction. At this crisis an opportunity offered, such as had never before occurred, of terminating the dominion of the English in Ireland, but if the natives had ever conceived such a project, they were never sufficiently united to achieve it. The opportunity passed away and the disunion of the Irish saved the colony" - Excerpt from The Statute of Kilkenny, published by The Irish Archaeological Society, with introduction and notes by the late James Hardiman, Esq.,M.R.I.A

Chapter 8

A Tale of Two Kings

Art Mac Murrough, King of Leinster
If the name of MacMurrough was disgraced by Diarmuid MacMurrough, the twelfth century King of Leinster, then this disgrace was surely mitigated by his descendent Art Óg MacMurrough Kavanagh, who bravely sought to defend his homeland against the encroachment of the invader. Like his ancestor Diarmuid, Art succeeded to the throne of Leinster at a young age, in his case eighteen years, in the year 1375.

The English Pale – "Beholden to a Captain of the Enemy"
The King of Leinster had been accustomed to receiving "black rent" or an annual tribute from the English authorities for desisting from nuisance attacks against the Pale for despite many concerted attempts by the English to dislodge the Gaelic leader of Leinster from his mountain fastness of Glenmalure, victory eluded them.
In 1377, after Richard II became King of England, the authorities decided to withhold this payment from the new King of Leinster and this action provoked a violent reaction from him. Summoning all those Clans who owed loyalty to him, McMurrough launched a campaign against many Anglo-Irish settlements from his base in the Blackstairs Mountains and burned areas of Kildare, Carlow, Kilkenny and Wexford.

The government had no effective means at their disposal to deal with the threat that he posed to the security of the Pale and so had no option but to restore the payment of eighty marks a year to him.

In May of 1380, in order to bolster the waning fortunes of the English in Ireland, King Richard II sent a large army commanded by his newly appointed Lord Justice, Edmund Mortimer, who was married to Philippa Plantagenet, daughter of the Duke of Clarence. As the husband of the deBurgo heiress and de facto Earl of Ulster, Edmund Mortimer was determined to recover the vast Irish estates that the family had once possessed. His tenure in Ireland was short but frantic. He traversed the country from north to south, making war along its length and succeeded in recapturing the family stronghold on the Rock of Dunamase in Leix. On his arrival in Ulster, he was greeted in a peaceful fashion, but after laying hands on the Gaelic Chieftain Art Magennis who came to visit him, hostilities resumed. He died in Cork in December 1381, leaving as his heir an eight year old son, Roger, whom the childless Richard II later declared as his heir.

Around 1390, Art MacMurrough married the Anglo-Irish noblewoman, Elizabeth LeVeel, who was heiress to the Barony of Norragh. For this breach of the Statute of Kilkenny, his bride's sizeable estates were seized by the English government in Ireland, an action that greatly aroused MacMurrough's anger and the counties of the Pale suffered terribly as a result of his retribution.

The fact that the Pale as the centre of English rule in Ireland was beholden to a Gaelic King for its ability to live in peace was unconscionable to the Anglo-Irish. Realising that if this situation continued indefinitely, the country was in danger of reverting completely to Gaelic control, the residents of the Pale appealed to King Richard II for help, complaining of "the mischiefs and very great evils in the land of Ireland"[42]. Stating the weakness of English power in the country and warning of "a conquest of the greater part of the land of Ireland"[43] by the native Irish, they begged for "the coming of the King, our Lord in his own person."[44]

King Richard II Comes to Ireland

In 1394, after he had achieved a truce with the Scottish and peace with the French, Richard II was finally in a position to heed the pleas of his Irish settlers and give safety to the Pale, at least from MacMurrough and the other troublesome Leinster Clans that he controlled.

Despite numerous laws against absentee landlords, great swathes of Anglo-Irish territory were in the official ownership of English residents. Under pain of having their lands confiscated, these landlords were ordered to accompany the King on his Irish expedition.

The Submission of the Gaelic Chieftains

Two hundred ships ferried the single largest armed force ever to land on Irish shores. The King's army of 34,000 men disembarked at Waterford on the 2nd of October 1394. On receiving news of the King's arrival, MacMurrough decided to welcome him by launching an attack on the nearby walled English settlement of New Ross, which was set ablaze after everything of value was removed by his men. However, there was no prospect of a victory by the disunited Irish Clans over such an army as this and many of the southern native chieftains, MacMurrough included, yielded to the inevitable and submitted to Mowbray, Earl of Nottingham, in Carlow. Meanwhile, King Richard II marched up the East coast to Drogheda where the northern chiefs offered their submission to him in order to avoid being annihilated by this English army overwhelming in both strength and number.ⁱ

All told, seventy-five chieftains submitted. Excluding the Leinster chieftains, all others were confirmed in the ownership of their Irish lands on condition that they surrender the lands they had "usurped" from the English and acknowledge the King as their Liege and the Anglo-Irish Earls as their overlords.

King Richard II

The security of the Pale was of paramount importance to English interests in Ireland, so in order to achieve complete security for this area, the Leinster chieftains were offered terms of submission that included the abandonment of their native patrimony on a day of the King's choosing in return for a lifetime pension. Furthermore, as loyal King's subjects, they were then supposed to aid the King militarily in the pacification of the rest of the country where they would be allowed to compensate themselves with land captured from "rebels". Tongue in

---

ⁱ At this time Niall Óg O'Néill was the most prominent Gaelic ruler in Ulster. His father presented his written submission in latin to King Richard at the Dominican Monastery in Drogheda; "I, Niall Óg O'Néill, Captain of my Nation, have ordained in my plavce my beloved father, Niall Mór, giving him power in my name to appear before the illustrious Prince Richard, King of England, and Lord of Ireland, and before my lord Roger deMortimer, Earl of March and Ulster, and to treat of peace with them for me and my nation and subjects, and to surrender whatever lands, liberties, services and customs, I unjustly possess or allow other to possess, and especially the bonnaght (military service) of the Irish of Ulster"

cheek, Art MacMurrough agreed to these terms along with the other Clans of Leinster loyal to him, the larger of these being the O'Byrnes, O'Tooles, O'Mores, O'Dempseys and the Leinster O'Connors.

Deciding that the best way to secure his Irish colony was to bring the native provincial Kings into the fold of the King of England, Richard decided to knight MacMurrough along with O'Connor of Connacht, O'Néill of Ulster and O'Brien of Thomond. An English gentleman by the name of Henry Castide was instructed to take them under his instruction in Dublin for one month in order to teach them English ways.[i] Castide later recalled how they had submitted to the King "more through love and good humour than by battle or force"[45] sentiments that perhaps give us an indication of how the Gaelic princes viewed the whole proceedings.

The knighthoods, the days of feasting and the great display of English pomp and pageantry were all to no avail. To a man, the Irish Princes regarded the whole thing as something of a sham. Richard was not their King, and even though they would promise him whatever he asked, they did not feel bound to keep faith with him, as from the beginning the English had not kept faith with them. Richard's stay in Ireland was looked on in England as being a complete success but, like his predecessor King Henry II, he left Ireland on May 15th 1395 abord his ship *"Le Trinite"* with only extorted pledges.

---

[i] In describing his instruction Castide later wrote in part that the four Gaelic Kings "...would cause their minstrels, their servants and varlets to sit with them and to eat in their own dishes, and to drink of their cups, and they showed me that the usage of their country was good, for they said, in all things, except their beds they lived and worked as common men. So the fourth day I ordained other tables to covered in the hall, after the usage of England, and I made these four kings to sit at the high table and their minstrels at another table, and their servants and varlets at another... (at which)... they were displeased... and would not eat"

The Killing of Roger Mortimer

<u>The Emergence of the "Lancastrian Faction"</u>
Richard's father, Edward, "The Black Prince", had died without succeeding to the throne and Richard was still a teenager when he became King at the death of his grandfather, King Edward III. From the beginning, Richard's uncle, John of Gaunt, Duke of Lancaster, (and third son of King Edward III) eyed the throne jealously,[46] first for himself and then for his son Henry, whom Richard exiled to Calais.

<u>The Death of the Heir to the Throne</u>
King Richard II had been married to a Bohemian Princess called Anna who had died in 1494 without leaving Richard an heir.
In order to secure his reign and head off a potential conspiracy from the House of Lancaster, Richard had named his cousin Roger Mortimer as his heir, and it was the same Roger Mortimer whom he left behind as his Irish Lord Justice when he departed Ireland in May of 1395.
Once the King had departed, the Irish wasted no time in showing Lord Justice Mortimer how they regarded the "promises" they had made to his Sovereign. There was general insurrection on the part of the Irish, with mixed results. The decisive moment came in 1398 at Kenlis (Kells) in Co. Kilkenny when the Leinster Clans, including the army of MacMurrough, defeated a large English army. There, the Lord Justice and heir to the throne of England, Roger Mortimer was killed.

"MacMurrough – Dead or Alive"

Despite the fact that his reign was insecure due to the machinations of the Lancastrian faction led by John of Gaunt the rage of the King on hearing of the death of his heir at the hands of those Irish who had promised him their loyalty was such that he decided on a punitive expedition to Ireland with the primary purpose of chastising Art MacMurrough. This action was to cost him not only his throne but also indirectly his life.

Mistrusting all his relatives, he decided to leave the government of the country in the hands of the Duke of York whom he suspected the least.[47] By May of 1399, his army, which was almost as large as before, was assembled. On May 9th, he set sail from Milford Haven, bringing with him the son of the exiled Henry of Lancaster as a sort of hostage, perhaps suspecting trouble at home in his absence. Indeed, it seems that Richard felt that he would never resume a normal reign as, before his departure for Ireland, he made his will in which he set out the details for his own funeral. Richard had also arranged for the Duke of York's son, the Duke of Albemarle, to send more troops and provisions in his wake so as to keep his army supplied while in Ireland. The King's armada arrived in Waterford two days later on May 11th, 1399.

From Waterford, he marched to Kilkenny where he waited in vain for Albemarle's reinforcements and supplies. Unbeknown to Richard, Albemarle had betrayed his King in favour of Henry of Lancaster who at that moment was finalising his plans for his return to England.

Finally, the King could wait no longer and departed the city of St. Canice in order to march to Dublin, not by the most direct route but instead detouring through the Wicklow Mountains in order to track down the King of Leinster. The passage through these hills was slow for such a large force, but finally MacMurrough's army was spotted in position on the side of a mountain, observing the passage of the King and his army. During his previous visit, the Irish Chieftains had declared their affection for the King's standard, which consisted of the cross of St. Edward surrounded by doves, but now Richard marshalled his army before the wood and flew his personal standard of the three leopards. Over 2,000 people from the surrounding area were rounded up by the King's men and forced to cut a path through the woods while Richard amused himself by knighting the young son of Henry of Lancaster, later to be King Henry VI. Once the way was clear, the army marched into the forest in their bid to run the King of Leinster to ground.

The Entrapment of the King

MacMurrough knew well the path that Richard would have to travel. He had lured him into a part of the forest that consisted of bogs, hidden gullies and quagmires, in which the English soldiers sank up to their middles. While trying to force its way through the morass, the King's army was attacked time and again by bands of MacMurrough's men, who exacted a heavy toll on the King's army. It was at this moment that Albemarle's treachery hit Richard hard. Without sufficient provisions for man or beast and faced with MacMurrough's constant harassing attack, hundreds of his men and horses succumbed to weakness, sickness and even death. Some of MacMurrough's men who had been captured were returned to him with the message that the English King would pardon him and grant him "castles, towns and ample territory"[48] but the King of Leinster sent back the defiant message that "for all the gold in the world he would not submit himself, but would continue to war and endamage the King in all that he could"[49].

Hounded by MacMurrough's army, the King finally exited the mountains at the coast where, to his men's delight, three ships awaited them, containing provisions that had been sent from Dublin. The men did not wait for the distribution of the provisions but instead fought over them and gorged themselves, many getting drunk with the wine that was on board.

The march to Dublin continued but still MacMurrough would not let the King reach the city's safety in peace, so the journey proceeded as before. Before they had reached Dublin, emissaries from MacMurrough came into King Richard's presence, bringing the message that the King of Leinster wanted to parley. The news was received with joy by the English, and Richard appointed the Earl of Gloucester to meet with McMurrough's party. Taking a large guard of lances and archers with him, Gloucester set off, also bringing with him a man called Creton, a French visitor to King Richard's Court, who afterwards wrote an account of the meeting. Gloucester was the first to arrive at the appointed place, and then MacMurrough was spotted "...descending, accompanied by multitudes of the Irish, and mounted upon a horse without a saddle which cost him, it was reported, 400 cows. His horse was fair, and in his descent from the hill to us, ran as swiftly as any stag, hare, or the swiftest beast I have ever seen. In his right hand he bore a long spear, which when near the spot where he was to meet the Earl, he cast from him with much dexterity. The crowd that followed him then remained behind while he advanced to meet the Earl near a small brook. He was tall of stature, well composed, strong and active; his countenance fierce..."[50]

The parley was protracted and ended without agreement. Adamant in his refusal to submit, he told Gloucester: "I am a rightful King of Ireland, and it is unjust to deprive me of what is my land by conquest."[51] Whatever Gloucester was empowered to grant MacMurrough was not sufficient to satisfy him and the emissary returned to his King to report MacMurrough's refusal to surrender. On hearing this, Richard was enraged and swore by St. Edward that he would not leave Ireland until he had MacMurrough before him, living or dead. Finally, the English King reached Dublin, a huge force of half-starved men in tow. After his arrival in Dublin, Albemarle finally arrived with reinforcements, ostensibly so that the King could continue his Irish campaign, but in reality his mission was to detain the King in Ireland so that his first cousin, Henry of Lancaster, could proceed with his treachery undisturbed.

Richard proceeded in the reorganisation of his expeditionary force and let it be known to his men that 100 Marks would be the prize for whichever of them would deliver Art MacMurrough to him, dead or alive.

The Death of Two Kings

Before Richard's Irish campaign resumed in earnest, a messenger from England arrived with momentous news. The exiled Henry of Lancaster had returned from France with a small army some weeks previously and many English nobles had rallied to his cause. His Irish campaign now dead in the water, Richard returned to England with great haste, and on his arrival found no one that would help him. With only a personal bodyguard in tow, he was taken prisoner by his devious cousin at Flint Castle on August 19th and transferred to the Tower of London where he was subsequently murdered by starvation. Henry of Lancaster now had himself crowned under the title "Henry IV" on October 13th 1399.

After his accession to the throne, Henry IV was much reviled, being regarded not only as a murderer but also as a usurper and perjurer.[52] The upset caused by his accession to the throne both in England and Ireland was regarded as an opportunity by MacMurrough, who now continued his campaign with renewed vigour, although victory was not always the outcome. In 1401, the O'Byrnes were roundly defeated at the Battle of Bloody Bank in Bray, Co. Wicklow, with over 400 lives lost. Eventually, as a means of obtaining some relief from his attacks, the government paid him compensation for his wife's lands and he was restored to the barony of Norragh, but his raids continued. In 1405, two English settlements at

Castledermot and Carlow were plundered and burned. In 1407, MacMurrough suffered his greatest defeat when a large English army led by the Lord Justice Sir Steven Scroop met him in battle. Initially, the battle went well for MacMurrough, but the English gained the upper hand, and he was roundly defeated. In the wake of this victory, the English army marched on the stronghold of the Gaelic Lord of Ely, Teige O'Carroll, and caught his army completely unprepared. In the mayhem that followed, 800 of his warriors were slaughtered.

For a time, MacMurrough withdrew to renew his strength. In 1413, he resumed his war on the English, defeating their garrison in battle at Wexford. Following this defeat, the English again determined to bring to an end the menace that he was to their existence. In 1416, they met him again in open battle but once again he was victorious and, on this occasion, succeeded in capturing many prisoners. The day after the battle, the English sued for peace and surrendered hostages to MacMurrough, as a guarantee of their future tranquillity.

The epic of this great King came to an end not long after. In 1417, he spent Christmas in New Ross in the company of his deputy and Chief Brehon (lawgiver) O'Doran. In the time after Christmas, both of them fell ill and died shortly afterwards, McMurrough in his fortress of Ferns, as the Annals of Lough Cé record, "after the triumph of unction of penitence."[53] It was later recalled that during the Christmas festivities they had socialised and shared a drink served to them by a woman stranger who is reputed to have poisoned them.[54]

Art MacMurrough Kavanagh reigned as King of Leinster for forty-two years and is numbered among Ireland's greatest Kings due to his perseverance in the pursuit of freedom from the English. Although his kingdom was the antechamber of the Pale, he remained independent of the English and avoided becoming embroiled in the machinations with which they ensnared many other Gaelic princes. For the duration of his reign, he was always a factor that the English had to take into account when considering the security of their Irish seat of government, a fishbone which they could neither cough up nor swallow.

Chapter 9

Ireland During The Wars of the Roses

From Henry IV to Henry V

The reign of the new King Henry IV was largely taken up with troubles both in England and France. With the resources of the crown thus occupied, the decline of English power in Ireland that King Richard II had sought to arrest continued unabated. Towards the end of the reign of Henry IV, the speaker in the English House of Commons Sir John Tibetot remarked that the "greater part of the Lordship of Ireland hath been reconquered by the natives."[55]

The reign of Henry IV was further marred by his epilepsy and towards the end of his reign he suffered from one epileptic fit after another, the last of which occurred in March 1413, resulting in his death. His successor was his son, the 26-year-old Henry V (who had been knighted in the wilds of Wicklow by King Richard II). He set as the aim of his reign the firm establishment of the Lancastrian House on the throne of England by the return to French soil of English forces hoping for the reconquest of lost Norman French territory. To accomplish this reconquest, he proposed a large expeditionary force.

Regaining Lost Ground

Around this time, the Crown created a new title for the King's first minister in Ireland. Instead of Chief Justice or Justiciar, he would now be referred to as the "King's Lieutenant" or more commonly "Lord Deputy". The payment due for this high office also increased but such was the dire state of the King's Irish revenues that the stipend was often paid for directly from the London exchequer.

Before the departure of King HenryV for France, he gave the Irish baton to the very capable Sir John Talbot (Lord Furnival) who embarked on his duties with great vigour. Apart from defeating "the King's Irish enemies", he felt that his chief task was to steer Ireland away from the path of home rule advocated by James, the "White Earl" of Ormond.

The English of the Pale were delighted with Talbot's progress as he made great strides in securing the Pale's borders. Using aggressive military methods, he invaded the territory of the Gaelic Chieftain O'More in Leix and seized two of his castles. In order to secure peace terms, O'More had to give up his son as a hostage. The same methods were used against Oriel with MacMahon, the Chieftain of Oriel also forced to submit a hostage. The terms of peace obliged the surrendering chieftains to join Talbot under the King's standard and by this method Talbot hoped to break the Gaelic Lords one by one in their stance against English rule.

The joy of the Pale-dwellers was short-lived however, as the price they paid for their security was equivalent to if not in excess of the danger that they faced. In order to pay his army, Talbot quartered them in the Pale so that they could exact the much dreaded "coign and livery" in return for their services (which was in contravention of the Statute of Kilkenny). In 1416, Talbot's military leadership skills were required in France and on his departure the Irish attacks on the Pale resumed with the Pale-dwellers being once more forced to resume the practice of paying black rent in order to ensure their safety against Irish raids.

The Reign of King Henry VI

The English mistrust of the Anglo-Irish also continued and towards the end of the reign of Henry V Anglo-Irish law students were excluded from attending the King's Inns in London and many obstructions were also placed in the path of those among them who wished their sons to attend English schools.

Henry V achieved victory in his French war at Agincourt but did not live to see the glory of it. Only 36 years old, he suffered from the bad health that seemed to be inherent in the house of Lancaster and died in Paris in the spring of 1422. His son, the nine-month-old Henry VI, succeeded to the thrones of both England and France.

The start of Henry VI's reign coincided with the 250th anniversary of the coming of the Normans to Ireland. With the accession to the throne of the House of Lancaster, and the French war that ensued, the English had little in the way of military power to spare for Ireland and so the Gaelic Lords used this opportunity well in reclaiming lost territory. Unable to withstand the military campaign of the Irish seeking to regain their native soil, English settlers in many parts of the country abandoned their settlements and returned to England.

At this time, the Pale remained as the last English oasis in Ireland where English life, law and language were the order of the day. Outside of this, the three great Anglo-Irish Earldoms of Ormond, Desmond and Kildare along with some smaller Anglo-Irish holdings of twenty to thirty miles square approached the status of petty Gaelic kingdoms in their own right. Through generations of intermarriage and the adoption of Gaelic language and habits, these "degenerate English" straddled the line between the two traditions.

The Ulster Chieftains Attack South

Around the time that Henry VI became King of England, there was bitter feuding between the Anglo-Irish families of Butler and Talbot. The Talbots were led by the new Lord Deputy and Archbishop of Dublin Richard Talbot, (brother of Sir John Talbot) who was much distracted by the violent quarrel, and it was at this time that the Gaelic Ulster Lords of O'Néill and O'Donnell put aside their own intermittent feuding and together attacked the English stronghold of Oriel. They marched first to Dundalk and then onto into Meath where they routed Archbishop Talbot's army and captured a large amount of booty but did not press their advantage any further.

In May 1423, the King appointed Edmund Mortimer, (who was the son of Roger Mortimer that had been killed in battle outside Carlow in 1398) as titular Lord Deputy, while James, Earl of Ormond was appointed as his second in command.

The following year (1424), James Earl of Ormond arrived in Ireland with an English army determined to weaken the growing power of the Ulster Chieftains and reassert the previously strong presence of the Anglo-Irish in Ulster. After attacking northwards into Monaghan and Armagh, the O'Néills and O'Donnells were forced back into their native territory.

At the end of 1424, Edmund Mortimer was ordered to Ireland after a heated row with the King's Uncle, the Duke of Gloucester, and took over the duties of Lord Deputy himself. After his arrival in Ireland in January 1425, he held court at Trim Castle and five Ulster chieftains led by Eoghan O'Néill came to pay their respects to him. While the Ulster Lords were still at Trim, Edmund Mortimer fell ill and died. Immediately Sir John Talbot was reappointed Lord Deputy in his place. Never one to let an opportunity pass him by, the resourceful Talbot immediately took the chieftains prisoner until they would admit that Richard Plantagenet (Duke of York and

Edmund Mortimer's nephew) was Earl and Overlord of Ulster and its chieftains. Even after all this time, the English seemed not to have realised that the Gaelic chieftains never paid any regard to such promises that were not freely given. The "promise" was made, and the Ulster Lords were duly released, with O'Néill being let go before the others following payment of a ransom.

Some years later, the English had good cause to rue setting O'Néill at liberty as in 1430 he led his army into Louth and destroyed the castles built to defend Dundalk against the Gael. He continued his attacks southwards, advancing as far as Westmeath, destroying all the English settlements as he went and rallying many of the local Clans to his banner. The following year, he was formally inaugurated as Chieftain of the O'Néills at their ancient inauguration site at Tullyhoge following the murder of Domhnall O'Néill by the O'Kanes.

The Cancer of Feuding

What the Gaelic race desperately needed during these times was unity of action against the English. As a group, the Gaelic chieftains persisted in viewing the interests of their own areas of control as being of greater importance than the national interest and the opportunity of concerted action against the English was seldom taken. When such concerted action was taken (usually on a small scale), it often yielded results. At this time, as in previous times, if the Irish princes had only desisted from their internecine warfare and united their forces behind one common leader, they would very likely have succeeded in restoring native control on a national level.

Much more destructive than any war between the kingdoms was the constant strife inside many of them during the middle of the fifteenth century. The cancer that had earlier begun in Connacht among the O'Connors had by now spread far and wide.

It had been traditional for the Gaelic chieftains to name their successor during their lifetime in order to avoid disputes after their death and it was now more important than ever that this system continue in order to keep the clans united, but instead it widely fell into misuse or where it was still in use, it was much ignored. The result was that the Gaelic ruling families became divided as the inaugurated chieftains were often constantly in danger from the ambition of their kinsmen. In the case of Eoghan O'Néill, he initially had to defend himself again his kinsman Brian Og O'Néill. After that, his own son Henry turned traitor and succeeded in banishing him in 1455. In nearby Tirconnell, in 1452, the Chieftain Naghtan O'Donnell was murdered by two sons of his disinherited brother, while in Oriel Manus and Brian MacMahon vied for the position of Chieftain.

The Arrival of Richard Plantagenet

The Duke of York, Richard Plantagenet, was regarded by many as the lawful heir to the throne of England. Those who wished to maintain the pre-eminence of the House of Lancaster were afraid that his presence in England would be a source of danger and so thought to sideline him by sending him to Ireland. Richard was well aware of their stratagem and regarded his posting as an opportunity to gain support for himself among the Anglo-Irish and the Gael.

He arrived in 1449, accompanied by his wife cecily Nevill who was pregnant with the Duke's son George, who was to be the future Duke of Clarence. With an appointment for ten years as Lord Lieutenant, he set about his duties in a benign fashion and became well regarded by the native Chieftains due to his sense of justice for the Gael, so much so that a number of them were willing to supply him with their best sides of beef for his kitchen. On one occasion in 1450, he travelled to Killucan in Co. Westmeath at the head of an army in order to answer the call of groups of English settlers who were under threat from the son of MacGeoghegan, the local chieftain, who was burning English settlements. When the Duke encountered him, instead of attacking his army, he chose negotiation over battle and persuaded MacGeoghegan to cease his attacks.

The Irish kings and chieftains began to see in Richard Plantagenet something of the fair play that Henry II had promised the Irish centuries earlier but had failed to deliver. He succeeded in gaining the trust of some of those chieftains who had been loathe to grant it to his predecessors, such as the O'Reillys of Breifne and the MacMahons of Monaghan. Even the Clan O'Néill entered into a "entente cordiale" with the Duke and agreed to provide him with military help in the form of 1,000 men in the event of his having to fight abroad.

An Opportunity for Richard and the House of York

The reign of Henry VI saw the decline and fall of English fortunes in France. Following the French victory at the Battle of Formigny on April 15th, 1450, English power in France suffered a fatal blow. Nevertheless, some garrisons held on until 1452 and it was in one of these final battles at Castillon that Archbishop Richard Talbot was killed. The French defeats gave rise to anger among the population and rebellion had broken out in the South of England, led by an Anglo-Irishman by the name of Jack Cade. One of the rebels' aims was for Richard Duke of York to become King. Richard decided to leave Ireland in the hands of the Duke of Ormond and return to England, prepared when the time was right to claim the throne for himself. Two of the great Anglo-Irish families took sides in the ensuing War of the Roses. The Geraldines took the side of the House of York while the Butlers took the side of the House of Lancaster, with many members of both families leaving Ireland in order to fight for their respective causes in England.

Richard's Return to Ireland

While the gaze of the English was firmly on England, the Irish did not waste the opportunity and while the Anglo-Irish were occupied abroad, a substantial amount of land that had been in these families' possession was reclaimed into native hands.

By 1460, Richard of York was back in Ireland, having fled England following his defeat in battle at the "Rout of Ludlow". Being popular in Ireland (especially among the majority of the population of the Pale), he was welcomed and, despite being a wanted man in England, he resumed his duties as Lord Deputy. During his sojourn in Ireland, he summoned a parliament of the Anglo-Irish that met in Drogheda. This parliament enacted a law that freed itself "...of the burden of any special law of the realm of England..."[56] A coinage independent of that of England was also introduced. By these acts, the Anglo-Irish tried to free themselves from English laws, while retaining the link to the King.

Richard's Final Defeat

Through the efforts of the Earl of Warwick, the House of York regained the upper hand in England and Richard again left Ireland. This time, he brought with him large numbers of the Anglo-Irish nobility and gentry and several of the Ulster and Leinster Gaelic Chieftains and their men who felt that it would be in Ireland's interest if this fair-minded man were to gain what they considered to be his rightful inheritance. Most if not all of these suffered the fate of Richard himself during the Massacre of Wakefield at year's end, 1460. When the battle was over and Richard's forces defeated, Richard was beheaded on the battlefield and almost the entire remainder of his 3,000 followers who had not been killed in battle were put to the sword, including one of his sons. Richard's head was afterwards pierced with a pike and hoisted over one of the gates of York, bearing a crown made from gold paper.

An Anglo-Irish War of the Roses

Despite this stinging defeat, the House of York persisted in its bid to regain the English throne and by the end of spring 1461 they had triumphed and another of Richard of York's sons, Edward IV, became King of England. As supporters of the Yorkist cause, the Geraldines of Kildare and Desmond were high in the King's favour, while the Butlers of Ormond were stigmatised due to their support for the House of Lancaster (as The Duke of Ormond had led a sizeable force from Ireland in support of Henry VI).

In the spring of 1462, the tension between the Butlers and Geraldines resulted in open warfare. James Butler had been executed in England following the Battle of Mortimer's Cross in Herefordshire while his brother John managed to avoid capture and returned to Ireland. With an eye to the lands that the Butlers had taken from the native Irish, the son of the Earl of Desmond, Thomas Fitzgerald, decided to challenge him. In the spring of 1462, war broke out between them. In the course of the struggle, Westmeath was devastated and after recapturing the Butler's Irish holding, John Butler occupied Waterford. Once more, battle was joined between their opposing forces near Piltown in Co. Kilkenny. On the banks of the River Pill, the Geraldine crossbows took a heavy toll on Butler's men, who retreated into the river. Of those who did not drown, many were picked off by Fitzgerald's sharpshooters as they struggled in the mudflats on the farther shore. According to the Annals of the Four Masters, four hundred of Butler's men met their end here, not counting those who were "eaten by dogs and by the fowl of the air"[57].

The Geraldines Supreme

With the victory of the Yorkists seemingly complete, the Geraldines were now the premier party among the Anglo-Irish. King Edward IV seemed unwilling to undertake any measure against those Anglo-Irish who had helped him become King and the power of the Geraldines in Ireland seemed unassailable.

On the death of James Fitzgerald, his son Thomas became the 7th Earl of Desmond in 1462 and Lord Deputy in 1463. His chief ally during his tenure was the 7th Earl of Kildare, also called Thomas Fitzgerald. Despite the fact that the new Lord Deputy was popular with both Anglo-Irish (excluding the Butlers) and Gael alike, the native Irish did not reduce the pressure on the settlers in their attempts to regain lost territory, although they did not act in unison.

This state of affairs was exacerbated by a number of measures enacted by the Anglo-Irish Parliament. A 1465 act of Parliament stipulated that all Irishmen living inside the borders of the Pale had to shave and dress in the English fashion and adopt an English-sounding surname in the manner of a colour (Black, Brown, White etc.) or assume their trade as their surname (Smith, Carpenter, etc.). Other laws enacted in this period included the prohibition of English boats fishing in waters controlled by the native Irish so that no dues would be paid to them. The most despised law of all was one introduced as a measure to reduce plunderers from Co. Offaly who were in the habit of frequenting the Pale. The law allowed the decapitation of any thief either caught in the act or "...coming or going..." unless he had an Englishman with him[58]. A reward was to be paid by the local Mayor for all heads submitted to him. This measure gave *carte blanche* to any settler so inclined to kill any Irishman; and on producing the head, saying it was that of an Irish thief, a reward would be paid to him.

The Execution of Thomas Fitzgerald, Earl of Desmond

In 1466, the new Lord Deputy, Thomas Fitzgerald, suffered a major defeat in Offaly at the hands of his brother-in-law, the Gaelic Chieftain of Offaly Con O'Connor Ealy.

The defeat occurred after Fitzgerald travelled to Offaly with an army of the English of Leinster. It is possible that the Earl of Desmond was not seeking battle with O'Connor Ealy but was rather seeking out those thieves who were a scourge to the residents of the Pale. In any event, the two sides met in battle, with the English being roundly defeated. Desmond was captured along with his advisors and held prisoner at Carberry Castle in Kildare until a rescue was managed by an army unit dispatched from the Pale for that purpose.

However, it was not at the hands of the native Irish that Thomas Fitzgerald met his end as he was too much respected by them, but rather at the hands of the devious Earl of Worcester, John Tiptoft, nicknamed "The Butcher" because of his reputation for extreme cruelty when dealing with Lancastrians who fell into his hands during the Wars of the Roses. Tiptoft came to Ireland on a special mission – to engineer the downfall of Thomas Fitzgerald. The instigator of the plot against Fitzgerald was apparently the Queen, the commoner Elizabeth Woodville. The Earl of Desmond had been openly critical of the King's marriage to her, and it seems that it was on her secret instruction that Tiptoft came to Ireland seeking not only Fitzgerald's destruction but also his death. The King was persuaded that Fitzgeralds' ambition was such that he would soon proclaim himself King of Ireland.[i] In 1467, Tiptoft was appointed in Desmond's place as Lord Deputy and

---

[i] In his book "Geraldines", (a history of the Geraldine dynasty) Thomas Moore writes "...by no other crimes than those of being too Irish and too popular did (Fitzgerald, Earl of) Desmond draw upon himself persecution."

early the following year Desmond was arrested on a number of trumped up charges, including allying himself with the Irish and fostering his son with the Irish contrary to the "Statute of Kilkenny". Two of his sons were also arrested, tortured and executed, with Desmond himself being beheaded at Drogheda in February 1468. It seemed that his ally, Thomas Fitzgerald, Earl of Kildare might also go the same way, but he successfully managed to obtain a pardon from the king.

Ireland after Thomas Fitzgerald's Death

Anglo-Irish and Gael alike were outraged by the capture and execution of Thomas Fitzgerald since he had many friends among both. The Annals of Ulster recorded his passing with the words "Ireland never had a foreign youth that was better than he."[59] When news of the manner of Desmond's death reached England, King Edward's brother, the future Richard III, said of it that it had contravened "all manhood, reason and good conscience."[60] The Geraldines of Desmond rose up in rebellion and launched a number of attacks into the area of the Pale before the tumult subsided. After this, the Geraldines of Desmond went pretty much completely over to the Irish side, until their destruction over 100 years later during the reign of Elizabeth I.

His mission complete, Tiptoft was quickly recalled to England, where he later suffered the same fate that he had meted out to Desmond. When Henry VI of Lancaster made his return to the throne of England in 1470, the Yorkist Tiptoft had the misfortune to fall into the hands of the Lancastrians and was beheaded in 1470, a fitting end to the life of a man whose nickname was "The Butcher".

The return of the House of Lancaster to the throne of England was short lived. When the Yorkist Edward IV resumed the throne after the brief return of Henry VI, the Geraldine House of Kildare had a firm hold on power in Ireland. A succession of Lord Deputies was unable to alter this and apart from a short break during the reign of Henry VII, the House of Kildare would now reign supreme until its annihilation during the reign of Henry VIII.

During the years that remained to the Plantagenet dynasty until the crown of the slain Richard III was placed on the head of Henry Tudor (King Henry VII) at Bosworth Field in 1485, English military power in the Pale was nominal. In order to bolster the defences of the Pale, Sir Roland Fitzeustace formed a type of Yeomanry among the English residents called "The Brothers of St. George"[61] but even with this, the military strength of England's seat of power in Ireland was reckoned to be in the hundreds.

1500 AD - The Height of the Gaelic Resurgency

Chapter 10

The Rise and Fall of the House of Kildare

The Tudors come to Power

In 1471 King Edward VI resumed his reign and ruled undisturbed until his death in 1483 at the age of 41. He left behind him two young sons, Edward and Richard, both of whom disappeared into the Tower of London, never to be seen again, after they fell victim to the malignant designs of their uncle Richard. Richard now became King Richard III and the animosity felt by many over the manner in which he had usurped the throne became the catalyst for one Henry Tudor, who had no reasonable claim whatsoever to the throne of England,[i] challenging him in the name of the House of Lancaster, which was now without any leader of royal blood. Towards the end of August 1485, Henry's challenge succeeded when his mainly Welsh and French army, helped by a force

---

[i] Henry was the son of Edmund Tudor. Edmund Tudor was the illegitimate son of the widow of Henry V, Katharine of France, who had as a paramour one of her servants, Eoghan Tudor or Tyddr, a Welshman. Edmund Tudor married Margaret Beaufort who was the last heiress of the illegitimate children of John of Gaunt. The Beauforts were one of the legitimised bastard branches of the Plantagenets.

loyal to his stepfather, Lord Stanley,[i] defeated Richard at Bosworth and the 331-year rule of the Plantagenets as Kings of England came to an end.

One of the problems Henry VII faced on becoming King was that the English governance of Ireland was effectively in the hands of the Geraldines of Kildare who were avowed supporters of the Yorkist cause. After becoming king, Henry VII tried to get the Irish Lord Deputy, Garrett Mór Fitzgerald, to come to London to make a report on the situation in Ireland but Fitzgerald unsurprisingly did not trust the King's motives and sent his apologies, saying that his presence in Ireland was indispensable.[62]

The Pretenders

Lambert Simnel

George, Duke of Clarence, who had been born in Dublin in 1449 shortly after the arrival of his father, Richard of York, as Lord Deputy, died in 1478 leaving behind a son, Edward Earl of Warwick, who was now the legitimate heir to the throne of England. He was captured by Henry VII and held under close arrest preparatory to his murder.[ii]

In 1486, a young boy of about eleven years of age arrived in Dublin in the charge of his priest tutor, claiming to be the same Edward, Earl of Warwick. Although the boy had the attributes

---

[i] In early 1495 Henry had his stepfather executed during his attempts to scatter the supporters of the pretender to the throne, Perkin Warbeck.

[ii] In 1498 Henry planted a secret agent in the tower of London to worm his way into the confidence of Warwick (and also Perkin Warbeck whom we shall shortly encounter). The agent encouraged them into escape and rebellion. On the strength of the agent's testimony, both men were hung, drawn and quartered. According to the eminent English historian Hilaire Belloc this was a favourite method of obtaining information of all Tudor monarchs with the exception of Queen Mary.

and manners of a young prince, he was in fact one Lambert Simnel, the son of an Oxford tradesman. This imposter was welcomed to Dublin by Garrett Mór Fitzgerald and most of the Anglo-Irish of the Pale who appeared to fall for the fraud hook, line and sinker, the notable exception being the Anglo-Irish of Waterford who would have nothing whatsoever to do with him.

The following year, a German army of 2,000 men sent by the sister of Edward IV, Margaret Duchess of Burgundy (the apparent mastermind of the fraud), and under the command of one Martin Schwartz arrived in Dublin to assist Simnel and his Anglo-Irish followers in his bid to conquer England. Before departing for England, Simnel was crowned King Edward VI by the Bishop of Meath in Christ Church Cathedral before many of the great and the good of the Anglo-Irish establishment.

The commanders of Simnel's army hoped that, on landing on the Lancashire coast, the supporters of the House of York would flock to them and swell their ranks. However, this did not happen and their army numbering around 8,000 was easily defeated at Stoke in Nottinghamshire. Among those Anglo-Irish killed, were Lords Maurice and Thomas Fitzgerald. Simnel was captured and treated leniently, being sent to work in the King's kitchen as a turnspit and later as a falconer.

Lord Deputy Fitzgerald and the Anglo-Irish of the Pale now sent messages to the King begging for forgiveness. Henry VI, realising that he would drive them into rebellion if he did not pardon them, decided on discretion and sent Sir Richard Edgecombe to Dublin to exact oaths of allegiance from all concerned. To reward the Anglo-Irish of Waterford, the King granted them permission to take for their own whatever ships and merchandise they desired for their own use from his disloyal citizens of the Pale. Even today Henry VI's commendation of loyalty still remains in the city's coat of arms which bears the inscription: "Urbs Intacta Manet Waterfordia" or "Waterford Remains the Untarnished City".

Kildare was once again summoned to England, and this time he went, attending a King's banquet in Greenwich. For the banquet, King Henry VII summoned his new turnspit, Lambert Simnel, from the kitchen to act as waiter for Kildare and his companions.

In spite of the royal pardons and the oaths of allegiance taken, the King still had his suspicions about Kildare and in the early part of 1492 deprived him of his post as Lord Deputy, appointing in his place the Archbishop of Dublin, Walter Fitzsimons.

During the whole Simnel debacle, the Butlers of Ormond, being followers of the House of Lancaster, had stayed loyal to King Henry VII and Henry now raised Sir James Ormond to the position of Lord Treasurer. Kildare was incensed at his demotion and, in order to show his displeasure, he masterminded disturbances within the boundaries of the Pale and also withdrew his men from their duty of protecting the English who lived in Meath, an action that the Irish were quick to capitalise on, closing in on the settlers and destroying their properties.

Perkin Warbeck

Tidings of these disturbances in the Pale reached the King's ears around the same time that news came to him that many of the Anglo-Irish of Cork, led by the Mayor John Walter, had given their allegiance to a young man by the name of Perkin Warbeck, who was claiming to be Richard of York, one of the two young princes imprisoned by Richard III many years before. Incredible as it may seem that the Anglo-Irish were fooled twice by similar frauds, but in this case there is ample room for excuse as Warbeck had previously been entertained in the royal court of France as the legitimate heir to the throne of England and had been recognised by the Duchess of Burgundy as her nephew. Henry VII was now convinced that his suspicions of Kildare were justified and that many of his Anglo-Irish subjects were only too willing to rebel against him for any reason. He decided to send to Ireland a new broom in the form of one of his ablest advisors, Sir Edward Poynings, as Lord Deputy with a mission to clean house.

Poynings arrived in October 1494, bringing with him a host of English-born bureaucrats (who were to replace the Anglo-Irish officials) and also 1,000 men at arms (equipped with muskets and artillery) as, unlike the adherents of Simnel, the supporters of Warbeck were to be shown no mercy. On hearing of the arrival of Poynings, the more prominent of Warbeck's adherents fled to east Ulster and took refuge with two Gaelic Chieftains, O'Hanlon and Magennis. Poynings followed them north, bringing the reluctant Earl of Kildare in tow, but his expedition ended up chasing two different chieftains, John O'Reilly and Hugh Og MacMahon, who had lately defeated a force of English, killing sixty and taking many prisoners. On hearing of the large English force approaching, O'Reilly and Mac Mahon retreated deep into their territories, while Poynings vented his anger by pillaging. When Poynings resumed his search for the supporters of Warbeck, news reached him to the effect that he was heading into a trap to be sprung by O'Hanlon and Magennis, who were, according to the information received by Poynings, in league with Kildare. Furthermore, there was definite word that Kildare's brother James had launched a rebellion and captured Carlow Castle. Whether the news about Kildare being in league with the Gaelic Chieftains were true or not, Poynings could not be sure, but news of this rebellion in Carlow was reason enough for him to give up the chase for Warbeck's men. On reaching Carlow, it took a siege of ten days before the castle surrendered. Once the country was restored to relative calm, Poynings proceeded to the main business of his tenure.

Poynings Law – Anglo-Irish Power Annulled

As Lord Deputy, Poynings convened a parliament that took place in Drogheda in November 1494. Its chief aims were the undoing of the independence of the Anglo-Irish and the restatement of the Statue of Kilkenny which had more or less fallen into abeyance.

In order to effectively tie the hands of the Anglo-Irish, Poynings introduced a piece of legislation that became known as "Poynings Law". By this law, the parliament of the Anglo-Irish could not sit unless a list of all the acts that were to come before that parliament were submitted to the King of England and his counsellors and approved by them. Furthermore, all acts passed in England in the preceding years pertaining to the "public good" were to be retrospectively made law in Ireland and acts of the Anglo-Irish Parliament of 1460 were nullified. As well as reining in the Anglo-Irish politically, the act sought to rein them in militarily, with numerous restrictions being imposed, including the abolition of the Guild of St. George.

At the time, Poynings Law had no effect on the Gaelic rulers as, even if they had wanted to, they were forbidden from sitting in the Dublin parliament. However, for the Anglo-Irish, their ability to control their own destiny was completely nullified. When enacted, the law really only had any impact on the Pale, but in time its effects would be felt nationwide by Anglo-Irish and Gael alike – and for centuries to come.

Regarding the revival of the Statute of Kilkenny, there was one notable exception. Previously, the Anglo-Irish were forbidden to use the Gaelic tongue but now, as the use of it among them was almost universal, this measure had to be dispensed with. However, a new measure was introduced forbidding the use of Gaelic war cries by the Anglo-Irish after the fashion of the

Gaelic Clans. As the aim of the Statute was to engender division between Anglo-Irish and Gael, the adoption of the Gaelic style war cry by the settlers was considered to be over-identification with them.[i]

Poynings was still left with the problem of what to do about Fitzgerald, Earl of Kildare. Having passed such unpalatable laws, who knew what might happen if he left Kildare at large? Deciding to use the information received about the supposed collusion between Kildare and the northern chieftains, he had him and other members of his family arrested on suspicion of treason and personally brought Kildare to London where he was detained in the Tower. Even before his trial, the consequences of his arrest and imprisonment were significant for him as his wife Alison Fitzeustace died shortly following his incarceration, apparently of a broken heart.[63]

Garrett Mór Fitzgerald – "All but King of Ireland"
"The Fittest Man to Govern all Ireland"

Eventually, Fitzgerald was lucky enough to get to plead his case before King Henry VII. Before being cross-examined regarding his alleged treason, other charges were put to him by the prosecution, including that he had torched the church in Cashel. Kildare's disarming reply that he would not have done so had he been told that the Archbishop were not inside the church won favour with the King, sending him into fits of laughter. Kildare was also able to produce the Gaelic Chieftain O'Hanlon of Armagh in his defence, who confirmed that neither he nor Kildare were party to any type of plot against

---

[i] * The Gaelic war cry consisted of the name or slogan of the family or place of residence followed by the shout of defiance "abú" or "to victory". For example, the O'Néill war cry was "lámh-dearg abú!" or "red hand to victory" while the Anglo-Irish Fitzgeralds of Desmond had adopted the war cry "Cromadh-abú!" after their castle at Croom in Limerick.

Poynings. Impressed by Kildare, the King decided to give him more time to prepare for the remainder of the case against him and told him that he could choose his own counsel. Kildare disarmingly replied: "I doubt if I will be allowed to choose the good fellow I wish to select – I can see no better man in England than your Highness and I will choose no other."[64] On hearing this riposte, the King was completely won over to his side.

Finding that the issue of treason seemed to be a lost cause, the prosecution proceeded by listing Kildare's errant ways and his disrespect for authority, finishing with the words: "Not all Ireland could govern this man"[65], at which the King interjected: "Then he is the fittest man to govern all Ireland".[66]

The outcome of the proceedings was the appointment of Kildare as Lord Deputy and the restoration of all his titles and possessions. Furthermore, as an expression of the strengthening of ties between Kildare and the Royal House, the King arranged a marriage for him with his cousin, Elizabeth St. John, but in spite of this, Kildare always remained a fervent if secretive supporter of the Yorkist cause. The favourable impression that Henry VII had of Fitzgerald endured; until his death in 1513, Garrett Mór Fitzgerald was in effect Ireland's ruler since in the absence of direct interference from London his word was law, and he was free to use the resources of the Crown that were available to him as he saw fit. In his dealings, he pursued the aims of the Crown by trying to reconquer lands from the Irish that the latter had succeeded in recapturing. In general, he favoured neither Anglo-Irish nor Gael but sought through his methods to bring as many as possible from both parties along with him and therefore secured the personal loyalty of many Gaelic Chieftains with the O'Donnells of Tirconnnell being chief among his Gaelic allies. Although he became involved in many disputes involving the Gaelic chieftains, it was generally not with the intention of usurping territory but rather with one of restoring peace. He had many family ties among the Gaelic Chieftains. His sister Eleanora was married to Conn O'Néill, Chieftain of Tyrone, while one of his daughters was married to Domhnall MacCarthy Reagh and another to Mulrony O'Carroll, while his son Henry was fostered with Hugh Roe O'Donnell.

The Battle of Knocktow (Knockdoe)

The largest battle that occurred during Kildare's tenure as Lord Lieutenant took place in 1504. For many years, the Galway Chieftain Melaglin O'Kelly had been at war with Ulick (MacWilliam) Burke of Clanrickard and O'Kelly's efforts against him were on the point of being extinguished after Burke demolished his castles at Garbally, Monivea and Castleblakney. O'Kelly sent a plea for assistance to Kildare, which greatly pleased Fitzgerald on several accounts, chief of these being that Ulick Burke of Clanrickard was married to one of his daughters, and word had reached him that she had been mistreated by him. Furthermore, for some time Burke's power in Connacht had been growing unchecked and he had taken the city of Galway for himself. Kildare felt that it was high time this lord of Anglo Irish stock had his power checked, and used O'Kelly's plea as his excuse, being more concerned with settling his own scores than assisting a minor Gaelic chieftain. Crossing the Shannon with his own large force and that of the Anglo-Irish barons, Kildare was joined by many Gaelic chieftains who answered his call that they should help one of their own. From the midlands and Ulster, the Gaelic Chieftains came with their armies including Hugh Roe O'Donnell, O'Conor Roe, MacDermot, Magennis, MacMahon, O'Reilly, the O'Farrells of Longford (who were led into battle by the Bishop of Ardagh who was their chieftain), O'Connor Ealy and, of course, O'Kelly. Arrayed against them were some southern and midlands chieftains who had answered the call of Burke from Clanrickard, including O'Brien, MacNamara, O'Kennedy and O'Carroll. As well as his own force, Burke had also almost two thousand Gallowglass mercenaries in his army.

On August 19th 1504, about two miles from the Burke stronghold of Claregalway, the armies met on the rocky high ground of Knocktow[i] in what proved to be the last great medieval-style battle to take place on Irish soil. Armed with swords, bows, axes and spears, ten thousand men faced each other, with the advantage to the forces of Kildare. Although outnumbered, Clanrickard's army held its own for some considerable time before weight of number began to tell and the battle eventually turned into a rout for him. Out of Burke's almost two thousand gallowglasses, only two hundred remained alive, with losses on both sides running into many thousands. Even though many chieftains and their warriors had lined up behind Kildare to help him achieve his personal victory over Burke and the effective supremacy of the Pale in the West of Ireland, their contribution was not appreciated. With the battle won, the English mask was dropped. In the Anglo-Irish Annals, "The Book of Howth", Viscount Gormanstown is recorded as saying to Kildare after the battle: "We have slaughtered our enemies but to complete the good deed we must do the like with the Irish of our own party."[67] This remark clearly illustrates what a disaster the Battle of Knocktow was for the Gael.

In England, the battle was represented as a struggle between the forces of English government and Irish rebels and Kildare was made a Knight of the Garter in recognition of his exertions in the cause of the Crown in Ireland. Despite his being feted as a hero in London, he was involved with the Chieftain of

---

[i] Knocktow –from the Gaelic "Cnoc-tuagh" or "Hill of Axes"

Tirconnell, Hugh Óg O'Donnell,[i] in a bid to renew the fortunes of the Yorkist cause, as two nephews of Edward IV still remained alive.

"A Report on the State of Ireland"

In 1515, an English official in Dublin penned his opinions regarding the country in "A Report on the state of Ireland" which was dispatched to London. The report illustrates the level of "hibernisation" among the English.

He wrote in part: "There be sixty regions in Ireland, inhabited by the King's Irish enemies. Some regions there be as big as a shire, some more, some less, where reigneth more than sixty Chief Captains, whereof some calleth themselves kings, some king's peers, some princes, some dukes, that liveth only by the sword, and obeyeth no other temporal person save to him who is strong. And every one of the said Captains maketh war and peace for himself and holdeth by the sword, and hath imperial jurisdiction, and obeyeth no other person, English or Irish, except only such persons as may subdue him by the sword. Also in every one of the said regions there be divers petty captains, and every one of them maketh war and peace for himself without license of the Chief Captain. And there be more than thirty [families] of the English noble folk that follow the same Irish order and keepeth the same rule"[68]

---

[i] Hugh Og O'Donnell was son of Hugh Roe O'Donnell who died in 1505 aged 78. He had ruled Tirconnell for 44 years.

The Accession of Henry VIII
"He spared no man in his anger and no woman in his lust" – Peter Heylyn

When the usurper King Henry VII died in April 1509, he was succeeded by his second son Henry, his first son Arthur having predeceased him. The first act of the new King Henry VIII was to marry his brother's widow, the young Spanish Princess, Catherine of Aragon. With regard to Ireland, the young King was content to allow Kildare to continue in the position of Lord Deputy.

The Death of Garrett Mór Fitzgerald
Kildare continued with mixed fortunes in his bid to reconquer territory. In 1510, after invading Thomond, he attempted to retake Limerick but, on this occasion, the previously vanquished Burke of Clanrickard came to the assistance of O'Brien of Thomond and succeeded in routing the Earl's army, after which he was forced to retreat. In 1513, while laying siege to the castle of the Gaelic chieftain Ely O'Carroll, Kildare was taken ill from the effects of a musket wound received earlier at the hands of the O'Mores of Leix (Laois). After returning to Athy, he died shortly afterwards and was interred in Christ Church, Dublin.

Lord Deputy Garrett Óg Fitzgerald
Garrett Mór was replaced as Lord Deputy and Earl of Kildare by his son Garrett Óg (Gerald the Younger) who embarked on his appointed task with the sort of zeal that would have rivalled the most zealous of his predecessors. In short order, he defeated the O'Mores of Leix before turning his attention to the O'Reillys of Breifne. There, his forces killed in battle the Chieftain of the Clan along with fourteen Chieftains of the Clans allied to the O'Reillys. He also succeeded where his

father had failed, in conquering the castle and headquarters of the Clan Ely O'Carroll in Offaly.

In 1517, following up on a request of the Clan O'Néill, he took his army deep into Ulster and assisted them in capturing their fortress at Dungannon, which was the headquarters of a rebellious faction within the Clan led by Niall Óg O'Néill.

The Undermining of Garrett Óg Fitzgerald

The Butlers of Ormond, sworn enemies of Kildare, had kept their heads down after King Henry VII had re-appointed Garrett Mór as Lord Deputy at the end of his trial. However, in 1515, Thomas of Ormond died, and his estate passed in part to his grandson Sir Thomas Boleyn.[i] Sir Piers Butler claimed the Earldom of Ormond and he immediately re-hoisted the flag of opposition to the House of Kildare. Tales of mischief against Kildare were once again finding their way across to London and being bandied about in the Royal Court. At this time, Cardinal Wolsey became Chancellor of England, and, in the King's presence, repeatedly referred to Kildare as "The King of Kildare".[69] As a result of reports sent from Ireland by Butler, which were then passed into circulation by the Boleyns, a picture was gradually painted before the King's eyes of an over-powerful Irish Lord (Garrett Óg) reigning over semi-

---

[i] When Thomas Butler, (seventh Earl of Ormond) died in 1515 without a male heir, his vast English estates were split between his daughters Margaret and Anne. Anne was married to Sir William Bullen or Boleyn and Sir Thomas Boleyn was their son. By Sir Thomas Boleyn's marriage to Lady Elizabeth Howard, he was the father of Anne Boleyn, with whom King Henry later became obsessed, making the interests of the Butlers more important in the King's Irish considerations.

(In his book "The Rise and Growth of the Anglican Schism" the Rev Dr. Nicholas Sanders, who was Papal Nuncio to Ireland during part of the reign of Queen Elizabeth I, forcibly argues with much evidence that Lady Elizabeth Howard was at an earlier time also mistress to Henry VIII and that King Henry himself fathered Anne Boleyn.)

Gaelicised barons who cared little for the power of the Crown, but rather protected their own patch using the resources of the Crown for their own ends. Butler was excluded from this narrative as Kildare was also accused of trying to "extinguish the fame and honour of any other nobleman within that land"[70].

Garrett Óg Fitzgerald

King Henry VIII was fallow ground for the seed that those around him were planting and in 1519 Garrett Óg Fitzgerald was summoned to the King's Court to answer various charges, including that he had used the revenues of the Crown for his own purposes and exchanged treacherous correspondence with the King's Irish enemies.[i] At the encouragement of Cardinal Wolsey, the King appointed the Earl of Surrey and 2nd Duke of Norfolk, Thomas Howard (father of Elizabeth Howard), as King's Lieutenant and, reinforced with a large army, he left for Ireland.

Thomas Howard replaces Fitzgerald as Lord Deputy
After his arrival in Ireland, Thomas Howard led his army against the indefatigable O'More of Leix and ravaged his territory by burning property and ripening crops as he advanced. In the course of this escapade, the Duke almost fell

---

[i] Kildare was accused of writing to O'Carroll Ely, encouraging him to hold his fire until an English Viceroy should be sent over and then to "do your best to make war on the English".

into Irish hands. Shortly after his campaign against O'More, Surrey received word that Conn O'Néill of Tyrone was planning to invade the Pale territory of Meath, and so led his army northwards to forestall this threat. On hearing of the advance of this large, heavily-armed force, O'Néill retreated deep into his territory where the English could not follow without suffering devastating casualties.

Unsurprisingly, Howard quickly tired of Irish warfare. Even though he led a modern army equipped with the latest in musket and cannon, he was unused to the tactics adopted by the Irish in the heavily-wooded and sometimes boggy terrain. Even if the Irish appeared to retreat from his front, they quickly reappeared in flanking attacks or even from the rear. Surrey reported to the King that only by a huge conquest on a massive scale could he hope to bring Ireland into complete subjection. He reckoned the opposing Irish to be well in excess of 20,000 and advised the King that they would most likely band together if an English army of conquest landed with the mission of complete and total conquest. According to Howard, if Henry made any attempt at conquest he would face three major difficulties:

"First, to furnish the army, that your Grace will have here, with money until the conquest be perfected.

Secondly, how to furnish the said number with victuals, and carragie for the said victuals, ordnance, artillery, and all other stuff that must be occupied in building of strong fortresses.

Thirdly, how to find inhabitants in sufficient number, that will continue true subjects to your Grace and your noble successors."[71]

While Surrey was in the country, James, Earl of Desmond, attempted to invade the territory of the MacCarthys of Desmond and suffered a crushing defeat at Mourne Abbey between Mallow and Cork, losing 2,000 men. While serving to illustrate the points made to the King in his report to London, the defeat inflicted on Desmond pleased Surrey greatly and, in a letter to Cardinal Wolsey, he described the Gaelic Chieftains Cormac Óg MacCarthy and MacCarthy Reagh as "two wise men"[72]. He also encouraged the Crown to allow safe passage to all Gallowglass mercenaries on their way to fight for O'Donnell of Tirconnell in his interminable struggle against O'Néill of Tyrone as "it would be dangerous to have them both agreed and joined together...The longer they continue in war the better it should be for Your Grace's poor subjects here."[73]

Surrender and Regrant

Sir Thomas Howard's reports and letters greatly influenced Henry's deliberations on Ireland. He rejected the idea of a new conquest and instead came up with a policy that was to greatly serve in the corruption and downfall of the Gaelic chieftains and ultimately the Gaelic way of life. Called "Surrender and Regrant", it meant that all Gaelic Chieftains should be offered peace, persuaded to surrender their land to the King, and then receive it back as a land grant of His Majesty along with title, without losing any portion of it. In his letter to Surrey, the King instructed: "The Irish Lords may be told that though we are above the laws we will take nothing that belongs to them."[74] Surrey was also empowered to bestow a knighthood on all Irish chieftains whom he deemed suitable, and a collar of gold was sent from England to be bestowed on O'Néill of Tyrone. However, when Kildare returned as Lord Deputy, the policy was not immediately pursued.

The Return of Kildare as Lord Deputy

Meanwhile in London, Kildare succeeded, as had his father before him, in obtaining pardon from the King. However, Garrett Óg did not gain Henry's unequivocal confidence as had his father when he appeared before Henry VII. To his advantage, two factors worked in his favour when he appeared before King Henry. The evidence against him was inconclusive and, by his recent second marriage to the influential Lady Elizabeth Grey, who had powerful friends, the scales were firmly tipped in Kildare's favour, and he was set at liberty. He returned to Ireland to find that Norfolk had gone back to England due to ill health and that the post of Lord Deputy was occupied by his enemy, Sir Piers Butler[i] of Ormond. With Kildare absent, Ormond had wasted no time after his appointment in laying waste to Kildare's property, capturing and destroying several of his castles. Kildare was not going to accept this affront without response and, on his return, left Ormond in no doubt of his anger and outrage. In spite of the fact that Ormond had recently married Kildare's sister, the feud between the families was now as bad as ever. Ormond for his part defended himself by immediately sending new allegations against Kildare to the King. A Royal enquiry was launched into affairs between Kildare and Ormond, with the result that Kildare was once again fully reinstated as Lord Deputy. At his inauguration, the sword of state was carried into St. Thomas's Abbey by Kildare's brother in law, Conn O'Néill of Tyrone, whom he accompanied northwards after the celebration in order to attempt to make peace in the unending feud between the O'Néills and O'Donnells.

On resuming his old post, his first task was to apprehend his kinsman James Fitzgerald, Earl of Desmond, who was accused of treason[ii] and had also failed to answer a summons to

---

[i] Piers Butler was referred to by the Irish as "Pierce Roe" or "Red Pierce"

[ii] Emperor Charles V with the aim of bringing about the overthrow of King Henry VIII and the subsequent return to the throne of the House of York, whose claimant The Earl of Desmond along with O'Brien of Desmond had entered secret negotiations with King Francis I of France and Richard de la Pole was standing by in France. De la Pole died in 1525 while fighting alongside the King of France at the Battle of Pavia.

London. Kildare led an army into Munster in order to apprehend him, but Desmond succeeded in evading capture and Kildare quickly returned northwards without him, having avoided completing a task which he found distasteful.

The Fall from Grace of Garrett Óg Fitzgerald

Unlike his father, Garrett Óg was not left in peace. He was being constantly watched by his enemies, and tales of his real or pretended misdemeanours were making their way in an unending stream to the court of King Henry VIII. By 1526, sufficient charges against the Earl had been collected by Cardinal Wolsey in order to warrant a summons to London. Along with his failure to capture his fellow Geraldine, James of Desmond, he was also charged with colluding with the Irish Lords in a plot to relieve Ormond[i] of his territory and with being responsible for the hanging of certain loyal subjects because they were friends of Ormond. By getting his case heard before the Privy Council, Kildare skilfully defended himself and, despite being returned to the Tower of London after his trial, he was eventually set at liberty in 1530. A curious situation now prevailed. Kildare was removed from office and the King's illegitimate son Henry Fitzroy was given the dignity of the title of His Majesty's Irish Lord Deputy while Sir William Skeffington was empowered with the duties of the office and dispatched to Ireland as Fitzroy's deputy, with Kildare as his assistant. Initially, Kildare, realising the

---

[i] As the obsession of Henry VIII for Anne Boleyn increased so did the titles of her father Sir Thomas Boleyn. In 1529, King Henry VIII pressured Sir Piers Butler to renounce his claim to the title "Earl of Ormond". When Butler acquiesced, King Henry bestowed the title "Earl of Ormond" on Boleyn. Five days later, Butler was rewarded by being made "Earl of Ossory". After the Boleyn family fell from favour following the execution of Anne Boleyn, Piers Butler was made Earl of Ormond in January 1538 and, until Thomas Boleyn's death in March 1539, there were two Earls of Ormond.

weakened position in which he found himself, did not demur but when Skeffington decided to march northwards in 1531 to invade the territory of the O'Néill and make war on Kildare's friend and cousin Con O'Néill, it was about as much as Kildare could bear. Skeffington was all the while sending reports back to London regarding Kildare, so much so that the latter decided to go to England himself to see if he could not improve his situation. The ploy worked. Through skilful oration and the influence of his friends, the power of Lord Deputy was returned to Kildare for one last time.

Kildare cannot but have known only too well the tenuous hold he had on power. Trusting to his own abilities and the influence of his wife, he did not alter course. The fact that Cardinal Wolsey was dead also emboldened him, but he did not realise that he now faced a far deadlier foe in Thomas Cromwell, former secretary to the Cardinal and Henry's new Chief Minister. Whether or not he considered a complete rupture with England is a matter of conjecture, but the steps Kildare now took were not those of a man seeking to curry favour with his King. After replacing Archbishop Allen of Dublin with his friend Archbishop Cromer of Armagh, he made an alliance with two Gaelic Chieftains, O'Connor of Offaly and O'Carroll of Ossory, both of whom married Kildare's daughters. Aided by them, he attacked the territory of the Butlers while his brother James, assisted by Con O'Néill, attacked and burned English settlements in Louth. He also used his powers as Lord Deputy to reinforce his castles with military wares from Dublin. In 1532, his health was irreversibly damaged when he received a musket ball in his side at the siege of Birr Castle (the ball was removed from the opposite side some months later). When in the autumn of 1533, John Allen (secretary to Archbishop Allen and to the Council of State) was dispatched to England to report on Ireland, he also carried a secret dispatch that contained a list of criminal charges against Kildare. Shortly afterwards, Kildare was summoned to London once again but made excuses for not being able to depart Ireland. In November, he was again summoned, and this time sent his wife in the hope that her influence would excuse his attendance. Finally, in February 1534, on the receipt of more insistent orders, it was time for a decision. With a heavy heart, he embarked from Drogheda in the same month. Before his departure, the Council of State was summoned to Drogheda and, in their presence, Kildare appointed his son Thomas (who was not yet twenty-one) as his Deputy, entreating him most earnestly that he was, in his father's absence, to heed the advice of the Council. When Kildare arrived in London, he was immediately arrested and sent to the Tower. All was not lost – he had been here before and hoped that, as in the past, he would return to Ireland.

The Rebellion of "Silken" Thomas Fitzgerald
The Plot

Kildare's son, Thomas Lord Offaly, known to the native Irish as "Silken Thomas" (due to his fondness for fine clothing and the fabulous dress of his entourage) was ill-prepared for the trials of state. Lacking experience and with a tendency to rash action, he quickly became ensnared in the trap that was now set for him by his father's enemies, to the ruin of the House of Kildare.

A plot was hatched between the Butlers and certain pro-English members of the Council of State, the desired outcome being that Thomas would commit a treasonable act. Mingled with this plot was the angst already felt by the Fitzgeralds with regard to the rising schism of Henry with the Church of which the Geraldines wanted no part and which the Butlers were only too ready to support.

Only a few months later, around the beginning of June 1534, the plot was put into effect. False documents were circulated that reported the beheading of Kildare in the Tower of London. These documents were further backed up by letters to the effect that the same fate was planned for other prominent members of the House of Kildare.

The Revolt
Without waiting for definite confirmation from England and acting on advice from one of his father's counsellors, James Delahide, Thomas mustered a large force of men mounted on horses on June 11th and made for St. Mary's Abbey in Dublin where a meeting of the Council of State was due to be held. On entering the chamber with his men, he lay down the trappings of his office and renounced his allegiance to King Henry VIII. With tears in his eyes, his father's friend, the Chancellor Archbishop Cromer, begged him to reconsider. At that moment, Thomas's bard, O'Keenan, who had entered the chamber with him, was heard reciting in Gaelic a verse in praise of Thomas's actions and calling on him to avenge his father's death[75]. Thomas now turned and left the chamber.

"Silken" Thomas Fitzgerald

It is not apparent if Thomas had a premeditated plan of action. Initially, he despoiled the lands of his enemies. As word spread of his uprising, Gaelic Clans from the hinterland of the Pale came to his aid and they entered Dublin after promising that the citizens would not be harmed. After Dublin Castle was taken under siege, the former Chancellor, Archbishop Allen (who had been an intimate of Cardinal Wolsey and, like him, no friend of the Fitzgeralds), attempted to escape but was captured and killed after his ship ran aground at Clontarf. This incident cast a dark shadow on the enterprise as now a decree of excommunication was issued against Lord Offaly and all those associated with Allen's murder. The news of the rebellion, followed later by the decree of excommunication against Silken Thomas, was brought to his father in the Tower of London. This, along with the conditions there, did not help his already impaired health. He lingered until September 1534 when he died and was buried in the Tower Chapel of St. Peter ad Vincula (St Peter in Chains).

More Gaelic Chieftains now flocked to young Lord Offaly's standard, including O'Brien of Thomond and O'Néill of Tyrone, but many more stood aloof and O'Brien's help was tempered by the rebellion of his son Donough who was being aided by Butler of Ossory whose daughter he had married. However, the rebels were assisted by the inactivity of Sir William Skeffington who was suffering from ill health. Skeffington had returned to Ireland after being reappointed as King's Lieutenant and his inability to quickly come to terms with the revolt emboldened Offaly, who now sought help from abroad. He sent James Delahide to Emperor Charles V and envoys to Rome stating that, as the heretical King Henry was now in open schism with the Church, his lordship of Ireland, granted by the Pope centuries before, was now forfeit. This action (along with the later action of King Henry who would in 1541 abolish his title "Lord of Ireland "and replace it with "King of Ireland") was because of the widely held belief that Ireland was papal territory whose governance had been granted to King Henry II of England and his successors by Pope Adrian IV.

"The Pardon of Maynooth"
By the end of Winter months in early 1536, Thomas's rebellion was in trouble. His force that had occupied Dublin was attacked by many of its citizens and most of those who had not been captured were scattered piecemeal around the city. In March of 1535, Thomas was endeavouring to arouse resistance in the midlands when Skeffington attacked the main Fitzgerald stronghold at Maynooth. As Maynooth Castle was considered impregnable, the garrison consisted of only 100 men under the command of Christopher Paris. However, Skeffington had a new weapon recently arrived from England that was fatal to defences previously considered unassailable – artillery. After Skeffington's artillery bombardment, only 37 men of the garrison remained alive. In spite of his orders to hold to the last man if attacked, Paris now negotiated a surrender which included a promise that the remainder of the garrison would be shown mercy. Paris at the head of his men then approached Skeffington who asked him how Thomas Fitzgerald had treated him and what honours he had bestowed upon him. Paris, suspecting nothing, listed everything to which Skeffington replied; "And couldst thou then find in thy heart to betray his castle who has been so good to thee? Truly thou that art so hollow to him will never be true to us!"[76] Skeffington then ordered Paris executed while most of the remainder were executed the following day in front of the castle "as a lesson to all traitors".

With the help of O'Carroll of Offaly, Silken Thomas had mustered a small army of reinforcements and was returning to Maynooth when the news of the castle's capture reached him. Most of the men with him, on hearing the news of the fall of Maynooth, now considered his cause hopeless and abandoned him, Now left with only a handful of men, he sought refuge with O'Brien of Thomond.

The Capture and Death of Thomas Fitzgerald

With Skeffington's persistent ill-health still a stumbling block to the final quashing of the rebellion, the deceased Earl of Kildare's brother in law, Lord Leonard Grey, was sent to Ireland by King Henry VIII at the end of July to take charge of the army. Offaly, realising that his situation was now hopeless, sought to meet Grey so that he might give himself up on condition that his life was spared. Grey agreed with "comfortable words being spoken to allure him to yield".[77] At the meeting between the parties which was to be held during a banquet, Thomas was accompanied by his five uncles, three of whom were opposed to his rebellion from the very beginning. An old Norman ruse was now used to good effect. Having accompanied their nephew to the banquet, the five uncles were overpowered and arrested along with Offaly. Grey took it on himself to conduct the prisoners to England, but before they got to Windsor, they were intercepted and immediately committed to the Tower of London, where Offaly was left to rot without much food and no fresh clothing for eighteen months.[i] The conditions that his uncles endured are unknown, but they can hardly have been much better. All six were butchered, being hanged, drawn and quartered at Tyburn on February 3rd, 1537, without any form of trial.

In Grey's defence, he pleaded with the King for young Offaly's life to be spared and in previous times mercy would possibly have been shown to them all. But as the revolt had a Roman Catholic element to the extent that Silken Thomas was seeking

---

[i] In a letter sent by Thomas to a former servant in Ireland he asks the servant to request O'Brien of Thomond to send him money for food and clothing. "...I have neither hosen, nor doublet nor shoes, nor shirt but one...I have gone wolward and barefoot and barelegged divers times when it hath not been very warm and so I should have done still but that poor prisoners of their gentleness hath sometimes given me old hosen and shoes and shirts"

help from abroad against the heretical King Henry in order to keep Ireland attached to the Roman Catholic Church, there was no chance of clemency, as the Geraldines were seen as supporters of the Papacy.[78]

Following the executions, the lands formerly in possession of the House of Kildare were ordered to be officially incorporated into The Pale.

Massacre at Carrigogunnell Castle

In August 1536, Grey moved against Lord Offaly's allies, the O'Briens of Thomond. As part of his campaign he was determined to destroy a bridge that they had built over the River Shannon and which they were using to raid into English occupied territory. Aided by the Chieftain Conor O'Brien's treacherous son Donough, Grey was led on secret, undefended paths to the bridge, which he succeeded in destroying after the defenders were forced to retreat back across the Shannon. As a reward for his treachery, Donough O'Brien demanded that Grey should put him in possession of Carrigogunnell Castle in Thomond, from which the English had been ejected over two hundred years previously. Grey agreed and proceeded with his army towards the castle which was defended by soldiers from the army of O'Brien, assisted by men from the army of the Earl of Desmond. When Grey attacked, the Irish mounted a brave but futile defence and were ultimately forced to surrender. Grey then ordered that the entire garrison, including their women and children, be put to the sword, a deed that he included in his report of the battle that was sent to London.

Previously, only deaths of enemy soldiers would have been mentioned in such reports with deaths of non-combatants ignored, not because they were of no consequence but because they were not something to be proud of. Now for the first time it was included in a battle report, as something worthy of note.

For Grey to dispatch a report containing this information in the knowledge that he would not be reprimanded, it is likely that he was instructed on his departure from England to be ruthless beyond measure as he is also implicated in similar deeds during this period. This massacre was an was ominous portent of how the English would conduct their war against the Irish in the future, a war in which no one regardless of sex or age would be spared.

"The Geraldine League"

In spite of the efforts of the English to eradicate the male line of the House of Kildare, two male heirs remained at large, both half-brothers of Thomas Lord Offaly, sons of his father's second marriage to Elizabeth Grey, sister of Lord Leonard Grey. The youngest, Edward, who was only an infant, was quietly brought to England to the protection of his mother, while the elder, Gerald, who was the immediate heir of the House of Kildare, was around thirteen years of age and was being actively sought by the agents of the Crown with a reward being offered for his capture. At the time of the arrest of his uncles and half-brother he was ill, having contracted smallpox, and was in bed at Donore in Kildare in the care of his tutor Thomas Leverous. Fearing for his life, his tutor smuggled him out of Kildare to the safety of O'Brien in Thomond. The Gaelic lords and many of the Old English were determined that he should not fall into the King's hands, and to this end a Confederacy or League was formed with the prime object of keeping the heir of the House of Kildare safe and also with the aim of bringing to an end the Henrician reform of the Church in Ireland by defeating the English in battle and crowning Conn O'Néill of Tyrone as King of Ireland at Tara. To this second end, the Pale was attacked in 1539 by the armies of O'Néill and O'Donnell. After a successful raid in which they penetrated as far as Navan, the Ulstermen were returning home with much plunder, when they were overtaken by an English army led by Grey and defeated, with the loss of 400 men.

After a number of raids had been carried out by the English in search of young Kildare, O'Brien sent him at night to his aunt, Lady Eleanor MacCarthy, who lived in Kilbrittain in Cork. Eleanor was a widow, having been married to the Chieftain Mac Carthy Reagh, and, while Gerald was in her charge, the Chieftain of Tirconnell, Manus O'Donnell, sent her a proposal of marriage that she agreed to. That she accepted was in no small measure due to her desire to keep her nephew safe. She travelled with Gerald from Cork to Donegal and was protected the entire length of her journey by the Gaelic chieftains whose territory she passed through. All the while, the English were on his trail and secret agents were dispatched to locate him. Chieftains suspected of having harboured him had their lands destroyed. After a journey full of hazard, Tirconnell was safely reached. Grey was hot on his heels and sought to meet with the northern chieftains (who were all part of the League) to arrange for the handover of the boy. After they refused to meet, Grey launched an attack into Tyrone and captured Dungannon Castle. Using the castle as a base, he pillaged the surrounding territory for six days but his aim of capturing young Fitzgerald was not realised. It was during this expedition that Grey fell foul of the Crown-appointed Archbishop Browne of Dublin who, following the example of his confreres in England, had embarked on the destruction of the relics of the Irish Church of which more will be told in the next chapter. While passing through Trim, which had a shrine of Our Lady containing a statue of the Blessed Virgin before which many miraculous cures had occurred, Grey stopped and heard several Masses, an act which Browne held against him and included in his reports of him to London that contributed to his downfall.

Gerald Fitzgerald remained in Tirconnell until the middle of 1539, when Lady Eleanor, fearing that her husband's resolute stance in defence of the boy was weakening, brought him to France via the port of St. Malo and from thence onto Rome where he received asylum from Cardinal Pole. In 1554, during the restoration of Queen Mary, he became the eleventh Earl of Kildare but unfortunately his return was to prove a disappointment to the Irish. Doubtless aware of the destruction of his family by the English Crown, he seems to have resolved not to follow the path of courage taken by his forebears, and, under the reign of Queen Elizabeth, he acquiesced to the brutal policy undertaken by the English in Ireland, leaving unpaid the debt he owed to the Irish.

Chapter 11

Faithless Sons

"Let Erin remember the days of old, 'ere her faithless sons betrayed her" – Thomas Moore

Introduction

As the reign of Henry VIII entered the mid 1530's, two new and deadly elements were destined to be added to the Irish story – the Tudor policy of "Surrender and Regrant" which, although already mooted, was now to come to full fruition, and the Protestant Reformation, the latter determining English policy towards Ireland for the centuries that followed.

While the policy of "Surrender and Regrant" was to prove an English masterstroke in advancing their now stagnant conquest of Ireland and ultimately ending native governance, in the long run it was the Reformation which arguably was to have the greater impact, for Ireland's adherence to the old Faith was to be England's great excuse in the centuries that followed for relieving the Irish people of their land and possessions and visiting on them every criminal act known to man.

It is religion (or the lack of it) that is the predominant factor in determining a country's laws and outlook. Once official England had abandoned the Catholic Faith, it became completely intolerant of it, so much so that a man could lose his life for maintaining it. In its dealings with Ireland, it became the policy of the English government that the conquest and subjugation of Ireland would no longer suffice – she must also persecute her people. The conquest of Ireland was shortly to enter a new phase, for it was to become a pitiless war against Catholicism and the Catholic people of Ireland.

Although it is outside of the scope of this book, such was the effect of the Anglican Reformation on this country that in order to give the reader a fuller history and understanding of the subject, we must briefly recount its progress.

The Reformation in England
"A heresy and new error sprang up in England, through pride, vainglory, avarice and lust..." – Annals of the Four Masters.

The Reformation in Europe
Towards the end of 1517, during the reign of Henry VIII, the dam that held the pent-up discontent against the Church in Germany gave way. The initial breaching of the dam is often recounted: how a young Augustinian monk called Martin Luther nailed a list of 95 academic theses to be defended on the door of the Castle Chapel in Wittenberg, which was the notice board within that university for such disputes. Luther's document provoked a torrent of reaction that spread beyond Germany's borders and was to far exceed the questions contained in it. Initially, the worldliness and decay within the higher levels of the clergy along with the topical issue of indulgences and the laxity and abuses within the Church were the main points at issue, but very soon other things were attacked, such as celibacy and various Church doctrines, especially the doctrine of the Real Presence of Jesus Christ in the Blessed Sacrament which gave the clergy a special position in society because of their power of consecration of the bread and wine at Mass into the body and blood of Christ. Within a

short time, rulers of certain German states found that by throwing off the yoke of the Church, they could in turn dispossess her of her temporal wealth.

England and Ireland were initially beyond the reach of the crisis. Certainly, there was discontent at the wealth and power of the clergy and monasteries, but this was nothing new. King Henry, who prided himself on his doctrinal knowledge,[79] was critical of the European reformers' questioning of the doctrines by which the peoples of Europe had lived from time immemorial. Having studied theology in his youth, Henry wrote a book entitled "A Defence of The Seven Sacraments" for which he was given the title "Defender of the Faith" by the Pope.

"Bewitched"

However, a matter completely unrelated to the European situation was to change everything. By 1524, Henry's Queen, Catherine of Aragon, was no longer able to bear children and Henry, who had no legitimate male heir, had stopped living with her. He had long since had a succession of mistresses and now became completely infatuated with a young lady at court called Anne Boleyn (or Bullen) who, on seeing how consumed the king was with her, initially refused his advances, as she desired to play for higher stakes – that the King should endeavour to get the marriage with Catherine annulled and make her his queen instead. The King, who later described himself as being "bewitched"[80] by her, made a deal with Anne Boleyn sometime during the Summer of 1525 to the effect that come what may he would make her his queen. There followed a lengthy attempt by the King and his ministers, especially Cardinal Wolsey, to obtain from Rome an annulment of his marriage to Catherine, which ultimately ended in failure and the fall from grace of Cardinal Wolsey.

The Anglican Schism

Into Wolsey's shoes as the King's chief adviser stepped his secretary, Thomas Cromwell, who masterminded the break with Rome that now followed. After undertaking steps to cripple the Church financially, all revenues which were normally sent to Rome were withheld unless an annulment should be granted. After this failed, Henry was declared "Supreme Head of the Church and Clergy of England" and on April 23rd, 1533, Archbishop Cranmer declared his marriage with Queen Catherine null and void. After the Roman Consistory Court refused to declare the King's marriage to Catherine invalid in March 1534, the break was complete and by year's end it became treason to deny the King his new title as "Supreme Head of the Church in England". A reign of terror followed Rome's decision.

King Henry VIII

By this stage, Parliament had been transformed into an instrument of the King's will, and persecution against those who wanted no part of Henry's schism was the order of the day. An Act of Attainder was passed whereby any person or persons named could be put to death without trial.[i] Noblemen, bishops and abbots were butchered by being hanged, drawn and quartered for their refusal to acknowledge the King's title. Despite

---

[i] In 1540, Thomas Cromwell fell victim to an Act of Attainder after Henry's disastrous marriage to Anne of Cleves which he arranged.

maintaining his adherence to traditional Catholic teachings, it suited the King to adopt Luther's doctrine on the supremacy of scripture as it was by his use and interpretation of Scripture that he justified his desire for an annulment.[i] The veneration of relics and the practice of pilgrimage to places like Canterbury were attacked by the injunction of Thomas Cromwell in 1536 and, in 1538, the shrine of St. Thomas Becket in Canterbury was destroyed, an act that contributed to the decision by Pope Paul III to excommunicate King Henry.

For the common people, there was as yet little change; traditional doctrines were left untouched, and the traditional Mass in Latin continued as before. On the point of the Mass and the Real Presence, King Henry was to remain immovable in spite of the desire of Cromwell and Cranmer to undermine them. However, the monasteries which were a source of hospitality for travellers, medical care and alms for the poor were slowly disappearing as Cromwell closed them and seized their assets in punishment for their 'lax morals', a charge which he was unable to prove.

Henry VIII Extends his Schism to Ireland

For the accomplishment of his reformation programme in Ireland, the King had at his disposal a compliant triumvirate of Sir Piers Butler, Lord Grey and George Browne.[ii] Browne had formerly been a monk but was now the King's willing tool, Henry having installed him as his Archbishop of Dublin in place of the murdered Allen. Browne was disappointed with the appetite for reform in Dublin and complained bitterly to Thomas Cromwell about the "zealous blindness"[81] of the

---

[i] The King used verses 20 and 21 from the book of Leviticus.
[ii] King Henry VIII described Archbishop Browne, saying: "All virtue and honesty were almost vanished from him" (English State Papers clxxiv).

people. As his first goal, Browne set about dealing with Archbishop Cromer of Armagh who had pronounced an anathema against all who acknowledged the supremacy of the King in spiritual matters. Cromer's "treasonous" actions were denounced, and he was imprisoned. As Cromer had already sent envoys to the Pope (from whom an appeal to the Anglo-Irish was now feared), Browne decided that the best way forward was to summon an Anglo-Irish parliament

The Parliament of 1536

After Thomas Cromwell had assisted in the preparation of its programme, the Parliament was summoned on May 1st, 1536, with acts being passed or annulled to suit the King's whim. Civil issues were dealt with first. After an Act of Attainder was passed against the male members of the House of Kildare, the elements of the Statute of Kilkenny were restated, and all vacant lordships were granted to the King. The Parliament had just passed an act whereby King Henry's children by Anne Boleyn were declared his heirs, when a King's Messenger arrived from England with the news that she had been found guilty on numerous charges and had been beheaded. The act was rescinded without delay!

When it came to the implementation of the religious reforms, there was stubborn resistance from the clerical representatives from each diocese sitting in Parliament, and on the question of the spiritual supremacy of the Church in Ireland (which the King now proposed to take for himself), they would not give ground. The impasse continued for some time until finally in 1537, by act of the King, the clerical representatives were to be henceforth excluded from Parliament. Following the destruction of the House of Kildare, the secular members of the Irish Parliament were as putty in the King's hands and, although unhappy with the Act of Supremacy, they acquiesced. The King was declared Supreme Head on Earth of the Church in Ireland. Further acts were passed for the promotion of English order, habit and language and for the suppression of 13 monasteries within the area of the Pale. By law, Ireland was now at one with England in rejecting "the usurped authority of the Bishop of Rome" and the same draconian measures against the Church in England were now to be enforced in the English controlled areas of Ireland.

The enforcement of the practical aspects of the "Act of Supremacy" were entrusted to Archbishop Browne, who immediately sent out instructions that references to the Pope should be removed from the altar missals and other books. Regarding the dissolution of monasteries, he instructed that they be immediately closed down because "...the monks and nuns dwelling there being so addicted, partly to their own superstitious ceremonies, partly to the pernicious worship of idols, and to the pestiferous doctrines of the Roman Pontiff, that the Irish people may be speedily infected, to their total destruction, by the example of these persons..."[82]

As we have seen, as a result of English policy, the Church in Ireland was split into an Irish Element and an English element, so the enforcement of the measures of Church repression could never be uniform across the country. In many dioceses where the bishop was an English appointee, the bishop conformed, and monasteries were closed but other measures were not enforced with any great vigour. The native clergy were relatively firm in their opposition to the reforms, and in a lot of areas where the English writ did not run, the monasteries remained intact. A typical example might be the diocese of Kilmore (Kingdom of Breifne) where the English-appointed Bishop Nugent was in charge of the diocese. As a member of the House of Lords during the Anglo-Irish parliament of 1536-37, he had acquiesced to the legislation, and it was during his tenure that the Abbeys of Fore and Kells (both in his diocese) were dissolved while the abbeys of West Breifne remained intact as they were in Gaelic controlled areas. Many of Bishop Nugent's clergy still remained loyal to the Pope as Head of the Church and the papal courts and ordinances were still used by them in the case of disputes.

By 1540, Pope Paul III had enough evidence in his possession of Nugent's perfidy and appointed Fr. John MacBrady, Parish Priest of Kildrumferton, as his replacement. Nugent, who was supported by the establishment and also on good terms with the Gaelic Lords, continued to act as bishop. An accommodation was reached by the two men whereby Nugent who lived in the Pale allowed Brady to deal with the day-to-day affairs of the diocese.

Dissolution and Destruction

Eager to please King Henry VIII, Archbishop Browne was determined that the Reformation in Ireland should keep step with that of England where numerous Christian relics venerated for centuries by clergy and people alike were being destroyed and their valuable adornments removed into the coffers of the King. In the summer of 1538, he embarked on an orgy of iconoclasm and instigated the destruction of many Catholic relics and treasures, including the Shrine of the Holy Cross at Ballyboggan in Co. Meath which had a wooden cross that contained a portion of the True Cross. Also destroyed was the nearby shrine of Our Lady at Trim where the statue of the Blessed Virgin was publicly burned (described by Browne as "the idol of Trim"[83]) as well as Ireland's most important native Christian relic, the staff of St. Patrick. Numerous miracles were attributed to these relics[i] and their destruction greatly shocked

---

[i] For more information on the miracles attributed to these relics, please see The Annals of The Four Masters A.D 1381, 1397, 1411, 1444, 1464 and 1482.

both the Anglo and native Irish alike. The Annals of Lough Ce record Browne's actions as follows:

"The very miraculous image of Mary which was in the town of Ath-truim, (Trim) in which all the people of Eirinn believed...which healed the blind and deaf and lame, and every other ailment, was burnt by Saxons; and the Bachall–Isa (Staff of Jesus) which was in the town of Ath-Cliath working numerous prodigies and miracles...was burned...and there was not in Eirinn a holy cross or figure of Mary or an illustrious image over which their (Saxon) power reached that was not burned."

Not content that the Anglo-Irish could be trusted to dissolve the monastic settlements in their areas of control, a commission was appointed in 1539 to enforce the 1537 Act for the suppression of religious houses.

The commission's job was made much easier in East Ulster and Munster due to the presence of a large English army commanded by the Lord Deputy Leonard Grey. As part of his efforts to break up "The Geraldine League", Grey decamped to Munster (after a successful campaign against the Gaelic Chieftains of east Ulster) in order to break up the alliance between the Geraldines of Desmond and the O'Briens of Thomond.

As in Ulster, where he had attacked monasteries[i] and relics, monasteries that should have been beyond the reach of the English were targeted. For Grey, the mission was highly successful, and he received the submission of many Gaelic Chieftains and Anglo-Irish in Munster and in the territories through which he passed.

---

[i] In Monaghan town, the Guardian and some of the friars were killed during an attack on the monastery.

The Death of Lord Grey

Grey was recalled to London early in 1540 where he met King Henry who thanked him for his work in Ireland. However, he had made many enemies in Ireland and a file of accusations was prepared against him, the most serious of which was that he had not really tried to capture the heir of the House of Kildare, Gerald Fitzgerald, who was his nephew. Shortly afterwards, he was arrested and sent to The Tower of London. For his tireless efforts on the King's behalf, Grey was charged with high treason and executed as a traitor on Tower Hill in June of 1541.

After Grey's recall, Sir William Brereton was temporarily placed in charge of the governance of Ireland. Around this time, reports came to him that there was to be general muster of the armies of Ulster and Thomond, along with those of some of the other Chieftains, at the Abbey of Fore in Westmeath. A general alarm was sounded in the Pale and an army of ten thousand men of every conceivable occupation was assembled. Deciding to meet the threat head-on, Brereton marched towards Westmeath and reached Fore unhindered where there was no sign of the armed host. Deciding that the expedition should not be in vain, Brereton led his force into nearby Offaly, the territory of O'Conor Faly, where he destroyed all the crops and homes in his path for twenty days in succession, after which he was forced to return to the Pale since his rations were almost exhausted.

"Surrender and Regrant"

In the early 1520's, during the tenure of the Earl of Surrey as Lord Deputy, the policy of "Surrender and Regrant was first mentioned. Grey's replacement, Sir Anthony St. Leger, who was appointed in August 1540, was now to bring it to fruition.

If the policy of "Surrender and Regrant" had been designed to flatter the Irish Chieftains and appeal to their vanity while bringing them and their lands under English control, then it was most certainly an English masterstroke. While desirous to serve his King, St. Leger however had no hidden agenda, although the instructions from King Henry VIII imply that the act would be taken full advantage of by the English during a later reign. Henry recommended using "...circumspect and politic ways which things *must as yet* be practiced by sober ways, politic drifts and amiable persuasion..." The fruits of the policy were already apparent to the English by 1544, as a government official in Dublin was to write: "Experience showeth that the captainships (granting of titles) in Ireland are the undoing of the same."[84]

In the past, the native nobility had on many occasions found themselves in a situation where they had been forced to submit to the English. However, in the eyes of the Irish, this submission had not extended to the surrender of their lands, and land lost to the English was often successfully regained. With the use of cannon and sword now replaced by noble titles, allowances and fine clothes for the Gaelic Chieftains, the English sought to bring Ireland into line with England where all land was vested in the Crown and granted to the Irish nobility with their support. In England, the King was "Dominus Terrae" or "Lord of the Land", a notion that was totally alien to the Irish.

As well as pacifying the country, the act also sought to get the Irish Chieftains to recognise Henry's new title as "Supreme Head of the Church in Ireland". After all that had gone before, it should really have been obvious to the Gaelic Chieftains and their Brehons[i] with their separate laws, rights of succession and culture, that the act was full of danger for them.

The act was also used to set the greater Gaelic Chieftains against their vassal or dependent Chieftains as, once a petty

---

[i] Brehon – Law giver or lawyer of Gaelic law

King submitted to the English in his own right, he no longer felt himself bound to his former Gaelic master.

Sir Anthony St. Leger arrived in Dublin in August of 1540. Gone was the aggressiveness of Grey. Instead, St. Leger was conciliatory both in word and deed, and after the bruising few years which had just passed, where the Irish had failed to get the upper hand in any of their military engagements with Grey and where Grey had caused great destruction and despoliation in his bid to capture Gerald Fitzgerald, the Irish were positively disposed to concession and negotiation.

In a scene reminiscent of the visit of King Henry II in 1172, word of St. Leger's desire to come to terms with the Chieftains spread throughout the country after the first of them offered him their submission. Over an extended period, interviews were sought by the Chieftains with St. Leger and one by one they submitted, giving their lands into the hands of the King. Then these lands were returned to them with title, as was the case in England. Initially, around 40 of the Gaelic Lords submitted and acknowledged the King's claim to spiritual supremacy.

Also included in the provisions of the act were those early settlers who had become fully "Gaelicised", for they also desired to gain royal assent to the territories which they occupied. There was one exception. As an inveterate supporter and ally of Silken Thomas, the Gaelic Lord of Offaly, Brian O'Connor, was excluded and his land was confiscated.

The submission of the Gaelic Chieftains continued for some years. One of the last to submit during this period was Brian Ballach O'Rourke, Lord of West Breifne, who met with St. Leger in Maynooth in September 1542.

Henry VIII – "King of Ireland"

With the submissions in progress, St. Leger advised Henry that he should now abandon the title "Lord of Ireland" and instead

take the title "King of Ireland", "...for the Irish have a foolish opinion that the Bishop of Rome is King of Ireland."[85]
Following the promulgation in London of the Act by which Henry declared himself King of Ireland,[i] St. Leger summoned a parliament to be held on the 12th June 1541 and invited some of the loyal Chieftains to attend, for which purpose they were attired at the King's expense in fine clothing of the English style. The sight of the Irish dressed in these robes must have pleased St. Leger greatly for he was also tasked with clamping down on Irish language and culture and bringing English ways to the country.
As the entire proceedings were conducted through English, the Earl of Ormond, Piers Butler, translated them into Gaelic for the Chieftains. Among those attending were Kavanagh of Carlow (who now renounced the name MacMurrough), O'Reilly of Breifne and MacGillapatraic of Ossory (who also changed his name to the English form - "Fitzpatrick"). The act conferring the title "King of Ireland" on Henry VIII was passed unanimously and a general pardon was issued in the King's name by St. Leger. The following Sunday saw both the Anglo and native Irish nobility processing together to St. Patrick's Cathedral where a Solemn High Mass was sung by Archbishop Browne. After Mass, the new law announcing Henry VIII as King of Ireland was proclaimed and the *Te Deum* was chanted

---

[i] "Forasmuch as the King our most gracious dread sovereign lord, and his Grace's most noble progenitors, Kings of England, have been Lords of his land of Ireland, having all manner kingly jurisdiction, power, preeminence, and authority royal, belonging or appertaining to the royal estate and majesty of a King, by the name of Lords of Ireland, where the King's Majesty and his most noble progenitors justly and rightfully were and of right, ought to be Kings of Ireland...His Majesty, his heirs and successors, be from henceforth named, called, accepted, reputed and taken to be Kings of this land of Ireland, to have, hold and enjoy the said style, title, majesty and honours of King of Ireland, with all manner preeminencies, prerogatives, dignities, and all other the premises unto the King's Highness, his heirs and successors for ever, as united and knit to the imperial crown of the Realm of England." (Irish Statues Ch. 1 – 1786)

in thanksgiving. St. Leger was to write to Henry that after Mass "there was made in the city great bonfires, wine was set in the streets and there was great feasting in the houses."⁸⁶

Subsequent to the parliamentary sessions, submissions came from Manus O'Donnell of Tirconnell and Conn O'Néill of Tyrone. The submission of the O'Néill was a great triumph for the English as the Cenél Eoghan was one of the most resilient Clans in maintaining its independence from English rule. Having accepted Henry both as King and head of the Church, Conn O'Néill surrendered his lands, after which they were returned to him with the title Earl of Tyrone, while his illegitimate son Matthew (who was earmarked as his successor) was named as Baron of Dungannon. Two other Earldoms were also created around this time with the "degenerate English" Burke named Earl of Clanrickard and Murrough O'Brien Earl of Thomond.ⁱ

Murrough O'Brien is notable among the Chieftains for his zeal in the cause of the King's spiritual supremacy as he was anxious to get his hands on whatever religious spoils were going in his territory as a result of the dissolution of monasteries. His treacherous nephew Donough, the new resident of Carrickogunnel Castle, was made Baron of Ibrickan and promised the Earldom on his uncle's death. Nearly all of the Chieftains received an English title, most being created either Baron or Viscount depending on the size of their territory, with some of the titles being dubbed on the Irish by King Henry when they went to Greenwich Palace in London in July 1543 on an all expenses paid trip.

For his new Irish Lords, King Henry granted to each a house and land in Dublin for their accommodation when they would come to Parliament with their retinues.

ⁱ The previous Chieftain, his brother Conor had died in 1540.

However, for all their titles the native Irish Lords still had no say in the governance of the country, which was still in the hands of the Royal Council in Dublin. Prior to this general submission by the Gaelic Lords, the Anglo-Irish nobility of the area encompassing the Pale were members of the Council, but now the English Pale was much bigger than it had been before and included many of the Gaelic nobility; nevertheless, they were not to be included in its composition. In reality, by their submission they were little more than tenants of an English King. Furthermore, by their submission they had left themselves wide open to the King's policy against Gaelic tradition and language.

By the end of the reign of King Henry VIII, the actual area of the English Pale had encompassed all of Leinster and had crossed over into Munster. The Earl of Desmond was co-operating with the Earl of Ormond as to the suppression of the native Brehon law and the introduction of English law. Gaelic bards were also earmarked for suppression due to their renown for the part played by them in the decision making of their Lords.

For Shame

"Shame on you, men of the Gael
Not one of you has life in him:
The foreigner is sharing out your country among them
And you are like a phantom host

The O'Néills of Aileach and Navan
The King of Tara and Tailtéann
In foolish submission
Have surrendered their kingdom
For the *earldom* of Ulster

O Nobles of the Island of ancient Art
Evil is your change of dignity
O ill-guided cowardly host
Henceforth say nothing but "Shame"

(Anon – 16th Century)

Part 2

For Faith and Fatherland

Chapter 12

The First Plantations

The Religious Reforms of King Edward VI

During the last years of the reign of King Henry VIII, both England and Ireland remained Catholic in practice but were in schism with Rome because of the King's rejection of the papacy. To the end of his life, King Henry remained orthodox with regard to most Catholic teaching even publishing a volume entitled "The King's Book" which proclaimed his attachment to traditional Catholic doctrines, especially that of the Real Presence of Jesus Christ in the Blessed Sacrament.[i] However, there were many others in his kingdom who wished to advance the religious revolution much farther and they patiently waited in the wings for his death. When Henry died in 1547, his ailing son Edward VI who had just turned nine was crowned King. However, the real power in England was in the hands of the King's uncle Edward Seymour who became Duke of Somerset. Somerset led a council of 16 members who were due to govern until Edward reached 18. Most cared little for religion, and having tasted the spoils of confiscated Church

---

[i] In the last will and testament of Henry VIII he wrote: "We do earnestly require and desire the Blessed Virgin, God's Mother, with all the company of heaven to pray for us...and that there be provided, ordained and set a convenient altar honourably prepared and appareled, with all manner of things for daily Mass (for my soul) there to be said while the world shall endure."

wealth, wanted more. The only member of the council who desired to advance the revolution for religious reasons was the anti-Catholic Archbishop of Canterbury, Thomas Cranmer, who had kept his true sentiments hidden from King Henry.

Somerset's council decided to continue with the anti-Catholic reforms, but in a piecemeal fashion so as to try and avoid the popular revolts (like the "Pilgrimage of Grace") that had occurred after the declaration of Henry's supremacy. The first stage of the new reforms was to commence on June 9th, 1549, when the Mass was to be said in English instead of Latin. The idea was that, without actually denying the Real Presence, this would serve as a stepping stone to the next prayer book (1552) which, in addition to destroying the Mass, would also deny the Real Presence.

Opposition in Ireland to the Reforms

In Ireland, St. Leger was still Lord Deputy but was regarded by the Somerset-led council as being too even handed and as someone who would be unwilling to roll out the coming reforms. Sir Edward Bellingham was dispatched to replace him. When King Edward's new English prayer book was sent over, a meeting of the King's Irish council and bishops took place in Dublin. As expected, Archbishop Browne did not demur and said: "I submit to the King as Jesus did to Caesar"[87] (neglecting to mention that Jesus had submitted to Caesar in temporal matters only). The most serious opposition came from the Crown-appointed Archbishop Dowdall of Armagh who was also Primate of Ireland. He was unwilling to compromise further than the supremacy, and his outspokenness made him the leading voice for the Catholic party. He stated that if the Mass was to be said in English: "then shall every illiterate fellow read Mass"[88]. Many of the bishops rallied behind Dowdall, with Browne's only support coming from Staples of Meath, Lancaster of Kildare, and

Travers of Leighlin. Dowdall's opposition was such that no progress could be made and the hamstrung Bermingham was recalled. St. Leger was sent over again as it was hoped that he could achieve a breakthrough in favour of the reformers through his skills of tact and diplomacy. But he made no headway, in spite of his best efforts. Browne, who disliked St. Leger intensely, did not make life easy for him and after a short time made treasonous charges against him. He was quickly recalled to England and Sir James Crofts was sent over as his replacement. On Crofts' arrival in 1552, he called another meeting of the bishops and this time Archbishop Dowdall, as well as rejecting the Mass in English, went further than before, repudiating the King's declaration of spiritual supremacy by expressing his support for the authority of the Pope. Browne was furious at this and reported to London that Dowdall would have to be quickly sidelined. A Royal charter was obtained in short order, transferring the Irish primacy from Armagh to Dublin. Now Browne would be Primate with a free hand to proceed according to the government's desires. After these proceedings, Dowdall, knowing that he could be arrested for treason at any moment, quickly left Ireland and made for the continent.

The Edwardian reforms were only to make any headway among the officialdom of the Pale. Most of the other bishops kept their heads down and said nothing but did not make any move at introducing the reforms in their dioceses. As Crofts was to acknowledge in September of 1552: "...The olde seremonies yet remayne in meny places." Even those in favour of the King's reforms could do nothing as they faced unyielding opposition from their clergy and people. In Ossory, a new Bishop by the name of Bale was appointed in February of 1553, the first bishop to be introduced according to King Edward's second prayer book. When he spoke publicly in favour of the reforms and against the "Popish Mass" in

Kilkenny City, there was rioting and five of Bale's attendants were killed. Bale was escorted to safety and the local magistrate at the head of a body of soldiers was called on to restore order.

English Law Versus Brehon Law

When St. Leger had secured the allegiance of the native chieftains by the promise that they could have permanent possession of their territories under the King, he erroneously assumed that the chieftains were acting with the full authority of their people. According to Brehon law, the land belonged to the people with the chieftain having only an estate that he could rightfully call his own. Whatever the intentions of the chieftains in their submission, the people still regarded the tribal territory as theirs.

Furthermore, in their submission to the English many of the chieftains had presented the son they intended to be their successor and he had then been given a noble title by the English. This practice was according to English law where the eldest son succeeded to his father's estates without question. However, according to Brehon law the chieftain's successor, although coming from the ruling family, might or might not be his eldest son and in any event, he was to be chosen by the Clan and not the chieftain. It was of no significance to the Clan that the pre-ordained successor had been chosen with the blessing of the Crown and had a title of English nobility. The two systems were destined to clash head on and with violent results.

The Tyrone Succession

In 1551, Con "Bacach"[i] O'Néill, who was the Chieftain of the O'Néills of Tyrone, was old and infirm. According to the

---

[i] Gaelic for "lame"

English, his successor was to be his illegitimate son Matthew (known as Fedoragh to the Irish) as Con had nominated him and he had been created Baron of Dungannon. However, the Clan elders did not want Matthew and disputed whether or not he was actually Con's son at all.[i] They wanted Con's eldest legitimate son John, better known as "Shane", to be his successor. Con began to regret the favouritism he had shown to Matthew, but for his part Matthew would have none of Con's change of mind. He knew full well that the Crown title was useless if he was not "The O'Néill". He sent word to Crofts that his father had turned against him and asked for his help. Crofts came north and arrested Con, hoping that this would be enough to restore Matthew. However, Shane was not for turning and did not care what the Crown thought. According to Brehon law, he would succeed his father and that was all that mattered. Mustering his forces, he allied himself with the Scottish Clan MacDonnell, some ten thousand of whom had crossed over to Antrim after the "Lordship of the Isles" was taken away from John MacDonnell II in 1493 by King James IV of Scotland. Known as "Redshanks", they were sworn enemies of the English but had also caused a considerable amount of trouble for the O'Néills of Clandeboye and the McQuillans, rulers of a territory known as "The Route" in north Antrim. Crofts had already tried to throw them out of their northern base as a menace to English interests and another factor to be considered in the balance of power in Ulster. In 1551, out of four ships of English soldiers sent to

---

[i] Matthew (or Fedoragh) was the son of Alison O'Kelly, the wife of a Dundalk blacksmith. He was adopted by Con O'Néill after Alison's husband died when Matthew was fifteen years of age. He was reputed to be Con's son but Shane and many of the O'Néills regarded this as a deception which would deny Shane the chieftainship.

Rathlin Island to dislodge them, only one English soldier is reputed to have escaped.

In 1552, Crofts came north again, this time to Tyrone, at the head of a large army to try and secure Matthew's succession and caused great destruction but without any conclusive outcome. In the years that followed, as Con was still alive, the issue held no great urgency for the English especially as it was unlikely to be resolved without great loss of blood. As Con neared death in 1558, Shane decided that the time was ripe to get Matthew out of the way and made arrangements for him to be ambushed and killed.

In Thomond, a similar situation was also playing out. When the treacherous Donough O'Brien became Earl after the death of Murrough O'Brien in 1551, he received a letter from the King securing his line of succession as Earl of Thomond to his sons, as arranged. However, when Donough died in 1553, his son Conor, who by English law succeeded him, was left with nothing but an English title after his uncle, Domhnall O'Brien, made himself Chieftain claiming that he was the successor that the Clan had chosen. Domhnall then attacked Conor's stronghold at Doonmulvihill where he remained under siege there until the arrival of the Earl of Ormond. Donnell was eventually ousted in 1558 by Radcliffe, St. Leger's successor.

Meanwhile under King Edward, the English seizure of land extended where it could, with Offaly and Leix both being garrisoned by English soldiers as their chieftains had been refused the policy of surrender and regrant. Since 1548, a "Surveyor and Escheator General" had been appointed to survey and then allocate the stolen land into loyal hands.

Queen Mary Tudor
The Restoration of the Catholic Faith
After the death of King Edward on July 6th, 1553, the ruling council in England prepared to change dynasty and make Lady Jane Grey the Queen.

The council had decided that Henry VIII's Catholic daughter Mary was to be arrested and put to death. Then the unexpected happened. There was a mass movement of popular support for Mary, and when she arrived in London, huge crowds of common people followed her shouting that she was the rightful Queen of England. This large popular movement could not be ignored. The council were forced to give way and Mary became queen, after which the Catholic faith returned, and the recognition of Papal primacy was restored. Both Britain and Ireland were then absolved of their heresy by Pope Paul IV, with Queen Mary's cousin, Cardinal Reginald Pole acting as interlocutor between England and the Holy See.

In Ireland, the news that Mary had prevailed against her enemies was received with both joy and relief. As the Protestant Bishop Bale of Ossory recalled: "On Thursday, the last day of August, I being absent, the clergy of Kilkenny resumed the whole papism...they mustered forth with Sancta Maria, Ora Pro Nobis and the rest of the Latin Litany...they flung up their caps and banqueted all the day after..."[89].

While the Mass and sacraments were restored everywhere, monastic lands were not. The Queen would have liked to restore them in both England and Ireland, but it was obvious to her that such a move would lead to open revolt among the gentry. The courageous Archbishop Dowdall was recalled to the See of Armagh with the blessing of the Pope, while Browne and a few other bishops who had married or were outspoken in their Protestantism were replaced. Bale of Ossory fled the country. In Ireland, unlike in England, no action was taken against those of high rank or social position who openly adhered to Protestantism and some of those who felt endangered in England fled to Ireland.

The Chieftain of the Clan O'Conor Ealy was also released from his English prison after his daughter, Margaret O'Conor Ealy, went to London and had an audience with the Queen during which she begged for his freedom. He was arrested shortly after his return to Ireland on some pretext by the Queen's Irish administrators who were angered by the Queen's action.

King's County and Queen's County

Under Mary's reign, the diplomatic and gentlemanly St. Leger was initially restored as Deputy. However, because of his popularity and even-handedness with the Gael, government officials conspired against him, and he was replaced by Radcliffe, Earl of Sussex in 1556. On Radcliffe's appointment, he was instructed to begin the plantation of Offaly and Leix which had been seized and garrisoned under King Edward. They were now to be known as King's County after Mary's husband Philip of Spain and Queen's County after Queen Mary respectively. Two thirds of each county were to be planted with one third to be reserved for the native Irish Clans if they would stop resisting. Radcliffe's instructions read: "We desire also if the Dempsies and those rebels the Mores and the O'Connors shall call for grace, and do submit themselves unto order and mercy, that those countries shall be parted in three parts, and thereof to

Philip and Mary

assign unto the said O'Connor's, O'Mores and Dempsies, the thirds...."⁹⁰ However these Clans would not willingly surrender the lands that their families had held since time immemorial and resisted bravely but in vain to the murderous onslaught directed against them. Their struggle to regain their patrimony would continue until 1603, by which stage they were all but destroyed. In this first example of what would become an all too common pattern, their Chieftain Brian O'Connor had been declared a traitor and his lands declared forfeit to the Crown, after which they would be planted.[i] In this first plantation, the precedent for the future was set, consisting of three stages. Firstly, a declaration of treason by the Crown against the Gaelic Lord or a declaration that the Gaelic Lord did not in fact have title to his lands. This was followed by a confiscation of lands belonging to his Clan as well as the lands of those Clans loyal to him. The third stage was the forced removal of the native Irish, and finally plantation by loyal subjects, the more adventurous of whom would assist in the confiscation and receive larger spoils. Those to be planted had to meet certain criteria. They were required to be English born, or Irish born of English descent, and were not allowed to employ any Irish on their estates. They had to construct strong stone blockhouses and were also required to be ready to supply a certain number of troops to the Crown when called on to do so.

---

[i] This Act of the Crown read in part "Commission to Sir Henry Radcliffe Lieutenant of the King's and Queen's counties; to parle with and take pledges from and punish with fire and sword the Irish of the said counties otherwise called Leise and Offalery. Forasmuch as the O'Mores, O'Dempsies, O'Connors and others of the Irishry...by their sundry manifest treasons...their Majesty's Lord Deputy in Ireland, by sword evicted and reduced the said counties out of and from the wrongful and usurped possession as of right appertaineth...Be it therefore ordained, enacted and established that the said King's and Queen's Majesty's shall have, hold and possess for ever, as in right of the Crown of England, the said countries" – Acts of Philip and Mary.

The Death of Queen Mary

Already suffering from bad health on her accession to the throne of England, Queen Mary's health deteriorated rapidly after the English loss of Calais at the beginning of 1558. She lingered on during the summer, and by the onset of winter it was clear that her death was imminent. As her end approached, Mary was very concerned whether the outward piety of her half sister Elizabeth, whom she knew would succeed her as Queen of England, was in fact genuine since the state religion of England would depend on this. When Mary questioned her on this point, Elizabeth was vehement in her profession of faith, replying: "I pray God that the earth may open and swallow me alive if I be not a true Roman Catholic!"[91] Unfortunately for Ireland, Elizabeth's wish was not granted. Her reign was destined to bring decades of persecution, death and destruction to this country and would also sound the death knell for the old Gaelic order. Queen Mary died while attending Mass on the morning of November 17th, 1558. A few hours later, the death occurred of the man responsible for reconciling both England and Ireland to Roman Catholicism, her cousin Cardinal Reginald Pole.

Chapter 13

Shane O'Néill, King of Ulster

England becomes Protestant.
Even before the death of Queen Mary, plans were already afoot by the Secretary to the Royal Council, William Cecil – the man who was to be the chief advisor of Queen Elizabeth for the duration of her reign – to ensure that England would return to Protestantism. During Mary's reign, he had secretly drawn up a step-by-step plan entitled "A Device for the Alteration of Religion" whereby the Mass would be replaced by a Protestant liturgical service, Catholic preaching banned, and devout Catholic magistrates dismissed. In his document, he foresaw resistance in Ireland emanating from the native clergy when he wrote: "The Pope all that he may, will be incensed, but this will not go further than excommunication, interdicts, and intrigues with foreign princes, although by reason of the clergy so addicted to Rome, the Papal hostility will mean trouble in Ireland".[92]

As Secretary to the Council, Cecil was the leader of the prominent English landowners, and as such he had a vested interest in preventing the firm re-establishment of Catholicism, as all too many members of his group had become extremely wealthy through their appropriation of religious land, property and wealth. As for Queen Elizabeth, her professed Catholicism and outward piety during her sister's reign proved to be nothing more than a measure of expediency to ensure her succession. When the time came for her coronation, the growing disquiet among the English bishops with regard to her manifest hostility to Catholicism was such that none of them would crown her. Finally, the Bishop of Carlisle gave way and agreed to officiate at her coronation. During the ceremony, Elizabeth took the traditional oath to preserve the Catholic Religion intact but after her coronation, change followed rapidly. Cecil ensured that anti-Catholic peers were appointed to the House of Lords as replacements for a number of bishops who were imprisoned in the tower. Two thirds of the members of parliament were also new, and they were like putty in Cecil's hands. A new prayer book was introduced, which amounted to nothing less than the reintroduction of King Edward's second prayer book. When the new liturgy was introduced into parliament, it only passed due to Cecil's machinations. Various bishops were barred from sitting, others were in prison and seven sees were vacant. When a new Act of Supremacy was introduced, to which the new liturgy was appended, it was refused by all the remaining bishops who sat in the House of Lords. Following this, all except one of them were removed from their dioceses.

Scotland and Presbyterianism

Apart from the established church or Church of England, which would be replicated in Ireland, one of the many Protestant sects that arose during and after the reign of Queen Elizabeth was to have greater impact than the others. This sect was Presbyterianism, the new religion of the Reformation in Scotland, which in due course would have a direct impact on Ireland and its Catholics.

In the early years of the reign of Queen Elizabeth, a former Catholic cleric by the name of John Knox preached (unlike the Anglicans) a complete and full rejection of all things Catholic.

He had recently returned from the Continent to Scotland, his home country, where Catholicism still held sway but there was more ecclesiastical corruption here than had ever been the case in England. On the Continent, Knox had become an avid follower of Calvin and now preached his doctrines on the inefficacy of good works and that anyone who loyally adhered to his teaching was predestined for Heaven. Encouraged by the nobility who wished to see the Catholic Church in Scotland completely dispossessed, the lower classes of the Scottish Lowlands flocked to hear Knox's violent speeches and many of his adherents were joined by those who cared nothing for religion but were more interested in what booty they could gain. Mobs were formed, and in an anti-Catholic frenzy they torched churches and monasteries, wrecked statues and relics and destroyed the ancient St. Andrew's Cathedral in Fife.

Scotland had its own Catholic monarch, the teenage Mary Queen of Scots. She was in France when the storm erupted and was represented in Scotland by her French mother, Mary of Guise who remained precariously in control as the revolution gained traction. This revolution would finally overwhelm the Catholic monarchy when Queen Mary returned, after which she would flee to England to seek refuge with her cousin, Queen Elizabeth.

1560 – The Irish Reformation Parliament

Having first established her religious reforms and dealt with the opposition in England, Queen Elizabeth was now ready for their extension to Ireland. With this in mind, Radcliffe, Earl of Sussex, who had been retained by her as Lord Lieutenant, was instructed to summon an Irish Parliament in order to get approval for her changes. Radcliffe was no different to the majority of the aristocracy of the time whose consciences had proven to have no fixed abode – in the space of little more than six years, he (like many others) had changed his religion three times.

Compared to the previous parliament summoned by St. Leger, this parliament was notable for the absence of the Gaelic Lords who had accepted English title. Only two of them attended: O'Brien of Thomond and Fitzpatrick of Ossory. Most of the attendees were Anglo-Irish or English from the expanding area of English control in Leinster and those Munster counties bordering it. Spiritual peers (bishops) were also thin on the ground, with around eleven attending, mostly from the area of the Pale. Most bishops from Gaelic-controlled areas opposed the Crown-imposed change of religion and stayed away like their temporal masters. Of those bishops who did attend, most accepted the change, while a few spoke out against them. The most strident of these was the former tutor of Gerald Fitzgerald, Thomas Leverous, who was now Bishop of Kildare. Along with Bishop Lacey of Limerick and Bishop William Walshe of Meath, Leverous was deprived of his see for his opposition. These bishops then had to go underground in order to minister to their dioceses while Bishop Walshe was later imprisoned for his efforts in this regard. In those parts of the country where English governance existed, the local bishop either complied or was replaced. Where Protestant bishops were appointed, these "reformed" bishops were mostly to prove a scandal to the people. Afraid that the reversion to Protestantism might prove to be temporary, many plundered their bishoprics for their own personal gain to such an extent that it resulted in the amalgamation of dioceses. Others were forced to return to England or were deprived of their sees for crimes such as forgery, drunkenness and adultery.[i]

---

[i] William Knight the Co-adjutor Bishop of Cashel "excited the scorn and derision of the people" by his public drunkenness and was forced to return to England. (Ware's "Irish Bishops p.484) Marmaduke Middleton of Waterford was translated to St. David's for the forgery of a will. (Peter Heylin's Examen Hist).

Initial Effects of the Reforms

The acts passed by this Parliament included the Act of Supremacy (whereby the Church IN Ireland became the Church OF Ireland, with the Queen instead of the Pope as head) and the Act of Uniformity which abolished the Roman Missal and imposed the Book of Common Prayer in English. Attendance at the new Protestant service was made compulsory with a series of recusancy fines followed by imprisonment for non-conformance. A third offence against these laws was considered to be treasonous. Some Catholics within the English-controlled areas tried to circumvent these laws by secretly attending Mass on Sunday morning and then going to the Protestant service on Sunday evening. However, before long the established church authorities became wise to this practice and attendance at the Sunday morning service was made mandatory, with a church warden calling a roll and making a note of any absences for further investigation.

The Act of Supremacy also included an oath to be administered to all government officials and clergy. Most Catholic clergy were forced to abandon their churches and go underground, with many receiving help from the gentry of the Pale. Some years later in a dispatch to Queen Elizabeth, Sir Henry Sidney wrote of the many churches in Meath that were falling into decay because their Catholic pastors were forced to abandon them.

Although this difference in religion between the native Irish and English officialdom was not as yet destined to play a decisive part in Ireland's affairs, it was yet another obstacle between the Gael and the Gall. Protestantism became synonymous with the interests of the English establishment,

---

Richard Dixon of Cloyne was deprived for adultery, "propter adulterium manifestum et confessum" (Gilbert's History of Dublin Vol 1, p.114).

with the words "Sasanach" (Saxon) and "Protestant" amounting to the same thing.

Shane "The Proud"

Gaelic Ulster
Since the decline of the Norman earldom of Ulster, there had been many changes in the governance of the province of Ulster. An offshoot of the Clan O'Néill who were descendants of Aedh Buidhe O'Néill had separated themselves from the main Clan O'Néill and emerged from mid-Ulster, moving northwest, retaking the large area between Larne and Lough Neagh and also North Down. Meanwhile, the Clan MacQuillan had abandoned Down, moving to the north coast around Coleraine. The new O'Néill territory was called Clandeboye (from the Irish "Clann de Buidhe" meaning "The Yellow Family"), while the territory of the MacQuillans was referred to as "The Route". Meanwhile, having been ejected from The Lordship of the Isles, the Gaelic Scottish MacDonnells had settled in the Glens of Antrim where they built many castles and were determined to make it their permanent home. Ulster was in effect the most Gaelic part of Ireland, and powerful too, since brave and fearless Scottish Gallowglass warriors provided a very strong backbone for the armies of the Gaelic lords of Ulster. At this time very little remained to the English in Ulster except a few ports and the abbey lands of Newry monastery that were now under the control of Sir Nicholas Bagenal. The English also counted on the passive loyalty of the O'Donnells of Tirconnell.

Shane – "The O'Néill"
When Con O'Néill died in 1559, Shane O'Néill[i] was inaugurated "The O'Néill" at the ancient O'Néill inauguration

---
[i] Shane was known to the English as "Seán an Díomais" or "Shane The Proud"

site at Tullyhoge in Tyrone, in contravention of English law. As this affront to Her Majesty could not be ignored, Sir Henry Sidney, who was acting Viceroy at the time, prepared his army to move against the new O'Néill and immediately advanced as far as Dundalk. After a few minor engagements and before moving much further northwards where he would undoubtedly meet the men of Tyrone and their allies in battle,[i] he sent a message to Shane summoning him to Dundalk to explain himself. Shane ignored the summons, perhaps convinced that his death would be the result of it and returned the messenger with an invitation of his own: he asked if Sidney would come to Tyrone and be sponsor to one of his children. Trusting to Shane's honour, Sidney agreed, and travelled to the court of the prince of the O'Néill. While there, Shane expounded at length on Gaelic succession and, while declaring his loyalty to the Crown, he argued that the English had no right to trample on the rights of the Gael or the Gaelic way of life. Sidney was initially impressed by Shane and his arguments and promised him that he would not attack him with his army. Instead, he would travel to London and relate to the Queen what they had discussed. However, when Sussex, who was the appointed Lord Deputy, returned from England and resumed his duties, he decided that Shane should be dealt with by force. After reinforcements were summoned from England, he attacked deep into Tyrone. Realising that his army was not yet large enough to meet this danger, Shane retreated into the forests and evaded him.

---

[i] As *de facto* Gaelic King of Ulster, Shane had secured the loyalty of Maguire of Fermanagh and MacMahon of Monaghan, as well as a host of the smaller chieftains. O'Reilly of Breifne later swore allegiance to him after O'Néill invaded his territory on hearing that he and O'Donnell of Tirconnell were conspiring with the Crown to isolate and weaken him

The O'Néill at the Court of Queen Elizabeth

By this stage, Queen Elizabeth had received Sidney's report and now intervened directly. O'Néill was invited to London, where he stayed from January to May 1562, bringing with him 600 gallowglass bodyguards as a precaution. According to the eyewitness at court, William Camden, these warriors came: "...armed with battle axes, bared headed, with flowing curls, yellow shirts dyed with saffron...large sleeves, short tunics and rough cloaks, whom the English followed with much wonderment as if they had come from China or America".[93]

Queen Elizabeth I

During his stay, Shane explained to Elizabeth the law of Gaelic succession which was also recorded at Court by Camden: "The surrender made by my father to Henry VIII and the grant which Henry made by letters patent, was of no value, since Conn had no estate in what he surrendered save for his own life, nor could he yield it without the consent of the chiefs and peoples by whom he had been chosen to the dignity of O'Neill. Such letters patent are of no avail unless the true head of the family is first approved by the oath of twelve men, which in this case was not done."[94]

O'Néill submitted to the Queen and made various promises to her, including that he would fight against the Scottish MacDonnells who were now firmly embedded along the Antrim coast.

By all accounts, Shane's first and only focus was to keep the land of the O'Néill intact and free from direct English influence, with himself as King. "My ancestors were Kings of Ulster and Ulster is mine and shall be mine"[95], was his motto. The Queen pardoned him, and promised to make him an Earl, but this was never officially confirmed, and he went back to Ulster regretting some of the concessions he had made to her. After his return, all remained quiet for a time, but Shane made no effort to carry out the Queen's will regarding the extension of English ways and customs in the northern province. After the English accused Shane of bad faith, the stage seemed set for a showdown. However, the Ulsterman now fielded a formidable army and Sidney reported to London: "He is able to bring into the field one thousand horsemen and four thousand foot. He is the only strong man of Ireland…he armeth and weaponeth all the peasants of his country, the first that ever did so of an Irishman".[96] The Queen knew that any war against O'Néill's army would be a costly affair and instructed Sussex to come to terms with Shane, allowing him the advantage until the time was right to deal with him. Shane was amenable to Sussex's approach, and in November of 1563 Sir Thomas Cusack came to his residence at Benburb and terms of peace favourable to O'Néill were agreed on.

The Battle of Glenshesk

Following this, all was again quiet until Shane decided to enter battle against the Scottish MacDonnells. His motivation is unclear. Perhaps it was his fulfilment of one of Queen Elizabeth's requests or the fact that the MacDonnells had long become a menacing neighbour, frequently raiding into the interior of Ulster, sometimes penetrating as far as Armagh. Following a series of raids on them by O'Néill's men, battle was joined between the two armies at Glenshesk, deep in the glens of Antrim on May 2nd, 1565. The result was a resounding victory for the Cenél Eoghan, with 700 men killed from the army of MacDonnell, including their Chieftain, James

MacDonnell, who died from his wounds after the battle while a prisoner of Shane. News of the victory was received with joy in London, but this joy quickly turned to anger when word came through that Shane refused to hand over his prisoners (which included the new MacDonnell Chieftain, James' brother Sorley Boy MacDonnell) to the English. When two messengers from the Queen arrived at his court, Shane was uncompromising: "...I never made peace with her but at her own seeking...O'Donnell shall never come into his country, nor Bagenall into Newry, nor Kildare into Dundrum or Lecale. They are now mine. With this sword I won them: with this sword I will keep them..."[97] The English now advertised a reward of 1,000 marks for Shane's capture or death and launched repeated but unsuccessful attacks on Tyrone.

At this time, Shane was active in trying to secure French help so that he could defeat the English in battle. He wrote to King Charles IX, saying that both he and his successors would be: "...humble subjects to the Crown of France"[98] in return for his assistance. He also wrote to the Cardinal of Lorraine stressing the religious aspect to his struggle: "in defence of the Romish faith"[99], beseeching him to act on his behalf with the French King. But the English were not to be the ones to deal Shane the fatal blow that led to his death, but his Gaelic neighbour and long time adversary of the Clan O'Néill – the Clan O'Donnell of Tirconnell.

Farsetmore – Shane O'Néill's Last Battle

For centuries, there had been enmity and frequent war between the O'Néill and the O'Donnell since the Clan O'Donnell refused to acknowledge the old O'Néill claim of overlordship of their kingdom. Shortly after Shane became the O'Néill, he had successfully attacked into the territory of O'Donnell and captured the Chieftain, Calvagh O'Donnell and his wife, the Dowager Countess of Argyle, who subsequently became his mistress. This act had further inflamed tensions between the two Clans and the O'Donnells had subsequently actively conspired with the English to destabilize Shane's rule. When Calvagh O'Donnell died in 1566, he was succeeded by his brother Hugh Dubh. As the new Chieftain of the Clan O'Donnell, he was, as tradition demanded, determined to draw his first blood against the men of Tyrone. After a number of successful raids into Tyrone by O'Donnell's men in 1567, Shane, determined to protect his kingdom from all comers, decided to retaliate.

After amassing a large army, he crossed the estuary of the River Swilly at low tide on May 8th, 1567 and attacked Hugh Dubh's army at Farsetmore (Ardnagarry). Despite having the smaller army, Hugh Dubh, with the hardy gallowglass of the Clan Sweeny in his force, not only prevailed but succeeded in routing Shane's troops. The Tyrone men retreated to the estuary shore only to find that the tide had come in. They were trapped. In the action that followed, there was huge slaughter caused both by sword and drowning. Shane's army was annihilated. In the confusion, Shane escaped, running along the north embankment of the Swilly until he finally found a crossing point at the ford of Scarriffhollis.

The Death of Shane O'Néill

Shane made his way back home, a broken man with his army in tatters. Unsure what to do, he decided to try to mend a broken fence and seek refuge with a former ally in an attempt to strengthen his hand by proposing a new alliance. This former ally was the MacDonnells who he had attacked and defeated at Glenshesk.

Having arranged a meeting with them at Cushendun, Antrim, he sent his prisoner Sorley Boy MacDonnell on ahead of him as a good will gesture and departed Tyrone with his mistress[i] and a small bodyguard of his gallowglass warriors. Unknown to him, the MacDonnells had an English agent in their camp, a certain Captain Pierse who successfully aroused the anger of the Scotsmen against O'Néill. Shane had previously been their ally, he argued, and then defeated them with great loss. Now he was daring to seek refuge among them.

On his arrival on June 2nd, 1567, Shane was graciously received by the MacDonnells and a great banquet was held. During the banquet, he was drawn into a pre-arranged argument during which numbers of the Scotsmen rushed him, stabbing him and his bodyguard to death. His body was then thrown into a pit where it was subsequently retrieved by Captain Pierse who brought it to Dublin where he claimed the reward of 1,000 marks. In Dublin, the head was severed from the body and publicly displayed on a spike mounted on one of the towers of Dublin Castle. It was without doubt a lamentable and wretched end for this Captain of Tyrone. After his death, a Bill of Attainder was formally served against him, and the territory of the Clan O'Néill was formally confiscated by the Crown. Despite being encouraged by Sidney to confiscate the whole province and use the territory to create shires after the English fashion, Elizabeth declined since the native Irish of Ulster were still far too strong to attempt something of that magnitude. With the acquiescence of the English government, Shane's

---

[i] English histories of the period have traditionally dwelt on Shane's immorality in living with a mistress.
In his defence, he was renowned for his sense of law and order in his territory and also his charity and almsgiving. If money was taken from a poor person by robbery, he used to make good the loss out of his own pocket if the thief could not be found. One of his guests, Edward Campion, who later wrote a history of Ireland, wrote of Shane O'Néill: "Sitting at meate before he put one morsel in his mouth he used to slice a portion above the dayly almes and send it namely to some beggar at his gate saying it was meete to serve Christ first".

Tánaiste and second cousin Turlough Luineach O'Néill now assumed governance of Tyrone.

Chapter 14

Rebellion, Massacre and Plantation

Enforcing the New Religion

Since the Reformation Parliament of 1560, little progress had been made in Ireland with regard to the religious reforms introduced by Queen Elizabeth. Among the Gael there were few adherents, while among the old English there was considerable resistance. However, even if the adherents of the new religion were few, where the writ of the English administration ran, there were always willing government officials who enacted the policies of the Crown, proscribing priests, closing churches and shutting down those monasteries that had reopened under the reign of Queen Mary. During the reign of King Henry VIII, the common man had not been greatly affected by his takeover of the church primacy as the question of papal supremacy was not something that troubled him, but now altars were being replaced by tables and the Mass in Latin with both priest and people facing east was replaced by a communion service in English with the minister facing the people. This was something which even the common man felt was not right, and a feeling of unease gradually transformed into a general sense of anger, not just among the Gael but also among the old English, most of whom refused to adhere to the dictates of the Crown.

The Irish Catholic Church that was being steadily dispossessed at home was already flourishing abroad. New bishops were being appointed for vacant sees and colleges for the training of priests for Ireland were being set up all over Catholic Europe. The challenges posed by Protestantism in its various forms were now being met head-on as the teachings of the Council of Trent were disseminated. The laxity that had prevailed before was replaced by a new zeal, determination and energy which was injected into candidates for the priesthood, numbers of whom were already returning to these shores. The Catholic zeal of these men was later remarked upon by the Elizabethan poet (and author of "The Faerie Queen"), Edmund Spenser, when he contrasted it with the laxity of the ministers of the new religion: "Wherein it is great wonder to see the odds between the zeal of Popish priests and the ministers of the gospel. For they spare not to come out of Spain and from Rome by long toil and dangerous travelling, where they know the peril of death awaiteth them and no reward or riches are to be found, only to draw the people unto the Church of Rome: whereas some of our idle ministers having the livings of the country offered unto them without pains and without peril, will neither for the same nor any love of God nor zeal of religion be drawn forth from their warm nests..."[100]

The underground schooling of the Irish, some of whom would escape abroad to study abroad for the priesthood was attested to by the English Catholic Priest Edmund Campion (who was martyred in England in 1581) in his History of Ireland published in 1571: "They (the Irish) are sharp witted, lovers of learning, capable of any study...they speak latin like a vulgar tongue...I have seen them where they kept school, ten in some one chamber, grovelling upon couches of straw their books at their noses, lying themselves flat prostrate, and so chant out their lessons..."[101]

The Gaelic Order under Threat

On departing England at the end of 1565 in order to replace Sussex as Irish Lord Deputy, Sir Henry Sidney was given his instructions. As well as advancing the Anglicisation of Ireland on all fronts, he was particularly instructed to find the best means necessary to advance the cause of Protestantism in Ireland. With regard to the first of his tasks, he commanded those Gaelic Lords who had previously submitted but had failed to replace Irish customs for English ways, to remedy this situation and also to accept monetary payment as rent from their subjects instead of the various other methods of payment that were traditional and to which they were accustomed. He also re-introduced the policy of "Surrender and Regrant" for those Gaelic Lords who had not previously availed of it, but, it seems, without demanding any submission to the Queen with regard to the Act of Supremacy. By this stage, the policy of "Surrender and Regrant" was viewed by the Crown as a type of conveyance whereby lands in Gaelic control were brought under the control of the Crown, and then confiscated by it. Some years later Lord Mountjoy was to write of the policy: "...The titles of our honours do rather weaken than strengthen them (the Gaelic Lords)."[102]

War between the Earls of Ormond and Desmond

With regard to the advancement of the cause of Protestantism, Sidney decided that the best approach was to introduce a penal code. In order to give it legal force, a parliament would need to be called. But this was not immediately possible due to the terribly destructive war across the breadth of the country between the Earls of Ormond and Desmond, as well as a more minor conflict between the Earl of Clanrickard and his sons, in which various Gaelic Chieftains took sides.[i]

The conflict between Desmond and Ormond originated, not only in a dispute over land, but also in the age-old enmity between them which was exacerbated by the introduction of Protestantism. Ormond, who had stayed loyal to the government's position, had become Protestant whereas Desmond had remained Catholic and as such was much out of favour with the Crown. When Thomas, Earl of Ormond visited London in 1562, he received the Queen's blessing for his plan to defeat and take over the land of Desmond after telling her that he would pay her all feudal dues and suppress all Gaelic ways and laws, especially in relation to the bards. The latter, according to Ormond, "by their ditties and rhymes in commendation of extortions, rebellion, rape and ravin[ii] do encourage lords and gentlemen."[103]

In 1567, in order to restore peace among the warring parties, Sidney embarked with his army on a tour of the affected areas and employed a policy of ruthless severity towards them, capturing and imprisoning many but also hanging countless others. Of the state of Munster he wrote: "Like as I never was in a more pleasant country in all my life, so never saw I a more waste and desolate land...such horrible and lamentable spectacles are there to behold as the burning of villages, the ruin of churches the wasting of such as have been good towns and castles; yea, the view of bones and skulls of the dead subjects who, partly by murder, partly by famine, have died in the fields, as in troth hardly any Christian with dry eyes could behold."[104] With regard to the cause of the turmoil, he was unequivocal, blaming the governments "cowardly policy"[105]

---

[i] It was during this conflict that perhaps the largest abbey in Ireland, at Athassel near Golden in Co. Tipperary was burnt. The abbey was being used by Ormond as a base for his soldiers and was attacked by a force of men from Desmond.
[ii] plunder

that would "keep them (Ormond and Desmond) in continual dissension for fear lest through their quiet might follow I wot not what."[106]

Sidney, however, was not impartial in his pursuit of the malefactors. As Munster's Catholics looked to Desmond for leadership in resisting Queen Elisabeth's Protestant reforms, Sidney arrested him and left his brother John Fitzgerald to govern in his place. But John in turn was captured by Ormond, who sent him to London, and both brothers ended up in the Tower there until 1573. James Fitzmaurice, Desmond's first cousin, now took it on himself to lead the Munster Geraldines.

The First Geraldine Rebellion

<u>The Parliament of 1568</u>

With affairs in Ireland seemingly pacified, Sidney called a parliament towards the end of 1568 which met on the 17th of January 1569. It was once more badly attended by those Gaelic Lords who had accepted English noble titles. For the first time, an organised Catholic opposition of old English now appeared. This was led by Sir Edmund Butler who, unlike his younger brother the Earl, was a man of religious conviction and not just political expediency. When Sidney tried to introduce his anti-Catholic measures, the Catholic opposition pointed out that the legislation had not been submitted to London as Poynings law demanded. They did so in the knowledge that this measure would considerably lengthen the whole procedure. Sidney faced such resistance in this matter that he was forced to accept that he could not achieve the Queen's wishes. However, in all other matters the Parliament was wholly subservient. Other measures introduced by Sidney included a bill that legally extinguished the name of O'Néill, so that the Clan O'Néill would "only depend upon your imperial crown of England and yield to the same their subjection, obedience and services for ever"[107] and a parliamentary grant for the maintenance of the army so that "coign and livery" could no longer be demanded. State schools were also to be established in the country's dioceses, whose teachers were by law to be English Protestants.

English Intentions Laid Bare

However, it was three other measures introduced by Sidney that would spell the greatest threat to the Gael and would lay bare the intentions which the English had for Ireland. The first of these was the division or "shiring" of all lands into counties after the English fashion. The implications of this measure were spelled out in a further act which was introduced for "taking away captainships and all exactions belonging thereunto from all lords and great men of this realm exercising absolute and regal authority within large circuits"[108] (which basically meant reducing the areas controlled by the Old English and Gaelic Lords). That these two measures were announced at this stage, even before the English had the power to enforce them, was due in no small part to the destructive land war that had taken place during the preceding five years. But it was also a shot across the bow for the Gaelic Lords as it signalled a dangerous English intent: the end of the external structure of large Gaelic territories and, consequently, of their ruling families, many of whom, the English knew, would not abandon the governance of their patrimony without a struggle. The last measure involved the introduction of presidencies in Munster and Connacht, the aim of which was to basically create two new "Pales" outside the existing Pale until all three could be united under English governmental control. These presidencies would have the power to override the local lords by their central decision-making and would speedily advance the Anglicisation of both provinces by rooting out Gaelic law and customs. The first appointed President of Munster was Sir

John Perrot (who was reputed to be an illegitimate son of King Henry VIII) while that of Connacht was Sir Edward Fitton.

These parliamentary acts signalled the arrival of a new breed of English adventurer in Ireland whose aim was to capitalize on the measures introduced by Sidney by claiming a slice from the areas of control he proposed to carve up. One of these new arrivals was Sir Peter Carew who claimed before the Council that he was the heir of the old Norman family of Fitzstephen. As such, he maintained that Carlow (which was then partly in the possession of the Gaelic Kavanagh family and partly under the control of Sir Edmund Butler) was his. Carew's claim had previously been made by an earlier generation of his family during the reign of King Edward III but had been rejected after investigation. This time, the Council (which was overly anxious to speedily advance its Anglicisation program) had no problem finding in his favour. Already weakened by their chieftain's acceptance of English title, the Kavanagh Clans had split into factions and so were in no position to resist. The same could not be said of Sir Edmund Butler who took great exception to the Council's decision and was determined to fight it.

Rebellion in Munster

News of the Parliament's proceedings caused great dismay around the country and when the newly appointed President of Munster, Sir John Perrot, declared the Earl of Desmond's "Liberty of Kerry" (control of Kerry) to be null and void, the stage was then set for the first Desmond revolt. As a reaction to the proceedings in Dublin, James Fitzmaurice, the *de facto* head of the Munster Geraldines, sent messengers to all the Gaelic Chieftains of Munster, summoning them to assist him in defence of faith and fatherland. Those who responded were joined by MacCarthy Mór of Cork (as Carew also laid claim to half of Cork) as well as Sir Edmund Butler who took up his sword saying: "I do not make war against the Queen but against those who banish Ireland and mean conquest."[109] Butler also persuaded his younger brothers Pierce and Edward to enter into this new Geraldine League. Messengers including the Archbishop of Cashel and Desmond's youngest brother James were sent to Rome to see what assistance could be garnered there. The alliance now attacked in many directions and caused much damage. Enniscorthy was overrun, as were the English settlements of Queen's County (Laois) but wherever there was a substantial English garrison (such as at Kilkenny), the alliance had no answer to English artillery and were defeated.

Slaughter of the Innocents

After the Battle of Kilkenny, Sidney set out for Munster on a punitive expedition with a large English army under the command of Colonel Sir Humphrey Gilbert. One after the other, the southern province's rebel strongholds were captured and their inhabitants, including women and children, were slaughtered, an action that Gilbert specifically recommended saying that: "the men of war could not be maintained without their churls and calliackes, old women and those women who milked their creaghts (cows) and provided their victuals and other necessaries, so that the killing of them by the sword was the way to kill the men of war by famine."[110]

A contemporary of Gilbert's wrote of him that while he was on campaign in Munster: "...his manner was that the heads of all those which were killed in the day should be cut off from their bodies and brought to the place where he encamped at night and should there be laid on the ground by each side of the way leading into his own tent, so that none should come into his tent for any cause but commonly he must pass through a lane of heads, which he used to terrorize – the dead feeling nothing more the pains thereby. And yet it did bring great terror to the people when they saw the heads of their dead fathers, brothers, children, kinsfolk and friends lie on the ground before their faces".[111]

The End of the Rebellion
Carew, who was eager to secure for himself the castles and territory of Sir Edmond Butler, stayed in Leinster where he successfully captured Cloghrenan Castle. While many of his adherents fell victim to Sidney, Fitzmaurice himself managed to avoid capture and death, successfully escaping to the Glen of Aherlow in the Galty mountains from where he attacked and destroyed the English garrison at Kilmallock in the Spring of 1571 with a large force of the Earl of Desmond's gallowglasses from the Clann Sweeney and Clann Sheehy. Perrot determined to, as he put it, "hunt the fox out of his hole"[112] and scoured the Galtee Mountains with a large force. Nevertheless, Fitzmaurice and his army still remained at large. His sources of supply were now attacked and cut off, and Perrot destroyed all his castles. After another attack on Kilmallock in 1573, which by now was rebuilt and reoccupied by the English, Fitzmaurice's force (suffering no doubt from hunger and the hardships of bad quarters) was heavily depleted. There was nothing left for him but surrender to the Lord Deputy in the ruins of the church of Kilmallock. The Earl of Desmond and his brother were then released from the Tower of London, but on their arrival in Dublin, the former was rearrested on some pretext. The rebellion of the Munster Geraldines was now over but Fitzmaurice, who had escaped to the continent, became determined that there should be a second.

Rebellion Provoked in Connacht
Meanwhile in Connacht, the new President of the province Sir Edward Fitton was succeeding in making enemies of all. His

manner was one of overbearing insolence and high-handedness towards everyone and he quickly succeeded in arousing the fury of both Gael and old English alike. After Fitton arrested the Earl of Clanrickard in 1572, following a failed bid to arrest his two sons, the sons took up arms against him and, joined by many of the disaffected and a large contingent of hired gallowglass mercenaries, they crossed the Shannon into Athlone and destroyed much of the English garrison town. After the Earl was released, their revolt died down and Clanrickard succeeded in having Fitton replaced, following a bitter complaint to the new Lord Deputy Sir William Fitzwilliam with regard to his incarceration and Fitton's methods.[i]

An English Plantation Attempted in Ulster
The Plantation of Sir Thomas Smyth
With affairs now progressing to her satisfaction in Munster and Connacht, Queen Elizabeth and her advisors now turned their minds to Ulster. That plantation of the province by the English was her aim cannot be doubted, as even during the rule of Shane O'Néill, she had remarked that his revolt served her well since in the long run it would leave more land for those who would be loyal to her. In 1570, her secretary Sir Thomas Smyth was granted the district of Ards in County Down, the area being described in her grant as "...parts of Her Highness's Earldom of Ulster...inhabited with a wicked, barbarous and uncivil people...some Scottish and some wild Irish and such as lately had been rebellious to her."[113] Smyth dispatched his illegitimate son who was also named Thomas to settle the area

---

[i] Even by English standards Fitton's conduct was so reprehensible that when his replacement Sir Nicholas Malby was appointed, he was referred to as *Colonel* of Connacht and not *President* of Connacht as Fitton had brought the title into such widespread disrepute.

along with a group of planters but the native O'Néills of Clandeboye did not take kindly to the new arrivals, and Smyth's son was killed shortly afterwards during a battle with them, after which the other settlers of the party struggled to gain ground.

Mass Extermination of the Irish in North East Ulster

A much larger enterprise was now entered into by the English, whereby a huge area incorporating the territories of Clandeboye, the Glens, Rathlin Island and the Route were granted to Walter Devereux, Earl of Essex. Essex arrived in the summer of 1573 with 1,200 soldiers, planning to eject not just the Scottish MacDonnells, but the O'Néills of Clandeboye as well. His intention was that after the "pacification" of the area was complete, his soldiers would then become planters, receiving a grant of land of between 200 and 400 acres. Despite the strength of his force, Essex was entering difficult territory, and the O'Néills of Clandeboye under their Chieftain Brian O'Néill succeeded in making life extremely difficult for Essex and his troops, attacking and continuously harassing them in unfavourable terrain. Essex became enraged by their tactics and now turned his attention to the inhabitants of the area. He began depopulating the entire countryside not only by fire and sword but also by starvation, destroying all those crops that his men did not need. Huge numbers of the Scottish MacDonnells were also massacred in order to clear the land, the most notorious case being the Rathlin Island massacre on July 26th, 1575. The MacDonnells had a garrisoned castle there but apart from that the island was used by them as a sanctuary for their women, children, elderly and infirm. After the castle on the island surrendered to Sir Francis Drake, the garrison of 200 men was obliterated in revenge for the casualties that the English had suffered. Then an English force under the command of Sir John Norris[i] scoured the island and its caves, brutally murdering around 400 civilians.[ii] Following this action, Norris received an army promotion from Queen Elizabeth while Essex was summoned to court for a special audience with her so that she could personally commend him for his actions.

The Murder of Brian O'Néill of Clandeboye

In spite of his campaign of murder and destruction, Essex was still unable to gain the upper hand in his battle with the O'Néills. Finally, he decided to enter negotiations with them, and a peace accord was reached. Following the signing of the peace treaty, Lord Essex invited Brian O'Néill and his court to a banquet. What followed is recorded in The Annals of the Four Masters: "…As they were agreeably drinking and merry making, Brian, his brother, and his wife were seized upon by the earl, and all his people put to the sword, men, women, youths, and maidens, in Brian's own presence…Brian was afterwards sent to Dublin, together with his wife and brother, where they were cut in quarters."[114]

After such an unspeakable outrage on the part of the English, no peace could be countenanced by the Irish. Essex, now forced to prepare for a full renewal of his war against the O'Néill's found his ranks greatly depleted as he had already lost a good number of his men, killed or wounded in battle, while others who were unfit or unprepared for his bloody campaign against non-combatants had returned to England.

---

[i] Mountnorris in Co. Armagh is named after him.

[ii] The wife and children of Sorley Boy MacDonnell died in the massacre. Francis Walsingham, secretary to Queen Elizabeth received a letter from Essex who reported that according to one of his spies, Sorley Boy had watched helplessly from the mainland and was "like to run made from sorrow, turning and tormenting himself, and saying that he had then lost all that ever he had"

He appealed to Queen Elizabeth for more men for the campaign but was turned down and eventually his efforts ground to a halt and he moved to Dublin. He died in Dublin on the 22nd of September 1576 apparently after having been poisoned.[i]

The Mullaghmast Massacre
"Righteous" Rory Og O'More

Since the initial efforts at plantation during the reign of Mary and Philip, Queen's County (Leix or Laois) and King's County (Offaly) had remained a battle ground where the native Gaelic families had stubbornly refused to let go of their patrimony despite decades of persecution. Sidney, who had resumed the position of Lord Deputy, wrote of the situation in both counties to the Council of State on December 15th, 1575, warning them that future plantations should be enacted more aggressively: "... Both countries[ii] (Leix and Offaly) are much spoiled and wasted, by the race and offspring of the old native inhabitors which grow great, and increase in number...This may be an example how the like hereafter is attempted, considering the charge is so great, and the honour and profit so small, to win lands from the Irishry so dearly, as these two counties have been to the crown".[115] After Sidney had written to the Council, a new danger to the English plantation now appeared in the form of the Chieftain of the O'Mores' – Rory Óg O'More. By his actions, he imitated Art Mac Murrough Kavangh for he struck fear into the hearts of the planters with his campaign of despoliation of English property, his band of men being more than a match for the English garrisons who guarded the

---

[i] Apparently the poisoning of Essex took place at the behest of the Earl of Leicester who coveted Essex's wife. Shortly after Essex's death, Leicester divorced his own wife and married Essex's widow.

[ii] Counties or petty kingdoms were generally referred to as "countries"

plantation settlements and the borders of the Pale proper. The best recorded exploit of his campaign took place on Christmas Eve of 1577, when after raiding villages in Offaly, he and his men made for the town of Naas in Kildare, the inhabitants of which traditionally celebrated Christmas Eve as the town's feast-day. The people of Naas had spent the day merry-making and as a result were much inebriated and completely off their guard. Rory O'More and his band approached the town with torches and, having successfully gained entry through its unguarded gates, they set about burning the low thatches of the planter's dwellings, the inhabitants of which were in no fit state to pursue the outlaw and his band. In time, many of the planters despaired of sufficient English protection to render their lives peaceful and returned to England. In consequence, the native inhabitants regained much of their land with the remaining planters being forced to barricade themselves inside guarded dwellings. The English government placed the culpability for this state of affairs at the planters' own door, blaming them for failing to account for their own defence by maintaining horsemen and footmen, which they were obliged to do as a condition of their plantation.

Mass Murder at Mullaghmast

When it became clear to the authorities that the very existence of their plantation settlements was under threat, a horrific outrage was committed by the English, the idea being that it would serve as a warning to others not to resist. At the end of December 1577, or on January 1st 1578, members of the Gaelic families of the seven Clans of Laois (the O'Mores, O'Kelly's, O'Lalors, Devoys, Macaboys, O'Dorans and O'Dowlings, along with some members of the Keating and Dunne family) were summoned with the knowledge of Lord Deputy Sidney and in the name and under the protection of Queen Elizabeth to a meeting with the English under the command of the Governor of Laois, Captain Francis Cosby, at the Rath of Mullaghmast, five miles from Athy in Kildare. By this time, Cosby already had a fearful reputation among the Irish of Laois, ruling them in a cruel tyrannical fashion, in which he was equalled by his son Alexander. Residing in the town of Stradbally where he had been granted a house and grounds which had belonged to the now dispossessed Franciscan order, he had an elm tree in his garden whose branches were all too frequently graced by the ropes which broke the necks of the local Irish. Cosby despised Catholics and took special delight in torturing them.[116] However, those summoned to Mullaghmast were not at war with the English or sought by them, and were called there on pretence of being of service to the Crown. Around 400 people assembled for the meeting and what followed is best described by quoting directly from the Annals of The Four Masters: "A horrible and abominable act of treachery was committed by the English of Leinster and Meath upon that part of the people of Offaly and Leix that remained in confederacy with them, and under their protection. It was effected thus: they were all summoned to show themselves, with the greatest number they could be able to bring with them, at the great rath of Mullach-Maistean; and on their arrival at that place they were surrounded on every side by four lines of soldiers and cavalry, who proceeded to shoot and slaughter them without mercy, so that not a single individual escaped, by flight or force."[117]

The veracity of this account was confirmed by an English officer, Captain Thomas Lee, who, in a memorial to Queen Elizabeth in 1594 entitled "A Brief Declaration of the Government of Ireland" (which is preserved in Trinity College, Dublin), mentioned among other acts of oppression and cruelty committed by the English in Ireland the massacre at Mullaghmast: "They have drawn unto them by protection three or four hundred of those country people under colour to do your Majesty service and brought them to a place of meeting where your garrison soldiers were appointed to be, who have there most dishonourably put them all to the sword and this hath been by the consent and practice of the Lord Deputy for the time being."[118]

After having served four terms as Lord Deputy, Sir Henry Sidney was replaced at his own behest by Sir William Drury on May 26th, 1578.

The Second Rebellion of the Munster Geraldines
<u>Fitzmaurice seeks help for Ireland</u>

After James Fitzmaurice escaped with his family to France, he made his home at St. Malo where he could easily have spent the rest of his days in peace. However, the fate of Ireland's governance and Catholicism was not something that he could willingly abandon, so he determined to seek help for Ireland in the courts of Catholic Europe. At this time, both France and Spain were at peace with England and were unwilling to disturb the status quo for Ireland's sake.

At the court of Philip II of Spain, he received no more than a recommendation that he should take his cause to Rome and the court of Pope Gregory XIII. Having left his sons in Spain, James Fitzmaurice went to Rome where he was warmly received by the Pope. Already in February of 1570, Pope Pius V had declared Queen Elizabeth an excommunicate and absolved all men from obedience to her, but Pope Gregory now went further and furnished Fitzmaurice with a Papal Edict declaring that Queen Elizabeth was no longer queen of England because of her heresy. In this document, Fitzmaurice recognised a powerful tool which he could use to draw the Catholics of Ireland to his banner. By way of material help, the Pope assigned to Ireland's cause, money, three ships and 700 soldiers, with the English adventurer Thomas Stukely as commander. Stukely, (who professed Ireland's cause dear to his heart) departed Civita Vecchia with his battle group, making first for the Port of Lisbon where he was to meet Fitzmaurice who was returning by the land route through Spain as he wished to go once more to the Court of Philip II in order to try and persuade him to give some additional help to that which he had received from the Pope. While in Spain, Fitzmaurice also purchased a number of small vessels and set sail for Lisbon with a very small contingent of around eighty Spanish soldiers that he had received from Philip II. However, the Spanish King also promised him that he would later send an expedition to Ireland.

Meanwhile, Stukely had arrived in Lisbon, where his spirit of adventure was being taken advantage of by the Portuguese. A knight errant who sought out the greatest glory, he allowed himself to be persuaded by King Sebastian of Portugal to first partake in his expedition to Morocco, stating that afterwards he would allocate him a much larger force for the Irish expedition, perhaps even leading the expedition himself. In Morocco, the Italian troops that should have been fighting in Ireland were instead annihilated at the Battle of Alcazar along with King Sebastian. Stukely himself was also killed early in the battle when both of his legs were severed from his body by a cannonball.

Fitzmaurice, doubtless distraught at the desertion of Stukely with the majority of his troops and all his money, nevertheless decided to proceed with his mission and departed for Ireland with his small force of Spanish and those Italians who had travelled with him over land. He was accompanied by Patrick O'Haly, the Bishop of Mayo, Cornelius Ryan, who was the Bishop of Killaloe, Rev. Dr. Nicholas Saunders, the Papal Legate, a Jesuit, Dr. William Allen, and a friar named Oviedo who was the chaplain to the small Spanish contingent. In order that the local chieftains and Geraldines in Kerry should have news of his imminent arrival, Fitzmaurice sent Bishop O'Haly on ahead of him, accompanied by Fr. Cornelius O'Rourke. On landing at Dingle, both men were shortly afterwards arrested as spies, tortured and executed.

The Rebellion is Launched

Fitzmaurice and his force arrived in Dingle on July 18th, 1579, and made their base on the opposite side of the promontory at Dunamore Fort (also known as "The Fort of Gold" from the Gaelic "Dún an Óir", to the English and called the "Fort del Ore" by the Spaniards) near Smerwick harbour where they fortified the area and prepared it for a further hoped-for Spanish landing. News of their arrival spread and aroused excitement and trepidation throughout Munster where the people were called on to join them. James Fitzmaurice issued a proclamation concerning "the justice of the war which he wageth in Ireland for the faith,"[119] stating: "Therefore now we fight not against the lawful sceptre...but against a tyrant which refuseth to hear Christ..."[120] James and John Fitzgerald, the brothers of the Earl of Desmond, both joined Fitzmaurice along with some of the Gaelic gentry including Domhnall MacCarthy Mór but many stood back and declared for Queen Elizabeth instead, including Cormac MacCarthy of Muskerry who was Sheriff of Cork and Brian O'Brien of Carrigogunnell. The Earl of Desmond also stood aloof from the rebels as he was fearful of being returned to the Tower of

James Fitzmaurice Fitzgerald

London and losing his position as Earl. However, his refusal to join the rebellion did not avail him among the English authorities, as, eager to be rid of him they constantly made it clear that they suspected his complicity. By their professed doubts and continuous false accusations against him, he seemed damned either way.

As news of the landing spread, more help arrived for Fitzmaurice from farther afield. As two hundred men from the Clan O'Flaherty came by sea from the coast of Connacht to answer his call for help, they were just in time to watch an English naval battle group from Kinsale under the command of Captain Courtenay destroy all of Fitzmaurice's ships. After witnessing this spectacle, the O' Flahertys turned around and retreated back to Connacht, as in their eyes the rebellion seemed doomed to fail. The rebel base at Smerwick was now in danger of being cut off and its defenders decided to abandon it and move inland where the three leaders, James Fitzmaurice and the brothers Fitzgerald split up, each taking a division of their troops with them.

The Death of Fitzmaurice

Fitzmaurice headed for Connacht where he hoped to gather more support for the rebel cause. As he passed through Castleconnell outside Limerick, he replaced some of his worn out horses with those of one William Burke, who on learning of this sent his two sons after him to reclaim them. When they caught up with Fitzmaurice, an argument ensued in which the latter was fired on and wounded, at which point he rushed the two brothers and ran his sword through both of them, killing them. The wounded Fitzmaurice died shortly afterwards with his chaplain Fr. Alan in attendance. The rebellion had suffered a serious blow, having lost its instigator and chief organiser.

John Fitzgerald now assumed command and, having travelled throughout Munster, he assembled a large army, many of whose members had deserted the forces of the Earl of Desmond. For the English, Sir William Drury, accompanied by Sir Nicholas Malbie, was also traversing Munster trying to summon all native and Anglo-Irish gentry to be loyal to the Queen and it was often the case that those who would have preferred to fight for the rebels were caught unawares and ended up being corralled into the government army through fear of what would befall their families and homes if they refused.

Part of Drury's army was now sent to search for John Fitzgerald and found him in command of a large force at Springfield in south Limerick. Battle was joined and the rebels won the day with the English force of some three hundred men under Captains Herbert and Price being annihilated, a success which gave the rebels great heart. Shortly after this battle, the Lord Deputy Sir William Drury fell sick at his encampment outside Kilmallock. After handing command of the army over to Malbie, he left for Waterford where he died on September 30th. Sir William Pelham, recently arrived from England, was appointed the new Lord Deputy.

The Battle of Manister

In England, news of the rebellion had been quickly acted on and a fleet of ships with 600 soldiers under the command of Sir John Perrott was dispatched to the port of Waterford. Meanwhile, Malbie determined to defeat the previously victorious army of John of Desmond and, having mustered all available forces, left Kilmallock for Limerick. As he approached Limerick around the beginning of October, he learned the location of John's army – the plains near the Abbey of Manister close to Croom. The Abbey itself was still active, although on a small scale, and a number of Augustinian monks resided there. By this time, many untrained Gaelic Irishmen had come out to swell the ranks of the rebels, and the foreign officers whom John Fitzgerald had placed in command of his army had succeeded in transforming them into an effective fighting force. When battle was joined, they twice managed to break the English line and the English were twice forced to retreat and reform before they finally prevailed. The Irish were in turn forced to retreat, with many of the Gallowglass Clan Sheehy accounting for their almost 300 dead. Malbie now turned his attention to the nearby abbey where the Irish wounded had taken shelter and, after shelling it with his artillery, his men advanced killing everyone they found both inside the abbey and in its precincts, including the Augustinian monks. The area was officially under the control of the Earl of Desmond and in order to provoke him into joining the rebels Malbie proceeded to destroy the entire district, burning the Abbey of Askeaton and the towns of Adare and Rathkeale. He also sent detachments of troops to occupy all of the Earl's castles in the surrounding area.

The Earl of Desmond joins the Rebels

After the arrival into the area of Sir William Pelham and the Earls of Ormond and Kildare, a message was sent to Desmond summoning him to their camp. He refused to comply, fearing for his own safety. Ormond, who was Commander in Chief of the army, now accused Desmond of harbouring the Papal Nuncio, Dr Nicholas Saunders (an Englishman), and called on him to hand him over. Desmond replied with a letter refuting the accusations made against him, after which Pelham declared him a traitor and immediately invaded Kerry and appointed Ormond Governor of Munster. Sir Nicholas Malbie returned to England where he reported to Queen Elizabeth that he "had hanged over four hundred people in Munster alone for the sake of peace".[121] Faced with this ruthlessness and well aware that he was already a "dead man walking", Desmond was now left with no choice but to join the rebellion.

While the English under Ormond savaged Kerry, burning its towns and villages and slaughtering its inhabitants, Desmond and his brothers invaded Cork where they captured Youghal after the men of the Gaelic Chieftain of the Bere Peninsula, O'Sullivan Bere, gained entry to the town by scaling its walls. The town was then burned to the ground. Ormond followed them, moving south through Cork and then north through Cashel, treating all areas inhabited by the native Irish as rebel areas with his declared policy of "burning every house and every stack of corn".[122]

As 1580 began, the English, who were now much reinforced, determined to take full advantage of the rebellion and planned not just to crush it, but to depopulate Munster by fire and sword with an eye to the future plantation. The rebels, some of whom were now in winter quarters in Desmond's castles, had no answer to this overwhelming force. Pelham set out with his army from Dublin for Limerick while Ormond marched on Cork, with a meeting between the two armies arranged for the Slieve Mis Mountains close to Tralee. The advance of the two English armies was marked by a path of total destruction and massacre of the native population, with neither women, children or the elderly being spared, and those that could fled into the forests and mountains even though it was the depths of Winter. Around this time, the rebels lost another of their leaders when James Fitzgerald was captured in Cork by the brother of MacCarthy, the Sheriff, and was afterwards hung drawn and quartered by Sir Walter Raleigh.

The Battle of Carrigafoyle Castle

After meeting outside Tralee without having had any major engagement with the rebels, the English now decided to head north to Carrigafoyle Castle (near Ballylongford) on the southern bank of the Shannon estuary. The Castle, which was known as the "Guardian of the Shannon" as its control was essential to the safe passage of shipping from Limerick to the Atlantic, was occupied by a force loyal to Desmond of 50 Irish and nineteen Spanish soldiers along with a number of women and children. The fortress was under the command of an Italian Officer, Count Julio. The huge English force that approached the castle was supported by a naval group under the command of Admiral Sir William Winter and their naval cannon made a large breach in the wall after two days of bombardment. Repeated attacks by the English foundered but finally succeeded after the castle's west wall collapsed, crushing many of the defenders, and the English soldiers commanded by Captains Zouch and Mackworth poured in. When the battle was over, there were six Irish and Spanish still alive as well as the Italian Count Julio, the rest of the defenders and inhabitants of the castle having been put to the sword. Julio and his six companions, including at least one woman, were later hanged in the English camp. On hearing of the fate of Carrigafoyle, other rebel garrisons including Ballyloughnane and Askeaton abandoned their forts in the sure knowledge that they would be next. The barbarity of the English forces knew no bounds for it is recorded that, following Carrigafoyle, Askeaton was occupied by Lord Deputy Pelham where an elderly man named Wall from Dunmoylan, who was blind since birth, and a man over 100 years of age, named Supple from Kilmacow were amongst those brutally murdered.[123]

Irish Victory at Glenmalure
During the summer of 1580, the insurgency received new energy. A large Irish army under the chieftain of the Clan Byrne, Fiach MacHugh O'Byrne, was mustered in Wicklow and was joined by James FitzEustace (Viscount Baltinglass) who, despite being numbered among the loyal English gentry of the Pale, now felt it his duty to take up his sword both in

defence of the Catholic Faith[i] and out of horror for the English policy being so brutally enacted in Munster. There was also an upsurge in activity in support of the rebels in the midlands. Rory Og O'More had reformed his fighting force and was once more very active in his attacks against the English, and was killed in one of these engagements. The extension of the rebellion into Leinster coincided with the arrival of a newly-appointed Lord Deputy, Lord Arthur Grey deWilton, who arrived in Howth on August 12th. Throwing caution to the wind, he decided to immediately take on the Wicklow insurgents and with a large army, headed for their reported rebel base at the Pass of Glenmalure. His lack of prudence did not however extend to his own person, for when the English arrived at the entrance to the defile where the rebels were reportedly located he remained there with Sir George Carew and the Earl of Kildare. His army, whose officers included the criminal Captain Francis Cosby (who was killed in the engagement), advanced about half a mile through the soft ground that was overlooked on either side by forested hills. From both sides of the defile, the English suddenly came under intense musket fire, which threw them into disarray. The firing suddenly ceased, and the Irish charged with swords and spears from either side. The English had no chance to mount any sort of defence and were practically annihilated, with only a few survivors emerging from this valley of death to report to Grey what had happened to his army. Now fearing for his own safety, Grey hastily retreated back to Dublin vowing vengeance.

---

[i] On July 30th 1580 Viscount Baltinglass wrote a letter to the Earl of Ormond in which he stated his opposition to Queen Elizabeth's reformation: "Questionless it is a great want of knowledge and more of grace, to think and believe that a woman, incapable of all holy orders, should be the supreme governor of Christ's Church; a thing that Christ did not grant unto His own mother"

Massacre at "The Fort of Gold"
<u>Spanish and Italian help for the Rebels</u>

As the winter of 1580 approached, the naval task force of Admiral William Winter returned to Kinsale, leaving the southwest coast clear for the arrival of further Papal and Spanish help. On October 1st, one huge ship capable of carrying 400 tons of supplies arrived along with two smaller vessels containing 700 Spanish and Italian soldiers under the command of the Spaniard, Sebastian de San Josef. Instead of moving inland, it was decided that the Fort of Gold would be reoccupied, and much time was wasted improving its defences. De San Josef had imagined that the local Irish would flock to their banner, but it was far too late for that, for they were either murdered or scattered by Ormond's troops who now occupied the entire area. The Earl of Ormond now watched and waited for he was unsure if he could handle the situation himself and decided to send word to Grey deWilton in Dublin to come to Kerry with all possible haste and force. The Spaniards, meanwhile, did not try to break out of the Dingle peninsula and when Grey arrived at the end of the month with a large army, he was met by the Earl of Ormond. Smerwick and the fort were quickly laid under siege. Admiral Winter was also summoned from Kinsale and brought by ship huge cannon which were landed nearby. The fort was then bombarded. After three days, de San Josef sought a truce, which was granted, and shortly afterwards the fort was surrendered so that the lives of its defenders would be spared. However according to the English, they surrendered without conditions. In any event, on the fateful morning of 10th November 1580, the Spanish and Italian troops emerged to face their captors.

The English Massacre their Prisoners

On November 12th, Lord Grey sent a dispatch to Queen Elizabeth in which he reported to her how events unfolded on the day of surrender: "From the camp before Smerwick, November 12th 1580...Morning came, I presented my forces in battaille before the forte. The coronel with ten or twelve of his chief gentlemen came trayling their ensigns rolled up, and presented them to me with their lives and the forte...I sent streighte certeyne gentlemen to see their weapons and armoires laid down and to guard the munition and victual them[i] from the spoil; then put I in certeyne bandes who streighte fell to execution. There were 600 slayne".[124]

The response of Queen Elizabeth to the massacre was to prefigure the response of a later ruler of England, Oliver Cromwell, when similar acts of atrocity were committed in Ireland. At the top of Grey's despatch, she wrote: "The mighty hand of the Almighty's power hath shewed manifest the force of his strength...in which action I joy that you have been chosen the instrument of his glory".[125]

While Grey ordered the massacre, Sir Walter Raleigh is charged with carrying out the massacre during which the 700 defenders of Smerwick were beheaded in a nearby field known ever since as the "Gort na gceann" ("Field of Heads") and their bodies thrown into the sea. During the reign of King James I, Raleigh fell into disfavour and, after being arrested, certain charges had to be found to put against him along with the main charge of plotting against the Crown. His role in the Smerwick massacre was recalled and charges relating to it were drawn up and put to him, to which he answered that he had been carrying out the orders of the Lord Deputy.

---

[i] In some English accounts the massacre has been excused on account of "necessity". The English had just about run out of provisions while the Spanish had only enough for themselves. Therefore the English had to kill them in order that they themselves would survive!

Some of the fort's inhabitants were not killed immediately and de San Josef and some of his officers escaped execution altogether. They were later allowed to return to Spain, arousing the suspicion that de San Josef had come to some sort of grubby arrangement with the English. A Mr. Plunkett, who was a servant to Bishop Saunders, was taken prisoner along with an Irish priest and a few others. According to Sir Richard Bingham who accompanied Grey, "their arms and legs were first broken, and they were then hanged on a gibbet on the walls of the fort"[126] after they refused to renounce their Catholic Faith.

The End of the Rebellion
As the year 1581 beckoned, Grey and his officers pursued the remaining insurgents with barbarous ferocity as the rebellion was looked on by the English as an opportunity to achieve their diverse aims. While continuing to fight the guerrilla attacks of the rebels, many of the Anglo-Irish of Munster, such as the Roches, Barrys and Purcells, were now attacked by the English on the pretext that they were providing clandestine assistance to the rebel cause. One of the worst atrocities against the Anglo-Irish took place at the Purcell estate in Kildimo, where English troops from Adare massacred 150 women and children who had taken refuge there.

In Dublin, "rumours" of a revolt against the English administration also provided an opportunity for the English to rid themselves of many troublesome Catholic government officials. Among those Catholic officials accused of treason and made to climb the scaffold was Judge Nugent, the Chief Justice of Common Pleas.

During the winter of 1581, the Papal Nuncio Dr. Saunders, whom the English longed to capture, died of dysentery in a woodland hut in Claenglass, attended by the Bishop of Killaloe. In early 1582, Captain Zouch, acting on information received from an Irish spy, set a trap for John of Desmond, one of the last principals of the revolt still at large. While trying to escape, he was mortally wounded when one of Zouch's men, Thomas Fleming, speared him through the throat.

By this stage, the rebellion was long since over, but still the English roamed the whole territory which they now extended to Connacht, where an army commanded by Captain Brabazon "pacified" the north of the province "to tread down all that standeth before them on foot, and lay on the ground all the stiffnecked people of that land."[127]

That Queen Elizabeth was fully aware of the barbarous policy of her Irish administration cannot be doubted for she had received from Grey and others a first-hand account of their doings. Many representations had been made to her concerning Grey's barbarity shortly after his arrival. These had gone unheeded until she finally decided to recall him in August 1582 when all of Munster was a charnel house and a wasteland of destroyed towns and dwellings. At the time of his recall, over 30,000 people had died of starvation alone in Munster in the year of 1582.

According to Wilton deGrey's secretary Edmund Spencer, Grey had brought the Irish of Munster "so low that he shall have no heart nor ability to endure his wretchedness...so pluck him on his knees that he will never be able to stand up again."[128]

One small matter remained however: to procure the death of The Earl of Desmond himself. He did not pose any threat and was finally hunted down and killed on the morning of the 11th of November 1583 at Glanageenty Wood in Kerry by a certain Daniel O'Kelly (from whose brother in law, who was an enemy of Desmond, the Earl had taken livestock) accompanied by a group of English soldiers. Munster was now ready to receive English settlers into a once "populous and plentiful country suddenly left void of man and beast"[129].

Grey was not immediately replaced but rather his powers were assigned to two Lord Justices, Wallop and Loftus (who was the Protestant Archbishop of Dublin), and a new policy was enacted, that of restoring the area to peace as the future planters from England would not stay long in a war zone. As the army began to stand down from its incessant destruction, the native inhabitants who had taken shelter in woodland and mountain began to reappear. Of this, Grey's Secretary, the poet Edmund Spencer, who would take 12,000 acres in Munster during the plantation which followed, was to write: "Out of every corner of the woods and glynes they came creeping forth on their hands for their legges could not bear them; they looked like anatomies of death; they spake like ghosts crying out of their graves; they did eate the dead carrions happy where they coulde find them; yea and one another soone after, insomuch as the very carcasses they spared not to scrape out of their graves; and if they found a plot of water cresses or shamrocks there they flocked as to a feast for the time..."[130]

The Plantation of Munster

In 1584, Sir John Perrott was appointed the new Lord Deputy. He arrived in Dublin on June 21st, bringing with him Sir Thomas Norris as President of Munster and Sir Richard Bingham as Governor of Connacht. In order to tie up the legal aspects of the Munster insurrection, Perrott summoned a parliament which, compared to previous parliaments, was attended by many of those Gaelic Irish who had accepted English title. For most of them, this was the last parliament they would ever attend.

The Parliament met on April 26th of 1585 and, despite some opposition, an Act of Attainder was passed against the dead Earl of Desmond and 140 others who were listed as his supporters. Also attainted was James Eustace Viscount

Baltinglass who had escaped to the continent (where he died shortly afterwards). All lands formerly in the possession of those attainted, amounting to almost one million acres, were seized by the Crown. The plantation of Munster could now officially proceed.

According to the Act of Plantation ("Articles for Repeopling and Inhabiting the Provinces of Munster in Ireland") almost 575,000 English acres were to be cleared of Irish people and made available to the planters. The Act declared that; "The heads of every family shall be born of English parents, and the heirs female, inheritable to any the same lands, shall marry with none but with persons born of English parents and no mere Irish to be permitted in any family there."[131]

During the year 1586, a proclamation was made throughout England inviting gentlemen to come to Ireland to be "Undertakers" of the plantation, with each Undertaker who was granted 12,000 acres agreeing to plant 86 English families on his plantation at the rent of two or three pence an acre, with no rent to be paid for three years and half rent for the following three years. In Kerry, a grant of 12,000 acres would cost the Undertaker a mere 100 pounds. For those undertakers granted a lesser amount of land (down to 4,000 acres), the number of families was reduced in proportion, with all estates to be populated within 7 years. In theory, no Undertaker was to be allocated more than 12,000 acres but in many cases the law was circumvented. Not content with the amount of land confiscated, through trickery and trumped-up charges, the English lawyers successfully managed to deprive many Irish who were not attainted by parliament out of their lands.

The land was liberally distributed to those who had leadership roles in the clearance of Munster. In the case of Sir Walter Raleigh, he finally accrued in the region of 40,000 acres, with other gentlemen, including Sir Thomas Norris, Sir Christopher Hatton and Sir George Bourchier, also amassing large grants.

The Undertakers were forbidden to have any native Irish as their tenants, but they could be employed as labourers. In spite of the favourable rents, the Undertakers were however unable to tempt English families to come over in sufficient numbers and some were forced to break the conditions of their undertaking, granting estates for rent to the native Irish in order to try and populate their undertaking and so make it commercially viable. It was around this period that much of Ireland was despoiled of its rich forestry by the Planters who proceeded to destroy them for their burgeoning industries such as the manufacture of charcoal for gunpowder.

Chapter 15

The Spanish Armada

Sir John Perrott as Lord Deputy
Since his return to Ireland, the new Lord Deputy Sir John Perrott (who had previously executed hundreds of people during his tenure as President of Munster) now determined to follow a more even-handed policy, deciding not to persecute the native Irish on account of their Catholicism. His approach flew in the face of the policy of Queen Elizabeth's Irish government, and its attitude towards him gradually changed from one of loyalty to one of bitterness and hatred. In his attempts to rein in the army, which under Grey's command had operated without any restraints whatsoever, he also had to endure the hatred and disdain of its leadership.

Reign of Terror in Connacht
Meanwhile, Sir Richard Bingham, who had arrived at the same time as Sir John Perrott, had proceeded to Connacht to take up his duties there. While Perrott tried to pursue a peaceful policy, in Connacht, Bingham was determined to pursue a policy of brutal severity, for he felt that if he succeeded in provoking a revolt among the native families, he could legally dispossess them.
In early 1586, Bingham presided at an assize in Connacht where he executed 70 men and women. In March of the same

year, he attacked the castle of the "Papist" Mahon O'Brien at Cloonoan in Clare, and, after a siege of seven days, O'Brien was killed on the battlements. When the castle surrendered after his death, Bingham ordered all the prisoners slaughtered. Following this butchery, Bingham proceeded to Hag's Castle on Lough Mask, in Mayo, which belonged to Richard Burke. He was intent on having another massacre here, but the castle's defenders managed to escape by boat to the opposite shore before his men entered the stronghold after it had been destroyed by bombardment. Bingham did however, capture Richard Burke's son, who was hanged. He also sent parties of marauding soldiers along the western seaboard and many innocent men, women and children were killed in this reign of terror.

Sir John Perrott

Perrott was less than pleased with Bingham's actions, which flew in the face of his own policy, and summoned him to Dublin to explain himself. A violent argument ensued between the two men in the council chamber, with the other members of the autocratic government council all supporting Bingham.

Around this time, the government decided on a policy known as "The Composition of Connacht". This was the imposition of a regular property tax due to the Crown for all lands held in Connacht, in return for secure tenure. While the Council was still in session, news arrived that the MacWilliam Burkes were resisting the payment of the newly introduced tax as Bingham's policies had provoked them into revolt against the government. Perrott wanted to go to Connacht to deal with the matter himself but was thwarted by the council and Bingham, whose bloody policy had caused the trouble in the first place. Instead, the council voted that Bingham himself should return to Connacht and suppress the rebellion. On his return, his first action was to execute all the hostages which the Burkes had given him as guarantee of their loyalty. Among those hanged by him was Edmond Burke, "a withered grey old man,"[132] whose sons were in revolt.

The Burkes had not risen against the English without preparation, having first secured the support of an army of 2,000 Highland Scots from the O'Donnell of Tirconnell. Sooner than face these formidable warriors in open battle, the wily Bingham surprised them in their encampment in the early morning hours of September 22nd, 1586, at Ardnaree on the River Moy after an all-night march by his men. The Scotsmen were caught completely by surprise and those who did not drown while trying to escape were either slaughtered or captured and hanged.

The Kidnapping of Hugh Roe O'Donnell

In the year 1587, all England watched and waited, as, following the execution of Mary Stuart, Queen of Scots, on a trumped up charge of plotting to murder Queen Elizabeth, it seemed certain that Catholic Spain would not let the outrage go unanswered. Furthermore, despite opposition from the Queen herself, Sir William Cecil had sent Sir Francis Drake to attack Spain from the sea and a Spanish attack on England was now expected in return. The Crown also feared a widespread Catholic uprising across England in the event of a successful Spanish landing. In Ireland, Perrott had already secured hostages from many of the Irish chiefs in order to ensure that they would not rise up should a Spanish attack happen, but no hostages were forthcoming from Sir Hugh O'Donnell of

Tirconnell. Furthermore, in the previous year the O'Donnell's had ejected from their territory an English miscreant by the name of Captain Humphrey Willis (of whom we will hear more later) and his force of 300 men who had been sent to Tirconnell to make trouble and provoke rebellion. The activities of Willis and his men were described by the English Captain Thomas Lee: "The rascals did rob and spoil the people, ravished their wives and daughters and made havoc of all."[133]

To the mind of Perrott, the O'Donnells needed to be kept in check, and he now hatched an ingenious plan in order to ensure that they would be more cooperative with the Crown. However, his actions were to have far-reaching consequences for it was to turn the hitherto acquiescent rulers of Tirconnell firmly against the Crown.

During the Autumn of 1587, a merchant ship apparently on its way back from Spain with a cargo of wine, entered Lough Swilly and set down its anchor close to Rathmullen, near where the young son of Hugh O'Donnell, whose name was Hugh Roe, lived in fosterage with the Gallowglass Clan Mac Sweeney. Young O'Donnell, then a lad of fifteen years of age, was, in spite of his youth, widely renowned for his wisdom and gentlemanly bearing.

In actual fact, this ship had been sent from Dublin by Perrott to kidnap Hugh Roe as an English hostage to ensure that the O'Donnells remained loyal. Its captain was a Dublin merchant, John Bermingham, and he had been given a crew of fifty armed men to execute his mission.

After word reached the MacSweeney household of the ship and its cargo, servants were sent in order to buy wine but returned with the message that all the casks were already sold or spoken for, but that if the men of the house wished to go on board, the ship's captain would be pleased to receive them, and they would be welcome to drink their fill. With a pleasant experience in prospect, a number of the MacSweeneys accompanied by Hugh Roe were brought out to the ship in a rowing boat and welcomed on board. Hugh's foster father, "MacSweeney na-tuath"[i] did not accompany them. On the party's arrival, the sampling of the Spanish wines began in earnest in the captain's cabin.

As the group was merry making, they felt the ship begin to move and, on jumping up, suddenly found themselves prisoners. While they had been in the captain's cabin, the vessel had prepared to sail, and the visitor's weapons had been quietly impounded. Distraught, the onlookers on the shore watched the ship move away. MacSweeneyrushed to the shore, shouting that he would give any ransom demanded to get Hugh Roe released, but to no avail. The ship set sail for the open sea while those on the shore looked on, powerless to do anything. On the boat's arrival in the Capital, Hugh Roe O'Donnell was taken to Dublin Castle and locked in a cell in the part of the Castle known as "Bermingham's Tower".

The Fall of Perrott

All the while, Perrott's enemies in Dublin were clamouring for his removal, sending to London report after report of his mismanagement. The most strident of his opponents was the Protestant Archbishop Loftus of Dublin who accused Perrott of treachery due to his refusal to tackle the growing number of prominent English Catholics in the Pale.

After his arrival, Perrott had tried to carry out his instructions with regard to the establishment of a Protestant University in Dublin, but Loftus had his own ideas on the matter and complained unceasingly to London regarding the Lord Deputy's mishandling of the project. After four years in his post, Perrott was recalled in mid-1588. A short time after returning to England, he was arrested on warrant of false

---

[i] "na tuath" – of the countryside

allegations of his being in league with the Spanish. He managed to disprove these allegations but was sent to the Tower anyway after his former secretary publicly accused him of making disparaging remarks about the illegitimacy of Queen Elizabeth. He died in the Tower of London in 1592.

His removal as Lord Deputy signalled the re-adoption of a much harder stance by the English in their dealings with the Gael. Those deputies who had supported Perrott on the Dublin Council were quickly replaced by appointees brought over from England, men for whom the furtherance of the Protestant cause in Ireland was paramount, and the now totally hard-line Council of State welcomed an equally hard-line Lord Deputy in the person of Sir William Fitzwilliam who officially succeeded Perrott on the 30th June 1588. Many of the Old English of the Pale who remained Catholic but loyal to the Crown resented or even hated the ever-growing influx of new officials and settlers, who regarded them with distrust and worse because of their adherence to the Catholic Faith.

The Spanish Armada

Fitzwilliam had been in the role of Lord Deputy for only a few months when the Spanish Armada foundered on the English coast and a not insignificant number of its ships managed to find their way to the ragged Atlantic shoreline off the west of Ireland where many of them ran aground and sank. Those ships that made it to safety along the western seaboard got a mixed reception.

Fitzwilliam issued a proclamation that all Spaniards coming ashore from the wrecked ships were to be executed on the spot. In Connacht, where Bingham presided over a reign of terror, a further edict was issued that anyone found harbouring a Spaniard was guilty of treason and as such liable to be executed. As a result, the Spaniards suffered many losses in the

western Province at the hands of the English, assisted by some of those Irish "eager" to show their loyalty to the Crown.[i]
Further north, the Spaniards fared much better. In Leitrim, Sir Brian O'Rourke gave refuge to 1,000 shipwrecked men under the command of Antonio deLeva, while Hugh O'Donnell of Tirconnell, assisted by Hugh O'Néill, gave help to around 3,000 men, many of whom perished in the *Girona* when she was shipwrecked on Bloody Foreland while attempting to return to Spain. One of the most prominent of the Spanish survivors of the Armada was Francisco deCuellar, Captain of the *San Pedro*, who wrote an account of the expedition after he escaped from Ireland and reached the Dutch port of Antwerp. DeCuellar came ashore at Streedagh Strand in Co. Sligo and, after walking a little inland, arrived at a monastery which, according to his narrative, was "deserted and the church and images of the saints burned and completely ruined and twelve Spaniards hanging within the church by an act of the Lutheran English who were prowling around in quest of us in order to finish all who had escaped from the disasters of the sea. All the monks had fled to the woods for fear of the enemies who were accustomed to leaving neither place of worship nor hermitage standing; for they had demolished them all, and made them drinking places for cows and swine."[134]
DeCuellar managed to find refuge with Brian O'Rourke who sent him to one of his chieftains, Manglana Mac Fhlannchaidh (anglicised as Clancy). Shortly afterwards, Bingham, at the head of 1,700 men attacked Clancy's castle and hanged Spanish prisoners in open sight in front of their lines in order to

---

[i] Sir Richard Bingham afterwards reported: "The men of these ships all perished, save 1,100 or more who were put to the sword, amongst whom were officers and gentlemen of quality to the number of 50 and whose names have been set down in a list. The gentlemen were spared until the Lord Deputy sent me specific directions to see them executed – reserving alone deCordoba and his nephew who were at Athlone."

intimidate the defenders. However the attack failed thanks to the assistance of DeCuellar and his compatriots.[i]

News of the wrecked Spanish ships was accompanied by rumours of treasure chests, and a special commission was set up by Fitzwilliam to recover the gold. Leaving nothing to chance, the Lord Deputy came to Connacht himself. Along with Bingham and an army of men, he carried out a search of shore and countryside, which continued for some time. Any Chieftains suspected of having given refuge to the shipwrecked men had their territories destroyed. Furthermore, many "Popish priests" were seized and sent to Dublin for trial, the common charge being that they had "sowed sedition and rebellion in the kingdom". Those who were not butchered by being hanged, drawn and quartered were left to rot in prison. Fitzwilliam and Bingham now crossed into Leitrim and Sir Brian O'Rourke, who had given refuge to so many Spaniards, was forced to go on the run. After O'Rourke had safely made his way to Scotland, King James VI had him arrested and handed him over to the English, who executed him for treason on the charge of having mistreated an image of Queen Elizabeth.

As there was no gold to be found, Fitzwilliam resorted to other methods in order to enrich himself. Hostages were taken and brought to Dublin. They included Sir John MacTuathal O'Gallagher and John Oge O'Doherty. O'Gallagher died as a result of his harsh imprisonment but O'Doherty was released after his father arranged for a large sum of money to be paid over to Fitzwilliam.

---

[i] After DeCuellar managed to escape into the care of the Bishop of Derry, Clancy was captured and beheaded. His head was taken to Sligo. Bingham reported to Dublin: "He was a most barbarous creature; his country extended from Grange to Ballyshannig: he was Ó Ruairc's right hand".

Chapter 16

Gaelic Ulster under Threat

"Torment it is to me that, in the very clan gathering, foreigners proscribe them that are Ireland's royal chiefs, in whose own ancestral territory is given to them no designation but that of a lowly outlaw's name." – Aongus Ó Dálaigh (1540-1600)

Ulster – The Last Gaelic Stronghold

As the English first appeared to grant peace and security to the Gaelic Chieftains by offering them "surrender and regrant", and then used this policy as a means of spreading the dark mantle of English control over the entire country, Ulster alone, due to the military strength of its native families that were greatly augmented by large numbers of Scottish mercenaries, remained relatively unaffected. In Most of Ulster, Gaelic rule still prevailed, and the old Gaelic ways and traditions were still in vogue, while the Catholic Church had for the most part escaped persecution. However, as the rest of the nation succumbed to English power and brutality, the Crown was now in a position to concentrate her efforts and resources on Ulster. Fatally weakened by Surrender and Regrant, the Gaelic Lords struggled to keep English law with its officials and sheriffs at bay. They fully realised that, once English rule gained mastery, open persecution against Catholicism would be the order of the day.

Already by the accession of Elizabeth to the throne of England, the O'Reilly's of East Breifne, who straddled Ulster's border, were coming under increasing pressure from the Anglo-Norman families of Nugent and Plunkett along their southern frontier in Co. Meath. In 1566, Aodh Conallach O'Reilly, Chieftain of the O'Reilly Clan, gave way to English coercion and signed the submissive "Treaty of Lough Sheelin" after which West Breifne was renamed County Cavan in 1579. Following this, the O'Reilly's became tenants instead of rulers of their territory.

The Overthrow of Gaelic Rule in Monaghan

In 1589, the newly-appointed Lord Deputy Sir William Fitzwilliam saw his chance to overthrow Gaelic rule in Monaghan when its Chieftain Ross MacMahon died. Only a month before his death, Ross had come to the attention of Fitzwilliam after driving Captain Humphrey Willis and his thieving, terrorizing, and raping band of men out of his territory.[i] Willis was used by the English as an *agent provocateur*, in most cases to take an English mile where the Irish Chieftain had given an inch. In Ross MacMahon's case, once he expelled Willis, Fitzwilliam arrived with an English army and ravaged and plundered at will[ii] until McMahon caved in, agreeing to a sheriff and an English gaol and garrison in Monaghan town. A few weeks later, he was dead.

Ross had no sons and, since taking English title, he had abandoned the old Gaelic law of succession whereby a Tánaiste was appointed by the ruling Chieftain. By English law, his heir was his brother Hugh Roe and, in order to officially succeed his dead brother, a visit to Dublin by Hugh Roe was deemed

---

[i] In his book "The Great O Neill" the renowned storyteller and historian Sean O'Faoláin describes Captain Willis and his band of miscreants as "The Scum of the Earth"

[ii] During this foray into Monaghan, Fitzwilliam and his army destroyed the monastic settlement and round tower at Clones.

necessary. When he arrived in Dublin, Hugh found to his dismay that Lord Deputy Fitzwilliam would not agree to his taking over the rule of Monaghan even though everything was legally in order. Fitzwilliam, who was adept at watching out for any opportunity to increase his personal wealth, relented after a short delay. All would be put right, he declared, if MacMahon handed over to him six hundred cows annually. After agreeing to the proposal, Hugh Roe made the necessary arrangements and part of the bribe was paid. Finally, everything was in order and Fitzwilliam then accompanied Hugh back to Monaghan to officially install him as ruler.

Some months later, Fitzwilliam returned to Monaghan and Hugh Roe was arrested on a charge of treason, for having used a party of armed men to forcibly collect rents due to him in Farney. The rents he was collecting were cattle to be used to pay the Fitzwilliam bribe. Fitzwilliam saw in this minor infraction of English law an opportunity to get Hugh Roe out of the way, take Monaghan directly into the control of the Crown and divide it, something which he now persuaded the other branches of the MacMahon family to be in their interest. After his arrest, Hugh Roe was brought first to Dublin and then back to Monaghan by Fitzwilliam for the trial.

Back in Monaghan, he was tried within two days, found guilty by a packed jury consisting of English soldiers and then immediately executed outside his own house. The object of Fitzwilliam's accompanying him back to Monaghan now became clear: he wished to dispense with any laws or procedures that would have inhibited the swift progress of his trial, as well as to arrange the composition of the jury.

Following MacMahon's execution, the usual English method of serving an Act of Attainder against him was used and Monaghan was confiscated, becoming the property of the Crown. Sir Henry Bagenal of Newry, who had succeeded his late father Sir Nicholas, was awarded part of the spoils, with the territory of Farney being given to those planters who had been lately ejected from Clandeboye by the O'Néills. Hugh Roe's private residence and lands were given to a Captain Henslowe who was appointed Governor of Monaghan. On payment of a substantial bribe[i] to the Lord Deputy, the territory was subsequently divided between four other branches of the Mac Mahon family and a MacKenna, who were required to pay the Crown an annual rent of ten pounds for every 960 acres.

The treatment of Hugh Roe MacMahon and his summary execution at the hands of the Lord Deputy confirmed to all the Gaelic Lords of Ulster that their policy of keeping the English at arm's length was entirely justified and that, in spite of the policy of Surrender and Regrant and the English titles that they held, the English establishment considered that the Irish had no rights to their lands under English law. The Earl of Tyrone, Hugh O'Néill was also perturbed at McMahon's unjust fate for such a minor infringement, commenting that: "cattle driving is merely distraining for his rights according to Irish custom."[135]

Hugh O'Néill – The Queen's Man?

The English Upbringing of Hugh O'Néill

After the murder of Shane O'Néill, his Tánaiste, Turlough O'Néill had succeeded him without any interference from the English, and since then Turlough had kept his head down, co-operating with the English when he felt he had to, thereby creating a situation which allowed the *status quo* to linger.

Back in 1562, in order to secure the rule of Shane O'Néill against the sons of Matthew (Fedoragh) O'Néill, Turlough had

---

[i] It is reported from the state papers of the time that Fitzwilliam in correspondence to Burghley calls upon God to witness that the bribes paid over to him were "meant for the profit of her majesty and not his own." (See Shirley's History of Farney pp. 88,89)

arranged for the assassination of the Baron of Dungannon, Brian O'Néill, who was Matthew's eldest son. Following Brian's death, the hopes that the English had for him as a man that they could use in the Anglicisation of Ulster were transferred to his younger brother Hugh. With this and Hugh's safety in mind, they removed him to Dublin, where he grew up as a ward of the English state in the household of the Hovendan family. After receiving an English education, he went to England where he attended the court of Queen Elizabeth and became the commander of a troop of horse. As time passed, he became extremely well-versed in all that the English state had to offer to a young man of ambition, including their arts of warfare, politics and all the methods that the Tudors used to achieve their goals by fair means or foul.

Earl of Dungannon
By all accounts, it seemed that Hugh had indeed become what the English wished him to be, for when he returned to Ulster, he assisted the English in their battles against the Scottish MacDonnells and also in their suppression of the Desmond Rebellion. In 1585, he was made Earl of Dungannon by Queen Elizabeth, but on being granted his estate he had to relinquish to the Crown over 200 acres at the ford of the River Blackwater where the English planned to construct a huge fortress to be called "Potmore Fort" on the Tyrone-Armagh border. Such was the confidence of the English that they had completely transformed this man of Tyrone into their own likeness, that when O'Néill requested that he be allowed maintain a standing army of six companies for the service of and paid for by the Queen in order to keep the peace in Ulster, it was granted. This force was six hundred men strong and was commanded by a cadre of well-trained officers. However, the enlisted men were rotated annually and in this way the Earl of Tyrone amassed a huge number of men, all trained in the English

methods of war. When, in 1590, his cousin Hugh Geimhleach O'Néill (who was a son of Shane O'Néill) tried to make trouble for him by sending to Fitzwilliam charges against him relating to an alleged plot against the Queen, Hugh O'Néill had him seized and executed by hanging, following a form of trial.[i]

While Sir John Perrott had viewed Hugh O'Néill with some affection, Fitzwilliam was more suspicious of him, fearing that he might not be the "useful idiot" that the English desired. Writing of him in 1587, Fitzwilliam noted: "As long as Sir Turloch lives he (Hugh O'Néill) is not dangerous, but when he is absolute and hath no competitor he may show himself to be the man which in his reason he has wisdom to dissemble"[136].

After the hanging of Hugh Geimhleach O'Néill, the Lord Deputy was anxious to use the episode to stir up trouble for the Earl of Tyrone but Hugh O'Néill forestalled this by going to London himself where he signed a comprehensive document undertaking to enact a full policy of Anglicisation in Tyrone provided that he remained unmolested. On returning to Dublin, O'Néill reported on what had taken place in London to Fitzwilliam and the Dublin Council, then proceeding to excuse himself from the immediate execution of the document until all the other Gaelic Lords of Ulster had made similar undertakings.

The O'Néill – Bagenal Marriage

In 1591, shortly after the death of his wife Siobhan O'Donnell (daughter of Sir Hugh O'Donnell of Tirconnell), Hugh O'Néill and Mabel Bagenal, who was the beautiful younger sister of Sir

---

[i] In accounts of Hugh O'Néill's life, it is often asserted that he himself executed Hugh Geimhleach (of the fetters) by strangulation. In fact, Hugh O'Néill procured a hangman from Meath as none could be found in Tyrone who would hang a son of Shane O'Néill.

Henry Bagenal, Marshal of Ireland, fell in love with each other after which Mabel then accepted his proposal of marriage.

Sir Henry Bagenal, who had himself already shed no small amount of Gaelic blood and hated the Irish with a passion, was vigorously opposed to the match, and sent Mabel away from their home in Newry to his friend Sir Patrick Barnwell in Dublin, who was married to Mabel's older sister Mary.

Undeterred, O'Néill tracked Mabel down, and on the 3rd August 1591 he arrived at Barnwell's house with an English confidant, William Warren. While Sir Patrick Barnwell entertained the Earl along with his other guests, Warren excused himself and found Mabel elsewhere in the house. He spoke to her, after which they both quietly departed the house without Barnwell's knowledge, making for a safe house in Drumcondra, to which they were later followed by O'Néill. That very same evening O'Néill and Mabel Bagenal were married before Thomas Jones, the Protestant Bishop of Meath, who later stated that he performed the ceremony "for the sake of the Lady's honour."

While the English government viewed the whole episode leniently, Sir Henry Bagenal was furious, a fury which can be determined from a letter he wrote to the Lord Treasurer that included the passage: "I cannot but accurse myself and fortune that my bloude which, in my father and myselfe hath often beene spilled in repressinge this rebellious race, should nowe be mingled with so traitorous a stocke and kindred."[137] The situation between Bagenal and O'Néill was hardly improved when Mabel converted to Catholicism shortly after her marriage to Hugh O'Néill. O'Néill had now made for himself an implacable and dangerous enemy in Bagenal, who made things extremely difficult for him, especially in the early 1590s when he intercepted his communications with London and always did his utmost to paint the Earl of Tyrone in a negative light in his reports to London.

Hugh Roe O'Donnell Returns Home
Escape and Recapture
Since his kidnapping at Rathmullen in the autumn of 1587, Hugh Roe O'Donnell had been incarcerated in Dublin Castle. The O'Donnells, although quite powerful militarily, had long been cooperative with the Crown, not wanting to give the English any excuse to interfere too much in the affairs of Tirconnell. However, while the action of Lord Deputy Perrott in ordering the kidnapping of Hugh Roe was intended to copper fasten their cooperation by force; it had instead filled them with distrust and resentment towards the Crown.

Hugh Roe O'Donnell was not prepared to sit out his imprisonment at Her Majesty's pleasure. In November of 1590, he and a few other prisoners' abseiled by rope from the castle to the drawbridge below before the night guard came on duty. After securing the castle door from the outside, they passed through the city towards Roundwood in Wicklow where O'Donnell, by now lame from wounds left by thorns and stones, had finally collapsed from exhaustion. While the other escapees continued on their way, one of them made for Castlekevin (Powerscourt) and the home of the local Chieftain, Feilim O'Toole, to get help for him.

Meanwhile, in Dublin, a hue and cry had been raised and English soldiers were hard on the trail of Hugh Roe. As Feilim O'Toole and some companions were on their way to bring the weary O'Donnell to safety, they realised that the woods through which they travelled were surrounded by English soldiers, with no route of escape through which they could escort him. As the enemy soldiers closed in, O'Toole was prepared to fight to save Hugh Roe from recapture, but his companions convinced him that this action would be to the ruin of all. They were instead forced to make a virtue out of necessity, and pretended to capture Hugh Roe O'Donnell, after which they handed him over to the English soldiers.

Brought back to Dublin Castle, Hugh Roe's feet were locked in iron rings joined by a chain so as to restrict his movements and he was placed in a more secure cell along with two sons of Shane O'Néill, Henry and Art.

The Second Escape

Unbowed by his ordeal, Hugh Roe was determined to try and escape a second time. A file was obtained either through a visitor or the bribing of a guard and a channel of communication was opened with the Earl of Tyrone, after which a plan of escape for Hugh Roe and his two companions was formed.

On Christmas Day of 1591, having filed through the chain that tied his feet together, he and his companions succeeded in reaching the bridge outside the castle wall with the help of a rope. As Art O'Néill descended, he injured himself, but nevertheless continued with his comrades. They now entered the stinking labyrinth of sewers that served the castle's latrines and, once out of the network, were forced by necessity to discard their dirty mantles. At the exit to the sewers, a servant of Fiach MacHugh O'Byrne of Battle of Glenmalure fame met them. He brought them along the city's streets and, after leaving the metropolis behind without encountering any trouble, they set off across country. The night was bitterly cold; it was snowing heavily, and the conditions were made worse by the fact that the escapees were already wet from head to foot. During their passage through the city or shortly after they left it, Hugh O'Néill became separated from his friends, who were forced to continue on without him.[i]

All evening and all night they walked through the sodden wilds of Wicklow, making for Glenmalure and the home of

---

[i] Hugh Mac Shane O'Néill (son of Shane) successfully managed to exit Dublin and finally returned to Tyrone where he was taken into custody by Hugh O'Néill.

Fiach Mac Hugh O'Byrne.The injuries that Art O'Néill had suffered now told on him and he had to be supported by the others, one on either side. Finally, the two escapees could continue no further and their guide left them to get help at Glenmalure. When a party of Fiach Mac Hugh's men returned, they found the escapees in a bad way. According to the Annals of The Four Masters; "Unhappy and miserable was the condition on their arrival. Their bodies were covered over with white bordered shrouds of hailstones freezing around them and their light clothes and fine threaded shirts adhered to their skin, and their large shoes and leather thongs to their legs and feet so that covered as they were with snow it did not appear to the men who had arrived that they were human beings at all, for they found no life in their members, but just as if they were dead."[138] The two men were also unable to swallow. After reaching Glenmalure, Art O'Néill succumbed to his wounds and died. Hugh Roe gradually improved but was unable to walk.

Having searched far and wide for Hugh Roe without success, the English now learned that he was in Glenmalure with Fiach MacHugh O'Byrne but were reluctant to follow him there. Knowing that he would try to move north, guards were posted, and search parties dispatched to try and prevent his escape back to Tirconnell. Furthermore, as a punishment, hundreds of English soldiers under Captain Humphrey Willis had entered Tirconnell and, after committing many terrible crimes, they had occupied the large monastic settlement at Ballyweel.

When news of O'Donnell's escape reached London, Queen Elizabeth was in no doubt as to how it had come about, for when she wrote to Lord Borough she said: "O'Donnell escaped by the practice of money on somebody...inquire who they are that have been touched by it."[139]

Home to Donegal
After the initial hue and cry had died down a little, Hugh O'Néill sent a young Chieftain by the name of Turlough O'Hagan to escort the former prisoner northwards. Although much recovered, Hugh Roe was still lame from frostbite and had to be lifted onto his horse. During their journey northwards, they were accompanied by O'Byrne's men to a deep and unused fording point on the River Liffey, after which Hugh Roe and Turlough then continued alone. They successfully evaded the English and reached Dungannon and the house of Hugh O'Néill after two days. Shortly afterwards, the last leg of the journey to Ballyshannon was completed, where Hugh Roe was received amid great jubilation.

Evicting the English
Within a short time, a massive crowd had assembled around him, and Hugh Roe invited them to accompany him to Ballyweel where English soldiers under the command of Captain Humphrey Willis were still in possession of the monastery. When Hugh arrived at the head of the people of Tirconnell, the English were told in no uncertain terms that their stay at Ballyweel was over and that they could leave unhindered if they left their plunder behind. Outnumbered beyond measure, Willis's men had no choice but to comply and were glad to have escaped with their lives,[140] considering what was the universal practice of the English in similar situations. The monks, who had managed to escape on the arrival of the English, were now able to return to their desecrated monastery.

"The O'Donnell"
On returning to Ballyshannon, Hugh Roe continued to undergo treatment for his frostbitten feet, but his doctors were unable to save them from permanent damage and the big toe

of each foot had to be amputated. The successful escape had come at a high cost for, in addition to the death of Art O'Néill, Hugh Roe was left more or less crippled with lameness. Injury aside, his cruel captivity and the ill treatment of his people at the hands of the English in spite of their efforts to remain at peace annoyed him greatly and played no small part in transforming what had been a carefree youth into an enemy of the English. His mother Finola[i] fervently embraced his cause and his father Hugh agreed not to stand in his way and abdicated the Chieftaincy in his favour on the 3rd May 1592, after which he was solemnly inaugurated according to the ancient Gaelic tradition of the O'Donnells.[ii]

It had long since been the tradition of the new Chieftain of the O'Donnells to lead an attack into the land of their ancient foe, the O'Néills of Tyrone. As the new Chieftain, Hugh knew that this was expected of him, and unwilling to break the old custom, a number of nuisance attacks into the O'Néill territory followed. When news of this reached Dublin Castle, English troops eager to take advantage of Hugh Roe's attacks quickly rushed to the county. Afraid of the consequences, Hugh O'Néill sent a message to O'Donnell to desist lest an ill-timed

---

[i] Finola was the daughter of James MacDonnell who was killed by Shane O'Néill at Glenshesk. Known to the Irish as "Inion Dubh" or "the dark lady / daughter", she was a significant factor in the politics of Tirconell, giving both advice and backing to her sons, especially Hugh Roe. The *Annals of the Four Masters* tells us that she was "like the mother of the Macchabees who joined a man's heart to a woman's thought".

[ii] The ceremony which took place at the Rock of Doone began in a local monastery with the singing of psalms. Hugh Roe then stood on the rock and recited an oath to protect the Catholic Church and the laws of the land and also to deliver his realm in peace to his Tánaiste. He then received from the Lawyer, O'Clery a book that contained the laws and customs of his realm and a straight white rod to symbolize the high standard of Christian morality demanded of him.

war with the English should be the result, a request which O'Donnell complied with.

Chapter 17

The Nine Years War 1– Years of Victory

1593 - The Road to War

In 1593, following the incursion of Hugh Roe O'Donnell into Tyrone, Turlough O'Néill agreed to relinquish the Chieftaincy in favour of Hugh O'Néill.

Still in the service of Queen Elizabeth, Hugh O'Néill was without doubt an object of suspicion to the English establishment in Ireland who had come to the realisation that as the current incarnation of an ancient family of Gaelic Kings, Hugh O'Néill wished to maintain some sort of freedom for his people and their Catholic faith and was not a man who would necessarily put English interests first.

As the situation in Ulster moved towards open conflict, O'Néill did his utmost to avoid it without compromising the rights of the Gael under his protection. The measures which he took to improve his military strength can well be viewed as prudent, for he wished to act from a position of strength, so that if the peace could not be maintained, then the people of Ulster might have a fighting chance if there was no alternative. Hugh O'Néill had seen the treachery and violence of the Queen's agents, including the execution of O'Rourke of Breifne and MacMahon of Monaghan on a trumped up charge, along with the confiscation of their lands. Since his youth, he had been a student of English ways – he knew only too well that in the long term England's solution for the rest of Ulster would be no different.

Captain Humphrey Willis is sent to into Fermanagh

Meanwhile in Fermanagh, the Gaelic ruler Hugh Maguire had managed to purchase an exemption from the presence of an English Sheriff in his territory by offering a bribe of 300 cows to Lord Deputy Fitzwilliam. Fitzwilliam, as corrupt as ever, had nevertheless proceeded to appoint one: the same notorious brigand and "agént provocateur", Captain Humphrey Willis, whom Hugh Roe O'Donnell had driven out of Donegal.

Captain Willis came into Fermanagh with 100 men at arms, along with their womenfolk and children. Billets were forcibly requisitioned by him and his men from the local populace, as well as all the other necessities of life required for man and beast. On top of the "Coign and livery" exacted by Willis, the sight of him traversing the territory with 100 men at arms stirring up trouble was more than Hugh Maguire could bear and he rose up in arms against him. Captain Willis escaped with his life for a second time: Hugh Maguire and his men had him and a troop of his soldiers under siege in a church, where they would surely have been put to the sword if Hugh O'Néill had not intervened on the captain's behalf, allowing him and his men to go free on the condition that they leave Fermanagh immediately.

The English in Dublin viewed this action of O'Néill as treachery, for O'Néill had not chastised Maguire for his actions against Willis, and Bagenal quickly forwarded a report of the incident to England.

Around the same period across the Fermanagh border, West Breifne (Leitrim) was also coming under renewed English pressure. Since the execution of Sir Brian O'Rourke in London, his son Brian Óg had taken charge. Sir Richard Bingham now came to West Breifne to collect Crown rents on unused wasteland and forcibly seized a large number of cattle after Brian Óg O'Rourke had informed him that no rents were due on unproductive acreage. The injustice of this had aroused the ire of the young chieftain who, already pushed to the limit by Bingham, now rose up in arms against him.[i] When his neighbour, Maguire of Fermanagh, became aware of this, he joined O'Rourke's revolt and led his army into Connacht in an attempt to free the people from Bingham's reign of terror. Having advanced as far as Tulsk in Roscommon, he ran into Bingham and his men. Among those who were killed in the resulting exchange of fire were the recently appointed Archbishop of Armagh Edward MacGauran[ii] who accompanied Maguire, and one of Bagenal's officers, Sir William Clifford.

Massacre at Enniskillen Castle

Having failed in his imposition of a Sheriff and with Maguire having joined O'Rourke in revolt, Fitzwilliam now saw his opportunity to gain the upper hand in Fermanagh. He summoned Bingham and the Earl of Thomond from Connacht to join him with their armies, his plan being that, with the help of the armies of Marshal Bagenal and Hugh O'Néill, they would drive Hugh Maguire out of his homeland.

---

[i] The injustice of Bingham's actions was compounded by the fact that MacMahon of Monaghan had previously been attainted and executed for the crime of forcibly collecting rents on productive lands.

[ii] Archbishop MacGauran and his assistant, Abbott Cathal Maguire were killed while ministering to the wounded. MacGauran had recently returned to Ireland having been appointed Archbishop of Armagh. He was dispatched to Rome the previous year by Hugh Maguire and Hugh O'Donnell to once more bring the plight of Irish Catholics to the notice of the Pope and King Philip of Spain. Ever since his return he had been a wanted man and the Earl of Tyrone, Hugh O'Néill, was accused by Bagenal of harbouring him.

Although vastly outnumbered, Maguire was determined to defend his native soil, and battle was joined between the two armies at a fording point on the River Erne near Belleek on October 10th, 1593. The more modern muskets of the English won the day as their range was much greater than the older Arquebus type used by Maguire's army and the English advance was held up for only a short time despite the deaths of around three hundred Fermanagh men. At the crossing of the Erne, Hugh O'Néill who led the English cavalry was injured in the thigh. The English now advanced into Enniskillen while the remnant of Maguire's army retreated. In Enniskillen, the English attacked Maguire's castle by river and successfully assaulted and entered it, after which the garrison surrendered. The garrison and the other inhabitants of the castle, including women and elderly, were all massacred.

Hugh Roe O'Donnell had received word of the impending battle and was advancing with all haste to Maguire's aid, intent on attacking the English force when Hugh O'Néill, aware of his progress towards Fermanagh, sent word to him to break off his advance, making arrangements for a parley with him on the following day. When they met, O'Néill told O'Donnell of his aversion for the proceedings and entreated him not to attack the English while he was in their ranks but to bide his time, after which O'Donnell agreed to hold his fire for the time being.

1594 – Ulster Declares War on the Crown

<u>The Fording of The River Arney</u>

After Hugh Maguire had been driven from Fermanagh, another Maguire – Conor Óg, who had cooperated with the English in opposition to Hugh, became puppet ruler of Fermanagh.

Early in 1594, Lord Deputy Fitzwilliam came to Fermanagh to install a new garrison of English soldiers in Hugh Maguire's castle in Enniskillen. Hugh Roe O'Donnell, who felt that he must now act either with or without Hugh O'Néill's blessing, responded positively to Hugh Maguire's plea for assistance in dislodging the garrison. Their joint armies marched on Enniskillen, laying the fortress under siege. On receiving news of this, Fitzwilliam ordered a heavily armed re-supply convoy under the command of Sir Edward Herbert and Sir Henry Duke, along with Henry Bingham, to proceed to Fermanagh. When news of the convoy reached the ears of Hugh O'Donnell, he appealed to Hugh O'Néill for reinforcements.

Shortly afterwards, Hugh O'Néill's brother Cormac appeared with a force of cavalry and foot soldiers, apparently without the Earl's blessing, and the English army was ambushed in early August 1594 at a fording point on the River Arney around the present day Drumane Bridge. The ambush was a complete success for the Ulstermen, who completely surprised the English and forced them to retreat, leaving the ground and river littered with provisions, which gave the crossing-point the name "Ford of the Biscuits". Around 300 English soldiers were killed in the engagement for minimal loss on the Ulster side. After word of the defeat reached Enniskillen Castle, the garrison capitulated and the chivalrous Hugh Maguire allowed them to leave his territory unhindered in spite of the massacre that the English had committed when they had captured the fortress the year before.

The Northern Alliance Goes West

Leaving some men in possession of Enniskillen, the Maguire / O'Donnell alliance departed on an expedition into North Connacht where Maguire's previous campaign against Sir Richard Bingham's reign of terror was renewed. As witness to the barbarism and desolation perpetrated by the English, they determined to fight fire with fire. All English settlements and castles that they came across were destroyed and every adult male who could not speak Gaelic was killed. Native governance was re-established in many parts of Connacht with O'Donnell (acting as traditional overlord of north Connacht) determining some disputed titles.

Hugh O'Néill goes to Dublin
Meanwhile in Dublin, Sir William Fitzwilliam was being replaced as Lord Deputy by Sir William Russell who was sworn in on August 11th. Shortly after Russell's arrival, Hugh O'Néill came to Dublin unexpectedly and was given a very frosty reception. He had come ostensibly to welcome the new Lord Deputy, but in reality to try and put him straight on the countless accusations of treason that Bagenal was forever laying against him. Russell was inclined to believe O'Néill, but Bagenal was more vehement than ever and charged him with many things, including training all the men of Tyrone in arms, as well as with storing large amounts of lead under the pretence of building a roof on his house so that he could manufacture vast quantities of musket balls in preparation for a rebellion. The Council debated as to whether or not they should seize O'Néill while they had him in their grasp, but some members were still friendly towards him, and he managed to leave Dublin unhindered. He could clearly see what way the wind was blowing and fully realized that his attempts to steer a middle course between the rights of the Gael and the intentions of the Crown in the matter of Ulster had reached the end of the road.

O'Néill Declares War "For Faith and Fatherland"
At the beginning of 1595, the English government decided to vastly reinforce the English army in Ireland. The decision was taken to send 2,000 veterans newly released from war on the continent along with 1,000 freshly trained men who were untried in battle. The army would be under the command of

Sir John Norris (of Rathlin Island infamy) who would be given the title of "Lord General". Lord Deputy Russell cannot have welcomed his appointment as he and Norris were old foes. In order that Russell would not interfere in his task, Norris, when informed of his appointment, demanded that his letters patent should stipulate that, while he engaged with the Ulster rebels, he would be outside Russell's jurisdiction.

The Capture of the Blackwater Fort
Deciding that he must act before this new English army arrived, Hugh O'Néill unsheathed his sword, this time not for Queen Elizabeth of England, but for Ulster and Ireland.
His first action was to send his brother Art MacBaron O'Néill with an army to capture the English fort on the River Blackwater which commanded the passage into Tyrone. The fort itself was a significant structure, constructed as an outpost of English power in the heart of Gaelic territory. Built in the form of a square, reinforced by towers, its earthworks were full of gun loop firing positions. Art O'Néill attempted to capture it by a *coup de main* operation, sending a small party of around forty men posing as English soldiers to the main gate with two "prisoners" in front, but the English guard opened fire on them after noticing that they had smouldering match-cords at the ready in order to fire their weapons. While the fracas at the main gate had the attention of the English, O'Néill's main force consisting of hundreds of men, succeeded in gaining access to the fort proper after scaling the earthworks. The English were forced to retreat into a wooden tower, agreeing to surrender only when Art O'Néill told them that the tower would be burnt if they did not come out. After their surrender, O'Néill granted the English garrison safe passage to Newry. Once the fort was in Gaelic hands, it was plundered for its war material and then burnt to the ground.

Hugh Roe O'Donnell under Siege in Sligo

Meanwhile, Hugh O'Néill ventured further south, raiding English settlements both in Cavan and Longford, while O'Donnell, joined by a Scottish army of 600 men under MacLeod of Ara, returned to Connacht, raiding as far as Tuam in Galway.

Sir Richard Bingham's brother, George, meanwhile determined to attack Tirconnell by sea while O'Donnell was in Connacht, and landed in Rathmullen where he plundered the Carmelite Monastery of the Blessed Virgin and also ransacked the Church of St. Columcille on Tory Island. However, he was killed shortly afterwards during an argument between himself and his men over the division of spoils.

As O'Donnell returned to Tirconnell from the west, he was hotly pursued by Bingham and the Earls of Ormond and Clanrickard. When he reached Ulick Burke's castle in Sligo, he and his army took refuge there and the pursuing English force put the castle under siege. The attackers constructed a movable gazebo made from timber taken from a local monastery, and after it was built, the gazebo was then moved in beside the castle wall so that it could be pierced without the attackers suffering heavy casualties. However, O'Donnell's men managed to destroy it by hurling huge rocks on top of it. Shortly afterwards, and with no plan of bringing the siege to a successful conclusion, the attackers retreated, fearful of reinforcements arriving from nearby Tirconnell. After their departure, O'Donnell abandoned the castle and destroyed it in case it should be later occupied by the English.

Attack on Monaghan Town

As soon as Lord General Norris arrived in May of 1595, he travelled north. Part of his army was sent to occupy the city of Armagh while Norris remained with the other part that included his artillery, which travelled to the large English army base in Newry. In Ireland's ancient apostolic city of Armagh, the members of the religious congregations remaining there fled for their lives ahead of the English troops who occupied their monasteries, stabling their horses in the city's churches which also had their statues and altars destroyed. In Dublin on June 28th, Sir William Russell issued a declaration pronouncing all the principals of the revolt as traitors.

In early summer, Hugh O'Néill, assisted by the MacMahons of Monaghan, turned his attention to the English of Monaghan and laid siege to its English garrison which had based itself in the monastery there. Sir John Norris, who was joined by his brother Sir Thomas (the acting Governor of Munster), now drew up plans to bring supplies and reinforcements to the beleaguered garrison in Monaghan from his Newry base, with the command of the relief force being given to Sir Henry Bagenal.

The Battle of Clontibret

The Monaghan-bound convoy of English troops and supplies consisted of around 1,800 men. Many of its officers and men were veterans of continental wars and as such were in no way fearful of any attack that the Ulstermen might mount against them.

Aware of their progress, Hugh O'Néill decided not to engage this force in a major battle on its way towards Monaghan but rather had a company of around 500 men harass them with sniper fire at the Crosdawlye Pass. At this point, the English detached a group of around 200 men under Captain Cuney to parry this assault while the remainder of the force made for Monaghan with Cuney following slowly, losing around fifty men, both killed and injured.

As the English approached Monaghan, the Irish who had the monastery under siege withdrew and the English successfully reinforced and re-supplied the garrison. However, on the following day, when the English, minus a full company of troops that remained in Monaghan, were returning to Newry from Monaghan via Clontibret, Hugh O Neill was lying in wait for them at the Pass of Clontibret with a large army of around 3,000 men from Monaghan, Fermanagh and Tyrone, as well as a large number of the intrepid Scottish Gallowglasses.

Long before the English had reached Clontibret, they were subjected to sniper fire from Irish sharpshooters, leaving them unsettled and eager to get away from the boggy Monaghan terrain into open country. As the English approached Clontibret an attack was launched on them from all sides on terrain favourable to the Irish.

During the ensuing battle, Hugh O'Néill's generalship and tactics left nothing to be desired as he used the various skills of his army to maximum effect. Once his foot soldiers had fired their muskets, they immediately retreated out of range to reload, at which point the cavalry following right behind them would close with the English front, then retreating themselves behind the foot soldiers who had advanced again with loaded muskets for another shot.

After the Irish attack began, the column was brought to a standstill as the English launched pike charge after pike charge to drive the Irish back, suffering heavy casualties in the process, as their column crept forward. After hours of this struggle, Bagenal decided to sacrifice his cavalry so that the rest of his men could get clear of this pass of death. In the ensuing cavalry charge, which was commanded by a very tall and powerful Captain named James Segrave, Hugh O'Néill was knocked off his horse by Segrave, who was himself unhorsed in the engagement. Both men now rolled on the ground, each trying to overpower the other, and fighting hand to hand, until O'Néill finally managed to retrieve a dagger from his person and plunged it into Segrave's abdomen below his armour, killing him. The English had meanwhile advanced and slowly managed to get clear of the Irish, their cavalry having been almost wiped out. With darkness falling, the English were forced to halt for the night but were not attacked again as O'Néill's men were almost completely out of gunpowder. The following day a relief force from Newry arrived to assist them.

Hugh O'Néill is Inaugurated "The O'Néill"

July of 1595 saw the death of Turlough Luineach O'Néill. After his demise, Hugh O'Néill took for himself the title "The O'Néill", an illegal title in English eyes, and one which Hugh had previously repudiated. However, all bets were now off, and Hugh O'Néill knew that his taking of the title would not just draw all the Irish of Ulster under his banner but would make clear to the entire country that he was not just fighting for Tyrone but for Gaelic Ireland too. Around the same time, he received a communication from the English asking for a parley in order to discuss the grievances of the northern chieftains. Taking sufficient precaution, he agreed to meet in an open field outside Dundalk and was met by two members of the Government Council from Dublin, Wallop the Treasurer and Chief Justice Gardiner. O'Néill outlined to them the intolerable oppression under which the country suffered and insisted that Catholics should be allowed to practice their faith freely and without restriction. However, though the English representatives were not

Hugh O' Neill

empowered to make decisions, they agreed that they would take O'Néill's grievances to the Queen.

The Battle of Mullabrack

Up to this point, Sir John Norris had led a distinguished military career, one which he had no intention of allowing Hugh O'Néill to tarnish. Nevertheless, the astute military tactics and generalship of O'Néill were to prove costly to him.
As the Winter of 1595 approached, Norris, accompanied by his brother Thomas was in command of a re-supply convoy destined for Armagh when the convoy was attacked at Mullabrack(close to the town of Markethill) by a force of O'Neill's cavalry. While the English struggled to parry the cavalry attack both Norris and his brother were wounded and the convoy was forced to retreat.
Queen Elizabeth had expected swift results from Norris following his arrival in May, but his failure to get to grips with the rebels before the Winter of 1595 heralded his fall from grace leaving Norris, after decades of service to his queen feeling morose and depressed. He complained bitterly "There is no soldier whom hath shedde as much bloode for Her Majesty as I."

A Truce

Following this, Hugh O'Néill remained on a war-footing but did not engage in any further offensive measures against the English. In October, arrangements were made for a truce which O'Néill and the English agreed should last until the new-year. O'Donnell meanwhile persisted in his efforts in Connacht and by year's end north Connacht was liberated from English rule after which the people pledged themselves to fight under O'Donnell's banner. In August, there was a mass breakout of Irish prisoners from Bingham's Galway prison but those that escaped were either shot by soldiers while trying to get free of the city or hanged on recapture.

Ireland was quiet during the winter of 1595-96. In England, the Queen and her council considered their options and decided that Sir Richard Bingham, who had caused such turmoil in Connacht, was not fit to master the situation and should be replaced, while negotiations should continue with O'Néill and O'Donnell.

In January of 1596, Sir Conyers Clifford arrived as Bingham's replacement and a further meeting between the English and the Ulster Chieftains took place near Dundalk. Along with demands relating to overbearing English interference, both men demanded freedom for the Catholic Faith to which the English negotiators offered concessions in all areas, excepting the right to practice the Catholic Faith freely. Although the negotiations ended inconclusively, it was agreed that the truce should be prolonged.

Hugh O'Néill and Hugh Roe O'Donnell never doubted that any concessions the English proposed to make would be but short lived, and that the English desire to gain complete and utter dominance over the entire country remained intact. They were well aware that theirs was but a delaying action to English intentions and that it was only a matter of time before the English would send enough troops to achieve victory. In concert with other chieftains, both men were in communication with King Philip II of Spain and proposed to him that "with your aid we may restore the faith and secure you a kingdom"[141] proposing to him that the Archduke of Austria could be King of Ireland.

O'Néill was also using the truce to try and rouse all of Ireland's chieftains into supporting a nationwide revolt, beseeching them to rise and fight in support of "Christ's Catholic religion."[142]

The War in Leinster
Massacre in Offaly
In Leinster meanwhile, the English had been on the trail of Fiach MacHugh O'Byrne (who was a friend of Hugh O'Néill) since the beginning of the year and had successfully penetrated as far as his home at Glenmalure. However, he had managed to escape. Roused not only by the actions of the English against him, but also by Hugh O'Néill's revolt, he resolved to unsheathe his sword once more, and was joined by Owny O'More, the son of Rory Óg O'More of Leix.

Another Chieftain who joined the revolt in Leinster at this time was Domhnall O'Madden, whose territory was in Co. Offaly. In March of 1596, Sir William Russell came to Offaly in order to destroy Madden's castle at Cloghan. On arriving there with a large English force, Russell sent Captain Thomas Lee as his envoy to the castle to demand that the Irish surrender. Lee shortly returned to Russell with the Irish reply: "If every man in his Lordship's company were a Lord Deputy, still we would not surrender"[143].

However, the bravery of the Irish did not make up for the English artillery and the following day Russell laid the castle under bombardment, during which forty-six of its defenders were killed. Nevertheless when the artillery went quiet, the Irish still held out but following resumption of the bombardment, the castle surrendered. After the surrender, the English, as was their practice in Ireland, showed no mercy. All the remaining Irish were thrown from the battlements of the castle so that not one of them remained alive.

On May 19th, 1596, Eóghan O'More and his men joined battle with a force of English commanded by the much reviled Alexander Cosby (son of Francis Cosby of Mullamast infamy), the engagement taking place at Stradbally Bridge. In the battle, O'More's Irish force successfully routed the English, killing Alexander Cosby and his son Francis.

A Plea to the King of Spain

In early May of 1596 the two northern Gaelic leaders were destined to have an unscheduled meeting. A Spanish ship had arrived in Killybegs with a cargo of ammunition for their cause and the Captain of the Ship Don Alonso Cobos wished to speak personally to them. A messenger was sent to Fermanagh to summon Hugh O'Néill, and after his arrival a meeting between the three men took place in Lifford. Following the meeting, a letter dated May 16th asking for Spanish aid signed by the two Gaelic Princes, was entrusted to Cobos to be delivered to the King of Spain's son, the Prince of Asturias. It read in part: "We have already written, most Serene Prince, to the Great King your father what we thought most necessary for our country. We implore that your Highness will aid in his clemency this most excellent and just cause, that of asserting Catholic liberty and of freeing the country from the rod of tyrannical evil and that, with the help of the Divine Majesty, he may win for Christ an infinite number of souls, snatching them from the jaws of hell, and may wholly destroy the minister of satanic fury."[144]

Since Sir Conyers Clifford's arrival in Connacht, he had replaced Bingham's reign of terror with a more conciliatory policy and, working along with O'Connor of Sligo who had just returned to Connacht (in December 1596) after a long sojourn in England, successfully managed to detach some of the province's chieftains, including MacDonough of Tireill, from their pledge of loyalty to Hugh Roe O'Donnell. O'Donnell did not take this change in allegiance lightly, and he returned to Connacht where he despoiled the territories of those who had not maintained their loyalty to him, venturing even further into the province than before, attacking both Athenry and Oranmore. Such was O'Donnell's vigour in pursuing those who had reneged on their declaration of allegiance to him, that the Annals of the Four Masters tells us that it was thought better "to have the (English) Governor in opposition than to be pursued by O'Donnell's vengeance"[145.]

The rebellion in Leinster now suffered a grave setback when, in May of 1597, the English successfully cornered Fiach MacHugh O'Byrne and killed him, apparently after his location was betrayed to them by a cousin of his with whom he had had an argument. So passed into eternity one of the bravest Irishmen of the sixteenth century.

Russell replaced by Borough as Lord Deputy

The tenure of Sir William Russell as Lord Deputy was short lived for, on the 22nd of May, he was recalled, and Thomas Lord Borough was appointed in his place. Almost immediately, Borough relieved Sir John Norris who had achieved little in the way of military success against the Irish. Shortly after being returned to his former job as Governor of Munster, Norris died, apparently broken-hearted at his dismissal.

Borough's arrival heralded a massive reinforcement of English troops in the country, now numbering seven thousand men, which he felt was enough to enable him to bring the rebellion to an end.

Hugh O'Néill, meanwhile, was determined to extend the rebellion as far south as possible. After extensive raiding, a path to the midlands had been thrown open and O'Néill dispatched two of his Captains – Tyrell and Lacy to this part of the country with a force of men.

After his arrival in Dublin, Lord Borough and his advisors set to work straight away on a strategy by which the rebels might be taken into hand. He devised a three-pronged attack. He himself intended to lead an army direct from Dublin marching northwards to retake the territory of the now abandoned fortress at Portmore so that a new fort could be established. From the west, Sir Conyers Clifford was to marshal his force at Boyle in Roscommon where he would link up with the Earls of

Thomond and Clanrickard among others and together they would march against Hugh Roe O'Donnell. Finally, from the midlands Lord Trimlestown of Meath was to command an army which would march northwards from Mullingar, engaging the enemy at every opportunity and eventually meeting with Clifford in Ballyshannon.

The Battle of Tyrrellspass
As Lord Trimblestown's army mustered in Mullingar and prepared to depart northwards on its campaign against the rebels, Trimblestown received news of a small force of Irish rebels to his south and decided to eradicate this menace before undertaking the main effort. Deciding that this" little task" was beneath him,[146] Trimblestown thought that it would be a good opportunity for his son and heir, the twenty-three-year-old Robert Barnewell to prove himself, and so the latter marched south in command of the army to dispose of the troublemakers while his father awaited their return in Mullingar.
The Irish force was larger than Lord Trimblestown had thought, as it actually consisted of around 400 men under the command of Captain Richard Tyrrell (of Norman and Gaelic descent and formerly of Queen Elizabeth's army) who, as a devout Catholic, had come over to O'Néill's side in defence of the Catholic faith. Tyrrell had his spies watching the English army and they kept him informed of its intentions and direction of travel. When he learned that the English were in pursuit of him, he formulated his plan of attack. As they came towards him, he waited until he knew that they had caught sight of him, and then rode on out of sight with his men into a hollow where he split his force in two at a place which is now called Tyrrellspass. One half of his force under Lieutenant O'Connor took up hiding positions in the hollow while Tyrrell, with the remainder of his men, rode back onto the main track

where they were soon spotted by the pursuing English. Totally oblivious of the presence of the other half of the Irish force, the English passed by the hollow. Leading his men out, O'Connor then pursued the enemy and proceeded to attack them from the rear as the fifes and drums of his company sounded out the agreed signal called "Tyrrell's march". On hearing this signal, Tyrrell turned and attacked the English from the front. Trapped between two hammer blows, the English army struggled to come to grips with its foe but was eventually overwhelmed and defeated with heavy loss.

After the battle, Robert Barnewell was taken prisoner and brought north to the camp of Hugh O'Néill. One English soldier escaped from the battlefield and returned to Mullingar to report to Lord Trimblestown the destruction of his army. Following this great victory, Tyrrell received fresh reinforcements from O'Néill, at which point he renewed his midlands campaign with great vigour and success, scoring another victory against an English force at Maryborough (Portlaoise), followed by a campaign against the Earl of Ormond.

The English rebuild the Blackwater Fort

Lord Borough had better success than Trimblestown, as O'Néill seemed to be taken unawares by his advance and did not engage him on his march northwards. After reaching Drogheda where his army was further augmented, he led this large force into Tyrone unopposed and successfully crossed the River Blackwater, where he made his encampment. Here he constructed a strong fort to replace the one that had been destroyed, while his army was continuously engaged in harassing attacks by O'Néill's troops. After the fort was constructed, it was garrisoned by 300 men under the command of Captain Williams. Elated with his success, Borough now returned south, boasting that he had regained the key to Ulster.

When London received this news, it was quickly spread abroad in an effort to avoid what the English feared most – a Spanish attack on Ireland to assist the rebels.

Borough had not yet got to Dublin when news reached him that his new Blackwater Fort was under attack by O'Néill, after which he immediately returned to the north where the siege of the fort was lifted at a high cost. In the engagement that took place before the fort with O'Néill's troops, the Earl of Kildare (who accompanied Borough) was killed, and Lord Borough was fatally wounded, dying on his stretcher before Newry was reached. However, the fort was further reinforced and supplied.

The Siege of Ballyshannon Castle

Meanwhile, Conyers Clifford was making good progress in his advance towards Ballyshannon, and by early August he had successfully passed through Sligo and crossed the River Erne at Belleek after heavy fighting. Here Clifford lost Murrough O'Brien, Baron of Inchiquin, who was shot dead by the Irish as he forded the river. On arriving at Ballyshannon Castle, Clifford immediately bombarded it using cannon that had arrived by sea from Galway. Nevertheless, the castle, under the command of the Scotsman Hugh Crawford, refused to surrender. On hearing of Clifford's advance, Hugh Roe O'Donnell mustered his army and made for Ballyshannon with all possible speed where he took Clifford's encampment under fire. At dawn on August 15th, 1597 Clifford abandoned the siege in great secrecy, hoping to escape from O'Donnell. O'Donnell was taken unawares, and gave chase as soon as he realised what was happening. Clifford's army was pursued in heavy rain and O'Donnell called a halt after his troops' powder became damp, returning to Ballyshannon where he found to his satisfaction that Clifford had abandoned his artillery and much of his supplies.

With only limited success in their northern campaign and the Lord Deputy dead, the English resolved to make a truce with the Irish and negotiations were reopened by the Earl of Ormond who had taken over the military duties of the Lord Deputy. The negotiations dragged on and it seemed that a deal might be done with O'Néill. A pardon was drawn up for him on April 11th, 1598, but O'Néill, seemingly unhappy with the proffered English concessions, broke off the negotiations.

The Battle of the Yellow Ford

The Trap is Set

On June 7th, 1598, the truce between the English and Irish came to an end. Two days later, Hugh O'Néill returned to the Blackwater Fort and once more placed it under siege. This time, he did not attempt to attack it, but instead surrounded it with deep, wide trenches topped with thorn bushes so that there could be neither entry nor exit from it without a battle. The roadway approaching the fort was also dug up so that no artillery could be brought to bear on the besieging Irish. After leaving a force large enough to hold the fort under siege, O'Néill departed in order to make further preparations for the arrival of the English, knowing that it would be only a matter of time before they would come to relieve it.

The fortress was still under the command of Captain Thomas Williams, and he had enough supplies to feed his garrison until the end of June. Williams was resolute in his defiance, absolutely refusing to surrender even after his stores were depleted. Word of his predicament eventually reached Dublin, and, after long deliberation, the Council decided to go along with Marshal Bagenal's plan, that he should lead a great army to save the garrison. Ormond had argued against the plan in the strongest possible terms, but his objections were described as shameful and timid by Bagenal who longed to defeat O'Néill in battle. Once again, fresh troops poured into the country from England, landing at all the major ports along the east coast of Ireland. One contingent of English soldiers that had arrived in the port of Dungarvan was making its way to Dublin, when it was ambushed by the Irish, with the loss of 400 men on the English side.

The insurgency in Leinster at this time was of such magnitude that the Dublin council now made a fatal mistake. Having gone along with Marshal Bagenal's plan to relieve the Blackwater Fort, the English now split their resources, dividing their troops between Ulster and Leinster. Bagenal would head north to Armagh with one division of 4,500 foot soldiers and 500 cavalrymen, while Ormond would stay in Leinster with another division and tackle the rebels there.

The Trap is Sprung

On Monday morning, August 14th, 1598, Marshal Bagenal's army left Armagh to the sound of fife and drum, with regimental colours fluttering in the summer breeze. His infantry was divided into six regiments grouped in three parts. The first part was led by Colonel Percy and contained his own regiment as well as Marshal Bagenal's; the second part consisted of the regiments of Colonel Cosby and Sir Thomas Wingfield, while Captains Cuynis and Billings commanded the two regiments in the rear. The English Cavalry was commanded by Sir Calisthenes Brooke and Captains Montague and Fleming.

The road to the Fort from the city of Armagh was five miles long, a path of uneven ground wooded on either side. Two miles along this roadway at the River Callan, there was a fording point at Bellanaboy called "The Yellow Ford" and it was at this crossing-point that the Gaelic generals Hugh O'Néill, Hugh Maguire, James MacSorley MacDonnell and

Hugh Roe O'Donnell[i] had assembled their army, with Hugh O'Néill in overall command. The Irish foot-soldiers were equal in number to the English although not as well armed and the number of Irish cavalry was a little larger than that of the English. O'Néill had also constructed a huge defence system on the approach to his main position at Drumcullen consisting of a trench one mile in length, four feet in width and five feet deep. The approach to the trench was strewn with felled trees and deep holes which were covered over with branches and vegetation.

The Irish were clearly aware of English intentions as on the night of the 13 to the 14th August, O'Néill had sent a group of around 500 men to take up sniping positions in the woodland outside Armagh. These snipers now harassed the English army as it advanced towards the besieged fortress. As there was no attack from the front, the march continued unabated. However, the sniping had its desired effect as the gap that had existed between the regiments and battle groups now opened ever wider.

When the great trench was reached by the first regiment (Percy's), the soldiers charged across the obstacle and forced their way to the other side unopposed, immediately reforming for the advance. As Percy's men continued the advance, they successfully reached the hilltop at Mullyleggan where they were spotted by a lookout at the distant fort. When the lookout reported that their relief was near, the spirits of the besieged men soared.

O'Néill now let loose an Irish charge that overwhelmed Percy's regiment which was forced to retreat back towards the trench

---

[i] Hugh Roe O'Donnell was accompanied by his poet and one of the authors of "The Annals of the Four Masters", Fearfeasa O'Clery, who encouraged the Irish with the words of St. Bearchan who had prophesied that at a place called "The Yellow Ford" the Foreigner would be defeated by a man named Hugh O'Néill.

in disarray, while Bagenal, who was at the head of the second regiment, was coming up behind them and led his men across the trench, undeterred by their retreat.

Hugh O'Néill was waiting for this moment and, as Bagenal's regiment gained the far side of the trench, an Irish cavalry charge was launched, with O'Néill at its head, determined to meet Bagenal in battle. As the latter raised his visor to survey this new threat, a musket ball struck him on the forehead and killed him.

The English were now split since their cavalry could not easily cross the trench. The infantry that had managed to cross did not have their support, while many who had fallen in the trench were crushed by those following.

As the second regiment (Bagenal's) was being engaged, an Irish force led by MacDonnell, Maguire and O'Donnell were outflanking the battlefield to meet with the third English battle group of two regiments before they came up to the main trench.

There was now heavy fighting all along the trench and, as the Irish gradually overcame the first two regiments, the third regiment under Cosby (which was almost at the trench) was not in time to save them from destruction. Cosby's unit in turn became the focus of Irish attention. The great error in Marshal Bagenal's tactics now became obvious for he had allowed the gap between each group of two regiments to go unchecked.

As Cosby's regiment fought, the English line of march to his rear became restricted when a huge siege cannon weighing almost 3,000 pounds became bogged down after the four oxen hauling it were killed. All efforts to free the cannon from the mire proved fruitless. As the fourth regiment struggled to circumvent this obstacle and reach the trench, a soldier who was low on gunpowder tried to resupply himself from a passing munitions wagon with a lit musket match-cord still in his hand. As he struggled with the match-cord, musket and gunpowder, a spark from the match-cord ignited the gunpowder and the wagon exploded in the middle of the English convoy, killing and wounding many of the advancing soldiers while the huge siege gun "moved from where it was to another place by the force and conflagration of the dry powder, when it blazed up fiercely to the clouds of the heavens...the hill too all round was one mass of dark black fog for a while after, so that it was not easy for any one to recognise a man of his own people from his enemies."[147] According to the English after-battle-report, in the aftermath of the great explosion the English army was "disrancked and rowted...wherewith the traitors were encouraged, and our men dismayed".[148]

While the battle was raging at the trench, the Irish had successfully come around the battlefield and now attacked the third group of two regiments from the flank while they were still on the approach to the trench. As some of the English struggled to keep the Irish at bay, others tried to dash forward to help their comrades at the front but, according to the English battle report, the majority of them "being hard sett to, retired foully (in disorder) to Armagh".[149]

By this stage, there was a desperate struggle along the whole length of the English column. In order to create greater confusion in the centre of the column, O'Néill withdrew from the front and went around the battlefield, taking with him about forty of his cavalry, followed by pikemen. When the centre of the column was reached, he charged into the fray.

It was plainly obvious to the English commanders that their mission had failed and, as the English casualties mounted, more and more men were abandoning the battlefield. By 1pm, a general rout of the English was in progress, with the Irish in pursuit. The pits and deep holes that the Irish had dug off the beaten track now ensnared many an Englishman struggling to escape his pursuers.

Of the 4,000 men that had set out from Armagh that morning, two thousand lay dead on the battlefield while a further one thousand had been wounded or had deserted. It was Ireland's greatest victory against the English and the worst military defeat suffered by Elizabeth in her forty year reign.

Among the English killed were Marshal Bagenal, 14 colonels and captains and 9 lieutenants. They had also lost all their artillery and the stores destined for the fort. The estimate of Irish losses in the battle varies from 300 to 700, depending on the source accessed.

After returning to Armagh, the English came under siege there. Two days after the battle, both Armagh and the Portmore Fort surrendered on favourable terms, with O'Néill granting the remaining troops safe passage and protection to Dundalk so long as all weapons, munitions, military stores and regimental colours were left behind.

Munster Rises Again

The resounding Irish victory at The Yellow Ford heralded a widespread nationwide rebellion against English rule. Areas that had previously been "pacified" now rose up in revolt, especially in Munster where O'Néill was already in contact with James Fitzthomas, nephew of the last Earl of Desmond (who had taken for himself the mantle of leader of the Munster Geraldines that had suffered so much in the Desmond Rebellion) and Florence (Fineen) MacCarthy Reagh, leader of the MacCarthys. O'Néill wrote to his midland Captains, Tyrrell and Lacey, urging them to go south with all speed and link up with the Munster chieftains and Fitzthomas. Along with Owny O'More, Redmond Burke and their army, they travelled south and before long the Irish and some of the Old English of Munster had risen up against their English rulers. Within two short weeks, the plantation of Munster was largely reversed with English Undertakers, planters and their families fleeing for their lives before the Irish wrath as they abandoned their appropriated lands.[i] 9,000 Munster men joined the revolt and the Irish Confederate Armies now numbered over 20,000 men. Fortified cities and towns, however, remained in the control of the Crown as O'Néill lacked the artillery he needed to take these on. He was, however, hoping that in time Spanish aid would remedy this problem as, after the death of Philip II in September 1598, his son Philip III renewed his father's promise of help. Philip II had done his utmost to help the Irish cause for in late 1596 and in early 1597 two Armadas[ii] had set sail for Ireland but both of them had been forced to turn back with loss after being broken up by severe weather.

An Ominous Portent

The first English reaction to the defeat at The Yellow Ford was the appointment of Sir Richard Bingham as Marshal Bagenal's replacement. This reaction speaks volumes as not long before this Bingham had been replaced as President of Connacht by Clifford due to the reign of butchery and slaughter he had masterminded against the Irish of that province. That he was now appointed as Marshal of the Army meant that the English were once more contemplating a war of scorched earth and murder. After arriving in Ireland with 2,000 men who had previously been earmarked for a naval landing on Lough Foyle, Bingham promptly died and was in turn replaced by Sir Samuel Bagenal. During the winter of 1598-99, the English remained largely holed up in the Pale and other walled cities,

---

[i] "The cause of this original hate is for that they were conquered of the English, the memory whereof is yet fresh among them and the desire both of revenge and also of recovery of their lands, is daily revived and kindled amongst them by their lords and counselors; for which they both hate ourselves and our laws and customs." – Edmund Spenser - A Brief Note of Ireland (London 1598)

[ii] Armada is the Spanish word for fleet.

while in England a massive army of Irish conquest was prepared.

"The Royallest Army"

In April 1599, Robert Devereux, second Earl of Essex (a man with whom Queen Elizabeth was besotted) was sent to Ireland as Lord Deputy with an army of 20,000 foot soldiers and 2,000 cavalry, the largest and best equipped English army ever to land on these shores, or in the words of Queen Elizabeth "the royallest army that ever went out of England."[150] He had been specifically instructed by the Queen that he was to go north and defeat Hugh O'Néill and construct forts at Lough Foyle in Derry and Ballyshannon in Donegal but the Council in Dublin, whose members had all their wealth, land and interests in Leinster and Munster, prevailed on him to go into the midlands and the south first to deal with the threat there.

Ambush at The Cashel Pass
Having sent reinforcements to the garrison towns of Newry, Drogheda, Dundalk, Naas and Wicklow, Devereux marshalled his army of 7,000 men on the Curragh of Kildare and from there began his campaign in the midlands. The movements of the Earl of Essex's large army were being monitored by Owny O'More and was harassed every step of the way by his force. Essex's first objective was Maryborough (Portlaoise) where the garrison there was being besieged by O'More's men. As Essex approached, O'More and his men withdrew. However, the following day (17th May 1599), as Essex's column made for Kilkenny, it marched through the Cashel Pass (about halfway between Portlaoise and Timahoe) and was ambushed there by O'More's men who allowed the advance guard of the column to pass unhindered, concentrating their effort on the rear of the column and the baggage train. In an engagement which lasted

around two hours, there were significant English casualties[i] before the English disengaged and cleared the Pass which is now referred to as "The Pass of the Plumes" as following the battle it was littered with English helmets adorned with plumes. Essex now made for Cahir Castle, home of a branch of the Anglo-Irish Butler family that had remained Catholic and sided with O'Néill. Here, after a three-day siege, Essex achieved the only military success of his campaign when the castle surrendered. He then followed a circuitous route around Munster in order to engage the Geraldine leader Fitzthomas and his army in battle but met with little military success, losing a lot of his own army piecemeal in ambushes and small battles.

Devereaux, Earl of Essex

Around this time, the President of Munster Sir Thomas Norris was also killed in an engagement against the Irish in Kilmallock as he awaited Essex's arrival. By mid-July, Essex was back in Dublin, returning from Munster along the eastern seaboard. Having departed the Curragh in May with 7,000 men, his army was reduced to less than half that number due to battle casualties and sickness. In London, Queen Elizabeth was growing impatient with his lack of progress[ii] while his

---

[i] The period historian Philip O'Sullivan Beare puts the number of English dead at 500.

[ii] Queen Elizabeth was also angered by the number of men Essex was knighting in Ireland. His detractors were known to quip: "He does not draw his sword except to bestow a knighthood".

many enemies at the Queen's court rejoiced at the Earl's fall from grace.

The Battle of The Yellow Pass

Meanwhile in Connacht, Hugh Roe O'Donnell was undertaking a siege against the castle of O'Connor Sligo at Collooney. After hearing that Sir Conyers Clifford had departed Athlone with an army to relieve the castle, Hugh Roe left the siege in the charge of his cousin Niall Garbh O'Donnell and departed for the pass of Ballaghboy (The Yellow Pass) in the Curlieu Mountains, through which he knew Clifford's army must surely advance. On the morning of August 15th, 1599, O'Donnell and his men were attending Mass for the Feast of the Assumption of the Blessed Virgin Mary on their hillside encampment. Mass had just concluded when O'Donnell's scouts reported the first sighting of the approaching English army. Hugh Roe then addressed his men on the importance of their fight for Faith and fatherland, after which the last preparations for battle were made.

Despite encountering O'Donnell's advance guard of javelin throwers and snipers, the English came on undeterred and were by now on a wide section of the track which led through the mountain on which they marched twelve abreast. When the track entered woodland where O'Donnell had situated his main battle line, he launched his attack and there followed a short but desperate struggle. The English front was led by Sir Alexander Radcliffe and after he and a number of other officers were killed, the vanguard broke and retreated into the centre of the column which continued forward undiscouraged. Although the Irish muskets were few in number, their fire was extremely accurate and when the English attempted to launch a charge at the Irish line, it broke up long before they had reached it. Following this, there was a spontaneous general retreat in the English ranks that Sir Conyers Clifford attempted to stop. As he tried to rally his men, Clifford was struck by a lance and died on the field. After the battle had been joined, reinforcements arrived for O'Donnell in the form of O'Rourke of Leitrim and his army, and these fresh men pursued the retreating English. English losses in the battle were significant and added to the angst already felt in the royal court as the stream of bad news from Ireland seemed endless. When news of a military defeat had arrived from Ireland on this or a similar occasion, Queen Elizabeth is recorded as remarking: "We receive naught else but news of fresh losses and calamities from Ireland. We disdain to bear affronts from a rabble of base cur".[151]

After the battle, Clifford's body was found on the battlefield and buried with honour at Lough Key Monastery. His severed head was taken to O'Connor Sligo as proof that he could expect no relief to the siege of his castle. Satisfied that his English friends could not relieve him, O'Connor Sligo surrendered, and the siege was brought to a peaceful conclusion.

The Earl of Essex Angers his Queen

While Clifford and his army succumbed to O'Donnell's men, Essex, who was in Dublin considering his next move, decided that it was time to go into Ulster. However, he found that the number of men at his disposal was insufficient for an advance on the province and he requested the Queen to send 2,000 more troops to bolster his army. Finally in September he departed Dublin for the north, telling the Queen in a dispatch that the most he could manage before winter was to set up a blocking force against O'Néill on the borders of his territory. After advancing as far as the Lagan at Annaclint (where Louth and Monaghan meet) he called a halt to the march after

O'Néill's sizeable army was sighted. No battle followed but rather a parley between the two commanders after O'Néill sent his adjutant O'Hagan forward under a flag of truce to make contact with Essex.[i] The following day, there were lengthy negotiations between the two parties and a truce was agreed until the following May after Essex noted O'Néill's demands.[ii] When news of Essex's truce with O'Néill was received in London, the Queen was furious. One of her aides wrote of her: "She walks much in her privy chamber and stamps much with her feet at (the) ill news, and thrusts her rusty sword at times into the arras (wall tapestry) in great rage."[152] Such was the Queen's displeasure at the truce that Essex returned to London without royal permission in order to justify himself before her, but was instead placed under house arrest. After encouraging a court revolt while imprisoned, he was charged with treason and executed on February 25th, 1601.[iii]

---

[i] Essex was much more favourably disposed to the Catholic religion than many of his predecessors, permitting the public celebration of Mass in out of the way buildings other than parish churches. He also released numbers of priests from imprisonment and did not demur from the appointing of "old English" Catholics to positions in the Irish government.

[ii] O'Néill's demands were freedom to practice the Catholic faith, that the principal officers of state and judges should be natives of Ireland, that half of the English garrison army should be Irishmen and that he and the other Irish leaders should be free to govern the land of their ancestors.

[iii] Essex was the last man to be executed in the tower of London. Ironically, his executioner Thomas Derrick had been previously pardoned by Essex on a charge of rape on condition that he became an executioner. Derrick botched the execution, having to strike three times with his axe before Essex's head was finally severed from his body. Also implicated and executed in the court revolt was Captain Thomas Lee whom we have encountered in our narrative several times.

Chapter 18

The Nine Years War 2 - Years of Defeat

An English Victory at any Price
As the year 1600 began, the English remained entrenched in Dublin and many other garrison towns while much of the country at large had once more returned into native hands.
The English had so far proved themselves incapable of overcoming the Irish Confederates militarily. However, if victory could not be achieved by military means alone, then other tried and tested methods such as scorched earth, man-made famine and the murder of civilians were now to be employed in order to ensure victory for the English.

The Death of Hugh Maguire
In January 1600, Hugh O'Néill, accompanied by Hugh Maguire and an army of 3,000 men, went south to Cork to give assistance and encouragement to the rebellion in Munster. Aside from a number of minor engagements, the journey was uneventful, and on their way south they visited Holy Cross Abbey in Tipperary where O'Néill and his army venerated the relic of the True Cross. O'Néill set up his encampment in Cork on the banks of the River Lee, and welcomed James

Fitzthomas[i] and many of the local Chieftains (O'Donohoe, MacCarthy, O'Sullivan Beare and O'Mahony) to his encampment. During their Lee-side sojourn, Hugh Maguire was wounded while out riding with only a few companions after stumbling upon 60 English cavalry, led by Sir Warham Sentleger. During the brief engagement, Maguire fatally wounded Sentleger with his lance after the latter shot him with his musket. Having fought their way through the English cavalry, the group returned to O'Néill's encampment where Maguire collapsed. His chaplain, who had accompanied him on the expedition, rushed to his side and gave him the last rites moments before he succumbed to his wound.

The Arrival of Blount and Carew

Towards the end of February, while he was still in Cork, O'Néill received word that a fresh English army of 20,000 men under the command of Lord Mountjoy (George Blount) had landed in Dublin. Mountjoy was accompanied by a man who possessed an intense hatred for the Gaelic race[153] – Sir George Carew, the newly appointed President of Munster. On his departure from England, Queen Elizabeth had expressly forbidden Mountjoy "the pardon of the arch traitor [O'Néill]"[154], calling him "a monster of ingratitude".[155]

The new English campaign against the Confederacy was to be split into two parts. While Mountjoy was to concentrate his efforts on crushing the rebellion in Leinster and Ulster, Carew was to do likewise in Munster.

---

[i] O'Néill conferred on Fitzthomas the title "Earl of Desmond". He was thereafter sometimes referred to by the Irish as "The Sugan Earl" or "The Earl of Straw"

Carew in Munster
It was less than twenty years since the people of Munster had suffered terribly from famine, despoliation and murder at the hands of the English during and in the aftermath of the Desmond revolt and now their suffering was renewed in like manner. As Carew turned his attention to the rebel strongholds, that attention was also directed at the houses and crops of the ordinary people of Munster in order to cause a famine. The common people of the southern province now fled to the mountains and forests in fear of their lives and, without food or the means of proper shelter, many thousands of them perished from starvation and deprivation. One by one, the rebel strongholds were attacked and taken, and their defenders massacred. At the beginning of July, Carew personally supervised the siege of Glin Castle, on the banks of the River Shannon. After a stubborn defence, the castle surrendered, and its defenders were slaughtered.

The Foyle Landings
Mountjoy's plan for Hugh O'Néill was to try and isolate him in Tyrone by attacks from both land and sea. In a brilliant tactical manoeuvre, Sir Hugh Dowcra was sent by ship from England with 4,500 men to land on the banks of the Foyle River. As O'Néill attempted to deal with this threat, Mountjoy marched north from Dublin as if to invade Tyrone, the result being that O'Néill was forced to split his army. After a successful landing, Dowcra succeeded in constructing several forts, at Culmore, Derry and Dunalong, the material for these being stone and wood taken from nearby churches and monasteries that the English first desecrated and then destroyed. Dowcra had also planned to send a large expedition under the command of Captain Matthew Morgan to Ballyshannon but abandoned this idea, feeling that the mission would not succeed. Further south, O'Néill succeeded in keeping

Mountjoy at bay with the help of an elaborate series of defences known as "Tyrone's Trenches."

Man Made Famine

Leinster and Ulster were now destined to suffer the same fate as Munster. In Leinster, following forty years of incessant struggle against larceny and plantation, the native Irish had regained much of their land and were enjoying some peace and prosperity. Most had not become embroiled in the recent conflict. However, in August 1600, as the crops were almost ready to be reaped, Mountjoy arrived. He came from Dublin with an army, armed not only with the implements of war but also with agricultural implements including sickles, scythes and special harrows called "Pracas" which were constructed with long pointed rods to uproot crops. The entire crop, which was supposed to ensure the people's survival through the winter and into the following year was ripped up and burned.[i] On August 17th 1600, as the gallant Gaelic Chieftain Owny O'More led his men against Mountjoy's army in Leix (Laois), he was mortally wounded by a musket shot. In the battles that followed, the overwhelming strength and power of the enemy ensured that his country of Leix fell into the hands of the invader once more.

When his task was complete in Leinster, Mountjoy returned north and attempted but failed to break O'Néill's defences at

---

[i] Mountjoy's secretary was a man named Fynes Moryson. Of Mountjoy's entry into Leix he wrote that the land in Leix was found well manured, the fields fenced, the towns populous and the roads and pathways in good condition, remarking that it was incredible that this should be achieved by "so barbarous inhabitants the reason thereof being that the Queen's forces during these wars never till then come amongst them". He then adds: "Our Captains and by their example the common soldier did cut down with their sword all the rebels' corn to the value of £10,000 and upwards, the only means by which they were to live".

the Moyry Pass (known as the "Gap of the North"). Regarding O'Néill's defences and resistance, Mountjoy observed that "these barbarous people had far exceeded our custom and our expectation."[156] Although unable to break through to Tyrone, Mountjoy nevertheless adopted the same procedure of scorched earth wherever he could, admonishing his Captains to "burn all the dwellings and destroy the corn in the ground"[157], which was carried out over a large part of the province so that by year's end almost the entire country was in the grip of a terrible famine.

Due to the nature of his barbarous tactics against the entire population, Mountjoy preferred to campaign in Winter as the cattle and sheep had been brought down from the upland pastures and were more easily slaughtered and burned by his men. Also, he could be sure that, after the destruction of stores of grain or potatoes, the people would starve as the countryside was naked of fruit and berries.

Treachery among the Irish

For centuries "Divide et Impera" (Divide and Conquer) had worked well for the English in Ireland and now they sought its use again in order to split the alliance. O'Néill and O'Donnell suffered a treacherous blow when a number of their captains were wooed by the English with promises of power and wealth if they would come over to their side. Arthur O'Néill (son of Turlough Luineach), Niall Garbh O'Donnell (grandson of Calvach O'Donnell) and Domhnall O'Cahan were bought by them. Niall Garbh was promised that he would become Earl of Tirconnell after the destruction of Hugh Roe. He had indeed long felt that but for Hugh Roe the rule of Donegal should have been his. He turned traitor along with his three brothers, Hugh Boy, Domhnall and Con and a significant number of adherents and offered much intelligence and local knowledge to the English, to such an extent that Dowcra admitted that little could have been achieved by the English without them.[158]

Ulster under Pressure

By the middle of 1601, using all means at their disposal, the English had successfully crushed the revolt everywhere except in Ulster and the founders of the Confederacy were now its last active adherents. Deciding to try once more to enter into O'Néill's heartland of Tyrone, Mountjoy successfully forced his way through the Moyry Pass running through Slieve Gullion between Newry and Dundalk during the summer of 1601. From here he attempted to advance towards Tyrone, burning and pillaging as he went. However, O'Néill's forces put up a desperate resistance and Mountjoy was forced to retreat. Nevertheless, he managed to occupy positions previously held by O'Néill at the Moyry Pass.

Meanwhile in Tirconnell, Red Hugh O'Donnell was besieged by enemies from both north and south. He struggled to parry English attacks both from Connacht and from Dowcra who sent the treacherous Niall Garbh at the head of five hundred English soldiers towards Ballyshannon to establish a fort. When they were attempting to turn Donegal Monastery into an English fort, Hugh Roe attacked them and forced them to retreat to Magherbeg.

In Tirconnell, Dowcra's tactics were similar to Mountjoy's. After failing to capture the Fanad stronghold of the Clan MacSweeney, he "hung up his hostages and made another journey upon him, burnt and destroyed his house and corn, whereupon winter approaching ensued the death of most of his people."[159]

By the end of summer 1601, the situation in Ulster was very bleak. Sir Hugh Dowcra was embedded along the north-western seaboard and gradually moving inland, while Mounjoy was poised at the Gap of the North and raiding into

Tyrone. A further threat came from the northeast where Sir Arthur Chichester had established a base at Carrickfergus and was raiding mid Ulster. Of one such raid, Chichester wrote: "...We have killed above one hundred people of all sorts, besides such as were burnt, how many I know not. We spare none of what quality or sex whatsoever and it hath bred much terror in the people..."[160] Chichester was also an advocate of the policy of starvation, as he found it killed all generations and many more people that his troops could murder. Writing to Queen Elizabeth's chief adviser, Lord Burghley towards the end of November 1601 he told him "...I have often said and written, it is famine which must consume them; as our swords and other endeavours work not that speedy effect which is expected, for their overthrow."[161]

But as the year of 1601 turned from summer to autumn, the epicentre of the conflict was destined to switch from the far north of this island to the far south.

The Siege and Battle of Kinsale – September 1601 to January 1602

The Arrival of Spanish Aid

Although their situation appeared bleak, O'Néill and O'Donnell nevertheless considered it worthwhile to continue the fight in the hope that Spanish aid would arrive before their struggle was extinguished. On September 23rd, 1601, the hoped for help arrived at the Cork port of Kinsale in the form of 3,400 men led by the Spanish General, Juan del Aguila.

That O'Néill and O'Donnell were disappointed with the size of this force and the location of its landing on the southern Irish coastline is beyond doubt. Even if a smaller number of well-armed troops had arrived in Donegal, much could have been achieved in an area where the rebellion was still active, but to land in a place where the rebellion had been completely extinguished and the people were in no condition to rise up and join the Spanish, was, to say the least a challenging proposition. However, with the memory of the Armada still fresh in their minds, the Spanish had chosen to land as soon as Ireland was sighted and, in spite of O'Néill's plea to King Philip to come to the north, the Spanish dread of the Donegal shoreline had won out. Added to this setback was the fact that disaster had already struck the Spanish convoy, for, after departing Spain, a severe storm had caused seven ships carrying artillery, muskets for the Irish and stores to turn back to Corunna.

After capturing Kinsale, General Del Aguila and Mathew of Oviedo sent an urgent dispatch to O'Néill to come south. Making no attempt to push inland, the Spanish waited in Kinsale and the surrounding country until the northern leaders should arrive. The only local leader who was in any position to offer them help was Domhnall Cam O'Sullivan Beare (Gaelic Prince of Beare – under English title, 1st Count of Berehaven) who contacted del Aguila at once and offered him 1,000 men to assist in the defence of Kinsale until the armies of the north should arrive.

O'Donnell's March

As the Ulstermen hastily prepared for a southward march the length of Ireland in order to link up with the Spanish army, Mountjoy and Carew, already having the advantage of position over the Ulstermen, did their utmost to cut off the Spanish by land and sea and also attempted to halt the expected march south of O'Néill and O'Donnell.

O'Donnell was first to leave the north and was joined on his march south by many Connacht Chieftains who brought with them almost 3,000 men. In spite of Carew's best efforts, O'Donnell, who was determined to reach Kinsale without a fight, succeeded in avoiding him. In a feat of endurance which amazed Carew, the Tirconnell men marched almost day and night, with their passage through the Slieve Feilim Mountains on the 23rd November only made possible due to sub-zero temperatures which hardened up the soft terrain. Carew described it as "...the greatest march with incumbrance of carriage that hath been heard of."[162] Giving up the pursuit of "so swift footed a General,"[163] Carew abandoned the chase to go directly to Kinsale where Mountjoy had the Spaniards firmly under siege.

In Kinsale, Mountjoy's artillery hammered away at the walls of the town but the Spanish drove back every attempt the English made to enter through the breaches which the artillery had created. After Carew had joined him, Mountjoy was further reinforced by the arrival of Sir Christopher St. Lawrence at the head of the Dublin garrison, 2,000 reinforcements from England and O'Brien, Earl of Thomond at the head of 1,000 men. By the end of November, the English had over 10,000 men in the area around Kinsale.

Spanish Landing at Castlehaven

The English navy under the command of Admiral Sir Richard Levison was also very active along the southern coast. When more Spanish ships under the command of Admiral Pedro Zubiaur arrived on December 3rd, they found the port of Kinsale completely blockaded and were forced to continue westwards along the coast to Castlehaven – twenty-five miles away from their comrades. Around 700 more Spaniards had arrived with Zubiaur and these were warmly welcomed by the local Gaelic Chieftains, Domhnall O'Sullivan Beare and Fineen O'Driscoll. O'Sullivan Beare gave the Spanish his castle at Dunboy for their use while O'Driscoll gave them his castle at Baltimore. Admiral Levison pursued the Spanish ships to Castlehaven and on December 6th a sea battle took place near Castlehaven during which the Spanish inflicted 300 casualties on the English, after which Levison retreated.

Hugh Roe O'Donnell had meanwhile arrived in the area but on seeing that the Spanish at Kinsale were not in imminent danger of being overwhelmed, he held back, awaiting the arrival of O'Néill who had been delayed by fighting in Meath. O'Donnell linked up with the Spaniards who had landed at Castlehaven and then awaited O'Néill in the vicinity of Belgooly, north of Kinsale. After O'Néill arrived, the Irish force numbered around 7,000 men, including 300 from Castlehaven under the command of Captain Alphonso Ocampo. On December 21st, the Irish army advanced to Belgooley where it took up positions in proximity to the English lines. The besiegers had now become the besieged, for the English were now hemmed in by the Spaniards on one side and the Irish on the other.

Disaster at Kinsale
By this stage, the English army at Kinsale was in a fairly poor state. Apart from being low on provisions, many men were suffering from sickness due to the severe winter weather. The number of men who were fully fit for active service had been drastically reduced through wastage and action to about 6,500 and Mountjoy, worried at their situation, began to give serious consideration to breaking out of his siege and making for Cork and winter quarters.

For his part, O'Néill was content to let the siege do its work but the Spanish in Kinsale were becoming impatient. Del Aguila sent a message to him proposing in the strongest terms that concerted actions both from Belgooley and Kinsale were required in order to bring matters to a favourable conclusion. In a council of war among the Irish Generals, O'Néill was strongly in favour of no action being taken, feeling that if the siege were maintained the English would be destroyed. O'Donnell took the opposite view and felt that they were honour bound to agree with del Aguila's request. Accepting to put the matter to a vote, O'Néill's position was outvoted by the other commanders, resulting in a decision to attack the English in concert with the Spanish. The attack was planned for the early morning of December 24th.

As preparations neared their conclusion, the English learned of the plan from two sources. The first source was a traitor in the Irish camp – Brian MacMahon – who sent a note to Carew. When the information in the note was confirmed by a dispatch from del Aguila to O'Néill which the English intercepted, the success of the Irish-Spanish attack was already in doubt.

The night of December 23rd – 24th was miserable, with the heavy rain only made worse by the driving wind, while thunder and lightning rent the air. The Irish left their trenches in three groups with Tyrell leading the first, O'Néill the second and O'Donnell the third, the plan being that the English entrenchments would be approached under cover of darkness and then attacked at first light. Everything now went badly wrong for the Irish, as the guides who were bringing them to their battle positions lost their way in the awful weather and the three groups lost contact with each other. As dawn was breaking, O'Néill saw the English lines with soldiers and cavalry all ready for action. Taken aback, he hesitated, wondering whether he should retreat to a more advantageous position or postpone the attack altogether as his men were by now soaked, exhausted and spread out and he had not yet linked up with O'Donnell's army. As skirmishing began, O'Néill sent his

O'Sullivan Beare, wearing Spanish armour

cavalry forward but after an eruption of musket fire from the English line they turned for their own lines and the Irish foot soldiers were forced to open their ranks and let them through. Any further decision was now taken out of O'Néill's hands, for in that moment the English cavalry charged from their positions and the disparate Irish struggled to offer an effective resistance. It was almost like the Battle of Yellow Ford in reverse, for the Irish were not in a strong enough concentration anywhere on the field of battle to offer sufficient opposition. Many of the Ulsterman were better used to hit and run tactics well practiced in the forested drumlins of home and did not adapt well to the open battlefield. To make matters worse, the Spanish, who should have been attacking the English line from the Kinsale side, had not done so in any great numbers, leaving the English free to devote most of their resources against the Irish. By the time O'Donnell arrived with his army, it was almost too late. For an hour, the Irish offered a fighting retreat but were eventually overwhelmed and completely routed, after which they were pursued by the English cavalry. Well over 1,000 men were killed, a loss that included significant numbers of the Scottish MacDonnells. All those whom the English took prisoner were afterwards hanged in the English encampment.[164]

Weary and dispirited, the Irish retired to Innishannon near Bandon to take stock of their situation. Having been in such a favourable position just a few days before, it now seemed that the damage to their cause was irreparable, and Hugh O'Néill was deeply dejected for perhaps the first time since the conflict had begun. Nevertheless, it was resolved to continue the struggle. Hugh Roe O'Donnell proposed that he would place his Chieftaincy of Tirconnell in the hands of his brother Rory and go to Spain immediately where he would directly appeal to King Philip III for sufficient forces to defeat the English, while Rory O'Donnell and O'Néill prepared to return to the north in all haste, as it would not be long before the whole strength of the English army was on their doorstep.

The Departure and Murder of Hugh Roe O'Donnell

On December 27th, Hugh Roe O'Donnell and a handful of companions boarded a Spanish ship at Castlehaven which landed in Corunna on January 14th. O'Donnell was treated with great honour by the Spanish with many noblemen donating great sums of money to him for the Irish Catholic cause. King Philip III also received him and made it known that he would endanger his throne to help the Catholics of Ireland. The King asked him to wait in Corunna until preparations could be completed for a further expedition. By the end of Summer 1602 O'Donnell had still heard nothing and decided to go to Valladolid where the King's court was being held in order to renew his plea but fell ill on the way after being poisoned by an English double agent called James Blake who had previously been an English secret agent in Spain in the 1590s .[i] Hugh Roe O'Donnell, one of the greatest heroes Ireland has ever known, died at Simancas on September 10th, 1602, and his remains were interred in the Cathedral of Valladolid. After his death, the Spanish formally abandoned any further plans that they may have had to intervene in Ireland.

---

[i] In 1870 it was discovered in the secret manuscripts of Sir George Carew that an English double agent called James Blake had followed O'Donnell to Spain with the intention of killing him. On May 28th 1602, Carew wrote to Mountjoy that he had spoken to Blake before he departed for Spain: "I applauded his enterprise, whereupon he departed from me, and is gone to Spain with determination to kill O'Donnell". In a letter dated October 9th, 1602, Carew wrote to Mountjoy: "O'Donnell is dead...poisoned by James Blake... whom your Lordship hath been formerly acquainted".

The Siege of Dunboy Castle
Spanish Treachery

In Kinsale, the Spanish commander, del Aguila, doubtless aware of the fate that had befallen the soldiers of the last Spanish expedition to Ireland twenty years before, was endeavouring to extricate himself and his men intact from the English blockade. The Irish had no idea that he was about to embark on this course of action as his situation in Kinsale appeared relatively secure. On January 2nd 1602, he sent proposals of capitulation to Mountjoy that greatly compromised the Irish who were still fighting in the area for he proposed that he would hand over to the English the Irish castles of Dunboy and Baltimore and also the port at Castlehaven intact if the English would allow him and his men to return to Spain unhindered.

Mountjoy, eager to neutralise the excellently situated and almost impregnable Dunboy Castle, assented but when Domhnall O'Sullivan Beare and his comrades heard of the terms of the Spanish withdrawal, their anger was aroused. They not only felt that the Spanish were abandoning them, but that they were endeavouring to make the situation untenable by the handover of strong-points which were not theirs to give. Acting swiftly to recover his castle, O'Sullivan Beare, Captain Richard Tyrell and eighty men went there at the dead of night while the Spanish were still in possession and, after secretly entering through a hole that they made in the wall, overpowered the Spaniards and ejected them. O'Sullivan Beare and Captain Tyrell then returned to their forces inland, placing the castle and its newly installed garrison under the command of Richard MacGeoghegan. With a garrison of 143 men, MacGeoghegan and his second in command, Thomas Taylor began immediate preparations for a siege. Del Aguila told Mountjoy that he would retake the castle himself and hand it over to the English, but Mountjoy, anxious to see the Spanish leave Ireland, told him that he would recapture it. Waiting until he had completely subdued all other resistance in the area, Mountjoy set out from Cork on the 23rd of April with an army of about 3,000 men. They were joined by Sir Charles Wilmot and his troops who had completed their task of eradicating resistance in Kerry. However, due to unforeseen difficulties regarding the shipment of troops, artillery and ordnance, Mountjoy's army, now numbering 4,000 men, was not in position on Beare Island until the beginning of June 1602.

The Dursey Island Massacre

After taking up positions in preparation for an assault on Dunboy castle, the English received information that a smaller garrison of around 40 men loyal to O'Sullivan Beare were in possession of a nearby fort on Dursey Island. Deciding to eliminate this fort first, Carew dispatched a shipload of troops to the island under the command of Captain Fleming. What followed bears a great resemblance to the Rathlin Island massacre for the island's defences consisted of a small garrison that was protecting the elderly and infirm of the Clan O'Sulivan Beare along with many of the wives and children of those men who were holed up in Dunboy. After successfully capturing the fort, the garrison was put to the sword. All others were herded into one group and then butchered. The women and children were tied back to back and hurled from a high point on the island onto the rocks below. Around 300 people were killed in the massacre.[i]

---

[i] The English record of the campaign entitled "Pacata Hibernia" makes no mention of this massacre. This account is based on the testimony of Philip O'Sullivan Beare, son of Domhnall O'Sullivan Beare, who recorded the story of the massacre in his account of the period entitled "A Briefe Relation of Ireland".

The Epic Defence of Dunboy Castle

Operations against Dunboy Castle commenced on June 6th once the English had completed the short crossing from Beare island to the western shore of Bearehaven. Domhnall O'Sullivan Beare was absent during the siege and ensuing battle, having travelled to Ulster to confer with Hugh O'Néill.

The Irish no doubt knew that there could only be one outcome to the siege but the gallant soldiers[i] of the Dunboy garrison never demurred, being determined to give a good account of themselves. Day after day, the English artillery thundered against the castle walls. By June 17th the castle was almost a complete wreck and MacGeoghegan, feeling that he had done his duty, sent a messenger to the English lines to negotiate a surrender that would allow the Irish to leave honourably and without molestation. On arriving at the English lines, the messenger was seized and hanged on Carew's orders. Feeling that nothing more could be accomplished with his artillery, Carew ordered the final assault to go in. For an entire day, a life and death struggle took place between the defenders and the assailants. The remains of the garrison fought desperately but the English numbers were overwhelming beyond measure. The eastern wing of the castle had escaped relatively undamaged, and it was here that the Irish made their last stand. For almost two hours, hand to hand combat took place at the entrance to the wing while the Irish hurled huge rocks from the tower on to the English below. Knowing that it was only a matter of time before they were overwhelmed, some of the defenders held off the English while others made an attempt to escape by swimming away, but they were spotted and cut down by musket fire. By nightfall, only the cellars of the east wing remained to the Irish, with 77 of them still alive.

---

[i] The castle's garrison also contained some Spanish gunners who had volunteered to remain in Ireland and serve the Irish cause.

The English called off the assault for the night while below them the garrison commander MacGeoghegan lay on the cellar floor, badly wounded. Taylor now assumed command. Knowing their situation to be hopeless, he allowed every man to decide his course of action for himself. Of the 77 who remained, 23 opted to exit the cellar and surrender themselves to the English. The following morning, Carew once more brought his artillery into action, directing his fire on the cellar. Knowing that it was only a short time before the cellar was turned into their tomb, Taylor finally surrendered at the behest of his men. As the English under the command of Captain Power descended to the cellar, they found the wounded MacGeoghegan with a lighted candle in his hand, struggling towards a barrel of gunpowder in the corner. Power grabbed MacGeoghegan by the arms while his men killed him with their swords.

When the battle was over, the entire number of Irish prisoners in English hands was seventy three. Of these, fifty eight were hanged the same day in the English camp, while the remainder (which included Thomas Taylor and the garrison chaplain Fr. Dominic Collins) were held back to be hanged individually so that any information they possessed on other matters might be extracted from them. Fr. Collins was afterwards taken to Youghal, the town of his birth, and hanged there. Of the entire garrison, not one man survived. Of the siege and battle Carew later wrote: "So obstinate and resolved a defence hath not been seene within this kingdom".[165] With all the garrison dead, Carew followed up with the punishment of the entire region. He later recounted that "…English regiments overran all Beare and Bantry, destroying all that they could find meet for the reliefe of men, so as that the country was wholly wasted."[166]

The "Cleansing" of Munster

As we have seen, the chief effect of the rebellion in Munster was the reversal of the Munster plantation. Following his actions on the Beara peninsula, Carew, as President of Munster, undertook a policy of removal, extermination and crop destruction in much of Munster in order to reverse the effects of the rebellion and drive out the Irish who had taken back their land. An example of this action was Sir Charles Wilmot now returned with his army to Kerry in order to cleanse entire districts of Irish. Wilmot issued an order to his men to execute all "suspected" persons without mercy[167]. On one occasion, after a district was forcibly cleared, large numbers of sick and wounded who remained behind were massacred in order to, as the English account describes; "put them out of pain."[168]

Sir George Carew

The Death March of the Clan O'Sullivan Beare

Since the destruction of Dunboy, Domhnall O'Sullivan Beare had continued to evade capture by the English and was living in the wilds of Glengarriff. Initially, large numbers of Irish had looked to him for help and leadership but following attacks by the English and the capture and removal of all his livestock, such was the dire situation in Munster that O'Sullivan Beare decided that the only chance both for his family and remaining followers was to abandon the southern province and go north as the English had an army of 2,000 men commanded by

Wilmot hunting for him and it was only a matter of time before he was tracked down.

On December 31st, 1602, O'Sullivan Beare accompanied by his family, 400 fighting men and their families, left Glengarriff to seek refuge with O'Rourke of Leitrim. All told, there were about 1,000 people in his party, completely lacking sufficient provisions for the journey as Munster was in the midst of a severe man made famine. O'Sullivan had plenty of money as funds had arrived from Spain during the previous summer with the Vicar Apostolic, Bishop Eoghan MacEgan. But he was unable to spend it since most common people had not enough to feed their own families and as fugitives, they could not approach any merchant. During the next two weeks, as they journeyed up the country in awful winter weather, they were repeatedly attacked by the English and those Anglo-Irish and Irish who either sided with the English or wished the fugitives to be out of their locality so that soldiers would not descend on it, and in order to protect from the starving refugees what little food they had remaining to themselves. The Clan O'Sullivan Beare were so short of food on their journey that they soon needed to kill their few horses for meat, which left the convoy without any means of conveying the elderly, sick or wounded, many of whom were left behind. As the refugees attempted to cross the Shannon in north Tipperary, they were attacked by the Sheriff of Tipperary Donogh MacEgan at the head of a force of men. At Aughrim, Captain Henry Malbie attacked the column but lost his own life in the process, while in Roscommon they were pursued by the Sheriff MacDavid Burke. Two weeks after the party of 1,000 people left Glengarriff, a mere 35[i] arrived at Leitrim Castle, the home of

---

[i] Philip O'Sullivan Beare later wrote: "They reached Letrim Fort about eleven o'clock being then reduced to 35, of whom 18 were soldiers, 16 were civilians of which one was woman. The other of the 1,000 had either perished or lingered on the road through weariness and wounds."

O'Rourke of Breifnee, with a few more arriving in the days that followed.

After reaching O'Rourke's Castle, O'Sullivan now planned to join up with O'Néill to continue the struggle but this plan was overtaken by O'Néill's surrender.

Following the end of the war, Domhnall Cam well knew that an English noose awaited him and successfully left Ireland by ship for Spanish exile. Once in Spain, he was received by King Philip III who made him a general of the army. Domhnall Cam O'Sullivan Beare remained in exile there until his death in 1618 when he was assassinated as he was leaving Mass in Madrid by an Englishman, John Bathe.[i]

The Surrender of Hugh O'Néill

By the summer of 1602, almost the entire country was in the grip of an English reign of terror and famine brought on by the repeated destruction of crops by the soldiers. By June 1602, Hugh O'Néill was overwhelmed by English soldiers who had succeeded in completely overrunning his territory. He now left Tyrone with 600 men at arms and made for an island fort on Lough Erne in a remote part of Fermanagh with his brother Cormac, while Mountjoy repeated in Ulster the destruction and wholesale murder undertaken by the English in Munster. At Tullahoge, Mountjoy destroyed the ancient inauguration stone of the O'Néills, afterwards writing that over a journey of seventeen miles "between Tullaghhoge and Toome there lay unburied 1,000 dead and since our first drawing this year to Blackwater there were about 3,000 starved in Tyrone...Tomorrow I am going into the field, as near as I can utterly to waste the county Tyrone...so that if O'Néill should

---

[i] The suspicion that Bathe was an English agent was afterwards confirmed by the fact that after his escape from Spain he returned to England where he was granted a pension of £500 by King James I.

return he would find nothing in the country but the Queen's garrisons"[169]. In Tirconnell, meanwhile, Dowcra would not accept the surrender of those Irish soldiers who wished to give themselves up, later writing that those who "came into my hands alive I caused the soldiers to hew into pieces with their swords"[170].

When news of the death of Red Hugh O'Donnell in Spain filtered through to Ireland, the last hopes of further foreign intervention evaporated, and his brother Rory and O'Conor Sligo surrendered to Mountjoy. The only two Irish commanders of significance that were now left at liberty were O'Néill and O'Rourke. The English were determined to neutralize O'Néill by fair means or foul but try as they might they could not track him down to his fastness as the few hundred soldiers he had left were determined that he should not fall into English hands. The closest they got to him was thirteen miles. Such was his reputation that, even though he was isolated, the English remained fearful that he might even at this stage contrive some means of further foreign intervention. In the Spring of 1603, despite Queen Elizabeth's reservations to enter into negotiations with that "most ungrateful viper", feelers were put forward to O'Néill offering him an honourable surrender, using Sir Garrett More as an intermediary.

After making contact with the Ulster Chieftain, the negotiations continued without conclusion until Queen Elizabeth ("Bloody Bess"[i]) died in the early hours of March 24th, 1603, propped up in the arms of her attendants as she refused to lie down in case she would die.

---

[i] This is the name given to Queen Elizabeth by the nineteenth century English historian and author William Cobbett. It is especially appropriate in the Irish context.

Immediately following her death, her cousin Carey travelled by horse the almost four hundred miles to the court of King James VI of Scotland in just over two days to advise him to come to London at once. James immediately left for London and was given the throne by Robert Cecil, son of William Cecil, who had put Elizabeth on the throne.

Lord Mountjoy

In the course of the war, when things were going well for the Irish, O'Néill had made representations to King James of Scotland and had received a not unfavourable reply to the effect that he would be happy to work with O'Néill "when it shall please God to call our sister the Queen of England to death"[171]. On hearing of the Queen's death and the likely ascension of James to the English throne, Mountjoy was at Sir Garret More's home in the grounds of the destroyed Mellifont Abbey in Louth. Realising that O'Néill might very well take a more hard-line stance in the negotiations and hold out for better terms if he was aware that Elizabeth was dead, he sent a message to O'Néill that everything was arranged for his submission on favourable terms and to come at once.

On March 31st, O'Néill formally submitted to the dead Queen before Mountjoy at Mellifont. In the Treaty of Mellifont, Tyrone promised full obedience, renounced all foreign powers, the title of "O'Néill" and all his lands, save what the Crown should grant him.ⁱ He was no longer permitted to resort to Brehon law but had to use English law instead and was also no longer allowed to maintain Gaelic Bards. In return, he received a full pardon, personal freedom to practice the Catholic faith and restoration in blood. It was not until April 5th that O'Néill finally found out that Queen Elizabeth was dead and that he had been taken advantage of, at which he apparently wept "tears of rage."[172]

ⁱ Following his submission, Hugh O'Néill wrote a letter of farewell to the King of Spain, also asking him to return his son Henry (then serving in the Spanish army) to Ireland, but Henry did not return. Henry was later in the court of the Archduke Albert and was murdered in Brussels the year after his father's death His murder was shrouded in mystery, and it was suspected that the English had a hand in it, fearing that the able youth might return to Ireland and become a leader of his people.

Chapter 19

The Flight of The Earls

King James I of England

Although a Calvinist, it was widely believed outside Scotland that King James did not harbour anti-Catholic sentiments. He had been baptised a Catholic and his mother, Mary Queen of Scots, had been a devout Catholic but had been forced to abdicate following her arrest by Protestant rebels, after which the now Protestant James had been crowned as King James VI of Scotland.

James's international policy as King of Scotland reinforced this belief as he had tried to gain the friendship of the Catholic powers of Europe and had also sent Lord Home, who was a Catholic, to Rome as his Papal envoy. However, in being friendly to foreign Catholic potentates, James only wished to limit the power of England under Elizabeth and he secretly approved of the execution of his mother at her hands.[173]

One of his first acts on becoming King James I of England was to unite the thrones of Scotland and England under one Monarch. This was something that was to have serious consequences for Ireland, as in the future plantation of Ulster by James I it would mean a veritable invasion of that province by Presbyterians from the Scottish Lowlands. Almost as soon as James united the thrones, two clever and wily Scotsmen, Sir James Hamilton and Sir Hugh Montgomery came to south

Antrim and North Down where they amassed considerable tracts of land by various methods on which they settled a Scottish Presbyterian colony.

James I - A Secret Catholic?

When news of James' accession to the throne of England became widespread in Ireland, there was great jubilation among the Catholic Anglo-Irish as they were sure that he would proclaim himself Catholic (which they believed he secretly was) and that the Catholic faith would be everywhere publicly restored as it had previously been under Queen Mary. Pre-empting this expected move, the Old English took back the Catholic Churches that had been previously wrested from them after the death of Queen Mary in towns such as Cashel, Cork, Waterford, Wexford and Limerick where Mass was once more publicly celebrated. As soon as Mountjoy heard of this "simplicity"[174] among the old English, he moved quickly to stamp out this movement saying: "If they do not desist from the celebration of the Mass I would think them fit to be prosecuted with the avenging sword of his Majesty's forces."[175] With an army of 14,000 men at his back, the towns were brought to a quick submission. After some public hangings of a number of pious Catholics, the churches were once more handed by the government back to the Protestants.[i] It was now abundantly clear to the Old English that their hopes had been in vain for there was to be no change in the state religion of England. It would remain to be seen what level of toleration King James would grant to Catholicism.

---

[i] In Waterford, the citizens of the town closed their gates against Mountjoy's troops, telling him that, under a charter of King John, their town was exempt from the presence of soldiers. Mountjoy retorted that he would "cut to shreds the charter of King John with the sword of King James".

The Act of Oblivion

With the Irish confederacy soundly beaten, James was determined that English rule would now be thoroughly established throughout all of Ireland in as peaceful a manner as possible. With this in mind, he published an "Act of Oblivion" whereby no legal action was to be taken against anyone who had taken part in the recent war on the Irish side provided they subjected themselves to the authority of the King and to all his laws and acts. For the first time since the Norman invasion well over 400 years previously, the entire country was to be subject to English rule and law[i] in absolutely every respect. Within a short time the last vestiges of the old Gaelic order had disappeared.

There was one caveat in James's declaration imposing English law to his Irish subjects: if any of his Irish subjects should not avail of his gracious offer, they were to be oppressed, "...everyone of them by all ways and means possible, to the utter extirpating and rooting out of them, their names and generations for ever..."[176]

Dispensing with the title of Lord Deputy, King James granted Mountjoy the higher title of "Lord Lieutenant of Ireland" with permission to reside in England. Leaving Sir George Carew as his deputy, Mountjoy returned to England in May of 1603, to the court of King James, accompanied by Hugh O'Néill and Rory O'Donnell where O'Néill was restored as Earl of Tyrone and O'Donnell made Earl of Tirconnell. Contrary to the expectations of many in the English government, their lands were not declared forfeit to the Crown. There was great anger about this in government circles and the army as most expected that O'Néill's territory in particular would be

---

[i] Brehon Law was abolished. All native titles were: "henceforth ceased... (and declared to be)...utterly abolished and extinct forever" These measures were further reinforced by the parliament of 1613 which also fobade all forms of Irish culture and their expression.

declared forfeit to the Crown at the end of the war. Many in high office now determined to bring about his ruin so that this end could be achieved, to such an extent that the Spanish Ambassador at the Court of King James declared: "I know they wish to kill him by poison or by any means possible"[177] O'Néill was unable to settle down and live out the remainder of his life quietly, in spite of his efforts to do so, for English officials made life intolerable for him and he was constantly subject to humiliation with spies keeping an eye on his every move. He wrote that there "are so many eyes watching over me that I cannot drink a full carouse of sack (wine) but the state is advised thereof within a few hours after"[178] For Rory O'Donnell of Tirconnell, the situation was little better. Furthermore, when Sir Arthur Chichester replaced Lord Mountjoy as Lord Deputy, the Catholics of those parts of Ulster who had heretofore been preserved from persecution on account of their Faith began to suffer what the rest of their countrymen had been suffering for decades.

Puritanism
During the early years of the rule of King James I, there arose in England a movement of Protestants within the established church who maintained that the Church of England had not been completely reformed and still retained far too many beliefs and practices associated with Catholicism (which they called "remnants of popery"). They advocated greater "purity of worship and doctrine" as espoused by the Calvinists and Presbyterians and believed that all practices not strictly rooted in the Bible should be eliminated. Renowned for their hatred of Catholicism and the Mass in particular, their overbearing strictness became an object of derision to some members of the established Protestant church. However as the years passed puritans occupied many important positions within both aristocracy and parliament.

The Gunpowder Plot

In the years leading up to the death of Queen Elizabeth, James as King of Scotland had promised that should he succeed Elizabeth to the throne of England he would allow Catholics freedom to practice their Faith. However, Robert Cecil, the man who had placed him on the throne, had other ideas: he was well aware that if toleration were given to Catholicism, many of "high birth" would return to the old religion and in time England might even return to the Catholic Faith. Since the beginning of James's reign, no royal effort at Catholic toleration had been forthcoming and when a plot to blow up the King and Parliament was hatched by a number of English Catholic gentlemen led by Robert Catesby, Cecil quickly became fully aware of it. Deciding to let the plot run its course and use it for his own ends, he nursed it along with the help of his agents so that when the time came, in the early hours of November 5th 1604, Guy Fawkes and the conspirators were killed or rounded up and executed as traitors. Following this, Cecil successfully incriminated a number of innocent Catholic priests in the plot. The outcome of the whole affair was the full and final establishment of Protestantism as the state religion of England and the wholesale purging of Catholics from official positions as potential traitors to a Protestant England.

The Effect of the Gunpowder Plot in Ireland

Due to the further machinations of Robert Cecil and as a consequence of the Gunpowder Plot, a proclamation was issued on July 4th, 1605, formally re-promulgating the Act of Uniformity and commanding all "Popish clergy" to depart the realm. Up to this point, the Old English of Ireland had been viewed by the Crown as a special case, as it was deemed necessary to keep them firmly on the side of the government. The anti-Catholic laws that had been pursued in England during the entirety of Queen Elizabeth's reign had also been pursued with vigour against the native Irish but not against the Old English. However, with the defeat of O'Néill's Confederacy and in the wake of the Gunpowder Plot, King James's administration felt that the time was right to fully invoke the Act of Uniformity and all the laws that it had at its disposal in order to persecute Catholics in Ireland especially those among the Old English. On September 28th, 1605, James ordered a proclamation published in Dublin, which read: "It hath seemed proper to us to proclaim, and we hereby make known to our subjects in Ireland, that no toleration shall ever be granted by us. This we do for the purpose of cutting off all hope that any other religion shall be allowed, save that which is consonant to the laws and statutes of this realm"[179]. Under the new measures any priest caught in Ireland after December 10th, 1605, was liable to be executed. Any man who harboured a priest was to be hanged outside his door. Furthermore, groups of soldiers were scattered throughout the country for the express purpose of priest hunting. The measures were strengthened in May of 1606 when a further edict was published to the effect that "All priests who would be detected, should without any subterfuge or further trial be hanged from the first tree or gallows that should present itself."[180]

Many of the foremost Old English of Dublin suffered as a result. When Sir Patrick Barnwell petitioned the King on behalf of the Anglo-Irish of Dublin to relax these draconian laws, the King responded by ordering him to be committed to the Tower of London, while in Dublin and many other cities and towns, many Catholics or "recusants" (as they were called) faced heavy fines and imprisonment for failing to attend the obligatory Protestant service. Fines due as a result of failure to attend were ruthlessly collected. One recusant recorded that in the search for money by the soldiers collecting fines "everything is torn open and whatever is of any value is set aside to be taken away; whatever is worthless is thrown in the streets and devoted to the flames."[181] Chichester himself took a personal interest in proceedings, using more than just words to invoke the Catholics to attend Protestant service. When a Catholic gentleman hesitated at the door of a Dublin Protestant church, and then would not enter, an eyewitness recounted: "Chichester told him savagely to go in, and seeing he could not prevail upon him, struck him a cruel blow on the head with his stick. Then the mace-bearer attacked him so savagely that he fell to the ground like a dead man, and the Lord Deputy had him dragged into the church, where he lay insensible and gasping all the time of the sermon, and no one dared to approach him. Some of his friends afterwards took him home, where he gave his blessed soul to God in two hours."[182]

This persecution of Catholics saw the emergence of an expanded Irish race. Chained together by fetters of suffering on account of their Faith, the Old English identified more and more with the Gael, both recognizing England as the cause of their mutual misfortune. By 1700, this identification of the Catholic Old English with the Gaelic Irish would be well-nigh complete especially within the middle and lower classes.

The Flight of the Earls
Robert Cecil's Plot for the Removal of the Ulster Earls

As the country recoiled under a new wave of anti-Catholic persecution, Robert Cecil, flushed with his success in The Gunpowder Plot (by which he had determined to brand all Catholics as potential traitors to the Crown), felt in early 1607 that the time was ripe to mastermind another plot, this time against the two Catholic Ulster Earls. If this plot was successful, it would see both O'Néill and O'Donnell executed or imprisoned in the Tower for life and their lands finally declared forfeit to the Crown.[i]

In order to execute his plan, Cecil enlisted the help of the Baron of Howth, Christopher St. Lawrence (who was later made a Lord). St. Lawrence in turn contacted Hugh O'Néill and Rory O'Donnell and arranged to meet them and some other Gaelic leaders in Maynooth, where he clandestinely informed them that even further severe persecutions were in preparation by the government against the Catholics of Ireland and that they should form a conspiracy with him against the authorities. How successful he was in drawing the two Earls into his nefarious web is uncertain but according to his own papers (which in the circumstances can hardly be relied upon) he met with some success[183]. Daniel O'Connell M.P. later maintained in his history of the period that the two Earls were suspicious of him from the outset and remained aloof from his proposal.[184] Some time after the Maynooth meeting, an anonymous letter was found at the door of the Council Chamber in Dublin addressed to Sir William Usher, who was Clerk of the Privy Council.[ii] The letter outlined a plot in preparation by persons

---

[i] In 1736, an English Protestant bishop Dr. Anderson, wrote a book entitled "Royal Genealogies" which was dedicated to the Prince of Wales. He recounted Cecil's plot, writing on page 786: "...Artful Cecil employed one St. Laurence to entrap the Earls of Tyrone and Tirconnell, the lord of Delvin and other Irish Chiefs into a sham plot which had no evidence but his. But these Chiefs being basely informed that witnesses were to be hired against them foolishly fled from Dublin and so taking guilt upon them, they were declared rebels and six entire counties in Ulster were at once forfeited to the crown which was what their enemies wanted".

[ii] The episode is well recorded by Protestant historians. An officer in Oliver Cromwell's army, later the Protestant bishop Jones of Meath, wrote the preface to "Borlase's History of the Irish Rebellion" which included this passage: "Anno 1607 – There was a providential discovery of another rebellion in Ireland, the Lord Chichester being Deputy; the discoverer not being willing to appear, a letter from him, not subscribed, was superscribed to Sir William Usher, Clerk of the Council, and dropt in the council chamber then held in the castle of Dublin;

unnamed for a general revolt that included the seizure of Dublin Castle and the murder of the Lord Deputy. The absurdity of the document was proven by the suggestion that the affair was to be conducted with the assistance of Spanish monks. Usher informed the Council of the letter, after which the Council proceeded as if they had evidence against the two Earls, and they were both summoned to Dublin to be questioned. [i]However, what they said hardly mattered for their fate had been sealed once the meeting with Baron Howth had taken place; his unnamed deposition would in all circumstances be preferred over theirs.

Hugh O'Néill is Summoned to London

By the end of June, Sir Arthur Chichester had received orders from London that Hugh O'Néill was to present himself there at the end of September or the beginning of October. Chichester presented the summons to O'Néill, writing afterwards that when he read it, "he did lose his former cheerfulness and grew often exceeding pensive."[185] Later, after fleeing Ireland, Hugh O'Néill informed King Philip III of Spain: "The King of England summoned us to London with the intention of either beheading us or putting us in the Tower of London for life"[186]. When news of O'Néill's English summons reached the ears of the exiled Gaelic Lord of Fermanagh, Cuchonnacht Maguire,

---

in which was mentioned a design for sieging the castle and murdering the Deputy".

[i] As the persecution of the English against Irish Catholics became more unbearable, the Church grew fearful for O'Néill's safety. In a letter quoted in O'Sullivan's Catholic History p271 which was dated May 1607 and signed by an unidentified bishop, the following passage was included: "Even the illustrious Earl of Tyrone, the Catholic Mardochai, already oppressed in various ways is now coming to Dublin under a citation from the Viceroy. It is not pleasant to foretell evil but the malice of the heretics towards him and their inveterate guile compel us at least, to have some fear for him".

he knew well that it more than likely meant the end of the two Earls. A gallant and noble man,[i] he immediately decided to return to Ireland to help his comrades. After travelling to Nantes, he hired a ship and crew and equipped it with fishing nets as a decoy in case it should be intercepted. From Nantes, he travelled to Dunkirk and from there to Tirconnell, taking with him Matthew Tully (O'Néill's official representative at the Spanish Court) and Donough O'Brien (a Catholic cousin of the loyalist Earl of Thomond).

Departure from Rathmullan

On September 4th, 1607, the ship entered Lough Swilly and docked at Rathmullan. O'Brien left the vessel and went straight to the castle of Rory O'Donnell to inform him of the ships' arrival, after which O'Donnell sent a messenger to summon Hugh O'Néill who was then in Slane to meet the Lord Deputy, Sir Arthur Chichester, regarding the details of his summons. O Neill received O'Donnell's message on September 6th and after two days in Slane he left to return home, stopping at the house of Sir Garrett Moore at Mellifont. Even after the end of the Nine Years War, O'Néill had remained on friendly terms with Moore and had placed his son John in fosterage with him. Before leaving Mellifont, O'Néill told Moore that he wished to bring John home with him, which made Moore suspicious. After O'Néill had left, Moore sent a message to Chichester regarding the boy's removal from his house, making Chichester think that O'Néill had "some mischief in his head"[187]. The thought that O'Néill might leave Ireland never occurred to him.

---

[i] According to The Four Masters, Maguire was "endowed with wisdom and beauty of person". Once, when asked at a banquet why he did not sit at the head of the table, he famously replied: "Where Maguire sits *is* the head of the table!"

After returning home, Hugh O'Néill left again with his family two days later for Rathmullan, travelling at night for fear of English spies. His party finally arrived at Rathmullan at daybreak on Friday September 14th where the ship was almost ready to depart.

Around midday on the 14th, ninety-nine passengers boarded the ship. Apart from the two Earls and their parties, there were some members of old English Catholic families who were personal friends of O'Néill and who wished to go abroad in order to escape the anti-Catholic persecution. There were also members of other Gaelic families: O'Hagans, Gallaghers, McDavitts, Kennys, O'Mahons and O'Loughrans, along with thirteen young men who wanted to go to Flanders to study for the priesthood.

The arrival of Cuchonnacht Maguire's ship at Rathmullan had surprised many of those who now wished to leave Ireland, not least Hugh O'Néill, forcing him into a quick decision. Many of the men who departed left wives and children behind, being unable to bring them to Rathmullan in time. Rory O'Donnell sent a messenger to fetch his wife Bridget Fitzgerald who was in Maynooth visiting her family, but the ship departed without her. Nuala O'Donnell, wife of Niall Garbh O'Donnell, also departed on the ship having previously separated from her husband once he became a traitor to his country.

A Forlorn Hope

Once on the open sea, the ship was assailed by a storm. As the storm increased in ferocity, O'Néill removed from his person a gold cross that contained a relic of the true Cross and trailed it in the water, at which point the storm subsided. This was recorded by one the passengers, O'Ciainain, who later wrote: "Only thanks to the Trinity who saved the ship and its occupants from drowning."[188] The ship made for the port of Le Havre where the exiles were received by the French with great respect. On hearing of their arrival, the English ambassador to the court of the French King Henry IV, Sir George Carew, requested that they be surrendered to the English as they were traitors to the English Crown, but the King would not entertain any such request. He refused to meet Carew for three days, preferring to go hunting instead, after which he informed him that the Irish party would not be restricted in their movements in any way, shape or form. The group proceeded on to Flanders[i] where they parted company with the students for the priesthood and from there they went to Rome by a circuitous route where they survived on pensions awarded to them by King Philip III of Spain and the Pope.

The following year, 1608, Rory O'Donnell died. Hugh O'Néill became blind a couple of years later and died in 1616. After their departure, Gael and Catholic Old English alike watched anxiously for their return at the head of a continental Catholic force which would make Ireland free. But this was not to be for there was never any opportunity for the Earls to raise such a force since the Spaniards were unwilling to endanger their recent peace accord with the English. Indeed, the Spanish were so concerned with maintaining this accord that they acceded to English demands that the exiles not be given a place of permanent refuge on Spanish soil, something which caused O'Néill and O'Donnell much sadness.

"Woe to the heart that meditated, woe to the mind that conceived, woe to the council that decided on, the project of

---

[i] On the continent, as in Ireland, both Gael and old English found common cause in the fight for the Catholic faith. An English spy wrote from Douai how those students for the priesthood who were descended from the old English of Ireland prayed every day for the Earl of Tyrone and "...all speak Irish...It is to be feared that those young gentlemen, the offspring of the colonies of the English conquest, may become in language and disposition fermented with the ancient hatred of Irish to English".

their setting out on this voyage without knowing whether they should ever return to their native principalities or patrimonies to the end of the world"
– Annals of the Four Masters for the year 1607.

Chapter 20

The Wholesale Robbery of Gaelic Land

"The reign of James the First was distinguished by crimes committed on the Irish people under the pretext of Protestantism. The entire of the province of Ulster was unjustly confiscated, the natives were executed on the scaffold or slaughtered with the sword, a miserable remnant were driven to the fastness of remote mountains, or the wild of almost inaccessible bogs. Their places were filled by Scottish adventurers, "aliens in blood and in religion." Devastation equal to that committed by King James in Ulster was never before seen in Christendom, save in Ireland. In the Christian world there never was a people so cruelly treated as the Irish."
– Daniel O'Connell

Ulster Seized by the Crown

After the conclusion of the Nine Years War the entire province of Ulster had been "shired" or split into counties after the English fashion. Following this, the old Gaelic system of land tenure was completely abolished and the English Landlord system introduced in its place. The introduction of this new system in Ulster gave the English a chance to inquire into and decide upon land ownership. Initially, in counties such as Cavan where the English had gained control as far back as the

1560's, the native Irish were more often than not officially recognized as legal freeholders.

The Attainder of Hugh O'Néill and Rory O'Donnell

Following the Flight of the Earls, two juries were summoned, one in Lifford to enquire into the departure of Rory O'Donnell and one in Strabane to enquire into the departure of Hugh O'Néill. In both cases, the juries consisted of English and Irish who were all loyal to the Crown. In O'Donnell's case, the foreman was Sir Cahir O'Doherty (known as "The Queen's O'Doherty") while in the case of O'Néill it was one of the sons of Shane O'Néill – Sir Henry Og O'Néill. Both Doherty and O'Néill had sided with the English during the latter part of The Nine Years War.

At the Assizes, both O'Néill and O'Donnell were found guilty of conspiracy and treason without a shred of evidence being produced. When these verdicts were returned, the London parliament duly passed Acts of Attainder against them and their lands were declared forfeit to the Crown, following which King James issued a proclamation notable for its lack of truth: "...We do hereby first declare that these persons above mentioned had not their creations or possessions in regard of any lineall or lawfull descent from ancestors of blood or virtue; but were onely preferred by the late Queen our sister of famous memorie and by ourselves, for some reasons of State..."[i][189]

King James I seizes Tyrone and Donegal

Up to that point, when similar cases had arisen, only the personal lands of the attainted had been seized by the Crown,

---

[i] Daniel O'Connell M.P was later to point our "If they had no title, their attainder could never have transferred a title to the King"

while the tenants on the land had been left intact as freeholders.[i] In this case, it was expected that the law would be applied following the precedent set in other cases, which would mean that Hugh O'Néill and Rory O'Donnell alone would suffer the loss of their lands. This outcome was especially expected since the Attorney General Sir John Davies had himself followed this precedent in the past.

Davies now turned completely about-face. Abandoning his previous practice (most likely under orders from above since the entire plot to dispossess the Earls now rested on Davies' actions), he made a decision that was both unlawful and unjust, ordering that the entire counties of Tyrone and Donegal be seized. He wrote that "both by Irish custom and the law of England, his Majesty may now seize these lands and dispose of them at his good pleasure".

This was completely untrue as, by Brehon law and Gaelic custom, the Chieftain did not own all the land of his country but only his own personal land, as we have already seen in Chapter 1.

King James Renounces the Act of Oblivion

The confiscation of Tyrone and Tirconnell was swiftly followed by the renunciation by the English of the solemn and general Act of Oblivion that had followed the Nine Years War. Having pardoned those involved in the Nine Years War, King James I now broke his word and proceeded to illegally seize a further four counties – Armagh, Cavan, Derry and Fermanagh – while Ulster was at peace, her people disarmed, and an English army of occupation in place. He accused the leaders in these counties of having previously been in rebellion against the Crown. In his seizure of Ulster, King James had been influenced by those

---

[i] This was similar to what happened in England: when a powerful man had an Act of Attainder served against him, only his personal lands were confiscated by the government and his tenants left intact and untouched on their farms.

King James I

who, like Francis Bacon, had told him of the "so many dowries of nature (considering the fruitfulness of the soil, the ports, the rivers, the fishings, the quarries, the woods and other materials, and especially the race and generation of men, valiant, hard and active) as it is not easy, no not upon the continent to find such confluence of commodities."[190] Robert Cecil's project was, however, set to exceed even his own expectations after Sir Cahir O'Doherty, who controlled the vast area of InishEoghain, revolted against his English friends. His rebellion was not a patriotic act against the occupying English but rather an act of revenge.

The Rebellion of Sir Cahir O'Doherty

When Sir George Paulett had taken over from Sir Henry Dowcra as Governor of Derry he had subjected "The Queen's O'Doherty" to taunts, accusing him of having advance knowledge of "The Flight of the Earls" and of saying nothing. O'Doherty's being "hand in glove" with the English had not worked to his advantage as the English had nevertheless determined to get control of much of the land that he had been awarded following the Nine Years War through various acts of legal spoliation. The final straw came when Paulett went so far as to hit him in the face during a meeting with him. O'Doherty, who was at this stage just twenty-one years old, could not take the insult and decided to take revenge against Paulett and the English.

The Seizure of Culmore Fort
Sir Cahir O'Doherty's uprising was a brief and especially bloody affair. Having worked for the English for some time, he was well acquainted with their methods and now turned them against his former friends.

His rebellion began with the use of an old English trick we have encountered many times in this history. On May 3rd, 1608, O'Doherty held a banquet at his house where he entertained the garrison commander of Culmore Fort, Captain Harte, and his wife. Towards the end of the banquet, O'Doherty's men seized them both. Cahir O'Doherty then threatened Harte with death unless he handed control of the Fort to him. Preferring death to dishonour, Harte refused, but his wife, fearful that her husband would be executed, broke down and agreed to go to the fort and persuade the guard to open the gate. After this happened, O'Doherty's men rushed the gate and quickly gained control of the fort. With the stronghold under his control, O'Doherty ordered the garrison to be slaughtered. Then, after removing the artillery, munitions and stores, the fort was abandoned, and O'Doherty and his men marched on Derry.

The Sack of Derry
The entry of O'Doherty's force into Derry took the English there by surprise. Here, the garrison was also slaughtered, Paulett killed, and the town sacked, after which O'Doherty and his men retired. From May to July, he held out in Tirconnell, parrying numerous excursions by English forces into the area. However, he was finally killed in an exchange of fire with an English army commanded by Marshall Wingfield, after which his head was sent to Dublin as a trophy.

Taking Advantage of O'Doherty's Rebellion

Already viewing O'Doherty's revolt as an opportunity to extend the area declared forfeit to the Crown, the English then arrested two other Irishmen who had pledged their allegiance to the Crown, Niall Garbh O'Donnell and Sir Domhnall O'Cahan, accusing them of being complicit in the revolt. O'Donnell was sent to Dublin for trial where he was found not guilty for lack of evidence, but this did not suit the English plans. Following the verdict, the Attorney General Sir John Davies announced: "We must have an English colony, for the Irish will never condemn a principal traitor."[191] Both O'Donnell and O'Cahan were sent to England and afterwards dispatched to the Tower of London where they remained interned until their deaths some two decades later. The only dissenting voice on the English side concerning the treatment of these "useful idiots" was that of Sir Henry Dowcra, who had bribed them to join the English side in the first place, and now saw that the offers which he had made them in good faith were torn to shreds by others. The disappearance from the scene of these men (and others who were executed) was followed by the usual letters of attainder, which in turn was followed by the legal spoliation of vast tracts of Irish land.

Meanwhile, plans were proceeding apace in London for the accomplishment of King James' scheme whereby the Gaelic inhabitants of Ulster would have their patrimony taken from them, after which they would face banishment. This was because the founding principles of the proposed plantation were to be the exclusion of the native Irish and the eradication of the Catholic religion, in so far these were possible. The land would then be principally made available to English and Scottish Protestant Planters.

King James Bible, Exodus Chapter 20, verse 15; "Thou Shalt Not Steal"

The amount of Irish land stolen by the Crown in Ulster amounted to roughly one million English acres, around half of which was considered fertile land. The Lord Deputy, Sir Arthur Chichester, was given charge of the project after the proposals of Lord Bacon (which were deemed too lenient on the native Irish) were rejected. The project was to see the entire landmass of six counties taken by the Crown and distributed for rent to those deemed eligible after the native Irish had been ejected.

The Plantation of Ulster
According to the final plan for the Plantation of Ulster, the lots awarded were to be of three sizes: 2,000, 1,500 and 1,000 acres, with various ranks of "Undertaker" in charge of each grant. In the first rank, there were the wealthy gentlemen who were to be of English or lowland (inland) Scottish origin, all "well affected in religion". These Undertakers were required to build for themselves small blockhouse castles surrounded by a walled enclosure for protection. The second rank was made up of "Servitors". These were loyal servants of the Crown, civil servants, army officers and the like, all Protestant of course. Both the first and second rank were required to take the "Act of Supremacy" acknowledging King James as head of the church of England. The final rank also consisted of Servitors but with the exception that "Natives" or Irishmen who were considered worthy were allowed to be included. This rank was not required to take the Act of Supremacy. With regard to tenants, the first and second ranks were forbidden to take Catholics as their tenants. Rents varied. If you were an Undertaker or Servitor with Protestant tenants, your rent to the Crown was £5 6s 8d per 1,000 acres but if you were a Servitor who had Catholics as tenants, the rent due on the land

occupied by them was increased to £8.[192] The rent was even higher for the small number of Catholic Servitors, amounting to £10 13s 4d per 1,000 acres.[193] There were exceptions to these three classes with much larger grants being made in particular cases. Among the Gaelic Irish, by far the largest grant was made to Sir Turlough O'Néill of Armagh (a half brother of Hugh O'Néill) who was granted almost 10,000 acres. In return for his services as the director of the project, Chichester himself received the vast lands of the InishEoghain peninsula previously in the possession of Sir Cahir O'Doherty.

Immense tracts of land were also allocated to Protestant religious and educational foundations, including Trinity College, Dublin, while in every county land was to be set aside for a Protestant "Royal School". In all, the established church received not far short of half a million acres, with each parish being assigned 60 acres of land as church property. In areas like Cavan where questions of land allocation had already been decided on by the Attorney General, ways were easily found to overturn these decisions and dispossess the Irish of their land, with the "premature" adjudications being generally reversed or greatly reduced. This even affected those who had proven useful to the English in the past, such as Conor Roe Maguire of Fermanagh (installed as puppet ruler of Fermanagh during the Nine Years War) who saw the amount of land that he owned reduced by two thirds, with the town of Lisnaskea, his ancestral home, being taken from him and given to a Scottish Undertaker. Similarly, in Donegal, the family of Niall Garbh O'Donnell (who had been detained in the Tower of London after having been found not guilty in Dublin of involvement in O'Doherty's rising) received nothing, despite having been previously in possession of almost 13,000 acres.

The greatest benefactors of the plunder were the companies and citizens of the city of London who were granted a much-enlarged Derry which they renamed "Londonderry". The grant was supposed to be of 40,000 acres but, due to failures in the measuring of the land when the plan was being drawn up, it was actually more than ten times that size. This area was especially rich in natural resources such as timber and fish, so freedom to export at will was also granted. Awarding such a vast amount of land to companies whose directors would remain in London ensured that the Ulster plantation would never be far removed from the attentions of the English government.

Of the land allocated by the Crown in the plantation, the native Irish received a mere 11.1% or one ninth of the total. Some Irish who had been confirmed in the ownership of their land after 1603 were allowed to retain it, at least for the present, which increased the total Gaelic share of land to closer to 20%, with few of the 286 Gaelic proprietors being awarded territory to which they had hereditary attachment. Of the 11.1%, many were given land only for their lifetime, after which it was allocated to British undertakers and planted. Others who could not cope with the constant demand for money from the Crown were forced to sell off parcels of land. In Co. Down, when the Magennisses of Iveagh were struggling to make ends meet, they accepted loans from the Planter families of Hill and Trevor at extortionate rates. When the loans could not be repaid, much of their land was seized. On the eve of the 1641 rebellion, the Gaelic share of land in the six planted counties is estimated at 14 percent.[194]

The Fate of the Native Irish

All other native Irish, those whose lands had been appropriated from them and those who were not accepted as tenants by the Servitors, were ordered to "depart with their goods and chattels at or before the first of May 1609 into what other part of the realm they pleased."[195] They received no subsidy nor were they recompensed in any way.

Due to the fact that the land survey undertaken before the announcement of the Plantation had been something of a shambles, some Undertakers were awarded far more land than they could initially cope with. This resulted in Undertakers and Servitors of the first and second rank taking Irish Catholics as tenants against the terms of their undertaking in order to make sure that the land awarded by the Crown to them was fully inhabited. As more Planters came along,[i] these Catholics lived in permanent fear of having their tenancy immediately terminated on the arrival of a more "suitable tenant", praying, according to Sir Toby Caulfield, that "so great a cruelty will not be offered as to remove them from their houses on the very edge of Winter, and in the very season when they are to supply themselves in making their harvest."[196]

When the English Protestants and Scottish Presbyterians flooded into Ulster, many were dismayed to discover that the land they were supposed to inhabit and farm had not been cleared of native Irish by war and famine (as they had been led to believe) but rather that the Irish vastly outnumbered them and in many cases had ignored the "disappear edict". This meant that the task of clearing the land of the native Irish fell to the Planter who, nevertheless, had the apparatus of the English state behind him in case the Irish refused to cooperate. While some Irish departed to an uncertain future elsewhere, many others, with hearts full of anger and bitterness, were forced into a terrible existence in the mountainous and unfertile areas of Ulster in which the planters had no interest. Many soldiers who had fought for the Confederacy during the Nine Years war also took refuge in the forested terrain around the

---

[i] Every year more and more Planters arrived, Scots especially. Sir William Alexander noted that "Scotland by reason of her populousnesse being constrained to disburden her selfe (like the painfull Bess) did every yeere send forth swarmes".

plantations. These "Woodkerne" survived by relieving the planters of livestock and poultry when the opportunity arose. The dispossessed Irish were always mindful of the land that was theirs, now occupied by the stranger[i] who generally despised the Irish on whose lands he now lived. The poverty, deprivation and increased mortality, especially among the young, added greatly to the sense of injustice felt by them. That the Plantation was sowing a terrible wind did not go unnoticed, and Lord Deputy Chichester was warned by Sir Toby Caulfield that "there was not a more discontented people in Christendom"[197] and also that the Gaelic Irish felt that the Plantation was "the greatest cruelty that was ever inflicted upon any people."[198]

In order to pay for the cost of keeping his Plantation secure, King James created a new Royal title, that of "Baronet", a novel means of getting the wealthy gentlemen of the Realm to pay the wages of thirty soldiers for three years, which amounted to the huge sum of over £1,000. In return, the gentleman was

---

[i] Regarding the nature and character of many of those who came to Ulster, the renowned historian W.H Lecky, quotes, in his "History of England in the Eighteenth Century" the writings of a Protestant clergyman, the Rev. Mr. Stewart who came from Scotland to Ulster during the plantation period: "From Scotland came many, and from England not a few, yet all of them generally the scum of both nations; who, from debt, or breaking or fleeing from justice, or seeking shelter, came hither, hoping to be, without fear of man's justice, in a land where there was nothing but little as yet of the fear of God. And in a few years there flocked such a multitude of people from Scotland, that these northern counties of Down, Antrim, etc., were in a good measure planted. Yet most of these people were void of godliness. On all hands atheism increased and disregard of God; iniquity abounded, with contention, fighting, murder."
Author's note - In more modern times, the Planters were described differently. In 1912 at a meeting of "The Belfast Liberal Association", the speaker described the first planters in the following terms: "Hardy pioneers, born of a sturdy race, trained to adversity, when brought face to face with dangers of anew life in a hostile country, soon developed that steady, energetic, and powerful character which has made the name of Ulster respected all over the world."

given the hereditary title and would be referred to as "Sir". Not content with having appropriated Gaelic land, the Crown also commandeered Gaelic heraldry, with Baronets being awarded a neck decoration whose principal symbol was the ancient banner of the O'Néills – the red hand of the legendary Gaelic warrior Cuchulainn. Furthermore, they were permitted to incorporate the "Red Hand of Ulster" into their family coat of arms.

Plantation and Persecution

Whenever the English army had attacked into Ulster during the Nine Years War, it had taken the opportunity to destroy all the Catholic churches and monasteries it came across. Some English commanders were extremely zealous in this regard and particularly sought out places of Catholic pilgrimage for destruction. One notable example was the Church of Down, home to the relics of Saints Patrick, Bridget and Columba, that was destroyed in 1599 after being set ablaze by Captain Edward Cromwell. As the war progressed and the English gained the upper hand in Ulster due to their barbarous tactics, so the travails of the Church had increased. By the end of the war, there was hardly an intact Catholic church left in the whole of Ulster. After the Plantation, many of these ruined churches were taken over and repaired by the Protestants for their own use.

Clergy too had suffered greatly along with the faithful and Catholic bishops were earmarked for particularly harsh treatment wherever the English had gained control. Those captured were generally tortured and hanged so that by the period of Plantation only three Catholic bishops remained in Ulster. This number was reduced to two when the Bishop of Down and Connor, Conor O'Devany, was captured in 1611 along with Fr. Patrick O'Loughrane, before they were both brought to Dublin to be executed. In Dublin, the hangman (who was Irish) refused to have anything to do with their butchering and left the city. The Council resorted to pardoning an English murderer on condition that he would undertake the executions, the sentence being that both bishop and priest should be hanged, cut down while they were still alive, disembowelled, their hearts cut out and their bodies quartered. In the face of this horrific sentence, Bishop O'Devany was afraid that Fr. Loughrane would waver in his resolve if he saw him executed first, so he asked that the priest should be first. But Fr. Loughrane refused, saying that "it was not meet that a bishop should be without a priest"[199]. Both men died, as the Annals of the Four Masters record, "for the sake of the Kingdom of Heaven."[200]

Attempted Conversion of the Irish to Protestantism
With the Plantation came attempts to convert the Gaelic Irish to Protestantism, but these attempts met with little success. Great things were expected of George Montgomery with regard to the conversion of the Irish to Protestantism after his appointment as Protestant Bishop of Derry. Sir John Davies hoped that he might even be "a new St. Patrick among them."[201] But he proved to be more interested in the income of the dioceses under his care than in gaining Irish adherents. Other imported Protestant bishops like the Scotsman Andrew Knox (who became the Protestant Bishop of Raphoe) were far more zealous and he arranged for Gaelic-speaking clergy to be sent over from Scotland so that they could preach to the Irish. But this also was to little avail as the ordinary people wanted nothing to do with the new religion. Knox's aim was to establish "a uniform order for the suppression of popery."[202] He set about destroying Catholic statues and relics at every opportunity, the most notable being the statue of the Blessed Virgin Mary at the Chapel of Agivey in Derry to which pilgrims from all over the country had come, as miraculous

cures through Our Lady's intercession had been obtained before it. In his own words, acts such as this succeeded in obtaining for him, not the people's conversion to Protestantism, but their "deadly hatred."[203] While many relics disappeared forever as a result of Puritan zeal, others were spirited away into hiding places and protected by Catholic families from generation to generation until better times might return.[i]

Along the East coast of Ulster, the Protestants met with some success. Here some Catholics who were well-to-do and eager to advance in a Protestant world conformed, but still the vast majority remained hostile to the "reformed" religion. This was despite being subject both to tariffs that were levied against those refusing to attend Protestant services and the tithe that was due to the established church. These levies were strictly enforced and proved to be something of a horrible shock to the native Irish who had never had to pay such exactions to the Catholic Church in previous times. They were collected not just in money but in kind, in commodities such as agricultural produce like milk. In the winter of 1614/15, it was approximated that one in five cows died as people struggled to pay the tithe. Where the native Irish refused to pay the tithe, the established church used the courts to enforce payment. Bishop Dundas of Down was particularly active in this respect,

---

[i] In Gaelic times Church lands were often occupied by a caretaker family, the head of which was called an "Erenagh" who paid rent to the diocese. This land remained in the family from generation to generation. After the Plantation, when these lands were given by the Crown to the Protestant church, many of these families remained in place as church lands were not earmarked for settlement by Planters but instead transferred to the Protestant church. Of these families, the O'Mulholland's of Tyrone kept safe the famous bell of St. Patrick and the Book of Armagh. Another Erenagh family, the MacMoyers of Armagh, kept safe St. Patrick's Confession. The famous Shrine of the Cathach of St. Columba, carried into battle by the O'Donnells of Tirconnell for centuries, was kept safe by the MacRorty family of Donegal.

using these tithes to build and restore Protestant churches in his diocese. Vast sums had to be handed over to the established church when a person died. Known as "mortuaries", these fines were excessive especially on the poor who were not excused. If a pauper died on a property, a mortuary of 2s6d was exacted on the tenant of the property. On one typical occasion, a man by the name of Dumnagh McConill died, with his burial being prevented until his wife handed over one of their three cows. Shortly afterwards, his wife also died, and the authorities seized a second cow from the family.

Chapter 21

Reasons for a Rebellion

Land Seizures in Leinster

Buoyed by their apparent success in the Ulster land seizure and plantation that had reduced the native population to a terrible existence in the woods, bogs and on the mountains, the view within the crown and government of England was that further land heists followed by plantations along similar lines in other parts of Ireland was the way forward. Munster was already largely secure. During a very brief period after the Irish success at The Battle of the Yellow Ford, the Irish of Munster had once again regained control of their native soil but after the English victory gained by famine and sword, they had been ejected once more into the wild and the Planters had returned.

The plan for all these plantations was that they would provide a loyal Protestant ascendancy within the country which in turn would elect dependable Protestant members for the Irish parliament and also provide candidates for public office, juries and the like. A further motivation on the part of the government for a more widespread plantation was their desire to eradicate the many small Irish freeholders and introduce into Ireland a system of landlordism which would be without the restraining features of the English method, an evil design which would under a later rule see a self-sufficient land owning agricultural class condemned to the depths of poverty and the tender mercies of an English landlord.

The Land Commission

Commencing in 1610, a commission of enquiry was ordered to be set up by the King whereby all titles and land rights going back to (but not further than) the reign of King Henry II would come under scrutiny. This, in spite of the fact that by the policy of "Surrender and Regrant" under King Henry VIII, the Irish Clans were supposed to have achieved security in the ownership of their lands. First in line were the Gaelic landowners of Leinster. Disarmed and powerless, they were at the mercy of the English government. The only recourse open to them was the Dublin courts but here they were up against judges who knew what side their bread was buttered on. This rapacious commission whose "Discoverers" swarmed across the province, seized upon the smallest thing in their investigations and any apparent flaw or informality was resurrected. Their enquiries were full of acts of fraud, perjury and deceit on the part of those leading them. As a reward for finding "flaws", the Discoverers were given a percentage of any rent increase or were sometimes awarded the lands in question, with the remainder being transferred by the Crown into the hands of British Protestants. Speaking of the commission of enquiry, the Protestant clergyman and eminent historian Thomas Leland (1722-85) wrote: "There are not wanting proofs of the most iniquitous practices of hardened cruelty, of vile perjury, and scandalous subornation employed to despoil the fair and unfortunate proprietor of his inheritance"[204]. As the enquiry progressed, the titles of those old English who had remained Catholic were also subject to scrutiny.

Initially, the Crown targeted those areas where the Gaelic Irish such the O'Tooles and O'Byrnes, MacMurrough Kavanaghs,

Farrells and O'Carrolls had always been predominant. These were Wicklow, Carlow, north Wexford, Longford and South Offaly respectively. In short order, 385,000 acres were identified as being suitable for confiscation; those who had their lands confiscated were transferred from the category of landowner to that of tenant, while receiving no compensation. Some landowners were transplanted to remote, unfertile and boggy areas of the country such as the Kerry uplands.

In the case of the Clan MacMurrough Kavanagh, so much land was seized by the Crown that the number of freeholders was reduced from 667 to 150[205], with the other 517 becoming tenants instead, mostly of new British landlords.

Once Leinster had been effectively dealt with, the King's commission turned its attention to Connacht, but the proceedings were put on hold when King James I died in 1625.

The "Packed" Parliament of 1613

With the Plantation of Ulster well underway and his plans for the establishment of a Protestant ascendancy in Ireland bearing fruit, the Lord Deputy Sir Arthur Chichester was determined that a parliament would be called which would pass legislation acceptable to the King, namely *post facto* legal measures for the attainder of the Ulster Earls and the legal establishment of the plantations.

A Catholic Parliament?

It was 27 years since a parliament had been held in Ireland and that parliament had contained a Catholic majority, as would this one. Or would it? Chichester felt that he could organise matters so that there would be a Protestant majority, despite the fact that since the last parliament 17 new counties had come into existence, many of which would return Catholic members. After being informed of Chichester's plan, the King agreed to his proposals. Preparatory measures would now be undertaken that would effectively rig the parliament in favour of Protestants. Once that was achieved, the parliament would be called. The key to Chichester's plan was the creation of forty new boroughs in the planted areas, 38 of them in Ulster. These were boroughs in name only, consisting of a tiny village or a scattering of planter dwellings but they would now be entitled to return their own members to parliament. For some of these "boroughs", the documentation for their creation had not even been completed by the time the election was officially promulgated, as the election date was announced with hardly any notice. A list of proposed legislation for the new parliament was also not forthcoming. The Catholic party, consisting of old English and Gaelic Irish, was extremely fearful that even more drastic anti-Catholic measures would be introduced.

A Rigged Election

However, even the creation of forty new boroughs would not be enough to ensure a Protestant majority in the Dublin parliament. Orders were given to the electoral officials to block Catholic freeholders from casting their vote. One example of this took place at the Shirehouse in Armagh. On the day of the election, Sir Turlough MacHenry O'Néill, of The Fews in Armagh, the most prominent Catholic in Ulster and the largest Catholic grantee of the recent plantation, arrived with many of his freeholders to cast his vote. As a candidate for one of the two county seats, he was guaranteed to be elected due to the high number of Catholic freeholders in the district. However, the election officials and sentries barred the way into the hall and forced Sir Turlough and his Catholic party away. Incensed, O'Néill's freeholders held their own election which returned Henry Mac Shane and Sir Turlough as members of the Dublin parliament. But of course this was not recognized, and two Protestants, Sir John Bourchier and Sir Toby Caulfield, were returned thanks to the rigged election, proving that the fair treatment of the so called "deserving Irish" was nothing more than a sham.

Pleading With the King

When Parliament met, the Protestant majority was 25. However, the Catholics withdrew almost immediately on account of a violent scene in the chamber during which the Catholic candidate for Speaker, Sir John Everard, was manhandled and had his garments ripped. After the Parliament was suspended, a delegation of Catholic members made their way to London to see the King. On their arrival, they were apprehended. Two of their number, Luttrell and Talbot, were sent to the Tower of London and the others to Fleet Prison.

After cooling their heels for some time, they were brought to the King where they were subjected to the ire of the "British Solomon" as his flatterers called him. "What is to you if I make many or few boroughs?" the King railed; "my Council may consider the fitness of it if I require it."[206] As regards their Catholicism, the King told them that because of it they were "but half subjects and therefore deserved only half privileges"[207]. The only public concession the King was willing to give was to dispense with the votes of the 11 boroughs for which the paperwork had not been completed before the election. Nevertheless, it appears that there were further concessions on both sides, most likely negotiated by Chichester as when Parliament was reconvened no further anti-Catholic measures were forthcoming from the government, and forced attendance at Protestant service was abolished: the government being content with maintaining the sizeable revenue stream from the recusancy fines. In return, the Old English Catholic party was, as had been the case during Queen Elizabeth's reign, willing to vote for all other measures, including the unjust Act of Attainder against the Ulster Earls. Large increases in taxation were also voted for and English law was legally extended to Ireland. Many wondered how long the Catholic party could survive under this system where the power of the Protestants grew from day to day.

Renewed Catholic Persecution

After the Parliament sittings were brought to a conclusion, a grateful King James relieved Sir Arthur Chichester of his role as Lord Deputy. For his loyal service to the Crown,[i] he was awarded further despoiled lands and given the title "Baron of Belfast". Having allowed Parliament to conclude without any new anti-Catholic legislation, the new appointee as Lord Deputy, Sir Oliver St. John (acting on the King's instructions), made life extremely difficult for the Catholics from almost his first day in office. By this time, the spirit in Britain was almost completely Puritan and intolerant of Catholicism and the King demanded that the same should be the case in Ireland. All the anti-Catholic legislation already passed was re-enforced to the letter of the law. Furthermore, the recusancy fines and penal taxes were increased by the addition of "administrative" fees which meant that a basic fine of twelve pence for non-attendance at Protestant service became a fine of ten shillings. It was the law that a portion of the recusancy fines was to be used for the relief of the poor, but in the case of Ireland this stipulation was ignored since the poor were themselves Catholics and therefore unworthy to receive charity. The view

---

[i] Chichester is remembered, not only as the engineer of the Ulster Plantation, but also for his guidelines relating to the punishment of jurors who failed to find in favour of the King in a court case when "sufficient evidence" was produced. For some, the punishment was to involve the "loss of ears", while others were to be "bored through the tongue" or "sometimes marked on the forehead with a hot iron".

of the Council was that they "ought to pay the like penalty themselves".[208]

The Loyal City

In 1617, Oliver St. John targeted the city council of Waterford, the members of which were immovable in their defence of the Catholic Faith and had steadfastly refused to take the Oath of Supremacy. Oliver St. John issued a proclamation which denied the city of its old charter and liberties granted at the time of King Henry VII when it had been named "Urbs intacta" or the "Loyal City".

The same proclamation renewed the restrictive measures on the diocesan clergy who continued to find their way into the country from abroad. A further proclamation was issued in 1622 ordering all "Popish Clergy" to depart the country, after which date they were liable to receive the most severe punishment. Keeping company with or talking to a priest was also proscribed.

The Court of Wards

The attention of the government also turned to the subject of land inheritance. The law was changed in order to force an upcoming generation of wealthy, mostly "old English" Catholics to embrace Protestantism. A "Court of Wards" was established in 1617 to ensure that any Catholic landowner who was underage would be educated as a Protestant. If he was overage, he could not legally succeed unless he took the Protestant Oath of Supremacy.

Following a tenure of six years, Oliver St. John was recalled in 1622 and replaced by Henry Carey, better known as Viscount Falkland.

The 'Graces' of King Charles I

After the death of King James I in 1625, his second son Charles succeeded him,[i] becoming King Charles I. When news of his accession to the throne reached Ireland, he was, like his father before him, hailed as someone who would hopefully grant a measure of toleration to Catholics. In the case of Charles, the hope for toleration was at least based on the influence of his Catholic wife, Henrietta Maria, who was the sister of the King of France, as well as on his attachment to so called "high church Anglicanism", which (as the religion of King Henry VIII) was regarded by Catholics as being more schismatic than heretical, because it still maintained many of the traditional Catholic doctrines rejected by the Puritans. However, as with his father before him, Catholic hopes were misplaced, for Charles's dislike of Catholicism in actual fact bordered on hatred.[209] His French marriage, which he had entered into for political advantage, had not yielded the expected results. To make matters worse, the King had broken his marriage treaty with the French Crown by ejecting from his house many of his wife's Catholic servants and chaplains. Nevertheless, Charles felt that the fact that Catholics thought he would grant them relief, could still be used to good advantage.

Tensions between Crown and Parliament

Ever since the early years of the reign of King James I, there had been growing opposition in Britain to the additional revenue-raising measures implemented by the King from the wealthy landowners and industrialists who were all members of the Westminster Parliament. The usual method for attaining these revenues was for the King to summon a parliament and expect its members to vote for what he demanded. Then each

---

[i] Henry, the eldest son of King James I had died in 1612.

member was expected to contribute their share as a sort of gift to King and country. Much of the royal revenues came from land duties but, as the value of money had declined so had the revenues leaving the Crown more reliant on the funds raised in Parliament. In the meantime, trade was continuously increasing, meaning that the wealthy classes were becoming wealthier. These influential members of parliament who engaged in trade planned to step up their efforts with Charles to reduce the amount of money the Crown demanded imagining that they would find in him a King without the experience and statecraft of his father.

King Charles I

After Charles' coronation, he summoned a parliament following the normal practice. To the annoyance of Scottish members, he announced the "Scottish Revocation" which would return to the Crown and the established Protestant Church much former Catholic Church land that had been in the possession of the wealthy Scottish landowning class ever since John Knox's revolution. This action had the effect of putting many wealthy industrialists all over Britain on their guard against the King, while in Scotland in particular it was the first step on a path to rebellion.

Meanwhile, the resistance to extra revenues in parliament continued, with the wealthy refusing to give the King any grant at all unless he had a number of priests, who had been caught saying Mass, put to death. In so doing, they were trying to outmanoeuvre Charles, knowing that he had secretly promised measures of Catholic toleration to his brother-in-law, the King of France. Knowing that his relations with the French Crown would be doomed if he complied with the demands of the parliamentarians, the King refused to execute the priests, the result being that no money was voted for the Crown. Matters then continued to deteriorate. When Charles's chief advisor Buckingham was murdered, he refused to give his full assent to "The Bill of Rights" which would lessen the amount of duty the Crown could expect on imports until finally Parliament was dissolved in 1628 following a violent scene. The last word of the wealthy Puritan party on leaving Parliament was threatening in the extreme – they pronounced that any merchant who paid customs was a traitor, while anyone who granted concessions to Popery was worthy of death. For the moment, the Crown was safe from trouble so long as Parliament was not recalled, and King Charles was determined to avoid its recall at all costs. However, he desperately needed to somehow make up the revenues that had formerly come from it. What was he to do? One of his answers was Ireland.

From His Majesty's Bounty
In 1626, Irish Catholic hopes of obtaining some relief from the incessant persecution were raised when the King mentioned during a speech "matters of grace and bounty to be rendered to Ireland"[210]. This pronouncement was swiftly followed by approaches from Falkland to the Catholics telling them that the King would look kindly on their plight if they would be willing to offer him monetary support in return. The Catholics agreed, never suspecting that they were in fact being duped by the King and that the offer was nothing more than a cunning scheme allowing the Crown to obtain vast sums of money from them by offering certain concessions regarding property and religion, while giving them nothing in return.

After Falkland had arranged for a meeting to take place in London between the King and a Catholic delegation, news of the proposal leaked out, arousing the fury of the Protestant hierarchy. Their Protestant Primate of Ireland, Archbishop Ussher, declared that to "grant the papists a toleration...to...profess their faith and doctrines was a grievous sin."[211] He prayed God to "make those in authority zealous, resolute and courageous against all popery, superstition and idolatry."[212]

In spite of this backlash by the established church, the negotiations between Catholics and Crown went ahead as planned, the King knowing that in the end he would give away nothing of importance. In 1627, an agreement was reached. In return for certain concessions, the Catholics were to pay the staggering sum of £120,000 over three years as a voluntary subsidy to the Crown. There were 51 concessions or "graces", including that Catholics would be allowed to practice law without having to take the oath relating to the Act of Supremacy, a simple act of allegiance to the King sufficing. Several of the graces also related to land and would see all discoveries of "land title defects" by any future land commission limited to 60 years. Furthermore, the so-called "Composition of Connacht", which dated back to the reign of Elizabeth, was to be confirmed by parliament. At the time of its introduction during the tenure of Lord Deputy Perrott, the Composition had taken land from many Catholics but in the face of the activities of the Discoverers, Catholics considered it to be by far the lesser of two evils and there was anxiety among them that the current authorities might seek to ignore it as it had never been promulgated by parliament. One of the most important of the "graces" related to the unending extortion and violent persecution of the Irish by the British army during marauding patrols from their barracks and also while supporting the Sheriffs and other authorities of the Crown as they carried out their repressive duties. These criminal activities by the army were to be "restrained"[213].

Following the agreement, a royal proclamation was issued outlining the agreement and stating that a parliament would be held to confirm its terms. Trusting the King's word, the Catholics returned home, expecting that the summoning of parliament was imminent and so immediately paid the first instalment of the amount. However, as the weeks went by, nothing happened, and enquiries only brought forth excuses from the government. Nevertheless, confident that the agreement would be kept the Catholics relaxed their guard and practiced their Faith more openly. For his part, Falkland did nothing to stop them even when the Dublin council urged him to take matters in hand. As the interlocutor between Crown and Catholics, he had never suspected that the whole scheme was a ruse. He was unwilling to persecute the Catholics on the pretext that that the graces had not as yet come before parliament, especially since they had already paid the first instalment of the agreed amount.

He eventually issued a declaration against the Catholics, but nothing more, and in 1629 the King recalled him at the behest of the Puritans due to his failure to enforce the laws against the Old Religion.

"Boyle's Law"

A new Lord Deputy was not appointed. Instead, the role was divided between two men, Lord Chancellor Ely and Lord Treasurer Richard Boyle, the Earl of Cork. Boyle in particular was a man who knew how to keep the Catholics in check. As a young adventurer, he had made his way to Ireland in the time of Queen Elizabeth and had quickly amassed a fortune for himself by "cunning and fraud."[214] Having purchased the estates that had previously been in the possession of Sir Walter Raleigh for a pittance, he had quickly ascended the greasy pole, amassing both wealth and titles. In Lodge's Irish Peerage, Vol.1, p.150, it is written of him with some pride that: "...he encouraged the settlement of Protestants, the suppression of popery, the regulation of the army, the increase of the public revenue and the transportation of many septs and barbarous Clans from the fruitful province of Leinster into the wilds of Kerry."

Richard Boyle

Without delay, the full rigours of the law were once more enforced in the entire country. All known chapels and Mass houses were targeted and, after having their altars and statues profaned, were either demolished or seized "for the King's use." Compulsory attendance at Protestant service (which had been dispensed with at the time of Chichester's parliament) was reintroduced.

Lord Deputy Sir Thomas Wentworth

King Charles I eventually decided on a candidate for the post of Lord Deputy of Ireland. His choice, Thomas Wentworth, was a man whose greatest ambition was to obey the King in his every wish and whim. He was utterly devoted to his lord and master, and as a result unprincipled, though certainly not the first Lord Deputy to hold these "qualities".

Wentworth had not always been this way, for in a previous existence he had led a group of squires in parliament who had sought to limit the power of the King. But he had changed course, deciding that the Sovereign must be supported above all else and Charles knew he could be absolutely trusted. He came to Ireland despising not only the Irish but those among the land grabbers and fortune hunters who had sought only to enrich themselves and not their King and country.

To cause further upheaval, pain and suffering to the common Irish was one thing, but Wentworth would go much further, garnering powerful enemies in his efforts to amass revenues for the Crown to ensure that King Charles I could remain independent of the English parliament.

Wentworth's Parliament

Although officially appointed in January 1632, Wentworth did not take up his position as Lord Deputy until July 1633. By his bearing and manner, he very quickly alienated many members of the Government Council, recognising in them gross inefficiency and corruption. He proceeded to dismiss some of the members, replacing them with men brought in from England.

Wentworth extracted a further £20,000 from the Catholics (who were waiting in vain for the King to keep his word regarding the "graces") in order to have the recusancy fines suspended for a year. He now had a choice to make. An Irish parliament needed to be called in order to raise further funds for the King, but how would he manage to parry the demand of the Catholics for the fulfilment of the King's promise regarding the graces?

The parliament assembled in July 1634 with a very large Protestant majority thanks to the ongoing gerrymandering of constituencies and various other measures employed by the Council. In his opening speech, Wentworth got the most important thing out of the way – money. He assured the members that the graces were coming but they would first have to vote more money for the King. He reassuringly told them: "Surely so great a meanness cannot enter your hearts, so

as to suspect His Majesty's gracious regards of you..."[215].
Further subsidies amounting to almost £250,000 were passed.

With the money secure, Wentworth proceeded to implement his plan of dealing with the question of the graces. The question of which ones were to be admitted and which were not was to be put before a committee consisting of Sir John Radcliffe and two Lord Justices. Since Wentworth had previously come to an arrangement with these gentlemen, he knew exactly what the outcome would be. With regard to the graces affecting the Catholics, the committee proposed that these were to be refused altogether, apart from a few watered down ones which could be admitted: for example, Catholics would be allowed to practice as lawyers but only in the very lowest courts of the land. As parliament was overwhelmingly Protestant, it was a trifling matter to get this passed. With regard to the graces affecting land titles, it was proposed by the committee that a commission for the examination of these should be re-established. Wentworth succeeded in passing this thanks to the Protestant majority. The whole procedure was completed without reference to the King, who was delighted with the outcome as the anger of the Catholics had been diverted away from him and on to Wentworth himself and the commission he had set up. In a letter to him, the King wrote: "Before I answer any of your particular letters to me I must tell you that your last public despatch has given me a great deal of contentment; and especially for keeping off the odium of a necessary negative from me, of those unreasonable graces that people expected from me."[216]

Dispossessing the People of Connacht

After dissolving parliament, Wentworth's reason for refusing to grant the Composition of Connacht became clear. His plan was twofold. If he appropriated Connacht for the Crown, then the King's revenues from Irish land would be substantially increased. His second aim was to introduce colonies of Planters into Connacht. The land settlement of Sir John Perrott in the reign of Elizabeth was completely discarded and the notorious Discoverers resumed their work. Ancient records, which had once had their homes in Norman monasteries and castles, were seized, examined, and amended where necessary. Naturally, the enquirers were only interested in the period after the Normans had taken control in Connacht. As with the rest of the country, the fact that the Irish had always lived there was of absolutely no interest to them.

The Discoverers maintained that since Connacht had been granted to Richard deBurgo, and since King Edward IV had descended from the deBurgo line, all the land of Connacht had therefore become the property of the Crown when King Henry VII had confirmed all land titles to himself. This was their finding, and they intended to "prove it" by organising a trial in each county whereby the King was to have the land confirmed to him. Sheriffs were instructed to select amenable jurors who were to have the sword of financial ruin hanging over them "in case they should prevaricate", as Wentworth put it.[217] They were instructed to find "a clear and undoubted title in the Crown to the province of Connacht".[218] Furthermore, the juries were told that if they came up with the right verdict, they could keep a portion of their own land. Matters proceeded to Wentworth's satisfaction. Juries in Roscommon, Sligo and Mayo all found for the King. In Galway, the jury would not be bullied and refused to find in his favour, facing Wentworth's wrath as a result. Along with the Sheriff who assembled them, they were summoned to appear before the Dublin Council where they were each fined £4,000 and had their land seized. They were also imprisoned until the fines should be paid. The Sheriff was also imprisoned and, being unable to pay the £1,000 fine demanded of him, died there. Wentworth continued undeterred, knowing he had the full support of the

English King, who, referring to the treatment of the Galway jurors, said concerning Wentworth: "...If he served Us otherwise then he would not have served us as We had expected..."[219]. With his treatment of the Galway jury held high as an example to other juries, the process continued.

By the 1630's, Ireland had established a highly successful and profitable trade both in fine woollen cloth and wool, mostly for export. This proved to be too much of a threat to the same industry in England and so, in order to protect it there, Wentworth enacted such draconian measures against the industry in Ireland that it was almost destroyed. However, for the English and Scottish planters of Ulster, Wentworth established the basis of a successful linen industry which would be of no danger to England's trade. Like a man possessed, he worked tirelessly for his King and his King was not disappointed. In a few short years, he had vastly increased the amount of customs duty he was able to send to King Charles I by harnessing Ireland's fishing and agricultural resources for him. Towards the end of his rule as Lord Deputy, the declining political Scotland edged towards armed conflict between the Scots and the English. In response to this, Wentworth enlisted a large army in Ireland mainly consisting of Irish Catholics. Well trained, this army waited in readiness to be used against the Scots.

Wentworth's Enemies and the Slide Towards the English Civil War

By his disregard for, and treatment of the Gaelic Irish, Wentworth had certainly made plenty of enemies among them. This was also the case with the so called "old English" in Ireland, Catholics from whom he had extracted vast amounts of money, granting them almost nothing in return. Both groups, having no influence or friends in high places, were powerless to do anything about him. However, this was not the case with the powerful Undertakers and Planters, and it was here that Wentworth, in his desire to please his King, would find the rock on which he perished.

The London Companies lose "Londonderry"

An example of Wentworth's indiscriminate approach with regard to his revenue-raising measures for the King's coffers may be found in the case of Boyle of Cork. Most other Lord Deputies would have hesitated to make an enemy of the powerful Earl, but not Wentworth. Having examined Boyle's land titles, Wentworth found that he owed the Crown the sum of £15,000 which he demanded to be paid. Furthermore, Boyle was forced to surrender Youghal College to Wentworth and the Crown.

For King James I, the Plantation of Ulster had been a project dear to his heart. This was not the case for his son Charles. When his father had heard that the rules of the Plantation were being broken, he was furious and had introduced fines in order to get the Undertakers to stick to the so called "Printed Book" which contained the Plantation regulations. However, many Undertakers had continued to break these rules in order to earn sufficient money to pay the fines and also to make a profit by keeping their land grant fully populated. Just before the death of King James I, a census had been carried out which had confirmed his worst fears. In every planted area of Ulster, the Catholic Irish were still in the majority. When Charles became King, gone was the dogmatic approach of his father with regard to the rules of the Plantation. Initially, his main interest was to extract as much revenue as he could from the project, and he was not particularly interested in the regulations so long as the fines due from the Undertakers and Servitors were paid. Nevertheless, official enquiries into the Ulster plantation, its rules and the neglect of them were still undertaken since more revenue in the form of fines could be exacted from the Undertakers and Servitors as a result of prosecutions.

It was in Derry that Wentworth was to make his most dangerous enemies, for "Londonderry" was controlled by the London companies, whose directors were either part of, or hand in glove with the powerful and wealthy parliamentarians who had recently refused to vote additional funds for the King in Parliament. In 1630 a commission of enquiry found that the London companies by their non-conformance had betrayed the trust of King James" by their non-conformance[220] and so imperilled the Kingdom of Ireland and "true religion"[221].

A "Star Chamber" trial was organised. Wentworth pressed for the removal of the London Companies' patent, knowing that if the patent were returned to the Crown, the Crown would at once be the direct recipient of all rents paid in the area of the Derry grant.

A Star Chamber trial in the Palace of Westminster meant a trial without a jury and could be expected to find in favour of the King, which it duly did. The London companies had their grant forfeited and were fined £70,000 with all customs and tariffs being immediately confiscated by the Crown. While the measure had gained money for a cash-strapped King, it had also succeeded in arousing great anger in the City of London against the Crown and Wentworth in particular.[i]

Scotland on the Brink of War

As a convinced Anglican, King Charles I desired to unite all the Protestant sects in both Britain and Ireland under his spiritual rule by bringing them into conformity with his own Anglicanism. The Scottish Kirk was far removed from what

---

[i] It is a great irony that the plantation of Ulster which was ordered by King James was to have a direct contribution to the later execution of his son King Charles I and ultimately the undoing of the Stuart dynasty.

the King desired, for the Presbyterians here were strongly Calvinist in outlook. Ever since the King had announced the Scottish Revocation, opposition to any church reform enforcing Anglicanism in the Kirk had hardened. When a new book of service was introduced into the country in 1637, it caused a riot in Edinburgh, and the bishop who was taking the service at St. Giles Church had to flee for his life. All levels and classes of Scottish Presbyterian society united in opposition to the reform and a binding Covenant was drawn up and signed by thousands demanding the abolition of the service, a free parliament and an assembly for their own Kirk. Even though their claims were granted, the Covenanters organised an independent Scottish government and prepared for war, feeling that their demands were only to be tolerated until the King could bring an army to bear on them.

Wentworth Introduces "The Black Oath" in Ulster

In Ulster too, the Presbyterians were coming under pressure. Many clergymen of the established church catered for their Presbyterian flocks and were Anglican in name only. Wentworth, who had no time for Puritans, now set up a commission under Bishops Bramhall and Leslie and they endeavoured to bring the Protestant Church in Ulster into line. Castigating the Puritan Clergy, Leslie preached: "…They have cryed down the most wholesome order of the church as popish superstition…"[222]

Thomas Wentworth

All clergy who would not

411

change their ways were dismissed. When the Scottish Covenant was signed, the Presbyterians of Ulster flocked to put their signature to it. Wentworth retaliated. He sent an army northward to encamp in Ulster and exact "coign and livery" from the Planters, thereby hoping that the "discomfort" would force them to return to Scotland. With the military in occupation in order to ensure that there would be no trouble, he also introduced the "Black Oath" whereby those who had signed the Covenant would be made to renounce it on their knees. Those who refused to take the Black Oath were excommunicated, fined and imprisoned. One large Antrim Undertaker, Sir John Clotworthy M.P. was responsible for the Derry grant of the London Drapers. A close friend of the parliamentarian leader John Pym, he had enough of Wentworth's persecution of the Presbyterian Planters and resolved to take action against him.

The Scottish War
Meanwhile, the King faced open revolt in Scotland. After the Covenant, the newly formed Scottish General Assembly had virtually taken over the running of the country, raising a large and efficient army officered by veterans of continental wars who had fought abroad as mercenaries. Curiously the anti-Catholic Covenanters had sought the financial aid of the powerful French Catholic, Cardinal Richelieu, who was more than happy to oblige any proposal that would make life difficult for the English. When a letter to him was intercepted by the English, war was inevitable as this treason could not be overlooked. The home army in England was in a dire state of repair, with many of these second line soldiers sympathising with the Presbyterians. In the battle that followed, the English were easily beaten back by the Scots who proceeded to occupy the north of England. To keep them at bay in the north, the

King offered to pay them £40,000 a month, an offer which they accepted.

The King Signs the Warrant for Wentworth's Execution

Thus hamstrung, the King recalled his loyal servant Wentworth, creating him Earl of Strafford. With insufficient funds to finance a Scottish war, the King was forced to do the one thing he did not want to - recall Parliament. Sooner than do this, he had attempted to raise funds by summoning a "Council of Nobles", but without success. Once parliament was recalled, his attempt to unite the country against the Scots failed for the parliamentarians who had been side-lined for over a decade were determined on revenge. Having locked the parliament door, Pym introduced an "Act of Impeachment" against Wentworth, accusing him of many and diverse crimes including his conscription of an army consisting of "Irish Papists" to be used against the Puritans. In reality, as far as the Puritans and the money power of London were concerned, his greatest fault was that he had for too long helped the King rule without Parliament, and this was the reason why he was condemned to death. In an attempt to save the country from civil war, the King signed the death warrant "in great anguish". After Wentworth's execution, parliament continued to pass more and more legislation, all of which the King found repugnant, feeling that it undermined his position. The drift towards civil war continued.

All these happenings were watched with great interest in Ireland. England's difficulty was seen as Ireland's opportunity for the recovery of Irish land into native hands and the chance to gain freedom for the practice of the Catholic Faith.

Finally, in January 1642, the King personally went to the House of Commons accompanied by 400 soldiers, determined to arrest five of the leading parliamentarians for treason. But they escaped before they could be seized, fleeing into the care of the wealthy London Merchants. War between the Crown and the Parliamentarians was now imminent.

Chapter 22

The Great National Rising of 1641-42

Ireland's Call

A Deteriorating Situation

Even before the end of the Nine Years' war, Ireland had been almost completely subjugated, the final phase of the war chiefly consisting of acts of barbarity and scorched earth by Crown forces accompanied by occasional guerrilla actions and small battles of final resistance. When the conclusion of the war coincided with the death of Queen Elizabeth, it seemed possible that the new monarch King James I, might try to govern Ireland with a measure of fairness and justice for he had generously not sought vengeance on Ireland's leaders. However, within a very short time, James had been influenced by his advisors at Court and England had instead resumed the path of robbery and despoliation for her own benefit. In every sphere of life, Irish people were excluded, existing only to be of use to their English masters as "drawers of water and hewers of wood". With the Irish disarmed and powerless, the agents of the Crown along with the army had free reign to degrade and terrorise the people, while seeking to eradicate Catholicism. Ulster, once the last bastion of the Gaelic way of life, had been stolen on the orders of King James, while in the rest of the country the Gaelic Irish were being squeezed out by agents of robbery and deceit called "Discoverers".

This was the situation in the late 1630's, and the signs for the future were ominous. However bad things in Ireland were at that moment, the rising power of the Puritan Party in England foretold even greater evil in the future. Some of the intentions of the Puritans were divulged in speeches. One such speech was delivered by the powerful Undertaker and Parliamentarian Sir John Clotworthy who stated that "...the conversion of Irish Papists can only be effected with the bible in one hand and the sword in the other..."[223] . In Dublin, Lord Justice Sir William Parsons (his tongue perhaps loosened by alcohol) had boasted at a party that, after the Parliamentarians in England had got their way, "...within twelve months there will not be a Catholic left in Ireland..."[224]

Government Plans to Drive the Irish into Rebellion

After King Charles had recalled his loyal Wentworth in November 1639, affairs in Ireland quickly deteriorated, for the King had replaced him with an absentee Lord Deputy –The Earl of Leicester. The real power was wielded by two Lord Justices named Parsons and Borlase, with the control of the army being entrusted to James Butler, the Earl of Ormond.

Initially, it seemed matters might improve and that any moves towards armed revolt on the part of the Irish were averted, for King Charles I, recognizing that he might need the help and support of Irish Catholics in his war with the Scots and his struggle with Parliament, had ordered Parsons and Borlase to prepare legislation for the granting of all the graces that he had promised. However, both Parsons and Borlase were of the Puritan and Parliamentary faction and the choice of them as the *de facto* rulers of Ireland was a disaster. Neither man had any intention of giving succour to the Catholics, preferring instead to prorogue the Irish Parliament with the intention of embarrassing the King and driving the Catholics into rebellion in the hope of crushing them completely. Once they were driven into insurrection, the government intended to do everything in its power to fan the flames of the insurrection so that the complete seizure of Catholic land would be the result. In letters written to Sir William St. Leger on January 27th and February 25th, 1642, the Duke of Ormond confirmed as much by complaining to St. Leger that the government's motives were too obvious[225]. In his reply to Ormond, St. Leger agreed, writing that "...the undue promulgation of that severe determination to extirpate the Irish and Papacy out of this Kingdom, your Lordship rightly apprehends to be too unseasonably published..."[226]

Planning an Insurrection

As of early 1640, small groups of powerless Gaelic Irish leaders were meeting informally with each other to discuss the dire state of affairs regarding both the spiritual and material welfare of their country. That these separate groups joined together to share their concerns and ideas can be traced to the efforts of Rory O'More, of the family of the Gaelic Chieftains of Laois. As always, Ulstermen were prominent, although in this case this is not surprising when we consider the suffering of the native Irish in Ulster at this time. Chief among the Ulstermen was Sir Phelim O'Néill who was in contact with several members of the Gaelic Clans of Ulster, while O'More himself won over Lord Conor Maguire, Baron of Enniskillen.

As the year progressed, their discussions turned to plans for action. The example of the Scots had its part to play in providing motivation for the Irish leaders, for the Scots had been successful thus far in their actions against the Crown. The feeling among the Irish was the King would find it difficult to fight both the Irish and the Scots at once. Unlike their Scottish counterparts, the Gaelic leaders were not strong enough to seek independence from the Crown. Justice for Ireland was their motive. Since their pleas against overwhelming repression had not been heard, their idea was to undertake a successful uprising that would allow them to gain redress by force. Then, acting from a position of strength, they hoped that the Crown would come to terms with them, granting what they most desired – freedom from English tyranny.

The group contacted more of the Gaelic leaders in the provinces, and also those prominent Irishmen who had fled abroad, many of whom were officers and gentlemen in the armies of Catholic Europe. Chief among these was a Colonel in the Spanish army who was stationed in the Low Countries and went by the name of "Don Eugenio O'Néill" – better known to his Gaelic kinsmen as Eoghan Roe O'Néill. Ireland's call also circulated among the many Gaelic priests and friars in Europe. In Rome, the call was enthusiastically answered by the founder of the College of St. Isidore for the training of Irish Priests, Fr. Luke Wadding, who became the chief organiser abroad for the Gaelic leaders, arranging both financial aid and political support for them.

The enemies of the Gaelic leaders now provided them with a favourable development. After Wentworth's trial and execution, the Parliamentarians had demanded the disbandment of his "Popish Army" of 10,000 Irishmen whom he had enlisted for use against the Scots, as the English Parliament would sooner see the Scots have their way than use an Irish Catholic army against them. With his back to the wall, King Charles I had little choice but to acquiesce. However, the English Parliament felt that it was too dangerous to let these trained fighters go free – they would have to leave Ireland. Permission was granted for them to depart the country to enlist in foreign armies. The matter was placed in the hands of officers who were to arrange the necessary paperwork, but as some of these were Irish Catholics, they had a higher loyalty than that which they professed to give the Crown. Among those sent over for the purpose of disbanding the "Popish

Army" were Sir James Dillon, Colonels Byrne and Plunkett and Captain Brian O'Néill. Seeing their opportunity, the Gaelic leaders of Ulster contacted these men and they agreed to help. Colonel Plunkett suggested that the primary objective of any revolt should be the seizure of Dublin Castle by a *coup de main* operation in order to capture the vast arsenal there and also as a means of neutralizing the centre of English governance in Ireland.

Plans for the rebellion were finalised. In both Leinster and Ulster, army forts and garrisons were to be seized simultaneously and weapons taken. The order was given that no one should be killed unnecessarily "…but where of necessity they must be forced thereunto by opposition…"[227]. With their plans complete, the date for the rebellion was set – October 23rd, 1641.

The Gaelic Insurgency

<u>Disaster in Dublin</u>

On the evening of the 22nd, several of the principals, including Conor Maguire, Rory O'More, Colonel Plunkett and Hugh MacMahon, had gathered in Dublin to direct the 200-man operation against the castle, when disaster struck.

Some time earlier, Conor Maguire had enlisted one Eoghan O'Connolly (who was his foster brother and a servant of Sir John Clotworthy) into the plot without knowing that Connolly had recently become a Protestant. On the day that the insurrection was to be launched, Connolly attended a meeting of the conspirators in order to gather the particulars of the plot and then immediately went to Parsons, who initially did not give much credence to the story as Connolly was intoxicated. Parsons brought Connolly to Borlase who decided to act, and immediate steps were taken to secure the city and the castle. Many of the Irish leaders had got wind of their betrayal and abandoned the Castle project and the city in time, but both

Maguire and MacMahon were captured.[i] Dublin was placed on high alert. All those in the city who had no permanent residence there were ordered to depart at once under pain of death. Sir Charles Coote was appointed City Governor and weapons were passed out to loyal citizens. An edict was issued against "this detestable conspiracy of evil affected Irish Papists"[228]. Some of the Catholic Old English objected to this, so another edict was issued explaining that the first edict was directed against the "...mere Irish...and none of the old English of the Pale."[229]

Ulster

In spite of the grave setback in Dublin, the rebellion proceeded as planned in Ulster. On the same evening that the plot was betrayed in Dublin, Sir Phelim O'Néill paid a surprise visit to Lady Caulfield at Charlemont Fort. As he appeared to be in no hurry, he was invited to stay for dinner. Later on in the evening, he surreptitiously admitted his men who quickly captured the fort and took Sir Tobias and Lady Caulfield prisoner along with the Fort's garrison. The same night, Dungannon was also taken using a similar stratagem. Within

---

[i] Both men were dispatched to London, where they were tried, found guilty and butchered at Tyburn. In court, Maguire told of how Rory O'More had convinced him to join the rebellion; "He began to lay down the case that I was in, overwhelmed in debt, the smallness of my now estate, and the greatness of the estate my ancestors had and...how the welfare of the Catholic religion, which he said the parliament now in England will suppress, doth depend on it."
Maguire's execution was notorious for its brutality as soldiers interfered with the "work" of the executioner. "...one of them cut the rope with a halberd and let the Lord Maguire drop alive and then called for the executioner to open him alive and very ill the executioner did it, the said Lord Maguire making resistance with his hand and defending himself with such little strength he had and such was the cruelty that for sheer compassion the executioner bore not to look upon him in such torment, and to have done with him, speedily handled his knife well and cut his throat." – Taken from Archivium Hibernicum (1949)

the following twenty-four hours, army forts and posts were captured all over the province. Castlecaulfield was taken by the O'Donnellys, Mountjoy Fort by the O'Quinns, Portadown by the MacCanns and Newry by Sir Conn Magennis. In Fermanagh Rory Maguire overran the county apart from Enniskillen Castle which remained an untaken English garrison under the command of the plantation undertaker Sir William Cole. In Monaghan, Castleblayney and Carrickmacross were captured by the MacMahons. In Cavan, the insurrection was led by its member of parliament, Philip O'Reilly,[i] who declared: "We rise for the Faith." Everywhere, the army bases were despoiled of their weapons and distributed to the insurgents. In Artrim, Lurgan capitulated, while Lisburn was taken under siege.

Proclamations and Letters
On the 23rd October, Sir Phelim O'Néill issued the following proclamation as he wished to make clear the intentions of the rebellion's leaders:[ii]

"These are to intimate and make known unto all persons whatsoever in and through the whole country that the true intent and meaning of us whose names are hereunto subscribed that the first assembling of us in nowise intended against our sovereign lord the King, nor hurt to any of his subjects either English or Scottish; but only for the defence and

---

[i] During the insurrection Philip O'Reilly undertook to house and protect all Protestants who put themselves in his care. One of those who availed of this was the Protestant Dean of Kilmore, Henry Jones, who as Bishop of Clogher in 1652 ordered all Catholics banished under pain of death from Monaghan town and its environs up to a distance of two miles from the town.

[ii] In his history of the period Professor Thomas Leland writes: "In the beginning of the insurrection it was decided that the enterprise should be conducted with as little bloodshed as possible"

libertie of ourselves and the Irish natives of this kingdom. And we further declare that whatsoever hurt hitherto hath been done to any person shall be presently repaired and we will that every person forthwith, after proclamation hereof, make their speedy repaire unto their own houses and under paine of death, that no further hurt be done unto any one under the like paine, and that this be proclaimed in all places"
   ----At Dungannon, the 23d October 1641---
    PHELIM O'NÉILL"[230]

Sir Con Magennis, who had just captured Newry, also put pen to paper writing to some of his English friends:

"To my loveinge friends, Capt. Vaughan, Marcus, Trevor and other commanders of Down these be deere friends – My love to you, although you think it as yet otherwise. Sure it is, I have broken Sir Edward Trevor's letter, fearing that any thinge should be written against us. We are for our lives and liberties as you may understand out of that letter. We desire no bloode to be shed, but if you meane to shed our bloode, be sure we will be as ready for you for the purpose."
I rest your assured friends[i]
   ----Newry, 23d October 1641---
    CONNOR MAGNEISSE"[231]

Meanwhile, at Charlemont Fort Phelim O'Néill had discovered the royal seal on a patent. Deciding to use this for the benefit of the rebellion, he had a fake royal commission from King

---

[i] The original of this letter by Conor Magennis was preserved in the Custom House, Dublin. However, during the burning of the Custom House by the IRA during The War of Independence in 1921, an act undertaken to paralyse the English governance of Ireland, vast amounts of ancient documents were lost in the flames.

Charles I made up. In the days that followed, he used the commission complete with seal to persuade various royalists to join him by telling them that the rising was for the King and against Parliament.

The Planters are Cast Out Without Mercy

Within a few days of the rising being launched a large part of planted Ulster was once more under Gaelic control. Army posts were captured and the English troops withdrew from the countryside to garrisoned forts. Within a short time the number of insurgents in Ulster numbered around 30,000.

Naturally the native Irish who had been despoiled of their land just over thirty years previously were anxious to reclaim it, and the cruelty that followed was not active policy on the part of the Irish commanders but rather indiscipline on the part of the many and varied groups and individuals who had joined the rising seeking justice and vengeance for the crimes committed against them over the previous half century. For many of them this was the opportunity they had been waiting for. With a fury born of long suffering they fell upon their native soil and cast out the planters without clothing or food into the winter weather where large numbers of them died from deprivation.

Massacres

According to the eighteenth century historian and Church of Ireland clergyman, Thomas Leland the first massacre of the period was perpetrated against the Irish of Antrim.[232] Carrickfergus had become the place to which many of the Planters had made for after being turned out of their homes as the Scottish garrison there was still intact. Around the beginning of November soldiers from the garrison accompanied by numbers of Scottishmen who had gathered there and at the village of Ballycorry said that "they had a warrant from the King to murder all the Irish and that they would kill any man who would save and protect the Irish."[233] They made for the nearby peninsula of Island Magee, a heavily populated Catholic district and massacred many hundreds[i] of the Catholics who lived there. Very shortly after this a second massacre also took place in Antrim after a failed attack by an insurgent army on Lisnagarvey during which large numbers of the insurgents were captured and later put to death. It was after word of this massacre spread among the Irish that there was a marked deterioration in their treatment of the Planters[234] resulting in maltreatment and murder.

Sir Phelim O'Néill

Through the actions of some of his subordinates and his role as a commander who did not take effective measures to control his men, Sir Phelim O'Neill has been rightly blamed as bearing ultimate responsibility for some of the murders committed against the English planters, a blame which he accepted at his execution in 1653 when he declared that: "the several outrages committed by my officers and soldiers in that war, contrary to my intention, now press my conscience very much"[235]

The most often recounted massacre of the period took place around the middle of November when around 100 Protestants were forcibly drowned after being driven off the bridge at Portadown at the point of sword and musket.

---

[i] Some accounts of the Islandmagee massacre put the number of those massacred at 3,000.

The largest massacre in Fermanagh took place in the countryside around Enniskillen at the end of October 1641 after Sir William Cole left the castle with a large number of soldiers After rounding up two hundred Irish in the locality they were all slaughtered. Fermanagh was also the scene of a second massacre two months later. On Christmas Day 1641 a party of Maguires returned to land taken from them in the plantation and murdered around 60 Protestants at Tully Castle.

Other massacres of Catholics took place in Templepatrick and at Ballydavey near Hollywood in Co. Down. Massacres of Catholics were to greatly increase following the arrival of the Covenanter army in the Spring of 1642 including the execution of Irish prisoners at Kilwarlin Woods outside Dromore, and the mass execution of Catholic civilians in Newry. On Rathlin Island, home to the Scottish Catholic MacDonnell Clan, many women and children were killed by Covenanters from the Clan Campbell.

Truth and fiction
Many Protestants left Ulster at this time and made their way to Dublin. There, the citizens were horrified by the stories told by many of those seeking refuge, grim accounts of people being roasted or buried alive and of the most terrible violations against women.

The two Lord Justices, Borlase and Parsons, established a commission to collect these stories which are to this day housed in Trinity College Dublin. They contain a mixture of truth, exaggeration, hearsay and lies Of the large number of submissions collected, very few of them were sworn while numbers of them described the same murder as if committed in different locations. Some people were reported as having been murdered but were found to be still alive several years later. Further submissions, including that of the later Protestant Bishop of Kilmore, the Rev. Robert Maxwell, related to apparitions of the ghosts of the murdered who had appeared with their hands raised to heaven crying for vengeance.

There are sixteen submissions relating to the Portadown massacre but of these only William Clarke's is an eyewitness account. Clarke recalled that: "He with such other English as they (the Irish) could find to the number of three score persons which belonged to the said parish of Loughgall and put them all into the Church there and did set a guard over them and from there took them to Porte of Douane and such English as they met did take alongst with the rest which were in all their coming...about a hundred persons where were all drowned at that time."[236]

Further submissions on Portadown include that of Catherine Cooke who recounted: "And that, about nine days afterwards she saw a vision or spirit in the shape of a man that appeared in that river in the place of the drowning, bolt upright, breast high with hands lifted up and stood in that posture there until the latter end of lent next following"[237]. Elizabeth Price testified: "...Then and there on a sudden appeared a vision or spirit...in the water, repeating the word Revenge! Revenge! Revenge!"[238] Such testimonies would hardly bear examination in a court of law.

Within a short time, England abounded with wildly exaggerated tales of what the Catholics of Ulster had done. The accounts of the depositions recorded in Dublin were regarded as gospel. One English writer by the name of Claredon maintained that "there were forty or fifty thousand Protestants murdered before they suspected themselves in any danger and that on the 23rd of October alone there were 50,000 Protestants murdered in Ulster."[239] Sir John Temple wrote that "one hundred and fifty thousand Protestants were massacred in cold blood in the first two months of the rebellion"[240], which was a number that exceeded the entire number of Protestants in the whole of Ireland at that time. With every retelling, the number increased, and the fury of the Puritan party grew. 200,000 Protestants had been put to death and their deaths had to be avenged. However, the official government dispatches from Dublin to London in the latter quarter of 1641 make no mention of massacres in Ulster, only of the despoliation of the Protestant planters.[241]

As regards how many Catholics were killed in massacres, no one appeared interested, least of all the officers of both Crown and Parliament. No figure for the massacred Catholics has emerged from history. In relation to the killings, the eminent historian William Lecky (1838-1903) later wrote: "It is far from clear on which side the balance of cruelty rests."[242] In any event, it is difficult to compare atrocities committed in hot blood by a long suffering people with the actions of the forces of the Crown.

So, how many Protestants were killed during the insurrection period? Around 1652, an English Protestant clergyman and historian, the Rev. Dr. Ferdinand Warner, undertook to minutely examine all the documentation, including the volumes of witness testimonies collected in order to arrive at a figure for the number of Protestants killed. Allowing for, in his estimation, the highest number possible, he records in his book "The History of the Rebellion in Ireland" that "...the number of persons killed out of war, not at the beginning only, but in the course of the two first years of the rebellion amounted altogether to 2,109. On the report of other Protestants, 1,619 more; and on the report of some of the rebels themselves, a further number of 300; the whole making 4,028. If we allow that the cruelties of the Irish out of war extended to these numbers, which considering the nature of several of the depositions I think in my conscience we cannot yet to be impartial, we must allow that there is no pretence for laying a greater number to their charge."[243]

Of the rising in Ulster, the eminent 20th century British historian Hilaire Belloc writes: "Acts of great cruelty took place against the victims as they flocked to seek refuge...How many (Protestants) fell in this insurrection has been a matter of dispute – 2,000 may be too low an estimate, 5,000 too high. But the story of a successful Catholic rising grew when it reached England to enormous proportions and men would have it in their fury, that hundreds of thousands had been put to death."[244]

In more modern times the Trinity College depositions have been re-examined and are now available to the public on the internet. It is now reckoned that the lowest estimate of planters killed during 1641-42 is 527 with the maximum number being put at 1,259.[245]

That the Irish were guilty of the wholesale murder of tens of thousands of Protestants in Ulster was to become part of the false narrative of English history for centuries to come, being used by successive English government to justify great massacres and crimes committed against the Irish people in the decades and centuries that followed, including the seizure of Irish land by Cromwell, and the refusal of King Charles II to return the land of Ireland to its rightful owners.

Atrocity Propaganda

In the years immediately following 1641, many books and pamphlets were published in England on the topic of the mass murder of Protestants in Ulster. These were illustrated with the most lurid pictures of apparent atrocities in progress. One of the Puritan leaders, Oliver Cromwell, often read these publications[246] and was doubtless influenced by them. His later invasion and "Settlement of Ireland" is one of the most terrible chapters in Irish history, termed by Cromwell as the "righteous judgement of God upon these barbarous wretches."[247]

In order to give some idea of the type of literature published in England before Cromwell's entry into Ireland, there follows an excerpt from one of these pamphlets published in London in 1647 by Stephen Bowtell. The effect of this and similar texts on those shortly to be let loose in Ireland can be imagined by the reader:

"...When the devil showed our Saviour all the kingdoms of the earth and their glory...he would not show Him Ireland but reserved it for himself...he hath kept it ever since for his own... They (the Irish) are the very offal of men, dregges of Mankind, reproache of Christendom, the bots that crawl on the beasts tail...I beg upon my hands and knees that the expedition against them may be undertaken while the hearts and hands of our soldiery are hot, to whome I will be bold to say ...Cursed be he that holdeth back his sword from blood: yea cursed be he that maketh not his sword starke drunk with Irish blood...that maketh not heaps upon heaps...Let not that eye look for pity, nor that hand be spared that pities or spares them and let him be accursed that curseth them not bitterly."[248]

The Insurrection Widens
The Catholic "Old English" are Goaded into Rebellion

Borlase and Parsons, far from being dismayed by the insurrection, welcomed it as England's chance to confiscate not just the lands still held by the native Irish but also those lands in the possession of the Catholic old English. Almost immediately, the old English who remained immensely loyal to the Crown, were treated with increased disdain and the weapons that had been handed out to them at the discovery of the plot to seize Dublin Castle were withdrawn as the government closed ranks against them the view being "that the more were in rebellion the more land should be forfeited."[249] Borlase and Parsons even went so far as to put plans in motion for the establishment of new plantations on the lands that would be seized once the insurrection was favourably concluded. In order to make a list of the "disaffected" among the Old English, the Government arrested numbers of their servants and resorted to that instrument of torture known as "the Rack" in order to obtain information.

Meanwhile, with Ulster largely under their control, the insurgents turned their attention to Drogheda which they took under siege after capturing Lord Moore's house at Mellifont, in Co. Louth on November 24th. Sir Phelim O'Néill, who was in overall command in the north, now took the title of "Lord General of the Catholic Army in Ulster".

As Drogheda was being taken under siege, the insurgents suffered a reverse when they failed to take Lisburn in a battle that ended with the massacre of a large number of Irish prisoners. Determined to lift the siege of Drogheda, Ormond quickly dispatched a relief force from Dublin under the command of Sir Patrick Wemyss, but the insurgent commanders learned of their approach and positioned a sizeable army under the command of two Cavan men, Philip O'Reilly and Myles "The Slasher" O'Reilly at Gillanstown Bridge, Julianstown, Co. Meath. The Irish lay in ambush as the English approached and the latter, taken by surprise, were completely routed after the Irish charged them in overwhelming numbers. As the battle commenced, the English cavalry abandoned the field rather than be swallowed up in the mass of Irish infantry.

Meanwhile in Dublin, the two Chief Justices assembled the garrisons of the army stationed in the Pale for active duty. They were sent out into the surrounding counties to encounter and destroy the rebels but according to Lord Castlehaven they were not overly particular with regard to whom they dispatched, "taking little or no care between rebels and subjects but killed in many places promiscuously men, women and children."[250] The Governor of Dublin, Sir Charles Coote,[i] led a portion of the army south ostensibly to secure Wicklow against the insurgents, but instead became mired in the bloody massacre of civilians, including young infants.[251]

Sir Charles Coote

After returning to Dublin, Baronet Coote became actively involved in efforts to drive the Old English Catholics into rebellion. Already completely marginalized by the Dublin government, the Old English decided to send Sir John Read (who was a King's Messenger) to London, his mission being to tell King Charles I of their loyalty and plead for his assistance regarding the course they should adopt with the Dublin government. Read never made it to the King however, as on his arrival in England he was arrested, imprisoned and later racked by the Parliamentarians in an effort to find out what exactly the King knew about the Irish insurrection before it was launched. Word now spread around the Catholics of Dublin that Coote

---

[i] To adequately recount the wanton barbarity and cruelty of Sir Charles Coote (for which he was renowned even among the English) would take up many paragraphs. His forays from Dublin are legendary for unprovoked, ruthless and indiscriminate carnage in which none of the Irish men, women or children he or his men encountered were spared. Rev. Dr. Warner writes of him that he "was a stranger to mercy, and committed many acts of cruelty without distinction." His crimes were not the crimes of an individual for the English government, knowing what he was like, first employed him and then commended him for his actions, raising him to a position where he was the overseer of Ormond who was in command of the English army in Ireland.

had proposed at a Council meeting that the insurrection should be met by the mass murder of Catholics. Such a thing seems incredible, but Coote's reputation was such that it was widely believed and a number of Old English gentlemen who were summoned to a meeting with the Council refused to attend, fearing that they would be arrested and killed. With no hope of assistance from the King and thinking they might at any moment be rounded up and imprisoned or worse, the Old English were slowly drawn into the rebellion as the Council intended, not against their King but against the tyranny of the Dublin government. Already, one of their number had suffered a terrible fate. When English soldiers had gone to Clongowes Castle in Kildare, the home of Sir James Eustace (who was known to be sympathetic to the cause of the insurrectionists), they had slaughtered everyone on the estate including the women and children. Even Sir James's ninety year old mother had not been spared. The soldiers, suspecting her of hiding a key in her mouth, promptly smashed in her jaw, after which she died.[252]

With the ongoing persecution of the Catholic Old English in progress, Borlase and Parsons had promptly seized the opportunity to ban any Catholic from sitting in Parliament. Treated as renegades and rebels on account of their adherence to the Catholic Faith, the friendless Old English now looked for help amongst the ranks of the Gaelic Irish.

At last, a meeting between the Gaelic leaders and the leaders of the Catholic Old English was arranged by Lord Gormanston at Crofty in Co. Meath, followed by a second meeting at the Hill of Tara. The Gaelic leaders knew that for the "Séan Ghall" (old English) there would be no question of any disloyalty towards the King. By the end of the second meeting, a union of minds between the two parties had been established – freedom for the Catholic Faith in Ireland under the King's and not Parliament's rule.

English Policy towards the Insurrection
In England, meanwhile, King Charles was under severe pressure from Parliament, Having allowed the genie to escape from the bottle by summoning Parliament, Its members now succeeded in gaining one demand after another from the Crown.

Having failed to unite England in its war against the Scots, King Charles now tried in vain to do likewise regarding the Irish, even proposing that he would go to Ireland himself in order to lead the effort against the rebellion. But Parliament would not allow such a thing, as they harboured the notion that the King himself was mixed up in the Irish insurrection in spite of all his condemnations of his "rebellious Irish subjects"[253]. Parliament now demanded control of the war in Ireland and the King was forced into another humbling submission, after which a resolution was passed in the House of Commons that they would "never consent to any toleration of the Popish religion in Ireland or in any other part of His Majesty's dominion."[254] While dispatching some troops to Ireland, Parliament could not afford to send those units upon which they relied, knowing that war with the King was coming ever closer as Charles would not brook their ongoing seizure of power forever. By continually ensuring that stories of Popish massacres against the Protestants of Ireland lingered, Parliament endeavoured to ensure that public anger remained aroused against the insurrection and undertook to enlist new army units under the pretence of their being sent to Ireland. In reality, these units were intended for Parliament's upcoming war against the King. Acts were also passed in the English House of Commons confiscating millions of acres in Ireland on the pretext that estates would be needed for distribution to the troops in lieu of payment for their services following the war. This measure was further advanced in February 1642 by the "Adventurer's Act", whereby confiscated estates in Ireland were to be offered for sale to English adventurers who would pay up front for them, thus providing funds for the putting down of the insurrection. In reality Parliament intended the funds to finance their war against the King.

It was Parliament's intention that when all wars were concluded, they would use the land and wealth of Ireland to pay their soldiers and repay their debtors. An essential part of the Act was the provision forbidding the King to pardon any of the rebels as otherwise the adventurers would not be able to receive a guarantee on their investment at the time of its making.

As 1641 drew to a close, the insurrection was still mainly confined to Ulster and Leinster. However, around the middle of December this situation was altered thanks to the actions of the Lord President of Munster Sir William St. Leger who sent troops of cavalry on the rampage, apparently in punishment for the removal of some livestock from his brother-in-law's estate following some punitive measures taken by him against the Irish. The cavalry had not held back but had slaughtered a large number of people. Sir William had been in command of one troop responsible for the murder of many innocent civilians, and the burning of houses.[255]

As the situation threatened to escalate, some of the Old English of Munster had offered their services to St. Leger in order to act as intermediaries with the Irish but this offer was soundly rejected, St. Leger telling them that he did not trust the Old English as "...they were all rebels..." and that he would rather "...hang the best of them..."[256] Following this, the situation quickly deteriorated and numerous massacres ensued with the garrison at Bandon being particularly notable in this respect. With the forces of the Crown treating everyone whom they came in contact with in the country at large as insurgents, the people had no choice but to rise in defence of their lives. Shortly after this, Cashel in Tipperary was seized by an ad hoc

Irish army led by Philip O'Dwyer as a place of refuge from those fleeing the atrocities of the Crown Forces.

That Munster should also join the insurrection was exactly what St. Leger intended, and for his friend the avaricious Boyle, Earl of Cork, the spoils of war were already being counted. The insurrection in Munster was still in its infancy when Boyle wrote to the Speaker of the English House of Commons regarding the confiscation of lands in Munster, including with his letter a list of 1,100 indictments against property owners, writing that "if the house please to direct to have them all proceeded against to outlawry, whereby his majesty may be entitled to their lands and possessions which I dare boldly affirm was, at the beginning of this insurrection, not of so little yearly value as £200,000." [257]

"Slay and Destroy"
The year 1642 began with a number of reverses for the Irish, both north and south. At the end of February, the English army made another great effort to lift the siege of Drogheda and this time they succeeded. By the end of the month, Dundalk was also in English hands. Borlase and Parsons, who continued to wield the powers of the Lord Deputy, now ordered that the war be brought to the people. This was a repetition of the tactics of pillaging and murder used by Mountjoy forty years previously, but with the caveat that the troops had to return to their barracks by nightfall.

The order handed by the Government to the Commander of the Army was as follows:

"It is resolved, that it is fit that his Lordship do endeavour with his Majesty's forces to wound, kill, slay and destroy by all the ways and means you may, all the rebels and adherents and relievers; and burn, spoil, waste, consume and demolish all places, towns and houses, where the said rebels are or have

been relieved or harboured, and all hay and corn there, and kill and destroy all the men inhabiting, able to bear arms
---Given at His Majesty's Castle of Dublin, 23rd February, 1642---

R. Dillon.	F. Willoughby.
Thos. Rotheram.	J. Temple.
AB. Loftus.	Robert Meredith"[258]

However, Ormond who was Commander of the army did not have sufficient stomach for the brutality desired of him and was on more than one occasion reprimanded by the Lord Justices for not carrying out their orders fully. In future, Sir Charles Coote was ordered to oversee the implementation of army orders and was instructed to accompany Ormond. Shortly after in the town of Naas, Co. Kildare, Ormond himself had taken into custody two priests, Frs. White and Higgins, who were imprisoned there until they should be transferred to prison in Dublin. Coote had the two clergymen removed from prison in Naas early one morning and, without reference to Ormond, executed them. Ormond protested to Borlase and Parsons but was told that Coote had not exceeded his power.

More of the Old English were now rising in arms against the government, and the most notable of these in the spring of 1642 was Richard Butler (Lord Mountgarret) who succeeded in rallying both the old English and Gaelic Irish of south Leinster and north Munster to his standard. Within a short period, he had overrun counties Kilkenny (where he captured the city without bloodshed), Waterford and Tipperary.

The success of the rebels in Cork was marred by the stubborn resistance of Crown forces in many places and also by divided leadership as the local Anglo-Irish leader, Gerald Barry, would not relinquish control of the movement in favour of Mountgarrett. Mountgarret returned with his army into Leinster where his largely untrained army was routed near

Rathcoole in Co. Dublin, with the loss of 600 men and a large amount of supplies.

The Beginning of the English Civil War

At the beginning of January 1642, the tensions between Crown and Parliament finally came to a head. Already the King had heard rumours that Parliament intended to impeach his Catholic wife Henrietta Maria, and now he received evidence that members of parliament were colluding with the Scots. When on January third Parliament failed to deliver up five of its members for treason after a request by the King, the following day the King personally went to the House of Commons accompanied by 400 soldiers, determined to arrest the five parliamentarians for treason. But they escaped before they could be seized, fleeing into the care of the wealthy London Merchants. Almost immediately the King was forced to flee London, and preparations by both sides for battle began in earnest.

A Scottish Army is Sent to Ulster

Although a truce remained in place between the English and Scottish armies, they were nonetheless still at war. A curious arrangement was now arrived at which clearly placed the importance of the Catholic rebellion in Ireland ahead of the Scottish revolt, even though the Scots had invaded and were in control of the north of England. The English Parliament now approached the Scottish leaders and asked for their help in the suppression of the Irish insurrection. The Scots, doubtless assured that the English would not take advantage of the situation and eager to assist their kinsfolk in Ulster, readily agreed and a Scottish army under the command of General Monroe was dispatched to Ulster, arriving in Carrickfergus in April 1642 where they joined forces with a large number of Planters before advancing towards Newry. The arrangement was sanctioned by the King, for neither he nor Parliament were willing to release Englishmen for service in Ireland as they would soon be needed on home soil since England was now on the brink of war.

General Robert Monroe was a man of vast military experience that he had accrued mostly in Germany. His advance on Newry was a trail of bloody slaughter of both prisoners and civilians in the districts through which he passed. At Kilwarlin, Loughbrickland and Newry, every man he captured was either shot or hanged. In the environs of Newry, his troops scoured the countryside, killing at will. In the town itself, his men murdered "sixty men, eighteen women and two priests"."[259] One of his officers wrote of Newry that all the Irish "...were cutte down with sume wyves and chldrene for I promise such gallants gotis but small mercie..."[260]

Chapter 23

The Catholic Government - 1642-1649

The Establishment of The Catholic Confederation
The Synods of Kells and Kilkenny

Due to their treatment at the hands of the government, the Old English had resorted to working with the Gaelic Irish for life and liberty and in defence of the Catholic faith. For both parties this arrangement was not without its difficulties. For the Gaelic Irish they would have to forego any desire which they had to use the rebellion as an attempt to achieve complete freedom from English rule not to mention regaining the lands of their forefathers much of which was occupied by the Old English, while for the Old English, they would have to put aside their misgivings about working with the Gaelic Irish. This was doubtless made easier by the fact that long before the insurrection they were as Catholics, already regarded as traitors to the Crown.

To ensure that this partnership would have a solid base, one built on the unity of faith between the two parties, the Archbishops, Bishops and Priests of Ireland now endeavoured to do all they could to ensure that this unlikely collaboration would accomplish its aims.

On March 22nd 1642 the first major step in this regard was taken when the Catholic Primate and Archbishop of Armagh

Hugh O'Reilly convened a provincial synod in the ancient monastic town of Kells, Co. Meath. The synod, whilst denouncing all criminal activity and murder, nevertheless declared the insurrection to be not only lawful but pious. Before the Synod concluded a national synod was called, to be held in Kilkenny City on May 10th.

Following the Kells Synod a meeting of Confederate Catholics took place in Trim, Co. Meath to lay the groundwork for the project. One of the items that exercised the minds of the participants was the many war crimes which the Insurgents had been accused of but had not committed, such accusations having been levelled against them in order to mask the crimes committed by the forces of both Crown and Parliament. Upon the conclusion of the meeting, a "remonstrance" or statement of protest was sent to King Charles which requested that at war's end a full investigation of war crimes would be undertaken. It included in part "...Forasmuch as your Majesty's said Catholic Subjects have been taxed with many inhuman cruelties which they never committed, your Majesty's said suppliants, therefore desire for their vindication and to manifest to all the world to have such offenders brought to justice, do desire that in the next Parliament all notorious murders, breaches of quarter, and inhuman cruelties committed of either side may be questioned in the said parliament if Your Majesty think fit; and such as shall appear to be guilty to be excepted out of the Act of Oblivion and punished according to their deserts"[261] On receipt of this plea the King rejected it at the insistence of the English Parliament.

When the three-day Kilkenny synod commenced on May 10th many of the country's Catholic prelates were in attendance including three out of the four Archbishops with the Archbishop of Dublin sending representatives. A manifesto was published which explained the motives of the insurrection and laid down rules for its continuance including severe penalties (excommunication) for anyone who should use the war for their own personal gain. Whilst stressing their loyalty to the King, a Plan for the governance of Ireland was also published, its ruling body being a General Assembly consisting of representatives both temporal and spiritual from all provinces and cities to include Old English and Gaelic Irish. This General Assembly would in turn elect a Supreme Council, a body which might be compared to a modern day ministerial Cabinet. The Supreme Council were tasked with carrying on the governance of Ireland on a day to day basis and with appointing officials such as Judges etc. Provincial Councils were also to be formed which would report to the Supreme Council. It was projected that the General Assembly of the Catholic Confederation would convene on the 24th October 1642.

The most important document emanating from the Synod was the "Oath of Association" that all Catholics throughout the land, regardless of background were asked to take as it cemented them together into a union to be known as "The Confederate Catholics of Ireland"

Massacre outside Naas

As spring 1642 turned to summer many minor battles took place especially in Leinster and Munster, where the siege of Limerick Castle by the Confederates commanded by Gerald Barry and Lord Muskerry continued. The castle finally surrendered to the Confederate army on June 22nd.

May 1642 saw a dreadful massacre committed by the English army in Co. Kildare when Sir Arthur Loftus, who was the Governor of Naas, led a force of cavalry and dragoons[i] into the hinterland and undertook a general massacre of the Irish. As

---

[i] Dragoons are mounted soldiers who generally dismount before engaging in battle.

the alarm spread through several villages many people escaped on foot onto a nearby hillside to wait there until the army should retire. However Loftus and his men pursued and surrounded them after which he ordered the mountain furze to be set ablaze resulting in the burning alive of many people.[i] The massacre was boasted of by Loftus to the brother of Lord Castlehaven who on investigation recorded that he: "...saw the bodies and furze still burning."[262]

Massacres in Meath

In early April 1642 the English were reinforced by the arrival of the son of the Earl of Leicester, Lord Lisle and 1,000 men. Coote decided they should go into Meath and set up a military base at the ruined Trim Castle that was in the possession of the Confederates. As this large force of fresh and heavily armed troops approached Trim the smaller Confederate force abandoned the Castle.

The English soldiers who now occupied Trim Castle earned for themselves a fearful reputation in the surrounding countryside for murder. From their headquarters at Trim they embarked on forays into the surrounding countryside, towns and villages killing all the Irish they came in contact with as far away as Navan, Slane and Dunshaughlin. Many people abandoned their homes, fleeing to wherever shelter could be obtained. In the parish of Rathcore, near Enfield in Co. Meath 160 people were murdered by soldiers under the command of Sir Richard Grenville.[263] During the summer of 1642, many people were murdered in the fields while attempting to save those crops which still remained in the ground[264]

---

[i] In the Appendix of his "History of the Irish Rebellion", published in 1720, the Duke of Claredon writes that the setting on fire of woods, thickets or furze in order to kill those taking shelter therein was common practice by the English soldiers.

Coote who accompanied Lisle and his army was killed around this time – apparently by one of his own men. Shortly after this the deceased Coote's son, also called Charles, was appointed "Provost Marshal of Connacht", and like his father was destined to play a barbarous role in Irish affairs for many years to come.

"Murrough of the Burnings"
The beginning of July saw the rise to prominence of one of the most monstrous and ruthless figures of the insurrection period –Murrough O'Brien (Lord Inchiquin). Ever since the "Surrender and Regrant" of King Henry VIII when the governing family of Thomond, the O'Briens, had eagerly seized Church and monastic lands in Thomond, they had thereafter effectively renounced their Gaelic identity and wholly embraced the process of Anglicisation becoming loyal to the Crown of England ever since. It was indeed difficult to associate them with King Brian Boru, from whose line they had descended, for every ounce of Gaelic empathy seemed to have deserted them.

A product of the School of Wards of King James I, Murrough O'Brien, had been raised in the manner of the English nobility, and as a staunch Protestant had married Elizabeth, the daughter of the Lord President of Cork, Sir William St. Leger. When St. Leger died at home on July 2nd 1642 O'Brien was appointed to succeed him.

If Murrough O'Brien had not inherited the Boru love of the Gaelic nation, he most certainly had inherited his fighting spirit for back in April when Cork was under attack by a confederate army led by Lord Muskerry, O'Brien at the head of about 200 soldiers had recklessly charged into and scattered a much larger force thereby bringing the siege of Cork by the Confederates to an end. Already by the time he was appointed to succeed St. Leger, he was known to the Irish as "Murrough of the Burnings" due to his penchant for razing to the ground the towns and villages of the Catholics.

The Return to Ireland of Eoghan Roe O'Néill

The mixed fortunes of the Confederates thus far now took a turn for the better with the arrival to Ireland of the experienced military leader and tactician, Colonel Eoghan Roe O'Néill in the middle of July 1642.[i] Aboard ship with him were about 100 trained Irish officers and a large amount of muskets and ammunition. Shortly after their arrival on the shores of Donegal, a convention of the Gaelic leaders of Ulster took place in Clones, Co. Monaghan, and it was here that Sir Phelim O'Néill formally handed over his military command to Eoghan Roe O'Néill. Immediately Eoghan Roe set about improving the organisation of the Ulster army in every way. Whilst Sir Phelim had turned a blind eye to some acts of atrocity, Eoghan Roe made it abundantly clear that he would not tolerate anything of the sort even as a retaliation. Within a

Eoghan Roe O'Néill

---

[i] Before departing the continent for Ireland, Eoghan Roe O'Néill had written to Fr. Luke Wadding in Rome: "I have received, Revrend Father, proofs of your well-known zeal for our fatherland. Time glides away and Ireland groans and suffers, worn out not so much by her miseries as by the weary hope of foreign help, long looked for and not yet come. I feel that I, at any rate, should make no more delay, and that in this hour of Ireland's troubles I should not be absent or seen wanting. I am girt up for my journey with many chiefs of my race. I bid goodbye to your paternity and return unbounded thanks for your unwearied exertions on behalf of Ireland and of myself."

short time the officers he had brought with were allocated commands within the army after which they dispersed in order to try and turn a largely untrained force into a skilled army and to improve the fortification of Confederate strongpoints.
The strength of the Confederate Army was further improved in August when more ships bearing Irishmen released from service on the continent arrived with stores of muskets, artillery and ammunition. At the head of this contingent was Colonel Owen Preston, the brother of Lord Gormanston.

For King or for Parliament?
At the commencement of the English Civil War at the end of August 1642, the Scottish General Monroe held the north east of Ulster for the parliaments of England and Scotland, while in the northwest there was a separate Royalist Planter force called "The Lagan Army" commanded by the Stewart brothers. The English civil war created a somewhat confused situation for English arms in Ireland as many commanders and officers had to officially decide whether they would fight against the Catholic Irish under the banner of King Charles I or under the banner of the Parliamentary forces. While the Duke of Ormond was a self professed Royalist his actions often betrayed his sympathy with the cause of the Parliamentarians. In Munster Inchiquin was initially royalist, but switched sides in 1644. In 1648 he was again to declare for the Royalist cause while Lord Broghill (Boyle) fought under the banner of Parliament. In Connacht, the Earl of Clanrickarde professed himself to be a Royalist but still tolerated the Parliamentary garrison in Galway which later in the war was responsible for a large number of atrocities in the region. Whether fighting for King or Parliament, both sides had but one aim – to eradicate the Catholic threat, as neither the Royalists or the Parliamentarians came to blows with each other on Irish soil until the war in England was long over.

"Pro Deo, Pro Rege, Pro Patria Hibernia Unanimis"
On October 24th 1642 the Catholics of Ireland, both Gaelic Irish and Old English officially united in defence of faith and fatherland. Drawn together by a lofty motive, and in spite of a promising start, the project was nevertheless to be under an almost constant cloud of rancour and division chiefly caused by the insistence of the Old English that their loyalty for the King of England was pre-eminent even when this loyalty threatened the very foundation on which the Confederacy was built.

The Parliament House for the General Assembly was in the City of St. Canice, – Kilkenny, at the home of Sir Richard Shea in the city's marketplace. The Assembly consisted of an Upper House comprising of eleven spiritual lords (bishops) and fourteen temporal lords, while the lower house was comprised of 226 members. The Speaker of the Lower House was Nicholas Plunkett while Patrick Darcy officiated as Chancellor. Fr Thomas O'Quirke, a learned Dominican Friar from Tralee was appointed as Chaplain.

The Confederacy was established as the provisional government of Ireland until such time as the injustices inflicted on the Catholics of Ireland could be remedied or as the assembly termed it "…'until His Majesty's wisdom had settled the present troubles"[265]. Having adopted the motto "Pro Deo, Pro Rege, Pro Patria Hibernia Unanimis" ("Together for God, King and our Irish Fatherland")[266] the Assembly set to work, its first task being the election of the Supreme Council [i] whose

---

[i] The members of the Council were; FOR LEINSTER – The Archbishop of Dublin, Lord Gormanston, Lord Mountgarret, Nicholas Plunkett, Richard Belling and James Cusack. FOR ULSTER – The Archbishop of Armagh, Bishop of Down, Colonel McMahon, Philip O'Reilly, Turlough O'Néill and Magennis. FOR CONNACHT – The Archbishop of Tuam, Bishop of Clonfert, Viscount Mayo, Geoffrey Brown, Patrick Darcy and Sir Lucas Dillon. FOR MUNSTER – Viscount Roche, Sir Daniel O'Brien, Edmond Fitzmaurice, Robert Lambert, Dr. Fennell and

President was Richard Butler. (Lord Mountgarret). The general body of English law was then adopted excluding all acts contrary to Catholicism and the common good. Initially at least the Assembly was careful to do its utmost to paper over the fault lines that existed between the diverse parties who were united in faith, passing a law which forbade any distinction to be made between Gaelic Irish and Old English.

Naturally the conduct of the war was foremost in the minds of members and various measures were taken in this regard and appointments confirmed. Eoghan Roe O'Néill was confirmed as the Military Commander in Ulster, Gerald Barry for Munster, Thomas Preston for Leinster and John Burke for Connacht, but to the great detriment of the overall military strategy of the Confederates, no supreme military commander was appointed. Many other items essential for the governance of Ireland were brought before the members and much work was set in motion such as the setting up of an Irish mint, the establishment of external trade, shipbuilding, taxes and duties, the establishment of affairs with other Catholic nations, conscription, the soliciting of loans and much else.

Gaelic culture was also to experience resurgence during the years of the Catholic Confederation with the re-emergence of Gaelic scholars and the printing of Irish books including the first Irish dictionary taking place on the continent.

The Assembly sat through the Christmas period, until January 9th 1643 with the intention of meeting again on May 20th.

George Comyn. The Earl of Castlehaven was added to the Council after his escape from prison in Dublin.

A Divisive Truce

Battles and Massacres

After a lull during the winter of 1642-43 fighting between the Confederacy and the array of forces which opposed them began once more during the spring of 1643.

In Leinster, Ormond's Royalist army attempted to advance south through Wexford. When they reached Timolin in Co. Kildare the Confederate garrison surrendered and were then promptly massacred on Ormond's orders. Ormond then continued his advance towards the town of New Ross in Co. Wexford but upon his arrival he failed to achieve a breakthrough and was forced to turn back towards Dublin through want of supplies and because of the advance towards New Ross of a confederate relief force under Colonel Purcell. While returning to Dublin Ormond had encountered Preston's much larger army and victory seemed assured for the Confederates However, Preston was too sure of himself and abandoned his strong position to advance, exposing his flanks. Ormond, the more experience commander was quick to seize his opportunity with Preston's army suffering the consequences - the death of 500 confederate soldiers.

In Ulster O'Néill had his hands full trying to contain the Scots, while at the same time doing his utmost to train new recruits. In May, Charlemont Fort very nearly fell to Monroe when he launched a stealthy attack on the base but the approach of the Scots had been discovered in time and they were thrown back. Shortly after this O'Néill had advanced south, to assist the army of Leinster and had successfully defeated a large English force under the command of Lord Moore at Portlester in Meath. During the engagement Moore was fatally wounded after being struck by a cannon ball.

The most decisive victory for confederate arms during the first half of 1643 occurred just outside Kilworth in Cork at The Battle of Funcheon Ford (Cloughleigh) when the army of

General Barry and Lieutenant General Purcell, in spite of being largely outnumbered inflicted a heavy defeat on the army of Sir Charles Vavasour. Vavasour was taken prisoner and about 600 English were slain. On the previous day some of Vavasour's men had engaged in a terrible war crime at Cloughleigh (Kilworth) Castle while requisitioning provisions. The inhabitants of the castle, 38 people in total, including 11 women and 7 children were butchered in cold blood.[267]

An Opportunity for King Charles I
The apparent stalemate of the Irish war caused King Charles I to sit up and take notice. However much he disliked the Old English Catholics of Ireland he knew that they were loyal to the monarchy and would do much to earn his favour. In his war against the Parliamentary armies of England and Scotland he could certainly do with all the help he could get from both the Confederates and his own soldiers who were fighting them. A truce in Ireland between his army and the Confederates might release both sides in the conflict to fight for him in England, if he could persuade the leaders of the Confederacy to come under his banner.
On learning of the King's intentions to come to terms with the Confederacy, Borlase and Parsons were dismayed as any agreement between the King and the Confederacy might spoil their own plans regarding the post war seizure of land and wealth. Faced with such a prospect they did all they could to sabotage the project but such were the straits in which King Charles I found himself he took a personal interest in the scheme and ordered the Earls of Ormond and Clanrickarde among others to receive proposals from the Confederacy. Thereafter affairs proceeded quickly and contact was established between the Crown and the Old English of the Confederacy.

A Truce is Signed

Having sent Ambassadors to Spain, France and to Pope Urban VIII, by May 1643 Ambassadors to the Confederacy were arriving from abroad. When Fr. Peter Scarampi arrived in Kilkenny as the Ambassador from the Holy See; he found to his dismay that a great deal of discord existed between the Gaelic Irish and the Old English. The topics under discussion were the peace feelers and apparent desire for a truce put forward by King CharlesI. While the Old English wanted to agree with the King's wishes, the Gaelic Irish supported by the clergy were of the opinion that any truce between the Confederacy and the Crown would be premature. As things stood, the Confederates were gaining ground in the military exchanges and it would do their cause a great disservice to agree to a truce now. However the Old English had one strong argument in their favour – in order to have any chance at freedom for the Catholic Faith, the Confederacy needed the King to win the English Civil War as the Parliamentary forces of England and Scotland completely detested Catholicism and Catholics, with many of them regarding the killing of Catholics as being God's work.

For some time now the King had earmarked Lord Justice Parsons for dismissal due to his repeated disloyalty. While the Assembly argued over the merits of a truce, Parsons was dismissed so that it would appear as a concession to the Catholics. The move worked. The Gaelic Irish reluctantly agreed to the wishes of the Old English and on September 15th 1643 a truce was signed in Naas, Co. Kildare between Ormond and the mostly Old English Confederate Leaders.

While the forces of Parliament were not a party to the truce, Ormond promised to ensure that it would be kept by their commanders but in reality did nothing.

When the King had previously signed a truce with the Scots he had agreed to pay them a large sum of money but with the

Catholics, for agreeing with the King's wishes they had to pay him a gift of £30,800 as a good will gesture, and also provide him with an army. The Confederacy now sent a delegation to England to meet with the King so that a firm agreement might be reached between the Confederacy and the Crown but the King would not be drawn and instead placated them with general assurances.

On receiving news of the truce and word that they might soon be fighting against Irish Catholics the English parliamentary leaders complained bitterly of the "popish counsels at court"[268] and two motions, one declaring that "a present cessation of arms with the rebels in Ireland is destructive to the Protestant religion"[269] and a second "that no Irishman should be shown mercy"[270] were passed in parliament..

This mandate was carried out to the letter. Shortly afterwards a Royal transport ship conveying Confederate troops for service in England was overtaken in the Irish Sea by a Cruiser of the Parliamentary army commanded by Captain Swanly who ordered that the passengers and crew of seventy men and two women (all of Irish birth) be thrown into the sea.[271]

The Bridge at Finea

"He fought till the red lines before him heaped high as the battlements lay;
He fell but the foot of a foeman pressed not on the bridge of Finea" – William Collins[i]

Following the news that the King was treating with the Catholic Confederacy in order to gain more troops for his

---

[i] In the village of Finea, there is a fine monument to Myles "The Slasher" O'Reilly, whose courage and leadership played a key role in withstanding the onslaught of Monroe. However, the monument wrongly states that the battle of Finea took place in early August 1646. Lord Castlehaven recounts the battle in his memoirs as taking place in the Autumn of 1644.

army, General Monroe in Ulster determined (or was ordered) to march south and meet the armies of the confederacy in battle and destroy them

At this time Eoghan Roe O'Néill was encamped with his army at Portlester near Trim when intelligence from Lord Castlehaven (who was in Granard, just south of Finea) reached him that Monroe's vast army, some 17,000 strong, were marching out of Ulster in a south westerly direction and would emerge into the midlands after crossing the Bridge at Feinnuagha[i] (anglicised as Finea, a village on the Cavan / Westmeath border.)

At this time O'Neill was still raising, training and organising his army and was far from prepared to meet Monroe's army in battle. Nevertheless his were the closest Confederate troops to the danger and he had to act. Calling together his best prepared units, O'Néill dispatched a task force under the command of Colonel John Butler to go north and attempt to prevent Monroe from crossing the River Inny at Finea. The force of around 100 cavalry (which were under the command of Brian Roe O'Néill) along with 600 foot soldiers, immediately departed Portlester for Finea. Following their departure hasty preparations were made for the departure of a second force to follow and reinforce Butler.

Arriving at Finea a day ahead of Monroe, Butler's small army prepared for the battle ahead. When Monroe arrived, his army quickly attacked the bridge's defenders who although greatly outnumbered fought back relentlessly and with great courage. All day long the battle raged but Monroe was unable to achieve a breakthrough in spite of the mounting death toll of the defenders and his overwhelming strength of numbers. The fact that the Irish were defending a bridge crossing meant that

---

[i] Meaning "The Hound's Ford"

Monroe was unable to use his superior numbers to outflank the defenders.

As the ferocious battle continued, one of the Irish Cavalry officers, Colonel Myles "The Slasher" O'Reilly (who had already played a key role in the defeat of the Royalist army of Sir Patrick Wemyss at Julianstown Bridge) crossed swords with a "gigantic Scotsman who thrust the point of his sword through the Slasher's cheek. The Slasher closed his jaw on the blade and held it as if in an iron vice while he slew his antagonist cutting him through steel helmet down to the chin with one blow both men falling together."[i]

Myles "The Slasher" O'Reilly

Just as the Scots threatened to finally overwhelm the Irish line, O'Néill's second force arrived from the direction of Granard behind the defensive line, taking Monroe by surprise and forcing his much weakened force to retreat.

Fearing that the arrival of this second force heralded the appearance of O'Néill's army, Monroe decided to withdraw back into Ulster retreating through East Cavan and Louth laying waste to the countryside as he went. He then tried to regroup and muster his strength for a new offensive south.

---

[i] Although the Finea memorial to Myles the Slasher (from which this quotation is taken) records him as having being killed at the Bridge of Finea, there is a local tradition in Cavan that after the retreat of Monroe, The Slasher was brought to Ross Castle on nearby Lough Sheelin where he recovered from his wounds. He is buried in the graveyard of the old Franciscan monastery in the centre of Cavan town along with Eoghan Roe O'Néill.

An Unrealistic Offer?

For their part the Confederates did their utmost to keep the truce. In Ulster however, Monroe ignored it. In order to fulfil the terms of the truce by which included sending supplied troops to England, Eoghan Roe O'Néill had been left without supplies for his men and as a result Monroe (as we have seen) succeeded in advancing south as far as Longford, before being forced to retreat at Finea. Monroe now returned into Ulster having despoiled the population of all their livestock during his retreat. In Munster, Inchiquin (O'Brien) and Broghill (Boyle) also committed acts contrary to the truce but in spite of this it was renewed.

By late Spring1645 King Charles I was desperate for more Irish help. In spite of ordering Ormond to offer concessions to the Confederates, Ormond prevaricated and the King decided to send over his own messenger, the Catholic Lord Herbert, Earl of Glamorgan. Glamorgan first met with Ormond telling him exactly why he was in Ireland. Immediately upon his arrival in Kilkenny Glamorgan wasted no time in negotiation. He offered the Assembly unrestricted public exercise of the faith without interference from either the Protestant clergy or the government as the measures would come under a decree of His Majesty. In return King Charles immediately needed 10,000 armed confederate troops to fight for him in England. Glamorgan stressed that the deal must be kept secret until such time as the Confederate troops were in England after which the King promised the concessions would be publicly promulgated.

In spite of Glamorgan's hurry to bring matters to a conclusion, some of the Confederate leaders, especially the Gaelic Irish were not inclined to be in such a rush. For one thing the current truce was not being maintained by either the forces of the Crown or the forces of Parliament as Ormond had promised. In Connacht, the Royalist Coote had joined forces with Stewart's Royalist Laggan army which had broken through from the north. Having crossed into Sligo their men were laying waste to the whole district, and killing at will.[i] In Munster, Inchiquin was living up to his name of "Murrough of the Burnings". Having crossed into Confederate territory he had proceeded to burn and destroy that year's crops which were still in the ground and had just been repulsed by a Confederate army under Lord Castlehaven.

The second problem that the Confederacy had with the King's offer was that the King had led them "up the garden path" once too often. The proposal was in itself acceptable but its liberality went far beyond what was realistic and there was absolutely no proof that the King would follow through with his side of the deal.

The Arrival in Ireland of Archbishop John Baptist Rinuccini

In early 1645 the Supreme Council of The Confederacy had sent one of their members Richard Belling to Rome to confer with Fr. Luke Wadding. Up to this time Fr. Wadding had been of inestimable value to the Confederacy and had sent vast amounts of money raised on the continent for the Irish Catholic cause.

While Belling was in Rome, Fr. Wadding arranged an audience for him with Pope Innocent X and having received a full account of how affairs stood in Ireland the Pope decided to send a Nuncio who would try and maintain concord and unity of purpose between the members of the Confederacy in their bid to gain freedom for the faith and from tyranny. For this

---

[i] In his history of the war, Lord Justice Borlase wrote that on entering Sligo, Hamilton "...burnt the town and slew in the streets three hundred of the Irish..." Edmund Borlase – History of the Irish Rebellion, p112. The Leitrim town of "Manorhamilton" is named after him (!)

mission the Pope picked Archbishop John Baptist Rinuccini[i] of the diocese of Fermo.

Rinuccini crossed through France visiting on his way the Queen of England at St. Germain. After embarking from La Rochelle on a ship laden with munitions and money (Fr. Wadding had sent over another £30,000) Rinuccini finally arrived in Kenmare on October 31st 1645 and from there went to Limerick where he offered a requiem Mass for the Archbishop of Tuam whose death had just been announced. The Archbishop had been in Sligo and had been killed by soldiers of the Royalist Lagan Army. Afterwards Rinuccini proceeded to Kilkenny where he was received with great honour.

Archbishop Rinuccini

When Rinuccini arrived in Kilkenny he found Glamorgan still trying to persuade the Confederacy to trust the King and send to England the troops which the King was so badly in need of. Glamorgan's biggest obstacle was Ormond, for Ormond had also come to Kilkenny and was publicly contradicting Glamorgan and watering down his proposals. Glamorgan now tried to persuade Rinuccini who although realising that the Catholic Confederacy needed a Royalist victory in England in order to have any chance for freedom for the faith

---

[i] Archbishop was a prominent legal scholar and had been Chamberlain to Pope Gregory XV. In 1625 he was consecrated Archbishop of Fermo by Pope Gregory XV.

nevertheless felt that the King was once more misusing and misleading the Irish and so the issue remained deadlocked.

"Ormondists" and "Rinuccinists"
Ormond Arrests the Earl of Glamorgan
During December 1645 Glamorgan went to Dublin and after Christmas the Confederate Assembly was thunderstruck to receive the news that he had been arrested by Ormond. It transpired that after the Archbishop of Tuam had been killed in Sligo, a copy of Glamorgan's proposals to the Confederacy had been found on his person. The document had then found its way into the hands of Coote who had sent it post haste to England where Parliament had wasted no time in making its contents public. Facing accusations not only from Parliament but from his own supporters of being a Papist, the King denied all knowledge of the document. When Ormond had learned of what had transpired in England he pretended to know nothing about the whole affair and arrested Glamorgan on the charge of high treason, accusing him of having exceeded his authority. The Confederacy now suspended all negotiations with Ormond until Glamorgan should be released after which Ormond agreed to bail him for £40,000.

A Split in the Confederacy
With Glamorgan now out of the picture Ormond continued to negotiate with the Confederacy These negotiations resulted in a wide open split in the movement caused by the limitations of what Ormond was prepared to offered, which were merely sops to the Old English (no obligation to take the Oath of Supremacy etc). Many among the Old English party felt that Ormond's proposals should be accepted as it answered some of their concerns and as they were English in outlook they felt compelled to assist their King to try and get out of the dire straits in which He now found himself.

Like the Gaelic Irish, Rinuccini rejected the deal as it did not offer the Catholics freedom to practice the faith or even that restrictions would be placed on the terrors committed by Crown Forces against the populace and as these were chief among the reasons why the insurrection had been launched in the first place, no peace offer without them could be countenanced. The Confederacy now deeply split divided into two groups labelled "Ormondists" and "Rinucciniists".

After much argument, the Old English party in the Supreme Council (which was the largest) prevailed and a deal was signed with Ormond at the end of March 1646. Many members of the Assembly especially the Gaelic Irish were subsequently in despair as the Confederacy seemed to be irrevocably split into factions. Worse still military disaster loomed as the Confederacy would shortly send its troops to England even while facing great danger on its own doorstep from both Coote in Connacht and Inchiquin in Munster. Still Rinuccini did not give up, and determined to do what he could in order to try and maintain some sort of unity of purpose among the Confederates who supported him by seeking to mobilise those Confederates who felt as he did - that they should act in Ireland's interest and try and secure even more than the initial aims of the insurrection – freedom for the faith, and with a Parliamentary victory in England now assured, Irish independence. The only sure way for Ireland to gain freedom for both faith and fatherland was to do her utmost to throw off the English yoke for once and for all. All efforts now needed to be put into a Confederate military victory. But many felt that with a large number of Confederate troops now departing for England, surely the time for this was past?

The Surrender of Bunratty

Just as Ormond was making preparations to ship the Confederate army to England, Chester, the last port in England that was still in the possession of the Royalists fell to Parliamentary forces. Following the Battle of Naseby, the Royalist cause was already hanging by a thread and by May 1646, with his resources at an end, King Charles I, surrendered to the Scots considering this the least evil option, as unlike the Parliamentarians, they still had great respect for the power of the monarchy. Rinuccini now encouraged the Confederate leadership to go on the offensive. The Confederate forces earmarked for England were now dispatched under the command of Castlehaven to Munster where numbers of them laid siege to a parliamentary army in Bunratty, Co. Clare. At first they were repulsed but Rinuccini pressed for a second attack, this time accompanying the army himself. After a siege of 12 days Bunratty surrendered.

The Battle of Benburb

"For God and Church and Country now, upon them every man,
But hold your strength until ye feel them scarce a pike-length's span.
Then, Red Hand ever uppermost, strike home your strongest blow!
And with a yell our feet outsped the words of Eoghan Roe"

Opposing Armies

In spite of the success of Parliamentary forces in England, Ormond who commanded the armies of the King stationed in Ireland still refused to march against Monroe's Parliamentary Army. In May 1646 Eoghan Roe O'Néill's army was far south of his ancient home territory of Tyrone, along the Ulster, Leinster border. Encouraged by Rinuccini, Eoghan Roe now determined to tackle Robert Monroe's army (that consisted of Scottish Covenanters and Ulster Planters) head on. Gathering together as large a force as he could muster – around 5,500 men, including 500 cavalry, O'Néill began his march north.

Ever since Eoghan Roe had taken command of the Ulster army there had been ill feeling between himself and Sir Phelim O'Néill. Rinuccini now brought about reconciliation between them before they would enter battle.

When Monroe found out from his spies of O'Néill's plans, he was making the final preparations for an advance southward. His army was in good condition and was much larger and in possession of much more artillery than O'Néill's and he looked forward with confidence to the upcoming battle. Leaving nothing to chance, Monroe sent a message to his younger brother George who was in command of around 500 cavalry in Coleraine and told him to rendezvous with him at Glaslough in north Monaghan. It was here that he hoped to meet and annihilate O'Néill's army as he advanced northwards.

Monroe was not the only one with spies and O'Néill also was informed of his enemy's plan. Before the Monroe brothers could meet up O' Neill had advanced through Glaslough and on into Tyrone, making his encampment where the home of Shane O'Néill had once been – Benburb. On this soil already saturated in the blood of many battles for the freedom of his homeland, O'Néill determined to make his stand. Two regiments under the command of Bernard MacMahon and Patrick MacNeny were dispatched to try and prevent the Monroe linkup by attacking George Monroe's cavalry unit, a feat which they successfully accomplished. Upon learning that the Irish were encamped at Benburb Robert Monroe attempted to approach stealthily from the east and south. Not knowing that his brother's cavalry had been repulsed he sent a dispatch rider to meet him to let him know of the new rendezvous.

"A Fight For your Native Birthright"

As June 5th dawned, Monroe's army approached Benburb. On the edge of battle the Irish army received absolution and attended Mass. The sun was strong, shining right into and blinding the eyes of O'Néill's men. Time needed to be bought so that open battle would not be entered into until such time as the sun had moved round off the faces of the Irish. A regiment under Colonel O'Farrell was sent forward to delay Monroe as his army approached down a narrow road. This ruse worked with Monroe being delayed for some time until artillery was brought up and the lane cleared by force. As Monroe advanced he was delayed several more times by episodes of sniping and light skirmishing until finally four hours had been bought. As Monroe closed in Eoghan Roe O'Néill addressed his troops:

"Behold the army of the enemies of God, the enemies of your lives. Fight valiantly against them today; for it is they who have deprived you of your Chiefs, of your children, of your subsistence, spiritual and temporal; it is they who have torn you, your wives and children from your land and houses and made you wandering fugitives seeking your bread and livelihood in strange places. Now you have arms in your hands as good as they have and you are gentlemen as good as they are. You are the flower of Ulster, descended from as ancient and honourable a stock of people as any in Europe. This land you and your predecessors have possessed for about three thousand years. All Christendom knows your quarrel is good – a fight for your native birthright and for the religion which your forefathers professed and maintained since Christianity first came to this land.

So now is the time to consider your distressed and slavish condition; you have arms in hands, you are as numerous as they are; and now try your valour and your strength on those who have banished you, and resolve to destroy you bud and branch. So let your manhood be seen by your push of pike and I will engage, if you do so by God's assistance and the intercession of his Blessed Mother, and all the holy saints in Heaven, that the day will be your own. Your word is Sancta Maria; and so in the Name of the Father and of the Son and Holy Ghost advance, and give not fire until you are within pike length"[272]

On the edge of battle, Monroe was not only looking forward to the fray but also confident of victory. He later wrote "All our army did earnestly covet fighting, which it was impossible for me to gainstand without reproach of cowardice, and never did I see a greater confidence than was amongst us"[273]

Before battle was joined a third force was seen approaching. Monroe thought it must be his brother with the cavalry, but the company made for the Irish encampment. It was in fact one of the units which O'Néill had sent towards Coleraine, but finding no further danger in that direction had returned. Deciding to wait until his brother should arrive, Monroe decided to withdraw a little.

The Battle

It was almost like Kinsale nearly half a century before except the roles were reversed. Seeing the enemy pull back a little, O'Néill ordered the charge and his men poured forward shouting their battle cry "Sancta Maria!"[i] Monroe's army turned to face them. Lord Blayney's regiment who were in the vanguard of Monroe's army were first to face the Irish charge. After a brief but stalwart resistance they gave way. Monroe now ordered his cavalry to charge and stem the tide but the Irish cavalry was also charging forward and had the better of the engagement. Within a short time the tide of battle turned decisively in favour of the Irish and Monroe's army began to

---

[i] "Sancta Maria" – "Holy Mary"

retreat, many of them being driven back towards the River Blackwater. As the Irish were already in possession of the fording point, Monroe's men were forced towards deep water, unsuitable for fording.

Confusion reigned in Monroe's ranks as the Irish were now among them with pike and sword. Monroe escaped the battlefield leaving behind his sword, cloak and hat, his verdict of the battle being: "For aught I can understand, the Lord of Hosts had a controversie with us to rub shame in our faces".[274]

The only regiment in Monroe's army which managed to retreat in good order was that of Sir James Montgomery. As the noise of battle waned around 3,000 of Monroe's army lay dead on the field of battle or drowned in the River. 300 men of O'Néill's army had been killed or wounded. Vast amounts of muskets, ammunition along with provisions and artillery were captured. The colours of 32 of Monroe's regiments fell into Irish hands. One of the Irish officers, Colonel Henry McTully O'Néill, later recorded the ending of the battle and its aftermath: "...The rout began two hours before night, in which the enemy left very rich booty of all sorts which hindered the execution much by the soldiers falling to plunder. My Lord Montgomery was taken prisoner and so was Major Cocheran, Captain Hamilton with several other officers were slain along with four thousand private men and in the pursuit that night and the next day about one hundred and fifty soldiers were taken prisoner and dismissed with a pass. To the best of my memory upwards of twenty colours were taken, their artillery being four field pieces with most of all their tents, arms and baggage left behind except Sir James Montgomery's regiment on their right who escaped...Next day O'Néill ordered My Lord Blayney's and Captain Hamilton's corpses to be interred in Benburb church with the proper ceremonies..."[275]

Rinuccini takes Charge
Ormond's Treaty Rejected

Following the Irish victory at Benburb, vast numbers of Ulstermen flocked to O'Néill's standard including many "Creaghts", a name given to Catholic farmers who had their lands stolen from them during the plantation of Ulster and as a result lived a nomadic existence with their families, constantly moving their few livestock and belongings from one area to another with no place to call home. O'Néill however did not press his advantage by advancing towards Monroe's main base at Carrickfergus but rather decided to go south with his newly named "Catholic Army" in answer to a request by Archbishop Rinuccini. In spite of his victory and the fact that there was no way that the Confederate troops could embark for England the dissension among the Confederates continued unabated and even threatened to spill over into violence due to the imminent official ratification and proclamation of the treaty with Ormond – a treaty that would see Confederate troops come under his command. In order to prevent this O'Néill determined to offer not just moral but also military support to Rinuccini. As it turned out this was not necessary for the people themselves were against the treaty – Old English and Gaelic Irish alike saw it as a complete sellout. In towns with a large old English population such as Limerick, Waterford and Clonmel there were demonstrations against the treaty. Rinuccini decided to settle the matter for once and for all by a national Synod which took place on August 6th after which it was declared that all who accepted the treaty were "Perjurers"[i]

---

[i] The declaration read in part "...all and every one of the Confederate Catholics that will adhere to such a peace, and consent to the furtherance thereof, or in any other manner or way will embrace the same, shall be absolutely as perjurers esteemed; chiefly inasmuch ass there is no mention made in the thirty articles, nor promise for the Catholic religion or safety thereof..."

as their acceptance of the treaty would break the Confederate Oath previously taken by them. Excommunication was threatened and sometimes used by Rinuccini. Following this many of the old English fell in behind him until finally on September 18th with O'Néill's army and the common people at his back he entered Kilkenny. Members of the Supreme Council were seized and temporarily imprisoned so that a new government could be formed without opposition. On September 20th, a new Supreme Council was formed consisting of four bishops and eight laymen with Rinuccini as President.

A Lost Opportunity

This ought to have been the end of the dissent, but Preston, the Commander of the Leinster army remained the fly in the ointment. Initially he had been a fervent supporter of the treaty with Ormond but after the Synod he had declared himself for Rinuccini and had so retained his command. When Rinuccini ordered an all out attack on Dublin before Ormond would hand control of the city over to the Parliamentarians, Preston demurred and actually accused Eoghan Roe O'Néill of harbouring the intention of attacking his Leinster troops. O'Néill, who had long condemned Preston's reluctance for offensive action was furious.

Due to Preston's prevarications, his mistrust of O'Néill and his unwillingness to attack the King's army under Ormond's command the opportunity was lost.

After much negotiation and debate, Rinuccini did his best to have the Confederacy make a fresh start but it was all to no avail for the dissension continued. Paralysed by rancour and opposing views the Confederacy lost whatever opportunity they might have had for military success.

The Confederacy Defeated
The Arrival of General Michael Jones
In February 1647, the Scots, never dreaming that they were ultimately sending him to his death, handed King Charles I over to an English parliamentary delegation in return for £200,000 in solid gold. By summer of 1647 Ormond had after token resistance handed Dublin over to an English Parliamentary army under General Michael Jones stating that he "preferred English rebels to Irish rebels". In return for betraying his King he received £5,000 after which he left Ireland for England after which he went to France.

An extremely capable if ruthless commander, Michael Jones had begun the war fighting for King Charles I but had switched sides. After landing in Dublin he immediately prepared his army for battle with the Confederates. By the beginning of August 1647 his army had been further reinforced by Planters from Ulster and now consisted of around 12,000 men and a 700 strong cavalry.

For the Ormondists in the Confederacy Ormond's departure and Jones' arrival on the scene served as something of a wakeup call as the dire situation facing the Confederacy became crystal clear. Up to this point the Confederacy seemed unable to comprehend that King Charles I might be beaten in his war with parliament. Now they realised that unless the forces of Parliament were defeated there could be no hope whatever of the least toleration for Irish Catholics. A sense of urgency at last possessed the Old English, but this was not to be enough. The initiative was now firmly with their enemies

Dungan's Hill
As Jones prepared for battle with the Confederates, Preston, who remained in command of the Leinster army braced himself for the onslaught. Jones in an effort to draw Preston into battle and also to break through the ring of fortified

positions in front of the city picked off various Confederate strongpoints in Meath, Seizing the opportunity to close on Dublin, Preston attempted to get between Dublin and Jones' army. On learning this, Jones quickly doubled back and located Preston at his encampment on Dungan's Hill, near Summerhill in Co. Meath. As both sides prepared for immediate battle, the Confederate army was disadvantaged by bad generalship on the part of Preston for he decided to abandon his strong defensive position atop Dungan's hill and attack.

As the battle got under way Preston's army charged down the hill directly into the ranks of the Parliamentary army, which they failed to break. Furthermore his artillery, which consisted of four pieces had been badly positioned and failed to do any real damage to the ranks of the enemy. As the battle became widespread a large part of the Confederate army were driven back towards one side of the battlefield where they became trapped in bogland. Here they were slaughtered without quarter even after they had surrendered and all resistance had ceased. Those who escaped through the bog were met on the other side by Jones's dragoons and killed. It was a dreadful scene of carnage. Over 5,000 Confederate troops were killed with minimal loss on the side of the English. The only prisoners taken were some officers who could be used as barter later.

As Jones now threatened the midlands, O'Néill was called upon (even by his enemies among the Ormondists) to restore the situation. At once he came south with his army of about 12,000 men but Jones retreated back to safety in Dublin, doubtless wary of O'Néill after his recent victory over Monroe.

The Sack of Cashel
Like a devil that had escaped from the fiery abyss of hell, Inchiquin, at the head of his parliamentary army was once

more laying waste the homes and properties of the Catholic population of Munster.

In this he was inadvertently assisted by the lack of unity among the Confederacy. When Rinuccini had become leader of the Supreme Council he had appointed Glamorgan to command the Munster army but Glamorgan was quickly replaced after the officers mutinied, insisting that Muskerry (Sir Donough MacCarthy) be reinstated. Muskerry, an Ormondist, had no desire to return to the command of the army, preferring instead to go to Kilkenny and take a hand in the political situation instead. He handed the command to the weak and vacillating royalist Lord Taffe (Theobald Taffe, Earl of Carlingford) who had recently joined the Confederacy. Taffe's efforts and strategy against Inchiquin was so weak and ineffectual that he was later accused of colluding with him as he was reluctant to engage with him in open battle or even harass him during his rampage.

Murrough O'Brien

At the beginning of September 1647, Inchiquin crossed the Tipperary border and in short order captured Cahir Castle which was reputed to be the strongest castle in Munster (as during the reign of Queen Elizabeth it had stood firm against the army of the Duke of Essex for two months in 1599). As September neared its end, Inchiquin, having destroyed around £20,000 worth of crops, was closing in on the ancient city of Cashel. As Inchiquin approached, Taffe, who was staying in Cashel, departed the city leaving behind a small and poorly equipped garrison that nevertheless refused to allow entry to Inchiquin unchecked. Their valiant if meagre efforts at resistance did not delay the entry of Inchiquin for long. As soon as his men had penetrated the cities defences they immediately set about the systematic slaughter of Cashel's defenders and its population without exception.

As the carnage unfolded hundreds of people ran from the streets up the hill towards the ancient cathedral on the rock in the hope that it might afford them shelter from the marauders or at least that the soldiers out of respect for its sacred precincts might desist from their devilish work. Inside the cathedral the panic stricken crowd looked for shelter in any hiding place that availed itself. When Inchiquin and his men reached the building the doors and windows were secured. After breaking them down, Inchiquin's men used them as vantage points and fired their muskets continually into the interior of the building until it appeared that everyone inside was dead. The soldiers then entered the building with pike and sword to search for any that were still alive. Men, women, children and priests were pulled from their hiding places and made to suffer a more terrible death than those who had died from musket fire. By days end around 3,000 people lay dead in and around Cashel.

As he departed with his army Inchiquin ordered the charnel house which Cashel had become to be set ablaze. Glutted with blood, Inchiquin and his men continued their march towards Fethard which opened its gates to him and afterwards to Clonmel which was defended by Sir Alexander MacDonnell[i] who had been a commander in Preston's Leinster army and had escaped the slaughter at Dungan Hill bringing with him

---

[i] An able swordsman with his left hand MacDonnell was given the nickname "Colkitto" from the gaelic "Colla Ciotach" or "Colla the left handed"

his Antrim Highlanders. Even though he was greatly outnumbered MacDonnell was determined to defend Clonmel at all costs. In the face of such determination and with his men doubtless exhausted by their recent exertions, Inchiquin returned to Cahir where he received from England fresh men, supplies and money for his parliamentary army.

The Battle of Knockanos

With Inchiquin rampant in Munster, Rinuccini and the Confederate leadership were fearful that he would advance on their capital – the city of Kilkenny. With O'Néill keeping Michael Jones pinned down in Dublin[i] and the Leinster army destroyed, Taffe and his Munster army were ordered by the Supreme Council to engage Inchiquin in battle so that his terrible campaign of butchery and destruction could be brought to an end. To give Taffe's army some backbone MacDonnell, who had been made a Lieutenant General was ordered to take his men and link up with Taffe.

The beginning of November 1647 found Inchiquin and his army of 6,000 soldiers and 1,200 cavalry and dragoons at Mallow while Taffe with a similar number of horsemen and 7,000 soldiers endeavoured to close with his army from the direction of Kanturk.

On learning of the approach of Taffe, Inchiquin left Mallow and advanced to meet him. Taffe meanwhile had assembled his army on the Hill of Knockanos. Atop the hill MacDonnell was in command of the right wing of the army which numbered around 3,000 men and two regiments of horse

---

[i] After Jones had retreated to back to Dublin in order to avoid O'Néill, O'Néill's men took up positions around the capital. Some time later men were dispatched to the battlefield of Dungan Hill in order to bury the bodies of the Leinster troops. According to the period historian O'Meallain numbers of the corpses were found with their hands tied behind their backs.

commanded by Colonel Purcell. Taffe himself took command of the left wing with the remainder. Once again the Confederacy were in command of the high ground with their enemy at a disadvantage.

When the battle commenced MacDonnell and his Antrim Highlanders followed their old custom. Once their muskets had been discharged, they were thrown aside and with sword in hand they charged the enemy. Faced with such a determined onslaught, Inchiquin's left wing broke and ran. MacDonnell at the head of his men pursued them, overrunning Inchiquin's artillery in the process and then continued the pursuit for almost two miles. However the same feat was not repeated with the men under Taffe's command. Inchiquin, had spotted an unguarded opening in Taffe's flank had sent his cavalry through it to the top of Knockanos from where they attacked Taffe in the rear. His Munster troops being outflanked and with the enemy both in front and behind them Taffe's wing of the army broke and ran after which they were pursued and killed. When MacDonnell and his men retraced their steps thinking that Taffe had won they day they found the English in control of the battlefield. Captured by the enemy, MacDonnell surrendered his sword to Colonel Purdon. However Inchiquin had ordered that no quarter was to be shown to the enemy and so the gallant MacDonnell and his brave men were slaughtered in cold blood after they had surrendered. Four thousand Confederate soldiers were killed, with many of them being murdered after the battle had ended.

The End of the Confederacy
"Sooner Defeat than O'Néill"
After having suffered heavy defeats at Knockanos and Dungan's Hill, the sense of foreboding which pervaded the Confederate Assembly did nothing to improve the declining morale among its members and Rinuccini found himself

unable to maintain unity. In spite of the fact that the army of O'Néill was all that stood between Kilkenny and outright defeat, many among the Ormondist faction nevertheless wished for his destruction.[i] When a book invalidating the sovereignty of England over Ireland and calling on the Irish to crown one of their own as King of Ireland and fight for complete freedom was circulated in Kilkenny, the Old English accused the Gaelic Irish of wanting to make Eoghan Roe O'Néill their King. In order to have their own way they sought to sideline the Gaelic members of the Confederacy by sending them abroad on missions for assistance to Spain, Rome and France so that the way might be left clear for the return of Ormond who was at that time at the court of the English Queen in St. Germain. to where Preston and Taffe, the only delegates with a serious mission were sent. Their mission was to get a form of words from the English Queen that would offer support to the Confederacy[ii] and also to persuade Ormond to return when the time was right.

---

[i] Some of O'Néill's enemies in the Confederacy forged a letter from O'Neill that attempted to show he was in touch with General Jones of the Parliamentary army after which a general appeal was issued against him: "Letters have been intercepted which beget in us a just suspicion of Qwen O'Neill and his party, which brought the British nation to their now sad condition, and who purpose to themselves at the end of this total subversion and ruin which, being made manifest, we have taken arms to reduce him and his adherents. We are of opinion no true-hearted Englishman, or any of that extraction, will join with such a party against us whose intentions never swerved from maintaining and submitting unto the Government, his intentions and proceedings being so well known to be averse unto that end, that the best and most of those of the same extraction as himself do abominate him and his actions, and are as active as any towards his reducement, and so we warn you against so false and perfidious a man as he is."
[ii] The Queen (who was being advised by Ormond) after condemning the Confederates for their rebellious conduct in rejecting Ormond's treaty, on which she blamed the King's misfortunes, told them that they would be allowed "whatever was consistent with justice and his majesty's honour".

With many Gaelic Irish members out of the way, Muskerry organised that their replacements in any vote would support the Ormondists. The aims and mission of the Confederacy were now lost. With England firmly in the hands of Parliament, Rinuccini, O'Néill and the Gaelic party saw the last chance for the Confederacy as being an all out effort against the armies of Parliament but the Old English would not countenance it for fear that it would return power to the Irish in whose hands it rightfully belonged. Their alternative was the return of Ormond and a truce with Inchiquin.

Inchiquin Switches to the Royalist Side
Following his victory at Knockanos, Inchiquin was promised £10,000 by the English parliament in order to pay the wages of his men and a further £1,000 for himself. However only a very small part of the money was paid, and the dispute that followed led to argument and rancour between the parties involved.

The matter was further complicated by the eventual fate of the King which still remained unclear. A prisoner of Cromwell, negotiations between the King and parliament regarding the role of the King in the future continued but many parliamentarians feared that the negotiations were nothing more than a sham that would eventually lead the King to the executioner's block. Many of those who sought more power for parliament nevertheless remained loyal to the King and wished to see the monarchy maintained, not destroyed and the issue was the cause of dispute among the Parliamentarians.

Having lost most of their fighting men, some within the Old English party of the Confederacy made treasonous contacts with Inchiquin with regard to a truce. Inchiquin did not dismiss them but instead saw his chance to get the funds he so badly needed. If the House of Commons would not pay his men's wages then perhaps the confederates would. Inchiquin now sent a message that a truce might be reached if the Confederates would pay him £4,000 a month.

Following this, in March 1648, Inchiquin sent a letter signed by his officers to the English House of Commons complaining about the meagre resources that England was sending him. Parliament sent a delegation to him to try and resolve the matter, but before negotiations between the parties had even properly got under way, Inchiquin decided to change sides, and fight for the King. Numbers of his officers, all loyal men of the Parliamentary army deserted him when he announced his change of course but he nevertheless managed to keep the bulk of his army together. By mid April the Parliamentary delegation had been withdrawn and Inchiquin declared a traitor by the English House of Commons.

Truce with Inchiquin – Death Knell of the Confederacy

As the underhand negotiations with Inchiquin developed, it was decided to put the issue to a meeting of the general assembly of the Confederacy. Rinuccini, already sidelined by the Ormondists, was in Waterford but was summoned to Kilkenny to be present. Having heard of the negotiations with Inchiquin he had already made known his feelings in a letter to the Council which read in part: "Europe is shocked at the atrocities of this man, and will you parley with him when you ought to avenge your brethren, sacrilegiously murdered and plundered by his brigands? You have an army ready to march – send it into Munster…and rescue the peasantry from the cruel and exorbitant taxation imposed by a man on whose sincerity you can place no reliance."[276]

When the proposed truce with Inchiquin was raised at the meeting of the Assembly it was wholeheartedly rejected by Rinuccini and the bishops, for to them a truce with a man such as Inchiquin who was guilty of the most monstrous crimes was unthinkable. All opposition to the proposal was ignored by the Ormondists and on May 20th 1648 the truce was signed in Dungarvan, Co. Waterford. With this act the Confederacy was effectively at an end for according to Preston, all those who did not support the truce were to be considered as traitors.

Having grasped Inchiquin's bloody hand, Preston now planned with him an attack on the army of O'Néill who was now seen as the common enemy. With the expectation of Ormond's return to Ireland, Clanricarde finally abandoned his neutrality and also marshalled his troops to march against O'Néill, the one military leader of the Confederation who had remained faithful to it aims.[i] Rinuccini now decided to use the only tool he had left against those who had not supported the truce but wished to see the Confederacy and O'Néill destroyed – excommunication.

A sentence of excommunication was now posted on the gates of Kilkenny against all who supported the truce with Inchiquin. Furthermore a papal interdict forbidding Mass and the sacraments was issued by him against all towns where the truce would be observed. Large numbers of troops who were not as Ormond termed it "excommunication proof" now abandoned Preston and went to Maryborough (Portlaoise) where O'Néill was based to join his army. They were joined there by Rinuccini, who had left Kilkenny for good. Rinuccini's harsh action saved O'Néill but it also split the Catholic hierarchy, some of whom appealed to Rome against the severity of his pronouncement.

Rinuccini leaves Ireland

After spending some days with O'Néill in Maryborough (Portlaoise) the Italian bishop whom O'Néill held in the highest regard departed for Galway preparatory to his return

---

[i] "Was it for this that glory guards Clanricarde's grave?"" – C.P Meehan in his book "The Confederation of Kilkenny"

to Italy. For O'Néill it was a sad parting for Rinuccini was pastor, friend and confidant to him, and more - he was also a true friend of Ireland.

In some accounts of Irish history he is not recorded as such, rather many accusations are placed at his door, the foremost being that he divided the Confederacy. The Confederacy was divided when he came and he sought in vain to see that all Confederates would remain true to the Oath that they had sworn. The Gaelic Irish were under represented in the Confederacy and he strove to see that justice would be done to them regarding the return to them of lands and livelihoods of which they had been despoiled and as a Bishop of the Catholic Church he tried to ensure that a solid base was laid for its future.

His biographer, Aiazzi, writes that on his return to Italy, Pope Innocent X sought to elevate him to a position within the pontifical court but that he refused, preferring to return to his diocese. In his home in Fermo, he organised the painting of frescoes of the battles of Ballaghmore, Benburb and Bunratty.

The Return of Ormond

Faced with the combined forces of the various English factions, Parliamentarians, Royalists and the Old English Confederates, Eoghan Roe O'Néill returned to Ulster[i] where he was destined to watch from the sidelines as his enemies engaged in battle with each other.

---

[i] Before he departed the midlands for Ulster, Eoghan Roe O'Néill received a visitor – the Dean of the Diocese of Fermo who brought with him the sword of Hugh O'Néill "which had rifted the field like lightning at Beal-an-atha-Buidhe" (The Yellow Ford). It had been in the possession of Fr. Wadding and had been blessed by the Pope who said that it should be given to Eoghan Roe O'Néill. When news of this reached Kilkenny, it was the signal for an outcry among the Old English. "O'Néill wants to be King"

In Ulster there was trouble within the camp of Monroe's Parliamentary army. Monroe was dismayed by events in England for although he was a Parliamentarian he had no desire to see Scotland and England without a King and was considering his options. Unbeknownst to him a replacement – George Monck, had been appointed to succeed him. Monck arrived in Carrickfergus unannounced and placed Monroe under arrest but Monroe would later be reunited with those Scots who wished to fight for the preservation of the monarchy.

On September 29th 1648 Ormond returned to Ireland, landing at Cork where he was met by Inchiquin and within a short time, he was being feted in Kilkenny. During the lengthy negotiations with the rump Confederacy, Ormond gave way on most points, but would not budge regarding the public exercise of the Catholic faith. There was also no movement on the question of the return of Gaelic land into the hands of its rightful owners, as the Old English were not in favour of its resolution. When an agreement was signed its terms did not fall that far short of those offered by Glamorgan and castigated by Ormond.

Shortly after the signing of the treaty between Ormond and the rump Confederacy in January 1649, King Charles I was executed by the victorious Parliamentary government in London. Ireland was now home to the last Royalist army. During the middle of February, Prince Rupert of the Rhine, one of King Charles most prominent generals arrived in Kinsale at the head of 16 frigates. For almost seven years Ireland had accommodated opposing Royalist and Parliamentary armies but they had never come to blows with each other preferring to engage instead with their common enemy. All that was now about to change.

Struggle for Supremacy before the coming of Cromwell

With peace now secure between Ormond (who was appointed as Lord Deputy by the Prince of Wales following the execution of the King) and the rump Confederacy, the joint armies of Inchiquin, the Confederates and the Royalists (including the Scottish Royalists in Ulster) now had a brief window of opportunity in which to try and achieve control in Ireland before the imminent arrival of Cromwell at the head of a large parliamentary army. It was agreed that Ormond would try and capture Dublin while Inchiquin would capture Drogheda which was under the control of Monck's Parliamentary army. Inchiquin easily succeeded and gave quarter to Monck's men, allowing them free passage to Dublin whereas Ormond feeling that he was too weak to launch an all out attack on Dublin decided that he would attempt to starve the city into submission. After having employed this tactic for almost two months, Ormond was expecting an attack by Jones in order to break the siege. His commanders, who should have been on high alert, were in fact taken unawares when on the night of August 1st 1649, Jones launched an attack out of the city in the direction of Rathmines. Ormond, who was sleeping in his tent was roused by musket fire. His whole command was in disorder. Struggling to prepare for battle and come to grips with the enemy, Ormond's men were easy prey and what was intended by Jones to be a raid upon enemy lines turned into a rout. Large numbers of Ormond's men were killed or taken prisoner and huge amounts of provisions, munitions and baggage were captured. Following this Jones marched on Drogheda but failed to recapture it and returned to Dublin just before the arrival of Cromwell.

Chapter 24

"With Bible and Sword"

Cromwell Comes To Ireland

The Killing of the King

As the war in Ireland between the Confederacy and the Crown came to an official conclusion, unimaginable scenes were being played out in England. After a bloody war between the forces of the King and Parliament, the army of Parliament had triumphed. As the war drew to a close King Charles I had sought refuge among his Scottish kin, but the Scots had handed him back to the English in return for a vast amount of gold.

Once the King was in the hands of the Parliamentary army, their leader Oliver Cromwell had woven a series of events designed to bring the King into close arrest after which his Parliamentary forces had occupied London. Then the King was tried and condemned to death after which one of Cromwell's colonels had spat in the King's face.[277] Outside the court, a woman who was protesting that the King should be spared was detained and publicly branded with red-hot irons. After all this, Cromwell still found it difficult to persuade his colleagues to sign the King's death warrant. Finally he shouted at them: "I will have your names and I will have them here!"[278] On the following Tuesday, January 30th 1649, the King was beheaded.

The Levellers

After the killing of the King, Cromwell hoped that he would be at last free to deal with Ireland, except that there was a movement within his own New Model Army that rejected such a move.

In 1645 a democratic and republican movement founded by John Lilleburn had gained increasing credence among Cromwell's soldiers. They were called "The Levellers" a term given them by their detractors, (which they later adopted) as it was said that they wished to "level men's estates"[279] or reduce all men to a common level, eradicating all social classes. Their program included equality before the law, economic reforms, security of tenure, and religious freedom. The Levellers were the first popular movement to use the distribution of leaflets and the collection of signatures as a means of garnering support, and they also had their own periodical newspaper called "The Moderate". As the re-conquest of Ireland was being prepared by Cromwell and his generals, the Levellers demanded to know what right had England to enslave a foreign people? On May 1st 1649 as preparations were underway for the invasion of Ireland the Levellers published a document called "An Agreement to the Free People of England" which stated that England had no right to be in Ireland. Cromwell was furious. He told the Council of States "...you have no way to deal with these men but to break them in pieces..."[280] Firm in their principles, a large number of the Levellers mutinied. Cromwell went into battle against the mutineers with troops who were loyal to him and defeated the Levellers in battle at Burnford on May 15th 1649, after which their movement declined.

Ireland - A Land Divided among British Factions

With England almost completely under his control, Cromwell's gaze was firmly fixed on Ireland for many reasons, the most important being the eradication of Catholicism[i] and the complete seizure of all Irish land. His other aims were retribution for crimes committed against the Planters during the initial insurrection period, the punishment of the Old English and Gaelic Irish and also his desire to achieve the final defeat of the monarchy, for Ireland was home to a sizeable Royalist army.

Following the beheading of the King Charles I, the Prince of Wales had been declared King Charles II by many of the prominent Royalists. As King Charles II he officially confirmed the treaty that Ormond had made with the rump Confederacy.

Although the Royalists were much more numerous in Ireland than the forces of Parliament, Parliament still had a sizeable army despite the fact that Inchiquin had changed to the Royalist side as had large numbers of the Scots in Ulster under the command of Monroe. Dublin also remained under the control of Parliament while Boyle in Munster and Coote whose forces were operating in Connacht and Ulster were both on the side of Parliament and had armies under their command. Coote was typical of those who had a weakness for the monarchy, but this weakness had been bested by his hatred of Catholicism and he had changed to the side of Parliament when the King had refused to cease negotiating with the Confederacy.

---

[i] On April 12th 1649, at the voting of funds for his Irish campaign during a meeting of the Common Council being held at the Guildhall the speakers "did rightly distinguish the state of war in that kingdom as not being between Protestant and Protestant, or Independent and Presbyterian, but Papist and Protestant; and that was the interest there; Papacy or Popery being not to be endured in that kingdom; which notably agreed with that maxim of King James, when first King of the three kingdoms: Plant Ireland with Puritans, and root out Papists and then secure it" – Acts of Cromwell, p55

Cromwell intended that his aims of retribution, conquest and the eradication of Catholicism would be completed simultaneously. Once these had been achieved, Cromwell intended to undertake his final Irish ambition; a colonisation of the entire country in order to bring Ireland to final submission and to pay off the debts he had incurred during the English Civil War.

The Arrival of Cromwell

On August 13th 1649 an armada of ships departed Milford Haven on the Welsh coast bound for Dublin. Aboard the fleet were around 9,000 foot soldiers and 4,000 cavalrymen along with artillery and vast amounts of stores of every type that were needed for making war. There were other weapons too, to be used in a later phase of his conquest – scythes, reaping hooks, rubstones and whetstones, to be used so that Irish crops could be harvested and destroyed thereby causing famine wherever the army deemed necessary.

After the army landed in Dublin on the 14th they joined forces with the army of General Michael Jones and prepared to march on Drogheda. Two decrees were issued by Cromwell to his troops; one against drinking alcohol to excess and the other forbidding the soldiers from engaging in plunder in the countryside, as he desired the country people to adequately provision his men while they were on the march by selling their produce.

"Cursed be he that Maketh not his Sword Starke drunk with Irish blood"

"This marvellous great mercy" – Drogheda, September 1649

Previously under the control of the Parliamentarians, Drogheda was now home to a Royalist garrison of 3,000 men under the command of a one legged English Catholic officer,

Sir Arthur Aston. The garrison was a mixed force consisting of Irish and English troops while the town itself was also mixed being home to a large number of Old English.

Oliver Cromwell

On August 30th Cromwell departed Dublin with 13,000 men and by September 2nd his army had been drawn up on the south side of the town in front of the River Boyne. Ormond was delighted with Cromwell's move, as Drogheda was heavily fortified and he envisaged Cromwell and his army being stuck outside the town for a protracted period just as Winter was approaching. However Ormond's view of warfare was somewhat outdated whereas Cromwell, fresh from the battlefields of England had the latest in heavy weaponry at his disposal. By September 9th, the heavy siege cannons that had been brought from Dublin by ship were in position. Cromwell now sent a messenger to Sir Arthur Aston who delivered it at eight o'clock on the morning of September 10th: "Sir, having brought the army belonging to the Parliament of England before this place, to reduce it to obedience, to the end effusion of blood may be prevented, I thought fit to summon you to deliver the same into my hands to their use. If this be refused, you will have no cause to blame me. I expect your answer and rest your servant. O. Cromwell."[281]

After Aston refused to surrender unconditionally, Cromwell's artillery commenced battering the town's walls. All that day and all the next the cannon fire was unrelenting. The chief targets were the town wall beside the cemetery of St. Mary's

Church and the south wall beside the elevated Millmount, which was the site of an ancient Tuatha dé Danann[i] burial mound. Both of these were on the south side of the town while the main part of the town was across the bridge over the river Boyne. By five o'clock on Tuesday 10th large breaches had been made in both places and storming parties comprising around 700 men were sent forward. On entering the breaches it was found that strong-points and trenches had been constructed behind the destroyed walls from which poured a deadly storm of musket fire at Cromwell's men who were forced to retreat. Some more artillery was used in order to try and break up the defenders and quarter was promised to all who would be taken prisoner. When the towns' cavalry commander, Colonel Wall was killed, the morale of his troops plummeted. Further attacks were launched by Cromwell's army, and finally the besiegers broke through the defences thereafter pouring through the breaches into the south side of the town. As he entered the town with General Jones over the bodies of his men who had fallen in the assault, General Jones said to Cromwell; "You have now all the flower of the Irish army in your hands"[282]

As Cromwell's men stormed through the two breaches, Sir Arthur Aston and his staff retreated into the Mill atop Millmount. For a while this well fortified position was defended but finally surrendered after the defenders were told that they would be taken prisoner. Of the taking of Millmount, Cromwell later wrote to the Speaker of the House of Commons, Sir William Lenthall; "The governor, Sir Arthur Aston, and divers considerable officers being there, our men getting up to them were ordered by me to put all to the sword; and indeed being in the heat of action, I forbade them to spare

---

[i] The Tuatha dé Danann were an ancient pre Christian tribe. The "Tuatha dé Danann" translates as "The folk of the goddess Danu"

any that were in arms in the town"²⁸³ After having surrendered their weapons, all were killed in cold blood. Sir Arthur Aston was clubbed to death with his wooden leg after Cromwell's soldiers, expecting to find gold inside, found that it was made of solid wood. After clubbing him to death, his body was hacked to pieces.[i]

As Cromwell's men swarmed into the town, the chance for blocking their entry over the bridge of the River Boyne into the north side of the town was missed due to the pell-mell nature of the retreat. Very soon Cromwell's men (who outnumbered the defenders by around 3 to 1) were everywhere, killing every enemy soldier in their path. However in buildings that were strongly defended, quarter was promised to all that would surrender and many soldiers were taken prisoner. The successful surrender of a few in a hopeless situation prompted the surrender of others who followed their example. However their surrender on the promise of quarter was not to avail them and the dishonouring of the promise of quarter troubled some of Cromwell's men. Ormond later wrote: "Cromwell's officers and soldiers promising quarter to such as would lay down their arms and performing it as long as any place held out, which encouraged others to yield; but when they had once all in their power and feared that no hurt could be done to them,

---

[i] "Aston was believed to have hid away his gold for security in his wooden leg. "This they (the soldiers) seized upon as a prize but finding nothing in it, they knocked out his brains with it and hacked his body to pieces" Memoris of Anthony Wood.
"The army put all they met to the sword, having positive orders from Lieutenant General Cromwell to give no quarter to any soldier. Their works and fort were also stormed and taken and those that defended them put to the sword also, and amongst them Sir Arthur Aston, Governor of the place. A great dispute there was amongst the soldiers for his artificial leg, which was reported to be of gold, but it proved to be of wood, his girdle found to be the better booty, wherein two hundred pieces of gold were found quilted." – Memoirs of General Edmund Ludlow.

the word "No Quarter" went around and the soldiers were forced many of them against their wills to kill the prisoners."[284] According to Cromwell himself some prisoners were taken after one of the towers incorporated into the town's wall successfully surrendered. Of this, Cromwell later wrote in his account to parliament; "The officers were knocked on the head, (clubbed to death) every tenth man of the soldiers killed and the rest shipped to the Barbadoes"[285]

When the town's defenders had been dealt with, Cromwell's men turned their attention to the civilians. In this case there were distinctions made, as his troops sought if possible to avoid murdering Protestants. In general all those of Irish birth were murdered as were all Catholic clergy and religious.[i]

St. Peter's Church was the largest church on the north side of the town, and it was here that more than a thousand people had gathered in the hope of finding refuge, but there was no refuge to be found. On the morning of September 11th everyone in the Church or its environs was brutally murdered. Some people had sought safety in the narrow wooden steeple of the church and as it could not be readily accessed by the soldiers, Cromwell ordered it to be set ablaze. When the soldiers entered the burial vaults underneath the church they found it to be the refuge of women of the town's nobility. None were spared.[ii] Cromwell justified the mass murder at the

---

[i] A Protestant clergyman, the Rev. Dr. Nalson, writes in his memoirs about a relation of his who was a Captain in Cromwell's army. Regarding the killing of children his relation told him that "if any who had some grains of compassion reprehended the soldiers for this unchristian inhumanity, they would scoffingly reply, Why? Nits will be lice! And so would despatch them" – Nalson, Memoirs, Vol II page 7.

[ii] One of Cromwell's officers, Thomas Wood who was the brother of the notable Oxford historian Anthony Wood, later wrote that he found in the vaults "...the flower and choicest of the women and ladies belonging to the town amongst whom a most handsome virgin, arrayed in costly and gorgeous apparel kneeled

church before Parliament by writing that: "...they had the insolence, on the last Lord's day to thrust out the Protestants from that church and to have the Mass said there..."[286] while in a letter to Speaker Louthall he refers to the Mass said in the church, adding "...and in this very place near one thousand of them were knocked on the head promiscuously but two."[287] For the best part of five days the killing spree continued.[i] After this the army was split into two parts, one to head north and the other to go back to Dublin. Once back in Dublin Cromwell wrote to Parliament of what had befallen Drogheda: "...this is a righteous judgement of God upon these barbarous wretches, who have imbrued their hands in so much innocent blood..."[288] He attributed his success at Drogheda to "the spirit of God."[289] As if to efface any guilt felt either by himself or any of his men for their unconscionable barbarity he added "...and therefore it is right that God alone should have all the glory"[290] On receipt of Cromwell's dispatch, the English Parliament voted a "day of thanksgiving"[291] and a letter of appreciation was sent to Cromwell in which it was noted that Parliament "...did approve of the execution done at Drogheda, as an act

---

down to save her life" Being moved to compassion he took her outside the church "...with the intention to put her over the wall to shift for herself..." but before the town wall was reached another soldier had plunged his sword into her body. Wood then writes how he "...seeing her gasping...(I)... took away her money and jewels and flung her over the works" In his record of the Sack of Drogheda Thomas Wood also writes how the soldiers "...when they were to make their way up to the lofts and galleries of the church and up to the tower where the enemy had fled, each would take up a child and use it as a buckler of defence, when they ascended the steps, to keep themselves from being shot or brained" - Life of Anthony A Wood - 1632-1672"

[i] "When the city was captured by the English, the blood of the Catholics was mercilessly shed in the streets, in the dwelling houses, and in the open fields; to none was mercy shown; not to the women, not to the aged, nor to the young" – Report to the Irish College in Rome (1649)

both of Justice to them (those killed) and mercy to others who may be warned by it"[292]

Venables Goes North

To face the Royalist Scots in Ulster, Cromwell sent an army under Colonel Robert Venables. Upon their march northwards they found that Dundalk, Newry and Carlingford had either already been abandoned by the Royalists or surrendered on their approach. Sir Charles Coote who was already in Ulster joined Venables and their joint armies engaged in a series of attacks on the Royalist Scots. Coleraine fell easily into the hands of Coote who massacred the garrison. With the exception of the fortress at Carrickfergus, Monroe's forces were ejected from Antrim and Down along with many of the Scottish Planters.

"This Other Mercy" – Wexford, October 1649

After his return to Dublin, Cromwell stayed there until September 27th after which he led his army south through Wicklow. They arrived at the walls of Wexford town on October 1st. Like Drogheda, Wexford was well fortified, for inside the town walls there was another large wall made of earth. The towns 3,000 strong garrison was under the command of Colonel David Sinnott.

As Cromwell prepared for the assault, negotiations between the two sides were entered into without conclusion and on Wednesday October 10th, Cromwell's large guns commenced firing on the town. By 12pm breaches had been made in the towns fortifications after which Sinnott decided to request further negotiations with Cromwell. When this was agreed to four men, Alderman Nicholas Cheevers, Captain James Stafford, Major James Byrne and Major Theobald Dillon crossed under the flag of truce to the enemy. While the terms were under negotiation, Cromwell found Captain Stafford to be very compliant and having separated him from the others bribed him to allow his men into the town's castle. Shortly afterwards the town's defenders were dismayed to find that they were under fire from the castle which was a cornerstone of the town's defence. Cromwell now launched his assault, his men scaling the town walls with siege ladders. After coming under cannon fire from their own positions, the town's defenders retreated into the town where they offered as Cromwell termed it "stiff resistance". As the battle continued thousands of men of the New Model Army were streaming into the town and the defenders were soon overwhelmed. Hundreds of the townspeople had flocked to the market square hoping for safety behind the ranks of the town's defenders. Once the defenders were overwhelmed Cromwell's soldiers massacred the civilians whilst shouting their battle cry: "Jesus and No Quarter."[293]

Even as the massacre of troops and citizens commenced the town's negotiators were still in Cromwell's encampment and the ink with which Cromwell had written down his own proposals for an end to the siege, which included life, liberty and freedom from pillage for the townspeople was barely dry.

As the soldiers of the New Model Army commenced their butchery[i], hundreds of people ran to the harbour and clambered aboard any boat that could be found there in order to try and escape but the boats soon became overcrowded and many sank. Soon Cromwell's men were on the quayside shooting into the water at those attempting to swim away.

The Catholic Bishop of Ferns, Dr. Nicholas French escaped the carnage because of illness. As Cromwell approached Wexford, Bishop French was recuperating in the countryside. For

---

[i] "...(We)...entered the town, where again the fight was renewed, and continued until those within were hacked down, and some of them, endeavouring to escape were lost without mercy" – Account of an officer in the regiment of Sir John Clotworthy

months afterwards he was on the run until finally he managed to escape from Ireland. In 1673 he wrote a letter from Antwerp to the Papal Nuncio which was published in the newspaper "The Nation" on October 8th 1859. He wrote how: "On that most calamitous day the city of Wexford, abounding in wealth, ships and merchandise was carried at the point of the sword and given up to the infuriated soldiery of Cromwell, that pest of the English government. There before God's altar, fell many sacred victims, priests of the Lord, some of whom were seized outside the precincts of the church, were scourged with whips; some were arrested and bound with chains; some were hanged, and others were cruelly put to death by divers sorts of torture. The best blood of the citizens was shed, till the very streets were red with it and there was scarcely a house that was not polluted with carnage and full of wailing. In my own palace a youth hardly sixteen years of age – an amiable boy – (and also) my gardener and sacristan were cruelly butchered; and they left the chaplain, whom I caused to remain behind me at home, transpierced with six mortal wounds, and weltering in his own gore. And these abominations were perpetrated in open day by impious cut throats"[294]

After the massacre was over, Cromwell once again wrote to the English parliament, telling the members that he had initially intended to spare Wexford, but then saw that "God would not have it so."[295] He informed them that he "thought it not good nor just to restrain off the soldiers from their right of pillage, nor from doing of execution on the enemy."[296] His dispatch to parliament concluded with the words "…it hath pleased God to give into your hands this other mercy (Drogheda being the first) for which as for all we pray that God may have all the glory."[297] By his own account he lost 150 men for 2,000 of the enemy, a figure that did not include the dead civilians.

Following the "battle" there lay dead on Wexford's streets around 1,500 civilians, including 500 women and children and all the Catholic clergy Cromwell's men could find.²⁹⁸ In recommending that parliament send over protestants to inhabit the town,ⁱ Cromwell adds "...of the former inhabitants, not one in twenty could be found to challenge any property in their own houses"²⁹⁹

After Wexford Cromwell's general policy was as follows. If a town surrendered and opened it gates to him without a fight there was minimum loss of life. If a town initially refused to surrender after being offered terms but then surrendered after minimum resistance, only the officers were put to the sword and if the town surrendered after vigorous resistance its entire garrison was killed. If quarter was granted to a town there were exceptions to this policy, for particular officers, Catholic clergy and religious etc.

Cromwell Continues His Campaign
The Killing of Eoghan Roe O'Néill
"They slew with poison him they feared to meet with steel" – Thomas Davis

For almost a year now Eoghan Roe O'Néill and his army had been ploughing a lonely furrow in Ulster. Rejected as an enemy by those who should have been seeking his assistance, he had gone so far as to make local deals with the Parliamentary forces of Monck and Coote, securing money to pay his troops and concessions regarding property and freedom to practice the Catholic faith in return for giving them some limited assistance against the Royalists when their forces were cut off or under siege. This had ended after parliament

---

ⁱ "God hath spoiled the spoiler; abundance of plunder and riches. It is a fine spot for some Godly congregation, where house and land wait for inhabitants and occupiers. I wish they would come." – Letter from Cromwellian Chaplain, Rev. Hugh Peters to the House of Commons

had gone wind of these local arrangements, because for a parliamentary commander to make deals with a papist was out of the question.

Since Cromwell's arrival, his murderous barbarity had come as something of a wake up call to Ormond who now realised that he could well do with an experienced commander like O'Néill, not to mention his army and contacted him. By this time Eoghan Roe O'Néill was seriously ill and unfit to lead his men but he was only too willing to help Ormond, as Cromwell's rule looked set to be the worst Ireland had yet endured. After brief negotiations with Ormond that were conducted by Eoghan's nephew Daniel, 6,000 men were sent south under the command of General Hugh Dubh O'Néill.

According to the testimony of Colonel Hugh O'Néill, Eoghan Roe's illness was due to a poisoned pair of boots. At the beginning of August 1649 he had received a gift of a fine pair of russet coloured boots (from one of the Old English, a man named Plunkett from Louth), which he had afterwards worn. Shortly afterwards he had fallen ill with blood poisoning and had gone to a castle of the O'Reilly's in Co. Cavan located on an island in Lough Oughter. According to the journal of Colonel Hugh O'Néill one or both boots had been poisoned. Colonel O'Néill wrote: "Plunkett afterwards boasted of the service he had done for England".[300] On November 6th 1649 Eoghan Roe O'Néill died from septicaemia. It was a heavy blow, not only for the Gael but for all who saw O'Néill as Ireland's last hope against Cromwell's barbarity. The remains of this great Irish General, in whom the native population had complete confidence, were taken by night to the old Franciscan monastery in Cavan town for secret burial in an unmarked grave lest his remains should be later exhumed.[i]

---

[i] Fr. McGeoghean who was Chaplain to the Irish Brigade in the French army in the early eighteenth century wrote of Eoghan Roe: "His ideas were clear, his perception accurate, his judgement very sound. He was dexterous in profiting

Ormond's Disastrous Strategy

The great weakness in Ormond's strategy against Cromwell was his fixation with defence. Every town and castle was garrisoned and with relative ease Cromwell now succeeded in rolling up his enemy as at each obstacle he faced a force much inferior to his own that he invariably managed to overcome. By deciding to forego the necessity of a field army and defend everything, Ormond defended nothing. His armies would have proven much more effective against Cromwell if he had abandoned many of the fixed positions and amassed one or two large armies with which he might have attempted to stop Cromwell. His general-ship was so lacklustre that many were convinced Ormond and Inchiquin were conniving together for no good purpose. Because of this Waterford refused to allow any of Ormond's men to enter the town and during the winter of 1649-1650 many southern towns would not even give his troops Winter quarters. Added to this lack of strategy was the great horror and fear that the Royalist / Confederate troops possessed of Cromwell's army after news of the great massacres permeated throughout the country.

Swift Progress for The New Model Army

After Wexford, Cromwell marched on New Ross. As soon as the artillery of the New Model Army began raining on the town, its Commander, Taffe immediately opened negotiations with the enemy. Taffe asked for liberty of conscience for the people to which Cromwell retorted; "I meddle not with any man's conscience but as for liberty to exercise the Mass, I must

---

of the advantages which were furnished by the enemy; he left nothing to chance and his plans were always well formed; he was sober, prudent and reserved; when occasion required he could disguise his sentiments; he was well acquainted with the intrigues of courts; and in a word he possessed all the qualities necessary for a great general."

tell you that where the Parliament of England has power, that will not be allowed".[301] Taffe surrendered on October 18th unconditionally. In the south, Inchiquin who had previously fought for parliament, had left garrisons at Cork, Youghal, Kinsale, Bandon and other towns who all now decided to mutiny and declared for Cromwell after being encouraged to do so by Roger Boyle who was a son of Broghill, Earl of Cork.. As a kindred spirit, Roger Boyle made a great impression on Cromwell and Cromwell appointed him his Master of Ordnance for his conquest of Ireland.

Outside New Ross, Cromwell ordered the construction of a pontoon bridge to allow his army to cross the River Barrow. Once across they captured Inistioge, Carrick and the fort at the village of Passage. Dungarvan also fell but Waterford continued to hold out.

The news was no better in Ulster. On December 13th, Carrickfergus Castle which had been under siege, surrendered to Coote. Ormond had sent Daniel O'Néill with 2,000 men to lift the siege but he arrived too late.

As the winter weather closed in Cromwell paused in Cork until the end of January as fresh troops and supplies were brought in from England, taking time to put pen to paper regarding his feelings on the Catholic Mass. "...I shall not, where I have power, and the Lord is pleased to bless me, suffer the exercise of the Mass where I can take notice of it..."[302]

The Defence of Clonmel

1650 continued for Cromwell just as 1649 had ended and by the beginning of spring much of Munster and Leinster was under his control. By mid March he was approaching the Confederate capital of Kilkenny where plague and death had seized the city, and as a result the number of soldiers defending it had fallen from 1,200 to 400. In spite of this, the greatly reduced garrison under the command of Major James

Walsh refused to surrender. On March 22nd Cromwell's siege of the town along with the positioning of his cannon commenced, with his attack starting some days later and by the 28th Kilkenny had had enough and surrendered. The next town in Cromwell's sights was Clonmel and it was here that Cromwell encountered the toughest battle of his campaign. As Cromwell prepared for battle at Clonmel, the Catholic Bishop of Ross, Boetius MacEgan was heading north for the town in command of a small army, the aim of this force being to assist the army of Colonel Hugh O'Néill who was defending the town. However Roger Boyle intercepted this force and captured the Bishop who was then brought to Carrigadrohid Castle on the Lee. Boyle had Carraigadrohid under siege and he wanted Bishop MacEgan to persuade its garrison to surrender but instead the Bishop called on the soldiers inside the castle to resist to the last. Boyle then ordered the Bishop MacEgan hanged before the castle within view of its defenders.[i]

Cromwell was much relieved to find out that Roger Boyle had intercepted and dealt with the relief force destined for Clonmel as he particularly didn't want a protracted struggle at the town. He had just received news from England that there was trouble with the Scots and was being summoned by parliament to return to England. Being influenced by this summons he did not subject Clonmel to a prolonged artillery bombardment but instead directed the artillery to fire specifically at the point where he wished his men to enter the town. At the artillery opened up Cromwell took part of his army and went around

---

[i] Carraigadrohid Castle was later captured by a clever ruse on the part of Boyle. Bereft of artillery he had his men construct fake guns out of tree trunks, which were pulled up to the castle by Oxen and emplaced. Fearing an artillery bombardment followed by attack and massacre, the Castle's garrison surrendered.

the town closer to its gates, which his men would open once they had broken through the breach in the wall being made by the artillery.

Within the walls, Colonel Hugh O'Néill withdrew his men from the area being bombarded. Once the artillery fire had ceased, his Ulstermen rushed forward and hid out of sight in the ruins of the destroyed buildings and previously constructed trenches. As the soldiers of the New Model Army entered the town there was an eerie silence, suddenly broken by the charge of the Ulstermen from their hiding places wielding weaponry more suited for close quarter fighting than the muskets of the enemy. Overwhelmed, those in the vanguard of the assault shouted to their comrades to fall back, but the men entering the town through the opening created by the artillery misheard them and continued to advance. As Cromwell waited patiently at the gates on the far side of the town, his troops entering through the breached wall were caught up in a bloodbath. After suffering severe casualties[i] Cromwell's men retreated and reformed, then charged once more into the fray but with the same results, this time their casualties being caused by heavy musket fire. After being ejected from the town a second time, Cromwell suspended the assault for the night. He did not take any blame himself for the terrible losses his army had suffered but instead told his men that they relied too much on their own ability and not enough on prayer or the power of the Lord, after which he imposed an overnight fast on his army. As Colonel O'Néill took stock of his own situation he made the decision to pull out of Clonmel during the hours of darkness as his stock of gunpowder was very low. He also knew that Cromwell, once his blood was up,

---

[i] The Cromwellian account of the battle admits to 1,000 dead. Carte, (who wrote the biography of Ormond) puts the number at 2,000.

would launch a fanatical and overpowering assault first thing in the morning.

By the following morning O'Néill and his men had escaped. As dawn broke the townspeople indicated their willingness to surrender. Cromwell, not realising that O'Néill's army had gone accepted the towns surrender promising the people that they or their properties would not be harmed. On entering the town Cromwell was dismayed to find that O'Néill and his men had escaped especially after the heavy losses he had suffered at their hands. In spite of this Cromwell nevertheless kept his word to the townspeople but dispatched many of his soldiers after O'Neill who "killed all they could light upon."[303] 2,500 of Cromwell's soldiers were dead and many more wounded. On Cromwell's departure for England his son in law, confidant and advisor, the cold and reserved Henry Ireton, already made Lord President of Munster succeeded him as commander of the army. Ireton, as Commander was anxious to bring the conquest to a conclusion so that in his own words "...the English nation might with justice assert their right of conquest..."[304]

At the end of May 1650, after his brief campaign unmatched for atrocity even in Ireland's bloody history, Cromwell left Ireland aboard the frigate "President Bradshaw". On his arrival at the port of Bristol five days late he received a welcome from the population of the city fit for a conquering hero.

The Battle of Scarriffhollis

After the death of Eoghan Roe O'Néill, the command of his army was assumed by his son, Colonel Henry O'Néill, until a convention of the army's officers could take place. On the 18th March 1650, at Belturbet in Co. Cavan the officers elected the Bishop of Clogher, Herber MacMahon, who was regarded not only as an able military commander but also as a compromise candidate between those officers who held differing opinion regarding the pact with Ormond.[i]

MacMahon was firmly convinced that Ireland's and Catholicism's best chance for survival was to wholeheartedly support the royalist cause. At a meeting of bishops which had taken place at Clonmacnoise at the beginning of December 1649, he had put forward the case for unity behind the royalist cause after which a declaration was published informing the people of Ireland "...how vain it was for them to expect from the common enemy commanded by Cromwell by authority from the rebels of England, any assurance of their religion, lives or fortunes...for God's glory and (your) own safety...contribute with patience to the support of the war against the enemy"[305] In spite of this declaration many continued to be wary of Ormond, and in many towns, including Limerick he was refused entry.

While a large part of the Ulster army had been dispatched south, MacMahon had remained in Ulster with the remainder fighting mainly against the forces of Coote and Venables with some success. By mid June, MacMahon and the army of Ulster were closing in on Coote who was at Lifford only to find out that he had just been reinforced by sea with 1,000 soldiers of the New Model Army under Colonel Fenwick who had sailed from Belfast.

The Ulster Army had their encampment on the Hill of Doonglebe overlooking the Pass of Scarriffhollis a few miles from Letterkenny. MacMahon's officers knew that although they slightly outnumbered Coote, Coote had a much stronger force of cavalry and his men were far better armed. The officers asked MacMahon not to consider open battle with Coote at

---

[i] That bishops were involved in the military campaign was not unusual because of the Cromwellian policy for the extermination of Catholicism. As we have already seen the Bishop of Ross was also in command of an army.

this stage, but MacMahon overruled them and the Ulster army came down from its strong point to engage the enemy where it found itself outflanked and unable to manoeuvre. It was not a situation into which Eoghan Roe O'Néill would have led the army.

Engaged by Coote on three sides, the Ulster army was annihilated, and while some managed to escape from the slaughter most preferred to stand, fight and die knowing Coote's reputation for butchery out of battle, which was afterwards realised.

Almost all those who escaped the battlefield were hunted down and killed. Bishop MacMahon managed to escape only to be recaptured after two days. On June 23rd he was promised quarter and made prisoner near Omagh by a Parliamentarian force under the command of Major King. However Coote was not prepared to see King's promise honoured and Bishop MacMahon was hanged on his orders. Also captured in the days following the battle was Eoghan Roe O'Néill's only son Henry. He was likewise taken prisoner after being promised quarter and was then murdered in cold blood. Following their overwhelming defeat at Scarrifhollis, the Ulster army had largely ceased to exist, continuing their struggle only in scattered pockets.

Perfidious Albion

After taking command of the army, Ireton continued Cromwell's successful military campaign by picking off more of the isolated garrisons. On August 10th Waterford, which was under the command of Preston surrendered while Duncannon Fort also fell into the hands of the Parliamentarians shortly afterwards.

Around the middle of August news reached Ireland that Charles II, who had come to Scotland at the end of June had signed an order publicly revoking the agreement made in his name by Ormond with the Confederacy (which Charles had afterwards publicly approved). His revocation stated "that he was convinced in his conscience of the sinfulness and unlawfulness of it, and of allowing them (the Catholics) the liberty of their Popish religion; for which he did, from his heart, desire to be deeply humbled before the Lord". This news caused consternation in Ireland, among the Confederates that the King's word should not be kept, and with Ormond, that the King should place him in such an invidious position. Ormond, whose currency was already very low in the country as rumours were abounding that he was endeavouring to make a separate peace with Cromwell for Royalist Protestants, tried to excuse the King by saying that he had found it difficult to brook the fanaticism of the Scots.

With this declaration the rug was effectively pulled from underneath the agreement which bound the Royalists and the Confederates to their common fight against Cromwell but in effect it changed little, for Cromwell was still the greater of two evils for the Catholics of Ireland.

The Flight of Ormond

By the onset of winter 1650, Cromwell's troops were in control of much of Ulster, Leinster and Munster. Although it would be some time before Ireland would be completely under Cromwell's control, some including Ormond were already planning on abandoning Ireland to join the King in France. In the company of Inchiquin (who after his relentless persecution of Catholics, would convert to Catholicism during his French exile) and about twenty others he departed Galway for St. Malo in France in the middle of December 1650, just when the winter weather was at its worst. A separate ship carrying baggage, servants and some other passengers was lost presumed sunk in the rough seas. Before his departure he passed on the role of Lord Deputy to Ulick Burke, the Earl of

Clanrickard, while the command of the Army was passed to Castlehaven.

The Siege of Limerick

With operations in Munster and Leinster all progressing satisfactorily Ireton's primary objective for 1652 was to capture the city of Limerick which he intended to use as a gateway into south Connacht. Already this had been attempted the previous Autumn, when Ireton had sent an army commanded by Sir Hardress Waller (who had signed the King's death warrant) to capture the city. When Waller called on Hugh Dubh O'Néill to surrender, he had refused and Waller, who was later joined by Ireton had begun a siege, which had to be ended in the face of the onset of Winter, after which Ireton had retired to Winter quarters in Kilkenny.

At the beginning of June 1652, Ireton returned to the isolated city on the Shannon in command of a huge force – almost 10,000 men and a vast amount of artillery.

In spite of this overwhelming strength, around five times what he himself possessed, Hugh Dubh remained obstinate and when Ireton called on him to give up he received the reply – "No Surrender"

In spite of the vast amount of siege artillery, Ireton had brought with him, it now proved to be of very little use to him for the city's walls were thickly buttressed with earth so as to deaden the impact of the big shells. Ireton resorted to various ruses and small attacks hoping to prise open a corner of the city's defence and thereby gain entry but to no avail. Amphibious attacks were beaten back and when he did capture the fort at Thomond Bridge, O'Néill's men destroyed the bridge to the fort.

After successfully crossing the River Shannon, Ireton's men brought Limerick under siege from two sides after Colonel Fennell gave up Killaloe without a fight. The plague, which had earlier ravaged Kilkenny, was now rampant in Limerick and many civilians who sought to flee the diseased city were captured by Ireton's men and executed or in some cases horsewhipped before being turned back.

After capturing King's Island, Ireton was further assisted by the Royalist Colonel Fennell. Fennell along with some other English Royalist officers duplicitously entered St. John's Gate and took control of the position, thereafter admitting 200 of Ireton's men and turned the strongpoint's guns away from the enemy and towards the city making the city's surrender inevitable. As this was happening members of the city's council were already in secret talks with Ireton regarding surrender, and after the capture of St. John's Gate the conditions he proposed were made compulsory. The ordinary soldiers were promised quarter and the townspeople that they would not be harmed.

On October 29th 1652, after a siege of five months, Hugh Dubh O'Néill surrendered Limerick. Following the surrender of the city 2,500 Irish soldiers, many of them seriously ill or dying from the plague left Limerick.

Ireton is Summoned into Eternity

Numbers of the city's Aldermen and Catholic clergy were found in hiding, including the Bishop of Emily, Terence O'Brien who was hanged. As Bishop O'Brien stood atop the scaffold, he summoned Ireton to follow him into death "to answer for his cruelties and injustice before the tribunal of God"[306] Following his execution Bishop O'Brien was beheaded and his head was prominently displayed in the centre of the city. Hugh O'Néill, the city's commander and also the mastermind of the defence of Clonmel was also supposed to be hanged but some of Ireton's officers objected to this, saying that he was a gallant soldier and a man of honour. In the face of this opposition, Ireton agreed to allow a second trial for him in which those officers who voted for clemency outvoted those who condemned him by a single vote.³⁰⁷ⁱ

Just over a week later Ireton fell ill with the plague and died on

Henry Ireton

November 25th complaining of his "unjust condemnation"³⁰⁸ by Bishop O'Brien on which he blamed his fast approaching demise. The public purse funded the repatriation of his body and the building of a great monument at Westminster. Until such time as parliament should decide on a new commander, Ireton was succeeded by the Lieutenant General of Horse, Edmond

Ludlow, who, like Cromwell accepted as fact the lurid anti Irish propaganda purveyed by the London news houses. Shortly afterwards Lambert was appointed as Commander but when Cromwell's daughter (who was also Ireton's widow) married Colonel Charles Fleetwood a few months after Ireton's death, Lambert's appointment was rescinded and Fleetwood was appointed instead.

The Conquest of Connacht

Coote, with his conquest of Ulster as good as complete turned his attention to Connacht, and its gateway town on the River Shannon - Athlone. Splitting his army into two unequal parts, the smaller section attacked Sligo in order to draw off

---

ⁱ Hugh O'Neill was sent to the Tower of London after which the Spanish government sought his release on the grounds that he was a Spanish citizen. He was finally released to the Spaniards and died in Spain during the reign of Charles II

Clanrickard's army from his main attack. Following a long route march over the Curlew Mountains, the main part of Coote's Army attacked and seized Athlone from the Connacht side, thus opening the main east-west route towards Galway after which Coote began his campaign in Connacht. After the capture of Limerick and the death of Ireton, Ludlow's army marched towards Galway to assist Coote who had already taken the city under siege. In command of Galway was General Preston. Realising that no force was available to lift the siege, he escaped by sea leaving the city's authorities to negotiate its surrender.

General Surrender

Even at this stage of the war the forces of the Royalist / Confederate alliance still at large numbered over 30,000 soldiers, distributed throughout various towns and strongpoints, which although cut-off from help continued to hold out. It was generally felt, especially by the common people, that any continuance of the war would be useless, although this opinion might well have been different if the full extent of Cromwell's plans for Ireland had been made clear to them at this stage.

Cromwell's army in Ireland numbered some thousands more than the Royalist /Confederate alliance, and was well capable of forcing the surrender of all these cut off towns and strongpoints in their turn, but this would take a long time and would inevitably hold up the implementation of Cromwell's plans for Ireland. How to get these soldiers to surrender was now the issue that Ludlow and his staff turned their attention to. The general terms of the policy which they came up with was to allow all enemy soldiers to leave Ireland and enter the service of any power that was not at war or a threat to England except for those who had taken up arms in the first years of the struggle, had belonged to the first general assembly of the

Confederacy or had taken orders in the Catholic Church. Mass surrender followed on an individual basis, without direction from either Clanrickard or Castlehaven. When Clanrickard sent Castlehaven to Charles II for instructions regarding what he should do, Castlehaven did not return but instead sent a messenger with the reply to make the best conditions for himself. On October 11th 1652, Clanrickard accepted Ludlow's terms which allowed him along with 3,000 followers to leave Ireland. Clanrickard chose to go to his estate in Kent where he died in 1657. Although a Catholic, his faith was tempered by his royalism, and he had often told Ormond of his hostility towards the Confederacy.

On April 27th 1653 the surrender of the last Confederate position took place at Clough Oughter Castle on Lough Oughter in Co. Cavan after the castle was besieged and bombarded by the artillery of the army of Sir Theophilus Jones. Some of Cromwell's officers now complained that too much leniency was been shown to their enemy, so much so that the Protestant Bishop Jones of the Diocese of Clogher (Monaghan) authored a report which once more brought to the fore many false stories of the atrocities committed by the Irish in the rebellion of 1641 in order to further harden the hearts of those who would now decide the fate of the Irish. Already in 1650 Bishop Jones had ordered all Catholics to leave Monaghan town and its environs up to a distance of two miles on pain of death.

The War Continues Against Tories and Priests

The war was now over but there were still many isolated bands of Irish soldiers who refused to surrender. They were known to Cromwell's men as "Tories" from the Gaelic word "toiridhe" meaning "one who is pursued". The existence of such bands had long been a feature of the Irish struggle against the invader, especially in Ulster following the end of the Nine

Years War and they engaged in raids and robberies not only against English army outposts but against the planted population.

Cromwell's men now waged a relentless and merciless war against them, a war that encompassed thousands of others not involved in their struggle. In 1651, with The New Model Army in control of Leinster, the Governor of Dublin, Colonel John Hewson, informed London that the soldiers "...doth now intend to make use of scythes and sickles that were sent over in 1649 with which they intend to cut down the corn growing in these parts",[309] a policy that would bring widespread famine and death. In Waterford alone, from the army stores there were issued to Cromwell's men eighteen dozen scythes and forty reaping hooks.[310] On every occasion when Cromwell's men went out searching for Tories, they invariably destroyed all crops that they encountered, either harvested or in the ground.

One account of the actions of Cromwell's men as they roamed the countryside in search of Tories is to be found in the memoirs of General Ludlow. He relates how at the end of 1652 when marching from Dundalk to Castleblayney, his troops discovered a cave in which people were hiding. His soldiers then attempted to smother the cave's inhabitants with smoke. However there was a stream in the cavern and those inside by holding their faces against the stream managed to escape suffocation. After closing all holes to the cave: "another smother was made"[311]. When the soldiers entered the cave fifteen were put to the sword and four dragged out alive. Inside the cave the soldiers discovered a crucifix, chalice and priest's vestments.[312] In a separate recorded incident a priest, Fr. Bernard Fitzpatrick, was pulled from a cave and beheaded.[313]

In 1652 a proclamation designed to exterminate priests was published in Dublin. By this proclamation; "every Romish priest so found was deemed guilty of rebellion and sentenced to be hanged until he was half dead; then to have his head taken off, and his body cut in quarters; his bowels to be drawn out and burned and his head fixed upon a pole in some public place"[314]

The public reward for the head of an Irish priest, was the same as for the head of a wolf – five pounds, and no matter what human male's head was produced the reward was given. Many priests were captured and killed – 4 bishops and 300 priests by the end of Cromwell's rule.[i] Many others survived, living a furtive and clandestine existence in order to be able to bring the sacraments by night to their scattered flocks.

Further measures were also introduced against Catholics who might be sheltering a priest or know his whereabouts. Any person who was caught hiding a priest was liable to be executed and the goods and chattels of the family were seized. Anyone knowing the whereabouts of a priest without disclosing it was liable to have their ears amputated. Even the private practice of the Catholic religion was considered a capital offence, with all these measures being renewed in 1657. Following the introduction of these measures, priests while saying Mass often had to hide their identity out of fear that an informer would betray them to the authorities. Nuns were ordered by the government to marry or leave Ireland.[ii]

---

[i] "We live, for the most part, in the mountains and forests and often too in the midst of bogs to escape the heretic English. Catholics flock to us, who we refresh by the word of God and consolation of the Sacraments; here in these wild mountain tracts, we preach to them constancy in faith, and the mysteries of the Cross of our Lord: here we find true worshippers of God and champions of Christ. In spite of all the precautions used to exercise our evangelical ministry in secret, the Cromwellians often discover it; and the wild beast was never hunted with more fury than the priest." – Fr. Thomas Quinn

[ii] "In the year 1649, there were in Ireland 23 bishops and four archbishops. In the cathderals there were as usual, canons and dignitaries; the parishes had pastors, a great number of priests and numerous convents of regulars. But after Cromwell had attained to supreme power, all were scattered. Over 300 were

Chapter 25

"To Hell or Connacht"

Transport! Transplant! My ears are deafened by English
Shoot him, kill him, strip him, tear him
A Torie, hack him, hang him, rebel,
A rogue, a thief, a priest, a papist.

Written in 1657 by Eamonn Mac Donnchadh

"I live a banished man within the bounds of my native soil; a spectator of others enriched by my birthright; an object of condoling to my relations and friends and a condoler of their miseries." - Roderick O'Flaherty (17th century Irish Poet)

"The sword of extermination had passed over the land, and the soldiers sat down to banquet on the hereditary possessions of the natives." –Irish historian, John Curry

---

put to death, 1,000 more driven into exile. Four bishops were slain, the others obliged to fly to foreign countries except the Bishop of Kilmore who was too feeble to be removed. In 1641, there were in Ireland 43 Houses of the Dominican Order and 600 religious. Ten years after, there was not a single house in their possession, and three-fourths of the religious were dead or in exile." – Burke in *"Hibernia Dominicana"*

"When victory was complete a deliberate plan was drawn up to destroy the Irish as a people" English historian - Hilaire Belloc

Ireland "…was the great capital out of which the Cromwellian government paid all debts, rewarded all services, and performed all acts of bounty" - Lord Claredon

Ireland at the End of War

As the Cromwellian conquest drew to a conclusion, it was plain enough to all how much the Irish people had suffered. One of Cromwell's officers, a Colonel Lawrence, who was a prominent officer of the rabid anti Catholic "Jesus and No Quarter" party, wrote in his memoirs; "About the year 1652 and 1653, the plague and famine had so swept away whole countries, that a man might travel twenty or thirty miles and not see a living creature…and when we did meet with two or three poor cabins, none but very aged men, with women and children…I have seen those miserable creatures plucking stinking carrion out of a ditch, black and rotten…"[315]

At wars end, the Physician General of Cromwell's army, Dr. William Petty (founder of the Lansdowne family) reckoned that the population of Ireland had in the eleven years between 1641 and 1652 been reduced by 616,000, of which 504,000 were native Irish. According to Petty, the native Irish were: "…wasted by the sword, plague, famine, hardships, and banishment…as for the bloodshed God knows best who did occasion it…"[316]

Some years later he altered his reckoning, estimating that the population had fallen by a further 140,000 people, as 100,000 men, women and children had been transported as slaves to Barbados and other colonies and a further 40,000 men had left Ireland to serve in foreign armies.

Cromwell's "Act of Grace" for Ireland

On August 12th 1652, an Act of Pardon following the war was passed in the English House of Commons. It was not really an act of Pardon at all as it was granted only to "all husbandmen and others of the inferior sort not possessed of lands or goods exceeding the value of £10"[317] but rather an act to make legal the mass robbery of Irish land.

After the Act pardoned those who had little or nothing, the Irish, Old English and Royalists were divided into a number of groups, all of whom would be treated slightly differently.

The first grouping was comprised of the largest landowners and Catholic clergy, all of whom were exempt from pardon, and as such their lives and estates were forfeit to the English government. A second grouping was all officers in the Royalist army. These men were to be banished and have two thirds of their land seized while the remaining one third was to be left in the possession of their families. A further grouping was composed of those not included in the first two. This category was described as those who opposed parliament but "might be found worthy of mercy".[318] They were to have two thirds of their lands appropriated from them, and were to be transplanted to a different part of the country where they would receive the equivalent of one third of their land: "wherever parliament might choose to allot it to them."[319] The final grouping were those who had taken no part whatsoever in the war but had not shown their "constant good affection"[320] to parliament. They were to have they their estates appropriated while receiving the equivalent of two thirds back wherever parliament decided. In essence all the Catholic landowners of Ireland were to have their ancestral land stolen from them.

In Ulster the robbery of King James was completed as the last of the native landowners were ordered on pain of death to depart their property, while in the rest of the country the work of the "Discoverers" was no longer required, for parliament had found a more effective instrument.

For those who had only part of their land stolen from them and wanted to receive back the remainder from the parliamentary commissioners, they were informed that they had to transplant themselves beyond the Shannon where they would be given back waste tracts of land in the province of Connacht or Clare, this being the most infertile land in Ireland, while the good land of Connacht remained with the government. All those departing were obliged to sign a declaration that forbade them or their heirs from seeking to reclaim their land in the future.

The three provinces of Ulster, Leinster and Munster with the exception of Clare were to be reserved for Protestant landowners.

After May 1st 1654 any former Catholic landowner who had not moved beyond the River Shannon, could, if not in the possession of the appropriate documentation, be killed by anyone without any form of trial or the order of a Judge.

In the town of Athlone which was partly built on the west side of the River Shannon, in the province of Connacht (Roscommon) many banished natives had erected small cabins and were eking out an existence on the outskirts of the town. The authorities now issued a further decree which forbade "all the Irish and other popish persons" from residing within fives miles of the town. In addition to this no Irish person was allowed to reside within two miles of the River Shannon for its entire length, within four miles of the sea (which denied the native population the right to fish) or in any city or town.

Those who moved beyond the River Shannon faced an extremely bleak future, for they had to depart with little that might assist them in their attempts to survive. Many of them especially the very young or old died from deprivation.

The first of the banished were ordered to go to the Burren in Co. Clare. One of Cromwell's commissioners wrote of the area that there was not "...water enough to drown a man, trees enough to hang a man or earth enough to bury a man..."[321] Even the system of assigning allotments to the "transplanted" was corrupt as much land earmarked for the transplanted was retained by the commissioners for their own benefit: "...Coles, Binghams, Kings, Gores and Lloyds who would do nothing except for money..."[322]

The Down Survey

As the mass expulsions and grand larceny got under way, Dr. William Petty was ordered to undertake a land survey of the entire country so that it could be distributed to parliament's debtors and to the soldiers of the New Model Army who demanded payment for their years of service. This survey became known as the "Down Survey" or the "Down Admeasurement" as Petty measured and wrote "down" his findings.

William Petty

Petty estimated the surface of the country to be 10,500,000 plantation acres (a plantation acre being roughly half of an English acre) of which 7,500,000 was arable land, the rest being waste or bogland. As of 1641, 5,200,000 acres of this arable land was in the hands of Catholics and separated Protestants, 2,000,000 acres was held by Planters and 300,000 acres by the Protestant Church. Of this land 5,000,000 acres could be safely appropriated, an amount which would adequately satisfy Parliament's needs and leave a surplus in the possession of the government, which could be rented to

Protestants. Whilst undertaking his survey and attempting to map out various baronies and districts it was necessary for him to have some local knowledge and in some cases when this was lacking, members of his survey had to go to Connacht and bring back banished people from the district to answer questions regarding historical land boundaries.

The Division of the Irish Spoils

For those individuals and investors in the City of London who had "adventured" money to parliament, a lottery for the allocation of the stolen land was held in 1653 in The Grocer's Hall London. For their protection, the lands allotted to investors were interspersed with lands allotted as payment in kind to the soldiers of The New Model Army

For those who had advanced £200 to Parliament, they now received from the government a thousand acres of land in Ulster, for £300, a thousand acres in Connacht, for £450, a thousand acres in Munster, and for £600 a thousand acres in Leinster with mountains, bogs and woods being added to the award without extra charge. The highest value set on any one acre of land was four shillings, the lowest being one penny. Numbers of others who had adventured significantly more money received vast estates, notably Sir John Clotworthy (later Lord Massereene) who was awarded an estate of 107,611 acres, previously in the possession of the Catholic Chieftain of the Clan MacDonnell, Randall MacDonnell (Lord Antrim). The 300,000 acres that had previously been in the possession of the Protestant Church now became government property as Cromwell had disestablished the Protestant Church.

Although Cromwell's rule was not destined to be of a significant duration, the measures of his "Act of Grace" were long lasting and many remain with us to this day. With Catholics expelled, cities and towns became Protestant centres of commerce and English Lords and gentlemen the "owners" of the real estate. As "owners" of great estates, with Catholics as tenants, the Catholics were barred from hunting and fishing, with Ireland's rivers and lakes off-limits to them. One of the greatest consequences of the "Settlement" was the firm establishment of an English landlord class in Ireland which ultimately meant the throwing of an ever-tightening noose around the necks of their rack-rented Irish tenants.

The Irish Slaves

While the families of the soldiers who had served in the King's Army were allowed to retain some land, the families of the soldiers of the Catholic Confederacy were not. As a result, there were thousands of women and children without a home, reduced to a state of abject poverty. The war and despoliation had also left many people homeless and without a livelihood. The answer of the government to this problem was the shipping of the destitute to the "West Indies", where they would be put to work in the tobacco plantations. There was certainly no shortage of destitute in Ireland, but the number of those dispatched is uncertain. In Irish accounts and by the account of Dr. Petty estimates are as high as 100,000. As no one, no matter how destitute, was going to volunteer for transport to the iniquitous tobacco plantations, force was necessary to collect them and many women lost their children to the gangs that roamed the countryside in search of them.

In the environs of Galway, the governor of the city, Colonel Strubber, raided the homes of the Irish at night in order to procure slaves for the West Indies.[323]

Force was not the only tactic used. In order to lure the destitute the new administration employed secondary persons to lure the destitute together on the promise of the distribution of free food whereupon soldiers would surround such groups and capture them.

After Jamaica was conquered Cromwell enquired about the possibility of peopling the new colony with "a stock of Irish girls and young Irish men".[324] Dublin Castle replied; "Although we must use force in taking them up, yet it being so much for their own good, and likely to be of so great advantage to the public, it is not in the least doubted that you may have such a number of them as you think fit"[325]

Cromwell's Slaughter Houses

Following the war the English government established two forms of tribunals. The first type was a general tribunal for the punishment of "rebels and malignants", while the second tribunal was for the punishment of "all massacres or murders done or committed since the 1st day of February 1641". For both tribunals the normal laws of justice were laid to one side.

The General Tribunals were scheduled to be held in all the major towns of the country with the first one being held in Kilkenny on October 4th 1652. It was presided over by Justice Donnellan, who was assisted by Solicitor Cook (who had acted as solicitor for Parliament in the trial of King Charles I) and Reynolds the Commissary-General.

Due to the frequent nature with which the death penalty was imposed, these tribunals became known as "Cromwell's Slaughter Houses"

The following February, a special court for trying "all massacres and murders done or committed since the 1st October 1641" opened in Dublin, presided over by Lord Lowther. However it did not try all massacres and murders but only those of which Catholics (native Irish or Old English) were accused of.

Since 1641 the Irish had been accused of the most terrible massacres of Protestants amounting to the deaths of hundreds of thousands of people. In spite of the courts best efforts and much corrupt evidence only two hundred people were convicted. In the province of Ulster where most of the massacres of Protestants took place, only Sir Phelim O'Néill was found guilty. Condemned to be hung drawn and quartered, he was repeatedly offered clemency if he would only say that the "Commission from the King" which he himself had forged in 1641 was genuine, the last offer being made to him as he ascended the scaffold. The temptation to keep his life in exchange for a lie was refused and before he died he declared that: "the several outrages committed by my officers and soldiers in that war, contrary to my intention, now press my conscience very much"[326]

The Governance of Ireland under Cromwell

Four administrators, Jones, Ludlow, Corbett and Weaver joined Fleetwood who governed Ireland under Parliamentary instruction. Some of these instructions were "to endeavour the promulgation of the gospel and the power of true religion and holiness" and to "allow no Papist or delinquent to hold any place of trust, to practice as barrister or solicitor or to keep school for the education of youth".

Any person who was absent from Protestant worship on Sunday was liable to a fine of thirty pence. Furthermore, the magistrate could order their children to be removed and dispatched to England for "education". All persons over the age of twenty one could be offered the "Oath of Abjuration" being the renouncement of their Catholicism which if refused could result in their indefinite imprisonment and the forfeiture of their possessions.[i] When on December 16th 1653, Cromwell

---

[i] Cromwell's oath of abjuration was ordered to be "administered" to everyone over the age of 16. Any official who neglected it was punished; "Each justice of the peace who shall neglect his duty in fully carrying out this order will be fined £20; each parish clerk will be fined for a like neglect £10; each registrar of assizes for each person that he omits in the registry £20; and of all of these

dissolved parliament and took for himself the title of "Lord Protector", Ludlow resigned from the civil administration as a measure of his displeasure.

In 1655, Cromwell's second son, Henry, was appointed Governor of Ireland. He is recalled as being a mild mannered man, disposed to Justice, but he nevertheless followed the government's dictates. During his governance, the transfer of Irish youths to the tobacco plantations continued unabated, with a letter of his to secretary Thurloe surviving which reads in part "Concerning the young women,...it is not in the least doubted that you may such a number of as you shall think fit...I think it might be like advantage to your affairs there (London) and ours here (Dublin) if you should think fit to send 1,500 or 2,000 young boys to the place aforementioned (Barbados)."[327] In reply Secretary of Parliament Thurloe writes "The committee of the Council have voted two thousand girls and as many youths to be taken for that purpose." Regarding

---

fines, one half will be distributed to the poor of the parish, the other half to the accuser."
The penalty for refusal to take the oath was confiscation of two thirds of everything the person possessed *every time* the oath was presented and the person refused to take it. The oath was as follows; "I A.B, abhor, detest and abjure the authority of the Pope, as well in regard of the Church in general, as in regard of myself in particular. I condemn and anathematize the tenet that any reward is due to good works. I firmly believe and avow that no reverence is due to the Virgin Mary, or to any other saint in heaven; and that no petition or adoration can be addressed to them without idolatry. I assert that no worship or reverence is due to the Sacrament of the Lord's Supper, or to the elements of bread and wine after consecration, by whomsoever that consecration is made. I believe there is no purgatory, but that it is a Popish invention; so is also the tenet that the Pope can grant indulgences. I also firmly believe that neither the Pope nor any other priest, can remit sins as the Papists rave. And all this I swear without any gloss, equivocation, or mental reservation. So help me God."
In April 1658 Fr. Richard Shelton reported to Rome: "...every effort is being made to compel the Catholics by exile, imprisonment, confiscation of goods, and other penalties, to take the sacrilegious oath of abjuration, but all in vain, for as yet there has not been even one to take it..."

the young women it was necessary "for their own good" that they should be "not past breeding"[328]

While the despoliation of Ireland at the expense of the Irish people continued under Henry Cromwell's rule, efforts were made to tempt the New England settlers to settle in Ireland instead.

Chapter 26

The Return of the King

The Restoration

A "Fortunate Day"

In 1653, after dissolving the "long Parliament"[i] and taking complete control of the English government himself, Cromwell attempted different forms of both central and regional government in England none of which were to his satisfaction. In what proved to be his final effort in 1658, he summoned a parliament during the middle of January, only to dissolve it two weeks later declaring it all to have been "a waste of time".[329] Later that same year his health began to fail, and when his daughter Elizabeth died, his own decline accelerated. Oliver Cromwell died on September 3rd – a day of the year he had often proclaimed to be his "fortunate day". Whatever about being Cromwell's fortunate day, it was certainly a fortunate day for Ireland, as the brevity of Cromwell's despotic regime could only be in Ireland's interest.

---

[i] The Parliament which King Charles I had previously summoned had up to this point never been formally dissolved.

The Recall of the Monarch
After Oliver Cromwell's death, an effort was made to begin a dynastic succession, and his son Richard, (nicknamed "Tumbledown Dick" by his detractors) who was somewhat lacking in the fanaticism of his father succeeded him with the support of the army. However, it was really the army who governed the country and when Richard Cromwell called a parliament, the army dissolved it, calling a parliament more to its own liking instead.

Watching these events from the sidelines was the Duke of Albemarle, George Monck, the commander of the army in Scotland.

His soldiers were personally loyal to him, and when at the end of 1659 he decided to march on London to bring an end to military rule, his march turned into a mass movement of the population. When Monck and his army reached London events moved quickly. The navy declared their support for Monck, as did the local administration in London and also the new parliament when it convened. After an army revolt was quashed, Monck wrote to Charles II summoning him to return from exile.

To the plain man it appeared that the return of the King was in fact a restoration of the Monarchy, but it was in effect part I of the last act of the civil war – the partnership of Parliament and Crown.

Tinkering with Cromwell's Irish "Settlement"
Great Expectations
After Oliver Cromwell's death, the desire for the return of the King among the English did not go unnoticed by Cromwell's lieutenants in Ireland. Both Charles Coote and Roger Boyle were cunning enough to see what was coming and declared themselves in favour of the return of the monarchy at the decisive moment.

Upon his return to England, King Charles II took the advice given him by Lord Claredon; "Make much of your enemies, for your friends will do you no harm"[330]
After the restoration, the Duke of Ormond returned as Lord Lieutenant, while Coote was made Earl of Mountrath and Boyle, Earl of Ossory. Along with Sir Maurice Eustace, both Coote and Boyle were appointed as Lord Justices. Considering that both men were violently anti Catholic, and that Boyle had a hand in the devising of Cromwell's Irish policies, it did not bode well for the Irish.

King Charles II

There was relief among the dispossessed and banished Catholic landowners at the return of the King as it was widely felt that the King would ensure that justice would be done to those Catholic landowners who had fallen victim to the regime that had killed his father. Already in England, the Royalists were regaining their estates by unceremoniously evicting the roundhead usurpers but when a few Catholic landowners in Ireland tried to return to their estates, the full rigours of the laws were enforced against them and those who had stolen their lands remained in place.

Still, there was cause for hope, as in his first speech to the English parliament, the King addressed the Irish saying that "...we expect (of the Irish) that they will have a care for Our honour and of the promise that We have made to them..."[331] However the King's promises to the Irish, that he had made in 1648 were never to be referred to again. Thereafter the King dampened down any expectations of justice, afterwards telling Catholics; "My Justice I must afford to you all, but my favour must be given to my Protestant subjects"[332]

Another "Act of Settlement"

> "This caps all their tricks, this statute from overseas
> That lays the switch on the people of Heber the Fair;[i]
> A crooked deal has robbed us of our land
> And all our rights in Ireland are swept away"
>
> (Séafra Ó Donncadha   1620-1678)

In November of 1660, a royal declaration outlining a new Irish act of settlement was made. In the declaration, the treaty with and the alignment of the Confederacy to the cause of the Crown during the Irish war against Cromwell was set to one side and the Adventurer's Act of 1642 was declared to be still in force. This new "Act of Settlement" was to be nothing more than an adjustment of Cromwell's "Hell or Connacht" policy.The royal declaration, promised the dispossessed Catholic landowners that they would have their land restored to them if they had not taken up arms in 1641 or joined the Confederation of Kilkenny. Whilst this might have restored many to their possessions, there was a caveat in the declaration. Those Cromwellian Planters, Soldiers and City of London investors who had received the stolen lands could not be dispossessed unless there were given an equal amount of forfeited land somewhere else. Naturally there was not enough land in Ireland to enact this measure in any meaningful way, and so very few of the Catholics got any land

---

[i] Heber the Fair was one of the sons of Milesius of Spain. It was believed that Herber and his brothers had originally settled Ireland with their families with Herber becoming the first King of Ireland.

back with those that did being in the main the "Old English". That the measure was designed this way was parliament's method of protecting England's powerful moneyed interests among the aristocracy and in the City of London, for it was the City of London who had adventured most of the money for Cromwell's wars, and had also lent vast sums to the Planters who had used the stolen lands as security for their loans. In the face of this, giving justice to the Irish Catholics did not enter the equation.Naturally there were those who the King would not allow to be overlooked and the adjustment favoured many who had accompanied and served the King while in exile. These were known as "Ensign men", but even of these, some Catholics among them received nothing. Others favoured by the new settlement included peers such as O'Brien of Inchiquin and the Scottish MacDonnell of Antrim who was restored in spite of the vociferous opposition of Ormond. It was particularly galling to the dispossessed when King Charles II awarded 120,000 acres in Tipperary to his brother James who was Duke of York.

A "Court of Claims" was also set up to adjudicate on all other cases, but the English Judges were too honest and in almost every case they found in favour of the dispossessed Catholics. Out of two hundred cases in the first sitting only nineteen were refused. Cromwell's Planters and soldiers were beginning to get edgy, but they had no need to worry as the caveat protecting both the Protestant and moneyed interest would shortly come into play. Under pressure from the English Parliament and aristocracy, who in the main hated to see even one Catholic get his land restored to him, Ormond dissolved the Court of Claims in 1667.

When the court wound up its proceedings around five thousand[i] native landowners were left without their land, and as they were excluded from both Parliament and Council there was nothing they could do except continue their lives in poverty. Of the four provinces, Gaelic Ulster suffered the most. In Ulster not one Gaelic landowner had his land restored to him. In fact the return of the monarchy heralded a mass influx of Scottish Presbyterians colonists into Ulster with around 80,000 arriving in the year 1672 alone.[333]
Fifteen years after the restoration of the monarchy Dr. William Petty reckoned that in Ireland Roman Catholics possessed one third of the land that they had possessed in 1641.

The Re-establishment of Anglicanism
The return of the Established Church and Parliament
During Cromwell's rule the Anglican Church had been disestablished and this was one of the first measures to be reversed on the return of the King. In January 1661 a mass ceremony for the appointment of Protestant bishops took place in St. Patrick's Cathedral, Dublin. Whereas Cromwell had not persecuted any but the Catholics, from now on only Anglicanism would be officially recognized by the state meaning that depending on the whim of the government, Protestant dissenters could be subjected to some form of persecution.

On May 8th the first Irish Parliament since the restoration assembled in Dublin. Although there was no official law in force barring Catholics, they were in effect barred as both speakers, Sir Audley Mervin in the Commons and Archbishop

---

[i] In a letter from Dublin dated June 23rd 1686 Chief Justice Nugent wrote "...there are 5,000 in this kingdome who were never outlawed, and out of theyre estates, yet cannot now by law be restored"

Bramhall in the Lords, insisted that the Oath of Supremacy was now in force thereby excluding them.

The Persecution of Presbyterians
Following the official re-establishment of the Anglican state church, an Act of Uniformity for the Protestants was passed, a measure that was to severely impact on the Presbyterian Planters in Ulster. Many ministers were dismissed as they were found to be not in accord with the established church. All the dismissed pastors lost the houses that were provided for them by the government, while some were fined, jailed or banished. For the ordinary Presbyterians the practice of Presbyterianism had to move underground for a time until they began to be tolerated after the initial persecution. The result of the persecution was that many Presbyterians left Scotland and Ulster for the new plantations in North America.

The Execution of Archbishop Oliver Plunkett
The Rise of Anti-Catholic Sentiment
Since the return of the monarchy, the level of persecution against Catholics both in Britain and Ireland had relaxed. As England was at war with Holland, King Charles II felt that it was an opportune moment to promote a greater toleration of Catholics so as to create greater national unity, but when he broached the idea parliament would not hear of it. In fact, so violent was Parliament's enmity that the very idea of a greater toleration seemed to promote even more strident anti Catholic rhetoric in both the Commons and the Lords that found its echo in the population.
In the midst of this the King appointed the unscrupulous Parliamentarian Ashley Cooper (Earl of Shaftesbury) as Chancellor as a means to quell parliamentary dissent, but in spite of this, Cooper remained violently anti Catholic and was dismissed from his post after he openly opposed the King. As

a result of this episode, the King made for himself a dangerous enemy.[i]

The Titus Oates Plot

A plot was now formed by the King's enemies, the aim of the plot being to increase anti Catholic sentiment to violent levels, following the manner of the Babington plot in the reign of Elizabeth. Titus Oates, "an accomplished villain"[334] was the front man of the plot and it is widely believed that Cooper was the prime mover although there is no hard evidence to support this. Certainly, once the initial accusations were made by Oates, Cooper became the most vociferous in their repetition, whipping up the whole tissue of lies to dizzy heights.

Archbishop Plunkett

During the middle of August 1678, King Charles received news that there was a plot to kill him. Oates, as the bearer of the tidings, was then questioned by the Council in London, and afterwards by a magistrate, by the name of Sir Edmund Berry Godfrey. Oates swore that he knew of a Jesuit plot to kill the King, and others, and that the aim of the plot was the re-establishment of Catholicism in England. According to Oates,

---

[i] Cooper was no stranger to treachery. After being made a Colonel by Charles I, he deserted to the forces of parliament, then as a member of the Cromwellian council he abandoned the government in favour of the monarchy. Following the restoration, during court proceedings he condemned some of his former friends resulting in their deaths.

Ireland was destined to play a significant part in the scheme. Shortly afterwards, on October 7th 1678, Berry Godfrey was mysteriously found dead.

The cry went up from Cooper and others that the Catholics were guilty of his death, and the story of the plot along with the prevalent anti-Catholicism gave way to a crescendo of hysteria. The Queen, who was Catholic, was now accused of plotting to kill the King. Another witness was believed when he gave evidence that an armada from Spain, whose ships were full of monks was on its way to invade England. Two thousand Catholics were imprisoned and 30,000 Catholics, who refused to renounce their Catholicism were expelled from London.

The Effects of the Plot in Ireland
When news of the Plot broke in Ireland, the country's Catholic Primate, Archbishop Oliver Plunkett and the country's clergy and faithful braced themselves for the persecution which they knew must surely follow. In October, Lord Lieutenant Ormond issued a Proclamation commanding all Catholic clergy exercising ecclesiastical jurisdiction to leave Ireland before November 20th 1678. The first to fall foul of the order was the Vicar Apostolic of Raphoe and Derry, Fr. Luke Plunkett, who was arrested before the end of November and an order for his transportation was executed. Shortly afterwards the Archbishop of Dublin, Peter Talbot was arrested in Maynooth, at the home of his brother Colonel Richard Talbot and transferred to Dublin Castle in a chair as he was very sick and infirm. Upon hearing this news, Archbishop Plunkett went into hiding at once, whilst doing his utmost to continue his duties as Primate. On the day by which all Bishops and priests in authority were supposed to have left the country, a further proclamation was issued barring Catholics from any town where there was an army post, while rewards were

offered; £15 for the arrest of a bishop or Jesuit, £10 for information regarding any army officer who had attended Mass since taking the Oath of Supremacy, and lesser rewards for information regarding the attendance at Mass of other army ranks.

As rumour followed rumour further measures were introduced including the banishment of any parish priest in whose parish a robbery or murder was committed except if the perpetrator had been killed or arrested.

On December 6th 1679, Archbishop Plunkett was tracked down to the cabin where he was living and arrested. News of the Archbishop's arrest greatly encouraged the Plot party in London and an intimate of Shaftesbury's, named Hetherington was dispatched to Ireland to try and make a good case against him.

In Dublin Hetherington found helpers in high places, including the rabid anti Catholic Bishop Jones of Meath. Jones helped Hetherington locate "witnesses" against Archbishop Plunkett in Dublin's jails and Lord Deputy Ormond arranged pardons for them after Hetherington had made deals with them. Of the criminals who were destined to give false evidence Ormond later wrote "They went out of Ireland with bad English and worse clothes and are returned well bred gentlemen, well-caroneted, periwigged and clothed"[335]

Among the willing accomplices Hetherington located with Jones's help were two apostate Franciscan monks named Duffy and McMoyer who had previously been disciplined by Archbishop Plunkett because of their vices. Both men indicated their willingness to make false and treasonous accusations against the Archbishop in return for freedom and gold.

The Trial of Archbishop Oliver Plunkett

As Hetherington felt that a trial against Plunkett would not succeed in Ireland, he had the Archbishop transferred to Newgate Prison outside London in October 1680, where "for six months, no Christian came near him, nor did he know how things stood in the world".

It was in London in June 1681 that the impossible charges and the false evidence were laid against him before an English court. Amongst other things, Archbishop Plunkett was accused of plotting to raise an army of 70,000 men, and of planning to bring 40,000 French soldiers into Ireland who were apparently going to come ashore in the village of Carlingford. Such was the evidence of the "witnesses".

Six of the most eminent English lawyers were his accusers while Plunkett was not allowed any defence attorney. Before the trial he had obtained some time to bring his own witnesses to London, but the time allocated fell far short of what was needed and so his witnesses were still on their way to London when his trial commenced.

When the trial was complete the jury deliberated for 15 minutes before finding the Archbishop guilty. The Chief Justice then addressed Archbishop Plunkett: "Look you, Mr. Plunkett, you have been indicted of a very great and heinous crime...The bottom of your treason was your setting up your false religion than which there is not anything more displeasing to God or more pernicious to mankind...a religion that is ten times worse than all the heathenish superstition"[336]

As it was blatantly obvious to all that a serious miscarriage of Justice was in progress, the Earl of Essex went to King Charles II to apply for a pardon telling him "Your Highness ...the witnesses must needs be perjured as what they swore could not possibly be true" to which the King replied; "Why did you not then declare this at his trial? I dare pardon nobody...His blood be upon your head and not upon mine"[337]

Archbishop Plunkett was sentenced to be hung drawn and quartered. The butchering of this innocent prelate was carried out on July 1st 1681 at Tyburn. For his work in uncovering the "plot" Oates received a pension of £1,200 per year but the pension was withdrawn in the reign of James II and he was sentenced to be flogged. However the pension was restored to one third of its previous level during the reign of William and Mary.

The Catholic King

The Change of Monarch

In the wake of the Titus Oates plot, toleration for Catholics returned and by 1685 King Charles II was enjoying some respite from attack by his enemies. On Monday February 2nd 1685, he fell seriously ill and by the 5th he was near death. As he lay dying his brother James asked him if he would like to see a Catholic priest. "Yes, with all my heart"[338] he replied after which the Queen's chaplain was summoned. By noon on the 6th he was dead.

King James II

Even though he was a Catholic, James assumed the throne without fuss by issuing a proclamation that he would support the established institutions as he found them. However it was not long before King James's attendance at Mass in the Queen's chapel was the subject of denunciation from the Protestant pulpits.

Growing Disquiet over King James's Catholicism

James hoped, that with the help of parliament, he would usher in an era where all those in the nation, whether they be Protestant or Catholic, would be allowed to live their lives freely and openly and that the result would be the tranquillity of the Kingdom under a popular monarchy. However, his efforts in this regard were rejected by most of the wealthy merchants and aristocrats who saw in his every move the advancement of Catholics. Two issues greatly enflamed the situation. The first of these was when the King tried to ensure that it would be possible for Catholics to obtain degrees from the universities and then secondly was his efforts to repeal the "Test Act" whereby those in public service and the army were required to take an oath denying the Catholic doctrine of Transubstantiation. However those opposed to the King seemed prepared to wait out his reign, sure in the knowledge, that James's Catholic Queen, Mary of Modena, (James's second wife) could not bear children, while his two daughters from his first marriage were staunch Protestants, Mary, who was married to William III of Orange (Holland), and Anne who was married to the Prince George of Denmark.

King James II – The Hope of Catholic Ireland

When James was crowned King, the Catholics of Ireland rejoiced, hoping that with a Catholic on the throne of England they might see some justice. Since 1641 the native Irish had lost almost all their land and whatever rights had remained to them. Now dispossessed they laboured as tenants-at-will under English landlords, who did not have the same restrictions imposed upon them as landlords in England did. Living in chimney-less hovels[i] and struggling to pay their

---

[i] In 1675, Dr. William Petty wrote that of the 184,000 homes recorded in his latest survey, only 24,000 had at least one chimney.

rents, they had resorted to a cheap root vegetable called the potato that grew easily in the Irish soil as their source of food. While they had suffered a violent religious persecution under Cromwell, things had improved upon the return of the monarchy but the practice of their faith remained greatly restricted.

Richard Talbot – Lord Lieutenant of Ireland

Since the return of the monarchy, the Catholic and Royalist officer Colonel Richard Talbot had acted for the Irish Catholic interest in London, on one ocassion being barred from the Royal Court as it was felt that he was having too much influence on King Charles II. A devout and zealous Catholic, he has been accused of putting his heart before his head resulting on occasion in imprudent decisions.

When James became King, Talbot was given the title "Earl of Tyrconnell" and newly promoted to Lieutenant General, he was dispatched to Ireland to take command of the army. Ormond had previously created a huge Protestant militia, but Talbot using many of the available Catholic gentry as officers created a permanent army. Talbot was quite definite in his aim – as Ireland was over 80% Catholic he wanted to restore Catholics to as many official positions as possible and also to fully repeal "The Act of Settlement". If Scotland was allowed to have

Richard Talbot

Presbyterianism as its state religion, why then should Ireland not be allowed to have Catholicism? King James had appointed his brother in law, Lord Claredon as Viceroy but Talbot felt that Ireland would do much better with a Catholic Viceroy stating that "Ireland is in a better way of thriving under the influence of a native governor than under any stranger to us and our country."[339] As King James continued to try and create a level playing field for the Catholics, Lord Claredon became more than uneasy. When Catholics were appointed to numerous civil bodies including town corporations and made sheriffs of most counties, Claredon indicated his unwillingness to co-operate any further and King James II recalled him. To say that there was Catholic delight and Protestant dismay when Richard Talbot was appointed to succeed him would put it mildly. As Lord Lieutenant, Talbot accelerated the introduction of further measures to restore Catholicism. In every court, two out of three judges were Catholic appointees while a large number of Catholics were appointed to the council of government.

The "Glorious Revolution" and the End of English Monarchical Rule

The Declaration of Indulgence

When King James published his "Declaration of Indulgence" in 1687, and again in 1688, establishing equality for all before the law irrespective of their creed and forbidding persecution on account of religious belief, the measure provoked a revolt among many of the Protestant Bishops of England who refused to read out the edict in their churches. The affair greatly excited the population against Catholics and by rhetoric and sermons the population were encouraged to believe that a plot was afoot to compel Protestants to become Catholics.

Already there was contact between the gentry, (who wanted to see the end of the monarchy except as a figurehead) and

Princess Mary's husband – William Henry Nassau, Prince of Orange (Holland). This contact changed to intrigue against the King when it was announced that his wife, Queen Mary was pregnant, as now there was the danger of a Catholic dynasty in England which the plotters insisted must be averted at all costs.

When Queen Mary gave birth to a son on June 10th 1688, William of Orange sent over an envoy called Zuylestein, apparently to offer congratulations on his and Mary's behalf on the birth of a male heir. In reality the real mission of Zuylestein's visit was to meet secretly with the intriguers[i] and make plans with them preparatory to a landing in England by William of Orange and his army.

As William prepared to invade England, King Louis XIV of France warned James II of the danger and promised him the assistance of the French fleet, but James who did not want to seem beholden to a foreign power refused, thus sealing his own fate.

The Arrival in England of William of Orange

William embarked for his invasion of England with 16,000 French, Dutch and German mercenaries, swearing that he did not intend to dethrone James and promising that in England he would do all he could for the freedom of the Catholics. On November 5th 1688 William's fleet landed at Torbay in Devon. King James was now surrounded on all sides by treachery. His ministers swore loyalty to him and the bishops loudly prayed for him but most were now secretly acting against him. His army vastly outnumbered the invaders but his officers led by Churchill who had only just sworn particular loyalty to him

---

[i] The leaders of the plot were; Lumley, Sidney, Compton, Danby, Devonshire, Shrewsbury and Russell.

largely deserted him Retreating to London ahead of William's army, King James was finally captured there on December 17th but succeeded in escaping from his imprisonment on the 19th after which he travelled to France. On assuming the English crown, (the flight of James being ruled by parliament as an abdication) William and Mary accepted the role of Parliamentary monarchs as presented to them by the aristocrats who had driven out James. Called the "Revolutionary Settlement", it passed all power into the hands of Parliament and its allies.

For the Catholics it was a disaster as power now passed completely into the hands of a parliament which was violently anti-Catholic. It was scene II of the closing act of the English civil war as Parliament now reigned supreme.[i]

---

[i] It is one of the lies of history that the "Glorious Revolution" of 1688 enshrined "civil and religious liberty for all" as it was instead a revolution that enshrined exclusion for Catholics.

Chapter 27

The Catholic Rearguard

Ireland Prepares for War

False Rumours

It should have been obvious to the English government that Tyrconnell and Ireland would fight for the usurped Catholic King but William of Orange received counsel from some of his English advisors, most notably John Temple, that Tyrconnell would not fight and so delayed any action while contacts were being made with Tyrconnell. When Temple realised his grave error he drowned himself.

While William had promised freedom for the Catholics, Tyrconnell was of the opinion that the English parliament would allow no such thing and was not prepared to entertain any other option than to defend Catholic Ireland and if necessary to put her under the protection of France. The interlude gave Tyrconnell time to raise a large army from among the Catholics of Ireland, with both native Irish and old English all rallying to the call, with many rallying to the call more in defence of their faith than in defence of King James II.

Once again munitions and the others materials of war were very much lacking and attempts were made to disarm all Protestants whom it was felt would not remain loyal to James II. While some Protestants left for England, many others went northwards with their weapons to join their brethren in Ulster who were already preparing for war. Unfounded and unchecked rumours now abounded among the Protestants that the Catholics were planning atrocities against them the most notable of these being an anonymous letter "found" lying on the street in Comber, Co. Down on the 3rd December 1688. The letter was addressed to Lord Mount Alexander and read in part; "Good my Lord, I have written to you to know that all our Irishmen through Ireland is sworn that on the ninth day of this month they are to fall onto and kill and murder man, wife and child..."[340]

The Apprentices Close Derry's Gates

Even as William of Orange was marching towards London with King James II in retreat ahead of him, Tyrconnell was endeavouring to ensure that all Irish garrison towns would continue being loyal to James II. Viscount Mounjoy who remained loyal to King James II (those who stayed loyal were called Jacobites) was in command of the Derry garrison whose soldiers were a mixed force of Catholics and Protestants. As Tyrconnell was dubious about the loyalty of Protestants to King James II, he ordered the entire regiment to leave Derry and march to Dublin to take up duty there, while MacDonnell, Earl of Antrim was ordered to take his regiment, consisting of Scottish Highland Catholics known as Redshanks into Derry to take up garrison duty. As Mountjoy's regiment departed Derry, Antrim's had not yet arrived and the city was left without a garrison. As MacDonnell and his regiment passed through the town of Limavaddy, about a day's march away from Derry, they encountered a certain Colonel Philips who quickly sent word on ahead to the city warning the city officials of the imminent arrival of the Catholic Lord Antrim and his Redshanks. As the Redshanks neared the city, Magistrates, Councillors and Protestant clergymen debated with each other as to what they should do. Citing the completely unfounded rumours of massacre including the Comber letter, the civilian administrators insisted that all Catholics should be kept out, but the Protestant clergymen took the opposite opinion insisting that James II was still King, and that being the case how could they keep a regiment of the King's soldiers from entering their garrison? The decision was taken not to hinder Antrim's men from entering the town.

Meanwhile numbers of the city's apprentices had already discussed the issue among themselves and decided to take the matter into their own hands. On December 7th 1688, taking the keys of the four city gates they closed and locked them thus keeping out Antrim and his men, a move which the city administration did nothing to counter. Finding he could not gain entry, and possessing only one regiment, Antrim did not have the strength to force his way in and so decided to go to Coleraine instead. Following on from this all Catholics were banished from the city and the mayor issued a proclamation against them which read in part; "...we have resolved to stand upon our guard and to defend our walls and not to admit of any papists whatsoever to quarter among us..."[341]

On hearing of what had befallen Antrim, Tyrconnell ordered Mountjoy to send back to Derry six companies of his regiment, half Protestant and half Catholic under the command of Lieutenant Colonel Lundy. When Lundy arrived he was only admitted on condition that all Catholics in his force were sent away. After complying he entered the city and assisted the Protestants in preparations for defence should Tyrconnell chose to try and take the city by force. The town of Enniskillen also followed suit, refusing to allow a regiment sent by Tyrconnell to enter the town. Aside from Carrickfergus and Charlemont Fort, the garrison towns of Ulster were now mostly in the hands of the Protestant supporters of William (Williamites). With Ulster defiantly refusing to acknowledge his authority, Tyrconnell felt he had no choice but to respond, and sent northwards an army of 2,500 men under Lieutenant General Richard Hamilton who successfully defeated a Williamite force at Dromore on March 14th 1689.

The decision to place Derry under siege was still some weeks away.

French Help for James II

In France, King Louis XIV saw the usurpation of James II as an opportunity. William of Orange was his enemy as were many other European leaders -all members of the "League of Augsburg", a league which included Pope Innocent XI who objected to French hegemony in Europe and particularly to Louis XIV as he had denied the right of the Holy See to have full control of the affairs of the Catholic Church in France.

For Louis XIV, James II was a tool that he could use to weaken the alliance of European leaders arrayed against him, for if he could manage to keep both William of Orange and England tied up in an Irish war so much the better for his military efforts against the league on the European mainland.

After a sojourn in France, James II landed at Kinsale harbour on March 12th 1689, bringing with him from France a large number of muskets, shot and gunpowder. Twelve hundred Irish and Anglo Irish exiles serving abroad also returned with King James. Those who disembarked included Patrick Sarsfield[i], John and Anthony Hamilton and Simon and Henry Luttrell. One hundred French officers also arrived including General DeRosen who was destined to act as second in command to Tyrconnell.

---

[i] An Irish hero, Patrick Sarsfield was descended on his father's side from an Anglo-Norman family of the Pale, while his mother was the daughter of the Gaelic patriot of 1641, Colonel Roger O'More. Sarsfield is seen as the epitome of the final union between the Gael and the Catholic Old English.

If Louis XIV really wanted to help James II defeat William, it was in fact a paltry contribution, for he could have sent over an army or deployed his overpowering naval strength to prevent William and his army from reaching Ireland. He had provided just enough help to ensure that William and his army would be kept busy for some time to come.

The Siege of Derry

Clearing the Passes

Upon his arrival in Dublin on March 24th, James II decided against Tyrconnell's advice that he should not to travel to Derrywas incorrect. James felt that if he as the rightful King appeared there, he would be able to bring the city to allegiance. As James II approached Derry two Jacobite forces under DeRosen and Hamilton cleared the way, DeRosen having victory at The Battle of Cladyford, while Hamilton had more difficulty at Castlefinn. The Passes being cleared, the Jacobites closed in on the city April 15th, but as they neared Derry, a Williamite convoy of ships led by HMS Swallow arrived in the city carrying troops and supplies.

"Lundy, The Traitor!"

Lundy, the city's military commander had been spooked by the defeat of his troops at "The Passes" and began to doubt if the city could hold out under siege. In secret talks with Colonels Cunningham and Richards, who had just arrived in the convoy it was agreed to abandon the city and not to unload the 1,500 soldiers who were in the troop transports. The local civilian leaders and military commanders, who had been kept in the dark about the negotiations only realised what was afoot as the ships prepared to depart. When the ships left Lundy was not aboard but remained in the city in hiding, afraid that if he showed himself, the local soldiers would lynch him. Heavily disguised he escaped the city a few days later, going to

Scotland. Henry Baker replaced Lundy as Derry's military commander, with the firebrand Protestant clergyman George Walker as his deputy.

James II at the Walls of Derry
When James II and his army arrived outside Derry, negotiations were arranged between the two sides in spite of the opposition of the townspeople but when DeRosen moved his men closer to the city than had been agreed to in the initial contacts, fire was opened on the Jacobite forces without warning from the city and a soldier standing next to James II was killed. As it was now blatantly obvious to James II that no talks would take place, he decided to return to Dublin after personally calling on those in the city to be loyal to him without any success. DeRosen accompanied the King while Hamilton stayed behind to keep the city under siege.

The Course of the Siege of Derry
As Hamilton possessed only some light artillery, taking Derry by storm was not an option. Hamilton decided the best course open to him was to blockade the city and try and forces its surrender through lack of food. Hamilton's humanity got the better of his strategy and he allowed all civilians who wanted to leave the city, do so unhindered, an action that probably ensured the failure of the siege as the food supply in the city would now last considerably longer.

The city's as hoc garrison was large, consisting of over 7,000 men and the besieged had considerably more artillery than the besiegers. Hamilton's army outside the walls also had to contend with a Williamite force under Colonel Wolseley that had been dispatched from Enniskillen and engaged in numerous nuisance attacks against the besiegers. This was a force comprising the menfolk of the Planter families in the Enniskillen area and also English mercenaries who were promised Jacobite gold for their service. The unit earned for itself a terrible reputation for war crimes, as it soldiers invariably took pity on no one so long as they were Catholic.

During April and May, sorties were made by both sides against the lines of their enemy with considerable loss of life, the largest being on April 24th, when around half of the troops in the city attacked the lines of their besiegers.

In Dublin James II was becoming impatient, and DeRosen, whom he had appointed as Marshal General of Ireland was sent back to Derry to try and bring the siege to a favourable conclusion. At Derry's walls DeRosen found only the same problems as the other commanders, lack of artillery and of the others weapons of war required. In a bid to reverse the effects of Hamilton's action in having let as many civilians as had wanted to leave the city, DeRosen ordered that all the Protestants that could be found were to be rounded up and brought outside the city gates to be left there without food or water. In a move that disgusted the Irish[342] he calculated that the city's defenders would not allow them to starve at the gates but would rather let them in to the city where the food stores would be used up more quickly. Three or four hundred Protestants were brought and abandoned outside the gates but the following day DeRosen's order was rescinded and the prisoners were let go after a gallows was erected atop the walls and a message was sent to DeRosen that unless the civilians were allowed to return to their homes all Jacobite prisoners held inside the city would be hanged. As the civilians departed, they were joined by many of the city's sick and elderly who had not left the city previously. When Hamilton reported the affair to James II, the episode greatly irritated him and he said of DeRosen that: "none but a barbarous Muscovite could have thought of so cruel a contrivance"[343.]

Along with the fact that DeRosen refused to give James II the extensive courtesy that he required as King this incident contributed to the souring of relations between DeRosen and King James II and by the following spring, James II had requested of King Louis that he be recalled to France.

The Breaking of the Siege

When the siege commenced, a boom to prevent the entrance of ships into Derry was pulled across the River Foyle, stretching from Culmore Fort on one side to a newly erected fort on the other. On June 13th a convoy of 30 ships arrived from England, under the command of Major General Kirke, and being unable to enter the city harbour took up a waiting position on Lough Foyle. By this time supplies of proper food in the city were dwindling and after all the horses had been used up domestic animals were used as a source of food. Dogs were being fattened on Jacobite corpses preparatory to their being slaughtered. As the shortage of food in the city reached a crisis near the end of July, Kirke at last decided to try and break through the boom. Four ships entered the river and while "Dartmouth" opened fire on the shore "Mountjoy" rammed the boom. Without any loss or much damage the boom was breached and the four ships arrived in the city and began unloading supplies.[i] Not having the military strength to storm the city, DeRosen immediately realised that the 105 day siege had failed and immediately prepared to decamp, a move that was completed by August 5th.

The "Patriot Parliament"

When James II had initially arrived in Dublin, he issued a number of decrees, one of which was the calling of an Irish Parliament. Called The Patriot Parliament it is either

---

[i] In the end the siege was broken with such ease that some historians have raised the possibility of the bribing of the Jacobite shore commanders by Kirke.

overlooked due to the brevity of Tyrconnell's administration, or unjustly criticised for what it sought to achieve.

It assembled on May 7th 1689, after James II returned from Derry and was to be the last time that Catholics would sit in a Dublin Parliament until the first Dáil in 1919. The Patriot Parliament was a true Home Rule Parliament, a representative body of the actual population of Ireland, consisting of members of many of the old Gaelic Irish, Gaelicised Normans and the Old English families. Most of its members were destined to meet an exiles death. Protestant bishops and Williamite loyalists were also called on to attend but only twelve chose to do so.

The parliament passed a good deal of legislation, establishing religious, judicial, legislative and commercial freedom for Ireland. Tithes were forbidden to be levied against any citizen in support of a church of which he was not a member. Poynings Law was repealed and appeals to the English parliament were forbidden.

With regard to property, the notorious Acts of Settlement were finally annulled and had there been a Jacobite victory in the war of the two kings, most Irish land would have to returned to the hands of its rightful owners. Henry Grattan, who was later responsible for the Home Rule Parliament of the unrepresentative Protestant Ascendancy in the late eighteenth century wrote of the parliament: "Though Papists, they were not slaves; they wrung a constitution from King James before they accompanied him to the field (of battle)"[344]

As many Protestants had already fled the country and their lands were vested in the crown, James II reluctantly gave way when a bill obliging them to return to Ireland within a limited time frame and prove their loyalty, or face the confiscation of the lands granted to them was proposed and later passed. Some of this land was to be set aside for the compensation of bona-fide landholders, who had purchased land during the time of Cromwell.

The Introduction of "Gun Money"

All the gold that could be availed of in Ireland (which was not much) was rounded up and kept for use so that war materials and stores could be purchased from abroad. A new coinage struck out of base metals (copper, brass, and pewter) was created, bearing James II's likeness and the royal inscription. This worthless currency was also inscribed with the year and month in which it entered circulation, the idea being that it would be withdrawn gradually after a Jacobite victory, when the correct gold and silver coinage would be introduced. Referred to as "gun-money" as some of it was made out of melted down obsolete cannon, it was only for domestic use in Ireland[i] and came with the promise that all would be put to rights after the Jacobite victory. It was very reluctantly received by the merchants who had no choice but to take it as

Halfcrown from February 1689

---

[i] The use of a base coinage in Ireland by English monarchs was nothing new. King Henry VIII introduced a law preventing the use in England of the base coinage he minted for Ireland while Queen Elizabeth's Irish shilling was valued by goldsmiths at twopence. The use of a base coinage by James II was, in the circumstances warranted. The most notorious case of base coinage was to occur during the reign of George I when "Wood's Halfpence" was introduced of which more will be told in Vol. II.

severe penalties were prescribed for anyone who refused to exchange it for commodities.

Confidence in this currency somewhat increased in January of 1691, when Tyrconnell returned from France with 18,000 gold pieces which were used to withdraw some of the base coinage from circulation.

Even before the end of the war William and Mary (or rather the English parliament) issued a proclamation declaring the coinage not to be legal tender so when the war ended all loss due to the use of this coinage fell on the Catholics of Ireland.

The Opening Phase of the Williamite War
Slaughter at Newtownbutler

As Derry was being relieved, a second Williamite victory occurred at the Battle of Newtownbutler on July 31st 1689, when the Planter force commanded by Colonel Wolseley (whose battle cry was "No Popery") encountered a Jacobite army commanded by Justin MacCarthy (Lord Mountcashel). The Enniskillen force was the same unit that had raided the besiegers of Derry, and they were a constant threat to any future Jacobite operations having been already involved in raiding Sligo, Clones and numerous isolated Jacobite positions. Already that morning Mountcashel had been defeated in a minor engagement near Lisnaskea and his dragoons were very much on the back foot as they were ordered to halt and face their pursuers at Newtownbutler. In the commotion an order "Right face" was given to face the enemy coming from the flank but was repeated by a subordinate as "right about face" (retreat) just as Wolseley attacked. A merciless slaughter of the Jacobites followed as Wolseley had ordered that no quarter be given and his men chased and killed the Jacobites during the rest of that day, that night and the following day with the Jacobite death toll being around 2,000. Many of Mountcashel's men fled towards the Erne, but were either drowned or hacked to death. Following the battle, Wolseley advanced as far as the Jacobite stronghold at Castle Saunderson (formerly Breifne Castle of the Clan O'Reilly) on the Fermanagh – Cavan border where the entire garrison was put to the sword.

Wolseley's breakthrough had other consequences for the Jacobites as it forced a withdrawal from Sligo of a small blocking force commanded by Patrick Sarsfield leaving north Connacht open. A more serious consequence was the fact that it left Ulster without a Jacobite army just as the Williamite Marshal Schomberg was preparing to land with his army.

Siege at Carrickfergus

On August 13th 1689 an unopposed Williamite seaborne landing was made at Bangor in Co. Down. In command of an army of 16,000 men, composed of English recruits, Hollanders, and French Huguenots was the octogenarian Marshal Schomberg who was General in Chief of Fredrick William of Brandenberg who was a member of the League of Augsburg.

After Schomberg's arrival the Enniskillen brigade came under his command. Chief among his objectives was the capture of the fort at Carrickfergus, a Jacobite stronghold under the command of Colonel Charles MacCarthy More. As the garrison refused to surrender, Schomberg began a siege which lasted until the strongholds gunpowder was almost exhausted (eight days) at which stage MacCarthy More successfully undertook negotiations with Schomberg which ended with the honourable surrender of the garrison just as the last barrel of gunpowder in the fortress ran out. As the Jacobites left the fortress with their families they were attacked by a Protestant mob. According to the Williamite Chaplain, Schomberg personally intervened being "...forced to ride in among them to keep the Irish from being murdered"[345]

Skirmishing in Dundalk

After taking Carrickfergus, Schomberg immediately moved south but was blocked in Dundalk on September 7th by a Jacobite army commanded by King James II who had kept for himself the role of Commander in Chief of his army. Schomberg had the misfortune to set up his encampment in the marshes on the edge of the town and when the weather turned very wet the whole encampment was flooded. Very soon a large number of his men fell sick with dysentery. Many fatalities due to illness followed both in Dundalk and in the Belfast infirmary to which the wounded were sent because of the unsanitary conditions there. Despite the poor weather it would have been an ideal opportunity for James II to launch an attack as Schomberg would have been in no position to respond effectively. Instead James chose to retreat to more comfortable winter quarters, a disastrous move, which allowed Schomberg to evacuate his army from the Dundalk Marshes.

The winter of 1689-90 was an opportunity lost for the Jacobites, as it was their last chance to make effective preparations before a vastly superior English army would strike them once the fighting season of 1690 opened but instead the winter passed in inactivity.

By February 1690, Schomberg had recovered his strength and having received supplies from England, his army was ready for battle. The same could not be said of the Jacobite army where almost everything, fodder for the horses, munitions, artillery and much else in the way of stores were in short supply.

The Battle of Cavan Town

As 1690 began almost the whole of Ulster was in the hands of Marshal Schomberg, the exception being Cavan town and the area of the county south of the town. As the most northerly town in Jacobite hands, Cavan was being used a staging post for the Jacobites for launching raids further north. In February 1690 Schomberg decided to neutralise it by dispatching the notorious Enniskillen brigade under Brigadier Wolseley to the town to destroy it. On learning of Schomberg's intentions, King James II sent an 800 strong blocking force consisting of soldiers from Longford and Westmeath commanded by Brigadier Nugent and another smaller force from Dublin under the command of his (illegitimate) son James Fitzjames, Duke of Berwick to Cavan, both units arriving in the town on February 10th, just ahead of Wolseley who was reported by a lookout to be advancing on the town from the direction of Belturbet on the morning of the 11th.

Marshal Schomberg

Fearing that Wolseley would try and take the town under siege, the Jacobites took up positions outside the town, but Wolseley successfully avoided them and after some skirmishing occupied the town himself. At the time, the streets of the town were divided by hedges and trees and Wolseley's men had excellent cover as the Jacobites, who attacked from the right and left, now sought to drive them out. Heavy fighting ensued but as the Jacobites were in the open and Wolseley's men were in cover, the Jacobites took heavy casualties and were finally forced to retire. Wolseley was well used to hit and run attacks and now saw his chance. The town was set ablaze from end to end and was completely destroyed with Wolseley's men retreating ahead of the flames after which they continued back towards Belturbet and onto Enniskillen.

Among the Jacobites, there were 200 dead including Brigadier Nugent, whose loss as a brave commander was very much regretted by his men. His Adjutant Captain Geoghegan was also killed. Wolseley's casualties were around 60 dead and 50 wounded.

The Siege of Charlemont Fort
In the same month of February 1690, Schomberg undertook a siege of the last significant Jacobite stronghold in mid Ulster – Charlemont Fort. Not unlike the siege of Carrickfergus, it's governor Teige O'Regan, refused to countenance surrender until the fortress's provisions were completely diminished almost two months later. The Fort's provisions had lasted so long because the soldiers had made do with very little while the bulk of the food was kept for the women and children. After negotiations took place in mid May, an honourable surrender was agreed to, after which 800 soldiers and 200 women and children left the Fort. Wolseley's Enniskillen regiment were at the scene, this time hurling abuse at and raining blows down on the Jacobite soldiers as they departed. Once more Schomberg intervened to save the prisoners and ordered that they be taken to Armagh and properly fed after noting their poor condition and that some of them were gnawing on horse-hide with hair attached.

The Battle of The Boyne
The Arrival of William of Orange in Ireland
With the fall of Charlemont, Ulster was now firmly under William's control and as Spring became Summer in 1690 he along with his many commanders both English and

continental[i] made the final preparations for the entry of his massive army into Ireland. A huge convoy, eighteen miles in length and consisting of 3,000 wagons made its way towards Chester where 300 ships were waiting to be loaded. This was no ordinary English army although there were many English in its ranks, it was rather an army of William's allies in the League of Augsburg being composed of Swedes, 6,000 Dutch, Prussians, Norweigians, Swiss and an army of 7,000 Danish infantry commanded by General Ernst Von Tettau. For Williams's purpose he preferred it that way, as many of the English, although Protestant still preferred to see James II on the throne, rather than a foreigner and William was suspect of their professed loyalty.

Leaving the port of Chester on June 11th 1690 the vast armada carrying 26,000 soldiers, hundreds of horses, powerful artillery and the necessary baggage and provisions arrived in Carrickfergus on the 14th, where William was met by Schomberg, in whose coach he journeyed into Belfast. His reception in Belfast was much warmer than when he had arrived in England. There the people had looked at him sullenly preferring an English Catholic as King to a foreign Protestant. In Belfast there were loud shouts of "Long live the Protestant King". At the welcoming ceremony in the city he received an address from the councillors urging him to "...pull the stiff neck of every papist down..."[346]

William was now in command of an immense army for along with the army of Schomberg and the Protestants in Ulster who had already taken up arms, the combined manpower of his force was over 40,000 men.

---

[i] Some of the notables who accompanied William of Orange to Ireland were Prince George of Denmark, the Duke of Wurtemburg and the Prince of Hesse-Darmstadt.

The Army of James II on the Eve of Battle

From the outset, James II's prospects of victory were poor in the extreme. Against a vastly superior foe, his army consisted in the main of recently recruited Irish footsoldiers, who although not lacking in bravery were inadequately trained, equipped and armed. So many of these units were raised without any possibility that they would be properly equipped that numbers of them were disbanded, being later formed into guerrilla units behind the Williamite lines where they attempted to disrupt the transport of supplies and also attacked enemy outposts armed only with pike and sword. These men were called "Raparees" by the English, the name being taken from the very name which the Irish had long used for the invaders themselves – "na rapairí" – meaning "plunderer" or "despoiler".

Certain sections of James II's army, especially his cavalry were admirable and equal to William's in all but manpower. The French Ambassador, Count Avaux, commented in his dispatches to France that: "...almost all the Irish gentlemen who have any military experience hold commissions in the cavalry, and by the exertions of these officers some regiments have been raised and disciplined... (and)... are equal to any I have seen...the inefficiency of the foot and of the dragoons is to be ascribed to the vices, not of the Irish character, but of the Irish administration"[347]

Aside from the Irish, James II had a contingent of Scottish Highlanders and a number of loyal Englishmen. This would have remained the case except that in March of 1690 at the behest of Tyrconnell, and with the agreement of the French, an exchange had taken place whereby Mountcashel's division had been sent to France in return for a well equipped French division under Count de Lauzun (who also took over from Avaux as Ambassador). Further equipment including 12 artillery pieces (James II's army had been devoid of artillery up to this point) had also been sent for the Irish, but the French Minister of War, Louvois, did not like James II and took care that only second rate material and low calibre artillery was dispatched. On the eve of battle it is reckoned that one third of the Jacobite foot-soldiers were not in possession of a musket, while a further one third possessed a musket which was unreliable.[348]

Lead-up to the Battle

When William landed at Carrickfergus on the 14th June 1690, James II prepared for immediate departure from Dublin. On June 16th, James II left Dublin with an army of 20,000 men and advanced to Dundalk where on June 22nd a strong reconnaissance force was dispatched northwards under the command of Colonel Dempsey. Around halfway between Dundalk and Newry this force lay in wait and intercepted a Williamite reconnaissance party of around 300. In the battle that followed the Williamite force suffered heavy casualties and prisoners were taken, with one of them, an English officer telling his captors that William had an army of 50,000 men. While James II proclaimed this number as being absurd, the following day he ordered his army to retreat to Ardee after which a further retreat behind the water barrier of the River Boyne was ordered as James had decided that it was here that his army would make their stand. His commanders and men were somewhat perturbed by his orders but James explained

William of Orange

that if he did not fight at the Boyne, then the English army would be able to enter Leinster unhindered. However, the summer of 1690 was especially dry and by July, the Boyne was not the barrier it might have been, and was fordable at many points.

The Jacobites set up their encampment at Donore with James II using a ruined church for his quarters. The centre point of the Jacobite line was Oldbridge, and positions were taken along the river, both towards Drogheda and inland but although the crossing point at Slane was brought to James II's attention, he dismissed it as being too far inland.

King William and his army arrived at the Boyne on June 29th, taking up excellent positions on the north side of the river. On William's approach his army was initially out of sight due to a receding plain uphill between the mountain ravines and the water. Artillery pieces were placed along the northern embankment and these artillery emplacements fired on the Jacobite army for long periods on the 30th.

As he prepared his battle plan, William and a group of officers were spotted close to the river and one of the few Jacobite artillery pieces – a six pounder, opened fire on the group. William was almost killed when the second ball fired from the gun grazed his shoulder causing a small flesh wound.

As William prepared to attack, James II, who was by far the poorer general, grew more and more nervous, even contemplating another retreat but finally deciding to stay once he assured himself that a way of escape was open. Of his twelve artillery pieces he ordered that six be sent back to Dublin (along with his baggage) presumably so that a secondary defensive position could be established should the Williamites break through and attempt to capture him. His complete lack of courage and will to fight, not to mention the sending away of the artillery cannot but have had a negative impact on his officers and men who could see that James II thought of nothing but the means to save his own skin. On the eve of battle, James II was once again advised of the danger of the unprotected crossing at Rosnaree, near Slane but he would only allow one regiment of dragoons commanded by Sir Niall O'Néill to leave and guard this River Boyne crossing four miles inland.

The Battle

July 1st 1690 (of the Julian calendar)[i] was a fine day. Early in the morning an exodus of around 10,000 troops commanded by Meinhardt Schomberg (son of Marshal Schomberg) took place from the Williamite encampment in the direction of Slane. When this movement was brought to the attention of James II, he realised his mistake in not having taken the advice of his generals to properly protect the Slane crossing. Now realising that he would be outflanked, he overreacted, and sent his entire left flank and part of his centre, including Lazun's French division and the six remaining artillery pieces to Rosnaree. Professing the belief that the main action must be here, James II followed after Lazun. At this point almost half of the Jacobite army had departed which was even better than what William intended, as his force heading for Slane was a diversionary attack intended to split the Jacobite army and when he saw the number of Jacobite soldiers departing what was to be the main field of battle he felt assured that victory would be his.[349] By 10am low tide had arrived and the main English army, with the elite Dutch Blue Guards in front, commenced crossing the river at the Oldbridge fording point while their artillery pounded the Jacobite army, who were now

---

[i] In 1582 Pope Gregory modified the ancient Julian calendar to correct the discrepancy between the Julian calendar and the solar year.
This new calendar (known as the "Gregorian Calendar") was adopted all over Europe, but seeing in it "a popish act"'" the English refused to adopt until finally accepting it in 1752.

totally bereft of artillery with which to disrupt the crossing. For nearly a mile of its course the Boyne was filled with thousands of Williamite soldiers, the water being so shallow, that the drums of the drummers did not get wet. Meanwhile the Williamite cavalry who could cross in higher water forded further downstream.

The Irish regiment defending the Oldbridge crossing were overwhelmed, and 150 of them were killed before the Jacobite Lieutenant General Hamilton who was in command of eight battalions reached them, and managed to scatter the Williamite infantry. Almost immediately the Williamite cavalry who had crossed upstream attacked them in the rear. The Irish cavalry now raced forward and the two opposing forces of cavalry crossed swords against each other while the Jacobite infantry withdrew a little to reform. An unequal combat now developed where time and again the Jacobite infantry attempted to stem the Williamite tide by one charge after another, while the Irish cavalry which was commanded by James II's son James FitzJames, Duke of Berwick[i] gave a good account of themselves by driving the Danish brigade and the Huguenot regiments back. Marshal Schomberg who was

---

[i] In his memoirs Berwick later wrote that his father had travelled towards Slane "...with the greater part of the army. Schomberg who remained opposite us attacked and took Oldbridge in spite of the resistance of the regiment which was stationed there, and which lost 150 men killed on the spot; whereupon Hamilton went down with the seven other battalions to expel the enemy. Two battalions of the Irish guards scattered them; but their cavalry having managed to pass at another ford, and proceeding to fall upon our infantry, I brought up our cavalry and thus enabled our battalions to retire; but we had then to commence a combat very unequal, both in the number of the squadrons, and in the nature of the ground, which was very much broken, and where the enemy had slipped in their infantry. Nevertheless, we charged again and again ten different times, and at length, the enemy, confounded by our boldness, halted and we reformed before them and marched at a slow pace to rejoin the King" – Translated from "Memoires du Maréchal de Berwick" – Vol 1-P70

watching on the north bank, saw the Huguenots fall back at which the eighty two year old raced into the water to rally them, just as a portion of the Irish cavalry attacked the Hugenot flank. The gallant Schomberg was killed[i] by a musket ball in the back of the neck fired by one of his own men.[350]

Around the same time, George Walker, the pastor who, by his speeches, had been so instrumental during the siege of Derry was shot dead in the middle of the ford as he rallied the Ulster Planters. On hearing of his death, which had occurred because he had deliberately put himself in harm's way, King William who had shortly before appointed him Protestant Bishop of Derry, replied "What brought him there then?"[351]

Retreat to Dublin

The crossing could not be stopped however and at length the Jacobite army now sought to extricate itself in good order which was fairly well achieved thanks to the cavalry who covered for the infantry as they withdrew leaving a force of Irish infantry, armed chiefly with the pike, as their rearguard to try and hold up their pursuers.

Meanwhile further inland the English army that had departed Drogheda that morning had split up. The cavalry successfully forced the crossing at Rosnaree despite a stout defence by Niall O'Néill, who was killed along with seventy of his men. At Slane itself, Williamite infantry and artillery under General Portland forded the river. When Lazun arrived he found the English army unable to travel towards Oldbridge due to a large area of bogland and so the two opposing armies took up positions on either side of the bog. Artillery was fired but no offensive action took place. When James II received word that the English army had crossed the Boyne he ordered Lazun's

---

[i] A pillar, 90 feet high was later erected in the River Boyne to mark the spot where Schomberg fell.

army to decamp and make for Duleek where they arrived in time to cover the retreating Jacobite infantry. At Duleek the Jacobite army once again formed up and the English army, by now in hot pursuit, was forced to call a halt. Shortly afterwards the Jacobite army resumed their retreat in good order as far as Naul in north county Dublin, where they took up positions for a last stand should William decide to attack once more. By now it was nine o' clock in the evening and the weary English were glad when they received the order to retire to Duleek.

Considering the differing strength of the two armies the losses of the day were remarkably similar. The Jacobites had lost around 1,000 men, including those left behind wounded and in the rearguard while the Williamite losses of dead and wounded were not far short of this number. According to a Dutch account the Jacobite soldiers who were left behind were cruelly treated by some of the Williamite soldiers.[352] The result of the day was an incomplete victory for William, who while now poised to take Dublin had not achieved a decisive defeat over his enemy.

While his army remained in the field at Naul, James II returned to Dublin along with some of the wounded and dead, making no mention to the government council of his own monumental tactical blunders, but rather blaming the Irish soldiers for his defeat. A well known anecdote recalls James II's return to Dublin where he is reputed to have met Lady Tyrconnell and told her "My troops have run away" to which she replied "If they have sire, your Majesty seems to have won the race"[353], while De Rosen (whom James II had wanted to return to France) told him "If your Majesty had a hundred kingdoms, he would lose them all"[354]

James II Leaves Ireland
On the following morning at 5am, after appointing Tyrconnell in command, James II left Dublin for Duncannon Fort in Wexford, taking two troops of cavalry with him. Both troops were left to guard the bridge at Bray in case the English army should send a strike force to follow him. From Duncannon he travelled by boat to Kinsale where he left for France aboard a French ship, arriving in Brest on July 20th.
The victory was seen in Europe as a defeat for Louis XIV of France and was greeted with joy in the capitals of the countries that belonged to the League of Augsburg but in Rome Pope, Alexander VIII, realising that fate of the Catholics of Ireland lay in the balance was anxious about the outcome of William's victory[355]
The opinion of the Jacobite General, Patrick Sarsfield, (whom James II later made "Earl of Lucan" in January 1691) was "Change but Kings and we will fight you over again"[356] This statement was a sure verdict on the poor generalship of James, compared to that of William which was anything but exemplary.[i]

"Enjoy the War for the Peace will be Terrible"

The Irish soldiers naturally greeted the news of King James II's flight with dismay, as when the commander flees it cannot but dishearten his men. Nevertheless it was determined that the fight should be continued, as for most of the men and commanders, the restoration of James II was not the only thing of importance. Fighting also for faith and fatherland, they well realised that surrender would mean that the usual acts of outlawry and attainder would follow, and most likely religious

---

[i] Following King James's cowardly conduct on the day of battle followed by his panicked retreat to Dublin and afterwards to France he received the igniminous nickname "Seamus an Chaca" or "James the Shit" from the Irish soldiers.

persecution since the English parliament would hardly permit King William to make a peace treaty that allowed for Catholic freedom. The determination of the Catholics to continue the fight was further reinforced when, following his arrival in Dublin, William issued a declaration excluding both Catholic gentry and Jacobite officers from any future act of pardon.
The same day that the King left, Tyrconnell decided to abandon Dublin and ordered all his senior officers to take their men to Limerick by whatever route they thought best. Fearful of persecution the Jacobite Governor of the city, Simon Luttrell evacuated the city along with a lot of the Catholics and the militia. The following Sunday, William of Orange, entered the city, where he was welcomed by the Protestants. Shunning the grand dining, the speeches and the state apartments in Dublin Castle, he returned to his military encampment at Finglas after attending a Protestant service.

The First Siege of Athlone
"I Will Defend Until I Eat My Old Boots!"
By the end of July the rest of the Jacobite garrisons in Leinster had either surrendered or abandoned their positions to go west. Athlone, which straddled the provinces of Leinster and Connacht remained in Irish hands, while the River Shannon was the Irish line of defence. King William now turned his attention to Limerick and Athlone, the two major strongholds which remained to the Jacobites. Travelling himself to Limerick he dispatched the Scottish General Douglas to Athlone, along with an army of 12,000 men, and a significant number of cannon and mortars with which to lay siege to the town's fortress. Arriving in Athlone on the 17th July, Douglas found that the Jacobite garrison under its commander Richard Grace had already abandoned the Leinster side of the town, and retreated to the west bank of the Shannon after ruining the bridge. Douglas sent an emissary under a flag of truce calling

on Grace to surrender but when he was taken to Grace, Grace fired a pistol over his head telling him "These are my terms; these only will I give or receive and when my provisions are consumed, I will defend until I eat my old boots"[357]

After this rebuff, Douglas immediately commenced bombarding King John's Castle and the Connacht side of the town, but after seven days he withdrew to Mullingar when he heard that Patrick Sarsfield was on his way to relieve Athlone.

General Douglas Massacres Irish Civilians

Travelling by a circuitous route around the Shannon through an area already occupied by the Williamites, Douglas headed for the south side of Limerick to link up with William. His journey to Limerick was marked by a trail of murder and destruction, as on his journey he rounded up and executed without ceremony both by hanging and by the sword, large numbers of civilians, who were taken both from their homes and from their work in the fields on the "assumption" that all of the Irish peasants were in some way involved with the Raparees. During the fourteen month war, almost two thousand civilians were killed in this way.[358]

The First Siege of Limerick

Limerick taken under siege by King William

The Fortress of Limerick now contained the bulk of the Jacobite army as the garrisons of many Leinster towns had collected there. Around 20,000 Irish foot soldiers, many without arms, were in the city while the Jacobite cavalry under their commander Brigadier General Patrick Sarsfield had set up their encampment to the north-west, just across the Clare border. The Governor of Limerick was a French officer named Boisseleau, who was an extremely able military tactician, well experienced in siege warfare and the construction of earthworks, trenches and barriers.

Just as William was marching towards the city, General Lauzun unilaterally decided to abandon the Jacobite cause. After declaring that Limerick's walls could be knocked with "roasted apples" Lauzun pulled his French division out of the city and marched to the Jacobite city of Galway from where he hoped to return to France. His actions were also designed to make Tyrconnell think twice about offering further resistance to the English army, for as far as Lauzun was concerned, his duty was to fight for James II, not the Catholic cause of the Irish, and with James II's departure for France, the Jacobite cause was lost.

After Lauzun's departure, an argument took place between Tirconnell and Sarsfield, regarding the ability of the Jacobite soldiers to defend Limerick. Tyrconnell doubted that the city could be held but Sarsfield insisted they should stand firm. In the end it was decided to defend the city.

On August 9^h, William of Orange, having earlier joined armies with those of Generals Douglas and Kirke, was at Singland on the south side of Limerick with almost 40,000 men. His army was in possession of some field artillery but his convoy of large calibre siege guns, ammunition and small boats had still not arrived.

"Sarsfield is the Man!"

The following day, August 10th, a French gunner in the English army deserted to the Jacobites and informed the Jacobite commanders of the imminent arrival of King William's siege artillery and equipment. On hearing this news Sarsfield immediately left Limerick and at his cavalry encampment enlisted 500 men for a special mission – to destroy the Williamite siege train. That same night with scouts ahead of him, Sarsfield and his men made their way eastwards through

Killaloe and on to Silvermines in Tipperary. His departure in great haste reached the ears of William by way of an informer called Manus O'Brien. Knowing that his siege train was in danger, William sent Sir John Lanier with 500 men, to get to the siege train before Sarsfield. Whereas Sarsfield had departed on his mission in great haste, Lanier took his time. By the time he left the Williamite encampment, he was almost twenty- four hours behind Sarsfield.

Patrick Sarsfield

As Lanier departed Singland, Sarsfield who had been guided through the mountains by a raparee known as "Galloping (Michael) Hogan" was closing in on the Williamite column which had halted for the night beside the ruins of Ballyneety Castle, close to the Tipperary border. Feeling secure in their encampment, the guard of the English soldiers was down. Hogan who now acted as a spy for Sarsfield, found a local woman who had sold apples to the encamped soldiers and she had overheard the password for the night, which was "Sarsfield". In the early hours of the morning of Tuesday August 12th 1690, Sarsfield and his men approached the encampment with Sarsfield in the lead. Asked for the password by the sentry, Sarsfield replied: "Sarsfield, is the word". As he continued into the encampment with his men, Sarsfield gave the signal: "Sarsfield is the man!" at which his men commenced their attack. The engagement that followed was short and one sided. Any Williamite soldier who resisted was cut down (about 60), while others, feeling that discretion was the better part of valour, managed to escape.

One soldier who was taken prisoner was promised his freedom in return for showing the Jacobite soldiers the workings of the gun mechanisms.

The siege cannon previously bound for Limerick now had their muzzles stuck in the earth after which they were charged with powder and fired, an action intended to tear open the barrels. Everything else in the encampment was destroyed before Sarsfield and his men undertook the circuitous journey back to Limerick.

The news of Sarsfield's escapade was received with great joy in Limerick and served as something of a tonic for the city's defenders. In the Williamite encampment the news caused consternation, but William was determined to remedy the situation as soon as possible. Knowing that Limerick's walls were fairly weak, he sent to Waterford for more artillery.

The Epic Defence of Limerick

The English army outside Limerick now began a steady program of artillery build up and emplacement, coupled with the neutralising of isolated Jacobite outposts. A system of trenches was also constructed which brought the besiegers very close to the city's wall. On August 24th, fire was opened on the besieged city from 36 cannon and four mortars and by the 27th a huge breach had made in the wall close to "St. John's Gate".

Behind the piles of masonry and stone, Boisseleau had constructed a trench behind which he had placed some artillery. Barricades had also been constructed in the streets.

William was now ready to undertake a massive assault on the city. The plan was set. At half past three in the afternoon, the storming party of 500 men would enter the breach, behind them there were ten thousand more to fill the shoes of the dead.

When the signal was given, five hundred Danish soldiers left their trenches and with grenade and musket in hand and stormed the breach while King watched with his staff from an artillery emplacement. Although expecting an attack, the Irish had no intelligence as to its time. As the assailants entered the breach, throwing their bombs, return fire erupted from the Irish positions, which momentarily slowed the attack. As the Williamite soldiers entered the town, those who were part of the defence party, but had not been on guard had by now grasped their weapons and the Williamite advantage was quickly lost in the face of a furious Irish defence. The hand to hand fighting just inside the city wall escalated as more and more soldiers from both sides rushed to join the desperate struggle that was now taking place. The citizens of Limerick, who doubtless, had both the massacres at Drogheda and Wexford in their minds, rushed to assist their soldiers. Of the women of Limerick, the Williamite chaplain, Rev. Story tells us that they: "…rushed boldly into the breach and stood nearer to the enemy than their own men, hurling stones and broken bottles…"[359] From atop the city walls a rain of projectiles also fell onto the heads of the attackers.

One of the Williamite units that followed the initial assault was the Brandenburg regiment, and they stormed forwards, successfully capturing an artillery emplacement known as "The Black Battery". Their success was short lived, for no sooner than they were in possession of the area than a huge mine was detonated. Rev Story writes that there were: "…men, faggots, stones and what not flying in the air with a most terrible noise…"[360]

The Williamite attack, coupled with the desperate defence, had continued for three hours when Colonel Talbot led an expedition of 500 Jacobite soldiers out of the city through one of the walls out-works and along the city wall to the opening through which the attack was made. The Williamite attackers now found themselves under attack from the rear but their rearward attackers were also attacked in turn when Colonel Cutts was sent forward by the Duke of Wurtemberg to repel them.

A huge plume of smoke reached out to the sky from the city in one continuous cloud. As nightfall beckoned the attack was finally called off. Of the aftermath in the Williamite line Rev Story writes "When our men drew off, some were brought up dead and some without a leg, others wanted arms, and some were blind with powder, especially a great many of the poor Brandenburghers looked like furies with the misfortune of gunpowder...the King stood nigh at Cromwell's Fort all the time, and the business being over, he went to his camp very much concerned, as indeed was the whole army; for you might have seen a mixture of anger and sorrow in everybody's countenance"[361.]

The End of the Siege

There is no great certainty with regard to the number of casualties suffered by the opposing armies during the attack of August 27th except that those of the English army were far greater than those of their enemy, reckoned to be around 3,000 dead and wounded against 500 for Limerick's defenders.

In the aftermath of this great effort by his army, not to mention the loss of some of his best troops, William could see no quick end to the siege and decided to lift it before the autumn rains raised the level of the River Shannon, which would turn the ground marshy and render his trenches un-usable. William was also doubtless aware that the English soldiers suffered terribly from sickness and disease if exposed to the winter weather – a fact illustrated all too recently by the army of Marshal Schomberg when they had wintered in Dundalk.

Another effort could have been made by the English army, before the autumn rains but the Ulster Protestants who had accompanied William to Limerick were very much against this fearing that a repeat of the defeat of August 27th might precipitate a nationwide Catholic uprising.

On August 31st, the English army marched away from Limerick's walls, with William making for Duncannon, in Co. Wexford to board ship for England. Before departing William placed Count de Solmes in command of the army, but he was shortly afterwards replaced with General Godert De Ginkell The end of the siege saw the arrival of French ships in Galway to take Marshal Lazun back to France with his division. Tyrconnell, departed with them so that he might give James II an update on the state of affairs in Ireland. Tyrconnell was by this stage not very popular among many of his officers because of his overbearing manner and his friendship with Lazun, while his pronounced Anglo Irish sympathies did not go down well with the native Irish. In his absence Brigadier Henry Luttrell along with some other officers attempted to increase bad feeling against him, but James II's son, the Duke of Berwick sent Luttrell to France on an errand to the court of his father to get him out of the way.

The Duke of Marlborough Captures Cork

Shortly after William left Ireland, The Duke of Marlborough, John Churchill, departed England with an army of 8,000 fresh men who landed near Cork at Passage West and afterwards joined up with 6,000 men of the Wurtemberg division. His objective was to capture Cork and Kinsale, thereby neutralising the two ports which the French would most likely use if landing further troops in Ireland. The garrison in Cork was completely unprepared for a siege, and had already been ordered to evacuate and move west into Kerry, but the City Governor, Lieutenant Colonel Mceligot had not yet done so. The siege began on September 24th and on the 27th, the Williamite artillery successfully breached the city's wall. The following day an assault was launched, led by the Duke of Grafton, Henry Fitzroy who was mortally wounded.

By this stage the city's garrison was down to two kegs of gunpowder, and Mceligot managed to call a truce for talks before the city fell at which he managed to achieve a surrender with terms. Despite surrendering on honourable terms whereby the citizens were not to be mistreated and the Jacobite prisoners were to be properly cared for, the English army sacked the place and terrorised the Catholics, before turning them out of the city. The Jacobite prisoners were stripped and kept under guard in a marsh without food for five days after which they were crammed into jails and churches where "...for want of sustenance and lying in their own excrements, with dead carcasses lying two whole weeks in the same place with them caused such infection that they dyed in great numbers daily"[362].

From Cork, Marlborough, who was anxious to achieve his objectives before winter began, quickly rushed to Kinsale. When he arrived the town was in flames, the garrison having retired to two forts outside the town. The old fort was captured on October 3rd with the new fort holding out until the 15th when they surrendered on condition that they were allowed to march to Limerick after which 1,200 marched out for the Jacobite headquarters.

The Second Siege of Athlone

The Arrival of The Marquis de St. Ruth

On May 8th 1691, a French fleet arrived in the Shannon, bringing war material to the Jacobite army, which was, since the departure of Lazun's division, almost completely composed of Irish soldiers. Following the battles of the previous year, war material, provisions and clothing were badly needed and by the Spring of 1691 the soldiers of the Jacobite army were dressed in rags, while muskets, gunpowder etc were (as usual) in short supply, not to mention decent provisions. There was no new French division aboard the ships, but there were three French generals; d'Usson, de Tessé and St. Ruth. Of these, Lieutenant General de St. Ruth (Charles Chalmont) was by far the most capable and experienced. St. Ruth was sent to take command of the Jacobite army and Tyrconnell had been instructed that regarding military matters, St. Ruth's decision was final.

While the Irish struggled to obtain even the most basic necessities of war, De Ginkell was meanwhile organising a massive army in Mullingar preparatory to launching his summer campaign. Huge amounts of money had been voted by the English parliament for the conduct of the war, and the latest models of artillery had been sent to Ireland along with new uniforms and equipment for the entire army.

The English army Advances on Athlone

By early June, De Ginkell was ready to commence his campaign, which was to see the return of the English army to the Jacobite town of Athlone. The town of Athlone is spread across the East and West bank of the River Shannon and was vitally important as it was the shortest gateway into Connacht. With an army of 11,000 men De Ginkell left Mullingar and set out for Ballymore, about a days march from Athlone where the most easterly Jacobite fortress was located, beside Lough Sewdy (called Lough Sunderlin in the Down Survey). Colonel Ulick Burke was the Jacobite commander of the castle and having only two small artillery pieces of Turkish origin, he was in no position to hold up the massive English army who arrived at Lough Sewdy on the 7th and commenced battering the castle with their heavy artillery. Col. Burke held out for a day, by which stage the castle was in ruins. DeGinkell stayed in Ballymore until he was joined by 7,000 foreign troops which were commanded by the Duke of Wurtemberg after which he marched on Athlone.

De Ginkell Enters the Town of Athlone

Arriving on the Leinster side of Athlone on the 19th June 1691, De Ginkell had his artillery quickly emplaced after which the bombardment on the town's walls commenced. The attack on the Leinster side of the town was of short duration as the town's walls were ancient and could not withstand De Ginkell's artillery. On the 20th, 4,000 men stormed through the broken walls while the remnants of the Jacobite garrison on the Leinster side of the town retreated ahead of them to the bridge over the River Shannon having already lost 200 of their number. As the Irishmen fought to hold the bridge, their comrades worked behind them in an attempt to destroy it. As two spans of the bridge teetered behind them, the Irish troops turned and ran, some not making it across as the bridge partially collapsed. The English now turned their fire on the Irish who had fallen into the waters of the Shannon but most succeeded in making the shore and safety.

At this stage St. Ruth was already on his way to Athlone with an army of around 15,000 men and upon arriving set up his encampment outside the town. The English meanwhile were busy emplacing their huge cannon after which the old King John's castle and the Connacht side of the town came under bombardment, the upper portion of the castle being almost destroyed. Siege mortars were also used, being filled with incendiary bombs called "carcasses" which were full of combustible materials, which easily ignited the thatched houses on the Connacht side of the town. Everything was levelled and there was no emplacement left standing from which the Irish could return fire. According to the Williamite chronicler, the Rev Story, the besiegers used 12,000 cannon balls, 600 bombs, tons of stones fired from the mortars and "nigh 50 tons of powder"³⁶³

"Are There Ten Men Who Will Die With Me For Ireland"?

DeGinkell's engineers, under cover of a massive artillery barrage began repairs on the bridge, throwing huge planks across the span until it was almost passable again. Realising the danger that now faced the Irish, Sergeant Custume asked for volunteers among his unit: "Are there ten men who will die with me for Ireland"?³⁶⁴ With his ten volunteers Custume dashed out under fire in an attempt to undo the work of Ginkel's engineers. As they attempted to once more wreck the bridge they were all killed, and a second group of volunteers rushed out to replace them and complete the work. Two men returned from the second group, but the bridge was once was once again impassable. De Ginkell was not to be outdone however, and once again a ferocious artillery fire was laid down on the Irish position to give his engineers a chance to commence repairs once more. De Ginkell also constructed a huge obstacle, referred to as a "gallery" whereby his men could work in safety while under fire but the Irish succeeded in setting it on fire.

Godert de Ginkell

According to Rev Story: "The 26ᵗʰ (June) was spent in firing, from seven batteries on the enemy's works, and a great many were killed in endeavouring to repair them. About 30 wagons laden with powder came to the camp; and that night we possess ourselves of all the bridge, except one arch at the further end, on the Connacht side, which was broke down, and we repair another broken arch in our possession; and all night our guns and mortars play most furiously...we labour hard to gain the bridge but what we got here was inch by inch, as it were, the enemy sticking very close to it, though great numbers of them were slain by our guns". According to an Irish officer, Colonel Felix O'Néill, the French generals who witnessed the Irish defence of the bridge said that "they never saw more resolution and firmness in any men of any nation; nay, blamed the men for their forwardness, and cried them up for brave fellows, as intrepid as lions"[365]

Athlone Captured

Growing weary of the Irish defence, De Ginkell now turned to the possibility that the River Shannon might be forded. After a possible fording point was established down stream three Danish soldier under sentence of death for cowardice was ordered to see if they could wade across and back while their comrades fired over their heads so that the Irish would assume that they were trying to desert. After the soldiers retuned, De Ginkell prepared his assault.

De Ginkell's plan was that 2,000 men should ford the river and fight their way into the town where they would hold back the Irish, thus allowing the bridge to be repaired and crossed by the bulk of the army. By now the Jacobite commanders were aware that something was afoot. St. Ruth ordered the ramparts on the Connacht side levelled so that if the Williamites broke into the town they would not be able to take up positions against his army, but d'Usson did not carry out the order. Meanwhile at the crossing point, two regiments commanded by Major General Maxwell, had just arrived to take over guarding the crossing point.[i]

On June 30th, just after 6pm deGinkell launched his attack. Under heavy artillery fire, the grenadiers crossed, with six battalions of infantry following behind them. Quickly overwhelmed, the Irish at the shore fired their muskets and retreated as the grenadiers entered the town and occupied the ramparts on the Connacht side, thus holding back St. Ruth's army until the Leinster side was secure. Within the hour, the town which in the preceding ten days had undergone the heaviest artillery bombardment in the history of Britain or Ireland was in Williamite hands. As the English army mopped up[ii] the only artillery they captured in the Jacobite side of the town were six ancient brass field pieces and two mortars.

The Jacobite Army retreats Westwards

St. Ruth was now in a precarious position, for if the English army pressed on and invaded his encampment, the result would be a massacre. He quickly dispatched General Hamilton to form a rearguard while his army retreated westwards to Ballinasloe behind the River Suck. Realising that Athlone had fallen in part because of bad leadership, St. Ruth was determined to efface the disgrace of it and to give battle once more. It was decided to set up encampment a further three miles west at Aughrim where the Jacobite army now consisting of around 15,000 men would stand and fight. For

---

[i] There are varying accounts of Maxwell's loyalty to the Jacobite cause – that he did not issue his men with sufficient ammunition and that he had had secretly reached an agreement with deGinkell. Another account states that he requested extra troops for the ford but was not granted them.

[ii] One hundred Irish soldiers are reported to have been murdered in cold blood in an outwork of the castle ruins.

this upcoming battle the Jacobite army had a total of nine pieces of field artillery.

Aughrim – The Decisive Battle

Battle is Joined

After the fall of Athlone, De Ginkell paused for a few days before re-commencing his advance. By July 10 he was approaching Aughrim, and on the morning of the 11th, his scouts spotted the Jacobite encampment, cleverly placed along the ridge of Kilcommandan Hill which was surrounded by a good part of its length by boggy ground, some of which was passable for infantry but impassable for cavalry except for a narrow pathway which led towards Aughrim Castle.

The following day, Sunday 12th as the Irish army attended Mass, the English army of over 20,000 men along with masses of artillery began to take up battle positions.

De Ginkell could clearly see the advantageous position of his enemy but with overwhelming artillery superiority, he hoped to overwhelm the centre of the Jacobite army by firepower alone. While his artillery bombarded his enemy, his cavalry and dragoons undertook probing attacks along their left flank at the Pass of Urraghree but these probing attacks turned into a larger battle with the Irish cavalry when the Williamites were lured into an ambush and this protracted struggle last until late in the afternoon. Meanwhile the opposing forces of artillery bombarded each other, and St. Ruth was painfully aware of his lack of artillery pieces. As evening was drawing on, De Ginkell now had a choice to make; to immediately launch a full scale attack as there were still three hours of daylight left or wait until the following morning. While some of his commanders urged him to wait, De Ginkell decided otherwise.

During the day, De Ginkell had the bog checked and now dispatched four regiments into it led by Colonels Brewer, Creighton, Erle and Herbert. The English advance towards the

Jacobite army was slow as the infantry had to wade through the bog and they quickly came under sustained musket fire from the Irish line. As they finally exited the worst of the bog, the Irish infantry charged them while the Irish cavalry attempted to cut them off in the rear. Those that could escape retreated back into the bog, attempting to return to their own lines while under fire. While these four regiments struggled others regiments attempted to cross closer to Aughrim and were also repulsed, but here the Irish pursued them right back to the English lines so that according to Rev Story the Irish infantry were "almost in a line with some of our great guns". Watching the retreating enemy; St Ruth exclaimed; "Le jour est á nous mes enfants!"[366] ("The day is ours my boys!") In his memoirs James II wrote "…St Ruth was in a transport of joy to see the foot of whom he had so mean an opinion, behave themselves so well and perform actions worthy of a better fate"[367]

Defeat from the Jaws of Victory

Upon seeing his attack repulsed, De Ginkell now endeavoured to use his numerical strength to good advantage, dispatching a great many regiments far beyond the Irish right flank as a diversion. Seeing the danger and fearing that he might be being outflanked, St. Ruth was forced to send some of his best regiments in that direction to keep an eye on them. In "error"[i] an officer ordered a regiment from the left centre to depart to the far right. Meanwhile De Ginkell had also sent his cavalry towards the narrow pathway that led towards Aughrim Castle

---

[i] This so-called "mistake" was made by Colonel Henry Luttrell, the same man that was dispatched to France to get him out of the way for being a troublemaker. A tradition of the "treachery of the general of the Irish horse that enabled the English to cross the bog" later arose. As we shall see from his action at Aughrim, Henry Luttrell was indeed a traitor to the Jacobite cause.

while also sending more regiments into the bog, this time armed with joined together sections of wooden planks called "hurdles" which made the crossing of the bog much easier. They successfully broke through and established themselves in a cornfield on the Irish side.

As the English cavalry approached Aughrim Castle, there was very little musket fire in their direction. It later transpired that the troops there had been issued with English musket balls for their French muskets, and in an attempt to fire on the enemy they had ripped off their buttons which they used as musket balls. The Irish cavalry reserve beyond the castle did not appear. Seeing the weak opposition at the castle De Ginkell dispatched further regiments under the command of Kirke and Hamilton into the bog beside the castle. Seeing the breakthrough. which was at this stage not beyond remedying, St. Ruth left his command post and rode with a cavalry brigade down the hill, stopping at an artillery position to direct fire. As he remounted his horse he uttered "They are beaten; let us beat them to the purpose."[368] The words were barely out of his mouth when a cannon ball severed his head from his body.

The only man who could have adequately replaced St. Ruth at this moment was Sarsfield. Since Athlone there had been tension between the two over the failure to hold the English at Athlone and before the Battle of Aughrim St. Ruth had personally ordered Sarsfield to stay with the cavalry reserve and not to move until directly ordered. This order had not been communicated by St. Ruth to anyone else and unaware of the demise of St. Ruth, Sarsfield remained at his post with the reserve.

As the English cavalry expanded their bridgehead at the castle and also in the cornfield, De Ginkell ordered an all out attack and the Irish cavalry were driven from the field. The Irish infantry in the centre and on the right fought stubbornly to hold their ground but when the enemy had crossed in sufficient numbers were forced to retreat. The Irish cavalry on the right wing fought on but eventually they too were forced to retreat. It was shortly after nine o' clock.

The Irish cavalry retreated towards Limerick while the infantry, many of whom had discarded their weapons and equipment to aid their flight also sought to escape the battlefield but were followed and massacred. The losses were enormous; the Irish had lost over 4,000 men while the English losses were not much less.[i] Furthermore the Irish had lost all their artillery, a huge amount of muskets, ammunition, tents and their entire baggage train. Eleven standards and 32 sets of battle colours had also fallen into the hands of the enemy. While the dead of the English army were gathered and buried, fifty years after the battle the bleached bones of the Irish soldiers still lay scattered on the plain of Aughrim[ii]

---

[i] One Danish soldier later wrote: "The blood from the dead so covered the ground that one could hardly take a step without slipping. This grisly scene of slaughter remained untouched and unchanged for several days, the horror of which cannot be imagined except by those who saw it."

[ii] There is an amazing tale of canine loyalty which was related by the Williamite chaplain, Rev. Story: "There is a true and remarkable story of an Irish wolfhound belonging to an Irish officer. The gentleman was killed and stripped in the battle whose body the animal remained by night and day; and though he fed upon other corpses with the rest of the dogs, yet he would not allow them or anything else to touch that of his master. When all the corpses were consumed, the other dogs departed; but this used to go in the night to the adjacent village for food and presently to the place where his master's bones were only then left; and thus he continued until January following when one of Colonel Foulke's soldiers being quartered nigh hand and going that way by chance, the dog fearing he came to disturb his master's bones flew upon the soldier who being surprised by the suddenness of the thing unslung his piece then upon his back and killed the poor dog"

Limerick – The Last Jacobite Bastion

The Capitulation of Galway and Sligo

Following the battle of Aughrim, three towns remained to the Jacobite army; Galway, Sligo and Limerick. While Limerick contained the bulk of the Irish soldiery, Galway and Sligo had only small garrisons and could not be defended for any length of time against the military might of the English army. After Aughrim, De Ginkell decided to quickly neutralise Galway and Sligo before attempting to deal with Limerick, which he knew only too well would be a tough nut to crack. Following the siege of the previous year, it was to his mind necessary to arrive at Limerick's gates as soon as possible to allow if necessary for an extended siege to do its work.

The English general, Mackay, was dispatched by De Ginkell to Galway and by the 20th July the town was surrounded on both sides. As resistance was futile the Irish agreed to a parley and terms of surrender which allowed the garrison to march to Limerick unhindered, were agreed to by De Ginkell, who even lent horses to the Irish to allow them pull their few pieces of artillery.

Sligo was taken under siege by a Williamite force commanded by Colonel Michelburne and once the town was completely blockaded, the Jacobite commander, Sir Teige O'Regan, who had previously held Charlemont Fort for months against the army of Schomberg, agreed to enter into negotiations. After protracted talks, O'Regan capitulated on September 14th and afterwards marched out of the town with his garrison for Limerick.

The Death of Tyrconnell

Following Aughrim, defeat beckoned the Jacobite army. There was however one last chance for the Irish; that they could hold out in Limerick until a French army would arrive. To this end, Tyrconnell immediately dispatched a message to James II telling him that all was lost unless help arrived. Tirconnell also warned his officers (and exacted promises from them) that no conclusion to the forthcoming siege must be entertained until such time as an answer to his letter had been received. Preparations were made to improve the city's store of food and to improve her defences by the building of new fortifications.

As Limerick prepared, De Ginkell advanced on the city, setting up camp at Caherconlish. On August 10th while at the house of General d'Usson, Tyrconnell took a stroke (more commonly referred to in those days as a fit of apoplexy) and died on August 14th, being interred afterwards in St. Mary's Cathderal. Described by the Duke of Berwick as "a man of much worth"[369] his death at this moment left a severe void in the Irish leadership. As a faithful supporter of King James and the Catholic cause, he had according to Berwick been offered generous terms of submission on several occasions but had rejected them.

After Tyrconnell's death, command of the army passed into the hands of General d'Usson who was Tyrconnell's second in command.

The Second Siege of Limerick Begins

The day that Tyrconnell died, the English army arrived at Limerick's walls. De Ginkell's greatest fear in undertaking the siege was the onset of the Autumn rains and he was most eager to obtain the surrender of the city under any circumstances. With this in mind, as his army emplaced sixty large cannon, nineteen mortars and 800 barrels of gunpowder, De Ginkell successfully established contact with the treacherous Colonel Luttrell, but this channel of communication was quickly discovered by General Sarsfield and Luttrell was arrested, court martialled and sentenced to death. However, through the influence of his friends, there was a stay put upon his execution until it could be confirmed by James II,[i] and he was instead put in prison.

When the first salvo of English artillery landed on the city on August 30th, De Ginkell's army occupied pretty much the same positions as King William's had the previous year, while once again (the remnant of) the Irish cavalry was in Co.Clare, outside the city. The morale of the defenders was not high as this was their last stronghold and they were vastly outnumbered. As the bombardment continued, the city was soon in flames and the outposts were forced to retreat. The people of the city had up to this point remained in the city and vast numbers of them retreated towards Co. Clare or to King's Island. On the 9th September, an attack was made from the beleaguered city, but was quickly driven back. By the 10th a huge breach had been made in the wall but the opening was protected by the waters of the Shannon and could not be immediately exploited.

Massacre at Thomond Gate

On the night of September 15th the English succeeded in constructing a pontoon bridge over the Shannon at Annabeg, due to the negligence or treachery of the Jacobite Brigadier Clifford who was entrusted with a large party of dragoons to prevent this. This crossing cut the pathway between Limerick and Clare and the Irish cavalry were forced to move their encampment to Six Mile Bridge, while many of those civilians who had sought refuge were now between the city and the English bridge and so were forced to return to the city.

---

[i] Following the war, Luttrell was awarded a pension of £500 by the government of King William and given the Luttrellstown estate near Clonsilla which was confiscated from his brother Simon, the Jacobite Lord Mayor of Dublin. He was murdered in mysterious circumstances on November 1st 1717 in Stafford St. Dublin.

However apart from cutting off the city from Clare, De Ginkell, made no immediate move to transfer a large part of his army to the Clare side of the city until the 22nd September, when three regiments under Tiffin, Kirke and Hamilton crossed and attacked the emplacements at Thomond bridge, which were fiercely defended by 700 Irishmen under the command of Colonel Lacy. At length the Irish were overwhelmed by the numbers attacking them and were forced to retreat back to the Thomond Gate, but the city commander, a Frenchman, who fearing that the enemy would enter and capture the gate along with the retreating Irish ordered the drawbridge raised, thinking that at worst these men would be forced to surrender. Unfortunately the result was quite different, for the English gave no quarter to the Irish and six hundred men were slaughtered at the city gate.

Capitulation
Following the massacre, the Irish feared further massacres if the English army should break through into the city proper. Sarsfield now advocated an honourable capitulation following a negotiatied agreement. This course was opposed by many others who felt that the army should fight on in the hope of help, and that any agreement the English would enter into would not be honoured.
Finally a consensus was reached that if Tyrconnell was still with them, then he too would recommend such a course as there was no help or message of any forthcoming help from the French.
Communication with the English was established under a flag of truce and on the morning of September 24th a three-day truce was agreed to by De Ginkell.
King William was especially anxious that a treaty should be concluded for he wished to move his army to Flanders as soon as possible. After the truce he instructed De Ginkell to "grant

all demands the Irish could make that would put an end to the war."³⁷⁰ Furthermore he already knew that a French fleet was on its way to Ireland with an army and that if this army arrived before a treaty was concluded the war might continue indefinitely.[i]

The Treaty of Limerick

On September 26th, hostages were exchanged between the parties and negotiations were opened between Sarsfield and deGinkell when Sarsfield was brought to the English encampment for dinner. For a full week the talks continued and on October 3rd 1691, the Treaty of Limerick was signed on a huge limestone block.[ii]

The treaty was composed of military and civil articles and while the military articles relating to the departure of the Irish troops were honoured in full, the civil articles which related to the rights of the Irish people to maintain their Catholic faith and to enjoy their property and positions in society at least insofar as they had during the reign of Charles II, will be forever memorable to the citizens of this nation for their disgraceful violation by the English.[iii]

For the Irish, the Treaty was signed by General Sarsfield, Viscount Galmoy, and Sir Toby Butler with Colonels Purcell,

---

[i] The French fleet would arrive two days after the signing of the The Treaty of Limerick with fresh men and weapons. Sarsfield, a man of high honour would not countenance going back on his word.

[ii] Sure that the English would never honour the Treaty, the Bishop of Limerick warned Sarsfield not to sign.

[iii] Since the Treaty of Windsor in 1175 when King Henry II of England pledged to the High King Rory O'Connor that he would halt the Norman expansion in Ireland, the English Crown had consistently not kept faith with the Irish, breaking every treaty or agreement as it suited. The previous treaty; The Treaty of Melifont at the conclusion of the Nine Years War in 1603 had also been broken resulting in the Plantation of Ulster.

Cusack, Dillon and Brown acting as procurators while for the English government, it was signed by Lord Scravenmore, Generals De Ginkell, Mackay and Talmash with Lords Justices Porter and Coningsby signing on behalf of King William. There were thirty-two articles in total; nineteen military and thirteen civil. The military articles allowed the Irish to march out of the city with all the honours of war – "with arms, baggage, drums beating, match lighted, colors flying, six brass guns, two mortar pieces and half the ammunition then in the place..." The Irish soldiers were to have their choice of either joining the army of King Louis of France or that of King William. Fifty ships were to be provided by the English government (with more if necessary) for the transportation of the Irish army to France.

The Civil Articles of the Treaty

Knowing that he was shortly to leave Ireland forever, Sarsfield was determined not to leave Ireland's Catholics without a guarantee for their future freedoms and so gave particular attention to the detail of the civil articles. It is maddening to recall that the ink signatures on the treaty were barely dry when a French fleet arrived in Limerick with a French army, 10,000 muskets and vast quantities of provisions but Sarsfield, who was as honourable as any medieval knight ever was, having given his word to the enemy, would not consider any course of action which would besmirch it.

The most important civil articles of the Treaty of Limerick may be summarised as follows;

The first article allowed that "the Roman Catholics of Ireland shall enjoy such privileges, in the exercise of their religion, as they did enjoy in the reign of King Charles II and that their majesties as soon as their affairs will permit them to summon a parliament in Ireland, will endeavour to procure the said Roman Catholics such further security in that particular, as may preserve them from any further disturbance on account of their religion". This article was in effect the most important part of the Treaty as it solemnly pronounced that no Irish Catholic should be offered any oath requiring them to renounce their religion, and that they would be free to practice their religion unhindered.

The second article secured to all Catholics in Limerick, Clare, Kerry, Cork, Mayo and Galway all their estates and properties, such as they were rightfully entitled to in the reign of Charles II, as also the free exercise of their respective callings and professions. (They would be entitled to sit in parliament, to vote at elections, to practice law and medicine, and to engage in trade and commerce).

The fifth article granted a general pardon for all "attainders, outlawries, treason, premunires, felonies & c incurred or committed since the beginning of the reign of James II".

In the seventh article, all those protected by the treaty were entitled to keep both horse and arms for their defence.

In the ninth article it was provided that Catholics who wished to enter the service of the English government would only be asked to take an oath of allegiance "…and no other" meaning that they would not have to take the oath of the Act of Supremacy.

Article No.10 stated that "No person who shall hereafter break these articles or any of them, shall thereby cause any other person to forfeit or lose the benefit of them".

Article 12 pledged that the treaty would be signed by the English monarchy within one year, and that it would also be fully ratified by the English parliament.

When the Lord Justices returned to Dublin after the signing of the treaty, they attended worship at Christ Church. The Protestant Bishop Dopping of Meath preached the sermon during which: "…the Sin of Keeping Faith with the Papists…" was solemnly denounced. It was a bad omen for the future.

When the treaty reached the hands of William of Orange and Queen Mary, the clause allowing the protection of the property of all those in counties where the Jacobites had garrisons had mysteriously disappeared, but King William found out about this and it was re-inserted. The monarchs signed the Treaty on February 4th 1692, attaching the great seal of England to it, and it was confirmed by royal letters patent on the 24th February 1692.

The Departure of the "Bone and Sinew of Ireland"

Some days after the treaty was signed the Jacobite army marched out of Limerick to the Clare side of the Shannon. It was here that the fighting men of Ireland decided their future.

Much to De Ginkell's disappointment only 1,000 of them composed of an Ulster regiment along with various men out of all the regiments chose to remain and join the English service while over 20,000 of them, "the bone and sinew of Ireland" chose to leave Ireland to enter the service of France to fight against England on foreign battlefields.[i] To this number must be added Mountcashel's division numbering 5,270 men who were already in France.

Afterwards, there followed a continuous stream of men to join them, so much so that in 1750 Fr. MacGeoghegan who was chaplain to the exiled army in France calculated that between 1691 and 1745, 450,000 Irishmen had departed Ireland to serve in armies abroad.

On December 3rd 4,500 Irishmen under the command of General Sarsfield boarded ship in the port of Cork and sailed to Brest, the first of many convoys bearing another generation of

---

[i] Of their departure, Sarsfield's Aide-de-Camp Gerald O'Connor wrote: "These men are leaving all that is most dear in life for a strange land in which they will have to endure much, to serve in an army that hardly knows our people; but they are true to Ireland and have still hopes for her cause. We will make another Ireland in the armies of the great King of France."

the "Wild Geese" of Ireland to France and further afield. Sarsfield did not long survive after his departure. In 1693, fighting for France, at the Battle of Landen, he was mortally wounded. Tradition tells us that his last words were "O that this were for Ireland!"

While some of the men had the good fortune to bring their families with them, most were forced to leave their families behind and there were many heartbreaking scenes at the ports of embarkation.

In France, the men were well received, and after enrolling in service of Louis XIV, they were all granted French citizenship, an honour renewed to all members of the Irish regiments upon the accession of Louis XV to the French throne, while from the hands of Louis XVI shortly before the end of his reign the remnants of the Irish brigade received a battle flag inscribed "Semper et Ubique Fidelis" ("Always and Everywhere Faithful")

Whilst remembering "The Wild Geese", we must not forget "The Raparees". These descendents of the "Wood Kerne" and "Tory" remained behind and continued a guerrilla war against the invader. In the decades that followed, they were feared by priest hunters, tithe proctors and tax gatherer alike. They also provided mountain shelters for those sought by the English. Often tarnished by the name of highwayman and robber, they were, following the departure of the Wild Geese, Ireland's last undefeated soldiers.

"Remember Limerick and Saxon Faith!"

"Like lions leaping at a fold when mad with hunger's pang,
Right up against the English line, the Irish exiles sprang.
Bright was their steel, 'tis bloody now, their guns are filled with gore;
Through shattered ranks, and severed files and trampled flags they tore.
The English strove with desperate strength, paused, rallied, staggered, fled-
The green hill-side is matted close with dying and with dead;
Across the plain and far away passed on that hideous wrack,
While cavalier and fantassin dash in upon their track,
On Fontenoy, on Fontenoy, like eagles in the sun,
With bloody plumes the Irish stand – the field is fought and won."

Excerpt from
"The Battle of Fontenoy" by Thomas Davis.

It is no exaggeration to say that in the decades that followed their exile, the brave deeds of Irishmen echoed up and down Europe and further afield. France benefited the most from these brave men along with Spain, Austria, Mexico, Chile and Cuba to name but a few. In the countries in which they sought their exile many Irishmen rose to positions of high command and honour.

While many battles were fought and much honour gained for the Irish Brigade in the French army during the battles of the war of the Spanish Succession at Blenheim (1704), Ramillies (1706), Oudenarde (1708), and Malplaquet (1709), it was for their charge against the English line at the Battle of Fontenoy on May 11th 1745 during the war of the Austrian Succession that the Irish regiments in the service of France gained immortal fame.

The Battle of Fontenoy

As the English alliance led by the Duke of Cumberland gained the upper hand, seven regiments of Irishmen shouting their battle cry in Gaelic "Remember Limerick and Saxon Faith!" charged and broke the English line thus securing victory for the French.

When the battle was over King Louis XV of France went immediately to his Irish regiments to thank them for their incredible bravery and to personally promote the non commissioned officer who had captured the English battle flag.

Upon hearing an account of the battle, King George II of England exclaimed; (with reference to the Penal laws which were then ravaging the Catholics of Ireland) "Cursed be the laws that deprive me of such subjects!"[371]

Almost 700 Irishmen were killed or wounded at the Battle of Fontenoy. This figure included half the officers of the Irish Brigade in the French army, the most senior being Colonel Dillon, who was the commander of his regiment.

References

[1] Martin Haverty – The History of Ireland Ancient and Modern, p142.
[2] Edmund Curtis – A History of Ireland from Earliest Times to 1922, p38.
[3] Martin Haverty – The History of Ireland Ancient and Modern, p169.
[4] Nicholas Furlong – Diarmait King of Leinster, P58.
[5] Thomas Wright – The Complete Works of Giraldus Cambrensis (London, 1905)
[6] Jonathon Bardon – A History of Ireland in 250 Episodes, p57.
[7] Seumas MacManus – The Story of the Irish Race, p324,325.
[8] Jonathon Bardon – A History of Ireland in 250 Episodes, p52.
[9] Thomas Wright – The Complete Works of Giraldus Cambrensis (London, 1905)
[10] Martin Haverty – The History of Ireland, Ancient and Modern, p179.
[11] Nicholas Furlong – Diarmait King of Leinster, p160.
[12] Nicholas Furlong – Diarmait King of Leinster, p9.
[13] Edmund Curtis – A History of Mediaeval Ireland from 1110 to 1513, p66
[14] Edmund Curtis – A History of Mediaeval Ireland from 1110 to 1513, p66
[15] Daniel O'Connell – A Memoir on Ireland Native and Saxon, p49,50.
[16] Daniel O'Connell – A Memoir on Ireland Native and Saxon, p55,56.
[17] Martin Haverty – The History of Ireland Ancient and Modern, p823.
[18] Daniel O'Connell – A Memoir on Ireland Native and Saxon, p49.
[19] P.W Joyce - A Concise History of Ireland, P88.89.
[20] Seumas MacManus – The Story of the Irish Race, p335.
[21] Hibernia Expugnata as quoted by Dr. Lanigan. Eccl. Hist. Vol IV p256.
[22] Annals of Kilronan as quoted in Haverty p222.
[23] Annals of Kilronan as quoted in Haverty p222.
[24] Edmund Curtis – A History of Ireland From Earliest Times To 1922, p69.
[25] As recorded in Haverty, p241,242.
[26] As recorded in Haverty, p241,242.
[27] Edmund Curtis – A History of Ireland From Earliest Times To 1922, p81.
[28] Edmund Curtis – A History of Ireland From Earliest Times To 1922, p81
[29] Hilaire Belloc – A Shorter History of England, p162.
[30] Irish Historical Documents until 1922 - Edmund Curtis and R.B McDowell
[31] Martin Haverty – The History of Ireland Ancient and Modern, p262.
[32] The History of Ireland Ancient and Modern – Martin Haverty, p273.
[33] The Story of the Irish Race – Seumas MacManus, p340.
[34] Ireland – A History – Robert Kee, p30.
[35] A Concise History of Ireland – P.W Joyce, p103.
[36] The Story of the Irish Race – Seumas MacManus, p339.
[37] The Story of the Irish Race – Seumas MacManus, p342.
[38] The Story of the Irish Race – Seumas MacManus, p342.
[39] A History of Ireland – Edmund Curtis, p98.
[40] A Concise History of Ireland – P.W Joyce, p107.
[41] A History of Ireland in 250 Episodes – Jonathan Bardon, p83.
[42] A History of Ireland in 250 Episodes – Jonathan Bardon, p87.

⁴³ I A History of Ireland in 250 Episodes – Jonathan Bardon, p87..
⁴⁴ I A History of Ireland in 250 Episodes – Jonathan Bardon, p87..
⁴⁵ The History of Ireland Ancient and Modern – Martin Haverty, p282.
⁴⁶ A Shorter History of England – Hilaire Belloc, p202.
⁴⁷ A Shorter History of England – Hilaire Belloc, p205.
⁴⁸ Harris's Hibernica taken from Histoire du Roy d'Angleterre as quoted in Haverty p284
⁴⁹ Harris's Hibernica taken from Histoire du Roy d'Angleterre as quoted in Haverty p284.
⁵⁰ The History of Ireland Ancient and Modern – Martin Haverty, p284.
⁵¹ A History of Ireland – Edmund Curtis, p113.
⁵² A Shorter History of England – Hilaire Belloc, p208.
⁵³ Annals of Lough ce as quoted in Ireland –The Struggle For Power, p125.
⁵⁴ The History of Ireland Ancient and Modern – Martin Haverty, p291.
⁵⁵ The History of Ireland Ancient and Modern – Martin Haverty, p289.
⁵⁶ Edmund Curtis - A History of Ireland, , p121.
⁵⁷ Jeffrey James - Ireland – The Struggle For Power., p130.
⁵⁸ P. W Joyce - A Concise History of Ireland – , p117.
⁵⁹ Jeffrey James - Ireland – The Struggle For Power., p132.
⁶⁰ Jeffrey James – Ireland, The Struggle For Power. Jeffrey James, p133.
⁶¹ Martin Haverty - The History of Ireland Ancient and Modern – , p230.
⁶² The History of Ireland Ancient and Modern – Martin Haverty, p. 304.
⁶³ The History of Ireland Ancient and Modern – Martin Haverty, p. 310.
⁶⁴ John Davidson – Ireland's Story Told to the New Democracy, pp. 76,77.
⁶⁵ The History of Ireland Ancient and Modern – Martin Haverty, p. 310.
⁶⁶ The History of Ireland Ancient and Modern – Martin Haverty, p. 310.
⁶⁷ The History of Ireland Ancient and Modern – Martin Haverty, p. 313.
⁶⁸ John Davidson – Ireland's Story Told to the New Democracy, p. 73.
⁶⁹ A History of Ireland From Earliest Times To 1922 – Edmund Curtis, p. 134.
⁷⁰ A History of Ireland From Earliest Times To 1922 – Edmund Curtis, p. 139.
⁷¹ State Papers of Henry VIII, Vol II, Page 73-75
⁷² State Papers of Henry VIII, Vol II.
⁷³ State Papers of Henry VIII, Vol II.
⁷⁴ A History of Ireland From Earliest Times To 1922 – Edmund Curtis, p. 140.
⁷⁵ A Concise History of Ireland – P.W Joyce, p. 129.
⁷⁶ John Davidson - Ireland's story told to the new democracy, p78
⁷⁷ John Davidson - Ireland's story told to the new democracy, p78
⁷⁸ A Shorter History of England – Hilaire Belloc, p. 281.
⁷⁹ Hilaire Belloc – A Shorter History of England, p258.
⁸⁰Hilaire Belloc – A Shorter History of England, p261.
⁸¹Martin Haverty – The History of Ireland Ancient and Modern, p333.
⁸²Jonathan Bardon – A History of Ireland in 250 Episodes, p102.
⁸³Martin Haverty – The History of Ireland Ancient and Modern, p334.
⁸⁴Edmund Curtis – A History of Ireland from Earliest Times to 1922, p155.
⁸⁵Edmund Curtis – A History of Ireland from Earliest Times to 1922, p146.
⁸⁶Martin Haverty – The History of Ireland Ancient and Modern, p333.
⁸⁷ Edmund Curtis – A History of Ireland from Earliest times to 1922, p.151.
⁸⁸ Edmund Curtis – A History of Ireland from Earliest times to 1922, p.151.
⁸⁹ Fr. Augustine, O.M Cap. – Ireland's Loyalty to the Mass, p.34.
⁹⁰ Constantia Maxwell – Irish History from Contemporary Sources, p.230.
⁹¹ Fr. Augustine, O.M Cap. – Ireland's Loyalty to the Mass, p.38.
⁹² Timothy T.O'Donnell – Swords Around the Cross p13
⁹³ William Camden – Annals of the Reign of Queen Elizabeth.
⁹⁴ William Camden – Annals of the Reign of Queen Elizabeth
⁹⁵P.W Joyce – A Concise History of Ireland, p145.
⁹⁶Edmund Curtis – A History of Ireland From Earliest Times to 1922, p161.
⁹⁷P.W Joyce – A Concise History of Ireland, p145.

[98] Constantia Maxwell – Irish History from Contemporary Sources 1509-1610, p172, 173.
[99] Constantia Maxwell – Irish History From Contemporary Sources 1509-1610, p173.
[100] Edmund Curtis – A History of Ireland From Earliest Times to 1922, p193.
[101] Edmund Campion – Historie of Ireland (1571)
[102] Edmund Curtis – A History of Ireland From Earliest Times to 1922, p155.
[103] Edmund Curtis – A History of Ireland From Earliest Times to 1922, p168.
[104] Martin Haverty – The History of Ireland Ancient and Modern, p362.
[105] Martin Haverty – The History of Ireland Ancient and Modern, p362
[106] Martin Haverty – The History of Ireland Ancient and Modern, p362.
[107] Constantia Maxwell – Irish History From Contemporary Sources 1509-1610, p174.
[108] Edmund Curtis – A History of Ireland From Earliest Times to 1922, p169
[109] Edmund Curtis – A History of Ireland From Earliest Times to 1922, p168
[110] David B. Quinn – The Elizabethans and the Irish
[111] Robert Kee – Ireland. A History. P32,33.
[112] Martin Haverty – The History of Ireland Ancient and Modern, p368.
[113] Martin Haverty – The History of Ireland Ancient and Modern, p370.
[114] The Annals of the Kingdom of Ireland- for the year 1574.
[115] Constantia Maxwell – Irish History From Contemporary Sources 1509-1610, p234.
[116] Macgeoghegan and Mitchel – The History of Ireland. Vol 1 p478.
[117] Constantia Maxwell – Irish History from Contemporary Sources 1509-1610, p236.
[118] Desiderata Curiosa Hibernica, Vol II, P91. See also Haverty p376.
[119] Constantia Maxwell – Irish History From Contemporary Sources 1509-1610, p169.
[120] Constantia Maxwell – Irish History From Contemporary Sources 1509-1610, p169.
[121] Sean O'Faolain – The Great O'Néill, p15.
[122] Martin Haverty – The History of Ireland Ancient and Modern, p384.
[123] Martin Haverty – The History of Ireland Ancient and Modern, p386.
[124] Martin Haverty – The History of Ireland Ancient and Modern, p389
[125] Jonathon Bardon – A History of Ireland in 250 Episodes, p119.
[126] Martin Haverty – The History of Ireland Ancient and Modern, p389
[127] Spencer – View of the State of Ireland
[128] Spencer – View of the State of Ireland.
[129] Spencer – View of the State of Ireland
[130] Spencer – View of the State of Ireland
[131] Acts of Queen Elizabeth
[132] Annals of the Four Masters for the Year 1586,
[133] Timothy T.O'Donnell – Swords Around the Cross p33,34.
[134] Recollections of Francisco deCuellar, Antwerp, October 1589
[135] Edmund Curtis – A History of Ireland From Earliest Times to 1922, p177.
[136] Edmund Curtis – A History of Ireland From Earliest Times to 1922, p179.
[137] Martin Haverty – The History of Ireland Ancient and Modern, p410.
[138] P.W Joyce – A Concise History of Ireland, p158.
[139] Timothy T.O'Donnell – Swords Around the Cross p
[140] Annals of the Four Masters for the Year 1592
[141] Edmund Curtis – A History of Ireland from Earliest Times to 1922, p183.
[142] Edmund Curtis – A History of Ireland from Earliest Times to 1922, p183
[143] Extract from the journal of Sir William Russell's diary published in "Hy Many" by Dr. O'Donovan p149, 150.
[144] Jonathon Bardon – A History of Ireland in 250 Episodes, p141,142.
[145] Annals of the Four Masters for the Year 1598
[146] The History of Ireland – MacGeoghegan and Mitchel vol 1 p513.
[147] Eyewitness account of Lugaidh Ó Cléirigh taken from "Beatha Aodha Ruaidh Ui Domhnaill"
[148] P.W Joyce – A Concise History of Ireland, p167.
[149] P.W Joyce – A Concise History of Ireland, p167.
[150] Edmund Curtis – A History of Ireland from Earliest Times to 1922, p185.
[151] Robert Kee – Ireland, A History, EP 1.

[152] Cyril Falls – Elizabeth's Irish Wars p241.
[153] P.W Joyce – A Concise History of Ireland, p170.
[154] Edmund Curtis – A History of Ireland From Earliest Times to 1922, p186.
[155] Edmund Curtis – A History of Ireland From Earliest Times to 1922, p186.
[156] Jonathan Bardon – A History of Ireland in 250 Episodes, p148.
[157] Jonathan Bardon – A History of Ireland in 250 Episodes, p150.
[158] Martin Haverty – The History of Ireland Ancient and Modern, p444.
[159] Annals of the Kingdom of Ireland for the year 1601
[160] Jonathan Bardon – A History of Ireland in 250 Episodes, p150
[161] Calendar of State Papers relating to Ireland.
[162] P.W Joyce – A Concise History of Ireland, p173.
[163] Martin Haverty – The History of Ireland Ancient and Modern, p445.
[164] Martin Haverty – The History of Ireland Ancient and Modern, p449.
[165] P.W Joyce – A Concise History of Ireland, p177.
[166] P.W Joyce – A Concise History of Ireland, p182.
[167] Pacata Hibernia – 1810 Edition, p449.
[168] Pacata Hibernia – 1810 Edition, p659.
[169] P.W Joyce – A Concise History of Ireland, p183 also Martin Haverty – The History of Ireland Ancient and Modern, p453.
[170] Jonathan Bardon – A History of Ireland in 250 Episodes, p154.
[171] Edmund Curtis – A History of Ireland From Earliest Times to 1922, p184.
[172] Fr. Augustine, O.M.Cap. – Ireland's Loyalty to the Mass, p70.
[173] Hilaire Belloc – A Shorter History of England, p345.
[174] Martin Haverty – The History of Ireland Ancient and Modern, p456.
[175] Fr. Augustine, O.M.Cap. – Ireland's Loyalty to the Mass, p72.
[176] Dorothy Macardle – The Irish Republic, p33.
[177] Jonathan Bardon – A History of Ireland in 250 Episodes, p159.s
[178] Liam Swords – The Flight of the Earls, p18.
[179] Fr. Augustine, O.M.Cap. – Ireland's Loyalty to the Mass, p73.
[180] Fr. Augustine, O.M.Cap. – Ireland's Loyalty to the Mass, p74.
[181] Jonathan Bardon – A History of Ireland in 250 Episodes, p157.
[182] Jonathan Bardon – A History of Ireland in 250 Episodes, p156,157.
[183] Moore – History of Ireland Volume IV p353.
[184] Daniel O'Connell – A Memoir on Ireland, Native and Saxon, p187.
[185] Liam Swords – The Flight of the Earls, p15.
[186] Liam Swords – The Flight of the Earls, p15.
[187] Liam Swords – The Flight of the Earls, p15.
[188] Liam Swords – The Flight of the Earls, p41.
[189] Daniel O'Connell – A Memoir on Ireland, Native and Saxon, p191.
[190] Dorothy Macardle – The Irish Republic, p32.
[191] Edmund Curtis – A History of Ireland From the Earliest Times to 1922, p197.
[192] Edmund Curtis – A History of Ireland From the Earliest Times to 1922, p197,198.
[193] Jonathan Bardon – The Plantation of Ulster, p194.
[194] Edmund Curtis – A History of Ireland From the Earliest Times to 1922, p197.
[195] P.W Joyce – A Concise History of Ireland, p188.
[196] Jonathan Bardon – The Plantation of Ulster, p191.
[197] Jonathan Bardon – The Plantation of Ulster, p192.
[198] Jonathan Bardon – The Plantation of Ulster, p192.
[199] Martin Haverty – The History of Ireland Ancient and Modern, p461.
[200] Annals of the Four Masters for 1611.
[201] Jonathan Bardon – The Plantation of Ulster, p199.
[202] Jonathan Bardon – The Plantation of Ulster, p200.
[203] Jonathan Bardon – The Plantation of Ulster, p200

[204] Martin Haverty – The History of Ireland Ancient and Modern, p465.

[205] Edmund Curtis – A History of Ireland From the Earliest Times to 1922, p201.
[206] Martin Haverty – The History of Ireland Ancient and Modern, p463.
[207] Edmund Curtis – A History of Ireland From the Earliest Times to 1922, p203.
[208] Martin Haverty – The History of Ireland Ancient and Modern, p464.
[209] Hilaire Belloc – A Shorter History of England, p360.
[210] Jonathan Bardon – A History of Ireland in 250 Episodes, p182
[211] Martin Haverty – The History of Ireland Ancient and Modern, p467.
[212] Martin Haverty – The History of Ireland Ancient and Modern, p467.
[213] P.W Joyce – A Concise History of Ireland, p188.
[214] P.W Joyce – A Concise History of Ireland, p192.
[215] Martin Haverty – The History of Ireland Ancient and Modern, p469
[216] Strafford's State Letters, Vol 1-p331.
[217] Strafford's State Letters, Vol 1-p442
[218] Strafford's State Letters, Vol 1-p442
[219] Carte's "Life of Ormond", Vol 3 – p11.
[220] Jonathan Bardon – The Plantation of Ulster, p258.
[221] Jonathan Bardon – The Plantation of Ulster, p258.
[222] Jonathan Bardon – The Plantation of Ulster, p259.
[223] John Curry – Review of the Civil Wars in Ireland, p147,148.
[224] Thomas Carte – A History of the Life of James Duke of Ormond, Volume 1, p235.
[225] Thomas Carte – A History of the Life of James Duke of Ormond, Volume 1, p263.
[226] Thomas Carte – A History of the Life of James Duke of Ormond, Volume 1, p263.
[227] Edmund Borlase – History of the Irish Rebellion, Appendix – Instructions given by Lord Maguire.
[228] Martin Haverty – The History of Ireland Ancient and Modern, p478.
[229] Martin Haverty – The History of Ireland Ancient and Modern, p478.
[230] Martin Haverty – The History of Ireland Ancient and Modern, p479.
[231] Martin Haverty – The History of Ireland Ancient and Modern, p479.
[232] Martin Haverty – The History of Ireland Ancient and Modern, p482.
[233] Deposition of James Mitchell – www.bbc.co.uk/history/british, Islandmagee Massacre.
[234] Nicholas Canny – Making Ireland British 1580-1650,p485
[235] John Davidson - Ireland's story told to the new democracy, p136.
[236] Deposition of William Clark, Trinity College manuscript 836
[237] John Davidson - Ireland's story told to the new democracy, p137.
[238] John Davidson - Ireland's story told to the new democracy, p137
[239] Daniel O'Connell M.P - A Memoir on Ireland Native and Saxon,p327,328.
[240] Daniel O'Connell M.P - A Memoir on Ireland Native and Saxon,p328.
[241] Daniel O'Connell M.P - A Memoir on Ireland Native and Saxon ,p329, 330,331,332,333.
[242] Moody, Martin and Byrne – Early Modern Ireland 1534-1591, p292.
[243] Rev. Dr. Warner – The History of the Rebellion in Ireland, p297.
[244] Hilaire Belloc – A Shorter History of England, p377.
[245] Peter Berresford Ellis – Eyewitness to Irish History, p108
[246] Peter Berresford Ellis – To Hell or Connacht, The Cromwellian Colonisation of Ireland 1652-1660, p20.
[247] Jonathan Bardon – A History of Ireland in 250 Episodes, p191.
[248] Daniel O'Connell M.P - A Memoir on Ireland Native and Saxon,p404,405,406.
[249] Lord Castlehaven's Memoirs , p26.
[250] Lord Castlehaven's Memoirs, p30.
[251] Thomas Carte – A History of the Life of James Duke of Ormond, Volume 1, p243.
[252] Robert Kee – Ireland – A History, p46.
[253] Martin Haverty – The History of Ireland Ancient and Modern, p486.
[254] Edmund Borlase – History of the Irish Rebellion, p34.
[255] Thomas Carte – A History of the Life of James Duke of Ormond, Volume 1, p265.
[256] Martin Haverty – The History of Ireland Ancient and Modern, p489.
[257] Francis Plowden – History of Ireland, Volume 1 – p375.
   Also Lord Castlehaven's Memoirs, p38.

[258] Thomas Carte – A History of the Life of James Duke of Ormond, Volume 3, p61.
[259] Thomas Leland – History of Ireland, Vol.3, P203.
[260] Jonathan Bardon – A History of Ireland in 250 Episodes, p193.
[261] Edmund Borlase – History of the Irish Rebellion, p191.
[262] Memoris of Lord Castlehaven
[263] Daniel O'Connell M.P – A Memoir on Ireland, Native and Saxon, p296.
[264] Daniel O'Connell M.P – A Memoir on Ireland, Native and Saxon, p296.
[265] C.P Meehan – The Confederation of Kilkenny,p43.
[266] C.P Meehan – The Confederation of Kilkenny,p45.
[267] Martin Haverty – The History of Ireland Ancient and Modern, p502
[268] Claredon – History of the Irish Rebellion, Vol 2,P323.
[269] Parliamentary History of England, Vol. III, p248..
[270] Parliamentary History of England, Vol. III, p248.
[271] Thomas Leland – History of Ireland, Volume 3 – p227.
[272] Padraic Column – A Treasury of Irish Folklore – p226,227. Also derived from the diary of Sir Phelim O'Néill.
[273] Martin Haverty – The History of Ireland Ancient and Modern, p512.
[274] Jonathan Bardon – A History of Ireland in 250 Episodes, p195.
[275] Padraic Column – A Treasury of Irish Folklore – p227,228.
[276] C.P Meehan – The Confederation of Kilkenny,p217.
[277] Hilaire Belloc – A Shorter History of England, p395
[278] Hilaire Belloc – A Shorter History of England, p395.
[279] Peter Berresford Ellis – Hell or Connacht, The Cromwellian Colonisation of Ireland 1652-1660, p.17.
[280] Peter Berresford Ellis – Hell or Connacht, The Cromwellian Colonisation of Ireland 1652-1660, p.18.
[281] Carte Manuscript Collection, Vol 3, p410.
[282] Thomas Carte – A History of the Life of James Duke of Ormond, Volume 2 - p84.
[283] W.C Abbott – Writings and Speeches of Oliver Cromwell
[284] Carte Manuscript Collection, Vol 3, p412
[285] Robert Kee – Ireland A History, p46.
[286] Martin Haverty – The History of Ireland Ancient and Modern, p532.
[287] Fr. Augustine, O.M Cap. – Ireland's Loyalty to the Mass, p110.
[288] Jonathan Bardon – A History of Ireland in 250 Episodes, p197
[289] Martin Haverty – The History of Ireland Ancient and Modern, p533.
[290] Robert Kee – Ireland A History, p46.
[291] Parliamentary History of England, Vol. III, p1334.
[292] Parliamentary History of England, Vol. III, p1334.
[293] John Davidson - Ireland's story told to the new democracy, p140.
[294] From the newspaper "The Nation" of October 8th 1859.
[295] Cary's Memorials – Vol. II, p180. See also the Cromwell Letter by Thomas Carlyle.
[296] Cary's Memorials – Vol. II, p180. See also the Cromwell Letter by Thomas Carlyle.
[297] Cary's Memorials – Vol. II, p180. See also the Cromwell Letter by Thomas Carlyle.
[298] Peter Berresford Ellis – Hell or Connacht, The Cromwellian Colonisation of Ireland 1652-1660, p.3,4.
[299] John Davidson - Ireland's story told to the new democracy, p140.
[300] Colonel O'Néill's Journal taken from Desirdata Curiosa Hibernica
[301] Edmund Curtis – A History of Ireland From Earliest Times To 1922, p215,216.
[302] Fr. Augustine, O.M Cap. – Ireland's Loyalty to the Mass, p110
[303] Bulstrode Whitelocke – Memorials of English Affairs (Oxford 1853)
[304] Peter Berresford Ellis – Hell or Connacht, The Cromwellian Colonisation of Ireland 1652-1660, p.22.
[305] Martin Haverty – The History of Ireland Ancient and Modern, p540.
[306] Dr. Burke – Hibernica Dominicana, p588.
[307] Edmund Ludlow – Memoirs of Edmund Ludlow esq, Vol 1-p379.
[308] Dr. Burke – Hibernica Dominicana, p588.
[309] Peter Berresford Ellis – Hell or Connacht, The Cromwellian Colonisation of Ireland 1652-1660, p.26.
[310] Peter Berresford Ellis – Hell or Connacht, The Cromwellian Colonisation of Ireland 1652-1660, p.26.
[311] Edmund Ludlow – Memoirs of Edmund Ludlow esq, Vol 1-p422

[312] Edmund Ludlow – Memoirs of Edmund Ludlow esq, Vol 1-p422
[313] Martin Haverty – The History of Ireland Ancient and Modern, p552.
[314] John Davidson - Ireland's story told to the new democracy, p150.
[315] Colonel Laurence's Interest of Ireland, Vol. II, p86,87.
[316] John Davidson - Ireland's story told to the new democracy, p136.
[317] Martin Haverty – The History of Ireland Ancient and Modern, p548.
[318] Martin Haverty – The History of Ireland Ancient and Modern, p548.
[319] Martin Haverty – The History of Ireland Ancient and Modern, p548.
[320] Martin Haverty – The History of Ireland Ancient and Modern, p548.
[321] John Davidson - Ireland's story told to the new democracy, p155.
[322] John Davidson - Ireland's story told to the new democracy, p155.
[323] A Collection of Irish Massacres – London 1660.
[324] John Davidson - Ireland's story told to the new democracy, p149.
[325] John Davidson - Ireland's story told to the new democracy, p149.
[326] John Davidson - Ireland's story told to the new democracy, p136.
[327] Irish Calendar of State Papers. – HMSO London 1903
[328] John Davidson - Ireland's story told to the new democracy, p149.
[329] Hilaire Belloc – A Shorter History of England, p42
[330] John Davidson - Ireland's story told to the new democracy, p157.
[331] Martin Haverty – The History of Ireland, Ancient and Modern, p556.
[332] Edmund Curtis – A History of Ireland From Earliest Times To 1922, p221.
[333] Peter Berresford Ellis – Eyewitness to Irish History, p124.
[334] Biographical History of England, Vol IV, p201.
[335] C.P Curran – Oliver Plunkett – The Trial of the Primate, p131.
[336] C.P Curran – Oliver Plunkett – The Trial of the Primate, p132
[337] Echard's History of England – Vol III, p681
[338] Hilaire Belloc – A Shorter History of England, p423.
[339] Edmund Curtis – A History of Ireland From Earliest Times To 1922, p228.
[340] Jonathan Bardon – A History of Ireland in 250 Episodes, p218.
[341] Jonathan Bardon – A History of Ireland in 250 Episodes, p220.
[342] Martin Haverty – The History of Ireland, Ancient and Modern, p577.
[343] Thomas Witherow – Derry and Enniskillen in the Year 1689,
[344] John Davidson - Ireland's story told to the new democracy, p157.
[345] Jonathan Bardon – A History of Ireland in 250 Episodes, p225.
[346] Jonathan Bardon – A History of Ireland in 250 Episodes, p226.
[347] Macaulay – History of England, Vol V, p43.
[348] Constantia Maxwell – A Short History of Ireland, p
[349] Keating- The Defence of Ireland, Ch5, P19.
[350] Hilaire Belloc – A Shorter History of England, p452.
[351] Martin Haverty – The History of Ireland, Ancient and Modern, p590.
[352] Rudolf Dekker - Observaties van een Zeventiende-eeuwse wereldbeschower, p45-47
[353] John Davidson - Ireland's story told to the new democracy, p166.
[354] John Davidson - Ireland's story told to the new democracy, p166.
[355] Edmund Curtis – A History of Ireland From Earliest Times To 1922, p233.
[356] P.W Joyce – A Concise History of Ireland, p218.
[357] Alfred Webb, Sketches of Distinguished Irishmen, p150.
[358] Memoirs of Sir John Dalrymple, Vol 1, p176.
[359] Martin Haverty – The History of Ireland, Ancient and Modern, p597.
[360] Martin Haverty – The History of Ireland, Ancient and Modern, p597.
[361] Martin Haverty – The History of Ireland, Ancient and Modern, p597.
[362] Rev Charles Leslie – Leslie's Answer to King, p162.
[363] Martin Haverty – The History of Ireland, Ancient and Modern, p604
[364] A.M Sullivan – The Story of Ireland
[365] Rawdon Papers, p346.
[366] Martin Haverty – The History of Ireland, Ancient and Modern, p609.

[367] Memoirs of King James II – Vol II, P457.
[368] Memoirs of King James II – Vol II, P459
[369] Memoirs of James Duke of Berwick – Vol I, p103.
[370] Patrick Moran – The Catholics of Ireland Under the Penal Laws in the Eighteenth century, p4.
[371] John Davidson - Ireland's story told to the new democracy, p172.

www.ingramcontent.com/pod-product-compliance
Lightning Source LLC
Chambersburg PA
CBHW060102170426
43198CB00010B/735